Constructive & Destructive Behavior

Constructive & Destructive Behavior

Implications for Family, School, & Society

Edited by Arthur C. Bohart

& Deborah J. Stipek

American Psychological Association

Washington, DC

Published by
American Psychological Association
750 First Street, NE
Washington, DC 20002

Copies may be ordered from
APA Order Department
P.O. Box 92984
Washington, DC 20090-2984

In the UK and Europe, copies may be ordered from
American Psychological Association
3 Henrietta Street
Covent Garden, London
WC2E 8LU England

Typeset in Goudy by D&G Limited, LLC

Printer: Data Reproductions Corp., Auburn Hills, MI
Jacket Designer: Ann Masters, Ann Masters Design, Washington DC
Project Manager: D&G Limited, LLC

Library of Congress Cataloging-in-Publication Data
Constructive and destructive behavior : implications for family, school, and society /
[edited by Arthur C. Bohart, Deborah J. Stipek].—1st ed.
     p. cm.
   Includes bibliographical references.
   ISBN 1-55798-740-8 (alk. paper)
   1. Aggressiveness. 2. Violence. 3. Helping behavior. I. Bohart, Arthur C. II. Stipek.
Deborah J., 1950–

HM1116.C654 2001
302.5'4—dc21   00-051063
                                                                                                    CIP

British Library Cataloguing-in-Publication Data
A CIP record is available from the British Library

Printed in the United States of America
First edition

DEDICATION

This book was written to honor two individuals who have influenced the developmental pathways both of psychology and of the individual authors. Norma and Seymour Feshbach have devoted their lives to understanding human behavior for purposes of creating a safer and more caring society. Seymour Feshbach has conducted groundbreaking research on the causes and control of aggression, and Norma Feshbach's pioneering research played a major role in moving empathy from an obscure concept to one of the most widely researched variables in prosocial development. Their thinking and research in these two domains provided the foundation for much of the psychological theory and research on constructive and destructive behavior discussed in this book.

This extraordinary couple has also influenced and enriched the lives of each of the chapter authors—as mentors, colleagues, friends, and, for one author, as parents. The authors have been inspired by their scholarship and the high standards they set for integrity and professionalism. They have been energized by their encouragement and commitment to research that can benefit society. And they have enjoyed their devotion and affection.

Just a few weeks before this book went to press this extraordinary couple endured the death of their son and one of our authors, Jonathan Bloom-Feshbach. A scholar and great man in his own right, his untimely death is a tremendous loss to family, friends, and the field of psychology. We dedicate this book to Jonathan in honor of his parents, two giants among scholars and human beings.

CONTENTS

CONTRIBUTORS

Paolo Albiero, Department of Developmental Psychology, University of Padua, Padua, Italy

Claudio Barbaranelli, Department of Psychology, University degli Studi di Roma, Rome

Arthur C. Bohart, Department of Psychology, California State University—Dominguez Hills, Carson, California

Jonathan Bloom-Feshbach (deceased), Washington School of Psychiatry, Washington, DC

Sally Bloom-Feshbach, private practice, Washington, DC

Beverley D. Cairns, Department of Psychology, University of North Carolina at Chapel Hill, Chapel Hill, North Carolina

Robert B. Cairns, Department of Psychology, University of North Carolina at Chapel Hill, Chapel Hill, North Carolina

Gian Vittorio Caprara, Department of Psychology, University degli Studi di Roma, Rome

Nancy Eisenberg, Department of Psychology, Arizona State University, Tempe, Arizona

Inger M. Endresen, Research Center for Health Promotion, University of Bergen, Bergen, Norway

L. D. Eron, Institute for Social Research, University of Michigan, Ann Arbor, Michigan

Robert A. Hinde, St. John's College, Cambridge, England, United Kingdom

Martin L. Hoffman, Psychology Department, New York University, New York, New York

L. Rowell Huesmann, Institute of Social Research, University of Michigan, Ann Arbor, Michigan

Alida Lo Coco, Department of Psychology, Vialle delle Scienze, University of Palermo, Palermo, Italy

Paul Mussen, Psychology Department, University of California at Berkeley, Berkeley, California

Dan Olweus, Research Center for Health Promotion, University of Bergen, Bergen, Norway

Concetta Pastorelli, Department of Psychology, University of Palermo, Palermo, Italy

Lea Pulkkinen, University of Jyvaskyla, Department of Psychology, Jyvaskyla, Finland

Meredith A. Reynolds, Centers for Disease Control and Prevention, Atlanta, Georgia

Myrna B. Shure, MCP Hahnemann University, Philadelphia, Pennsylvania

Deborah J. Stipek, Urban Education Studies Center, Education Department, University of California, Los Angeles, California

Sally J. Styfco, Department of Psychology, Yale University, New Haven, Connecticut

June Price Tangney, Department of Psychology, George Mason University, Fairfax, Virginia

Edward Zigler, Department of Psychology, Yale University, New Haven, Connecticut

Constructive & Destructive Behavior

INTRODUCTION

ARTHUR C. BOHART AND DEBORAH J. STIPEK

Americans were stunned when two high school students in Littleton, Colorado, shot and killed 12 of their classmates and a teacher, completing the massacre by taking their own lives. As we write this introduction, news reporters, political figures, and the public are still searching for an explanation. Analysts refer to the easy availability of guns, the breakdown of religion and morality, poor parenting, and schools' indifference to signs of emotional distress and tolerance of peer pressure and rejection. Video games are singled out as a training ground for violence—dulling children's empathic capacity and motivation to relate constructively to others and inspiring creative acts of aggression. Although everyone offers a different explanation, most acknowledge that the causes of such destructive behavior, to self and to others, are complex.

This book, *Constructive and Destructive Behavior: Implications for Family, School, and Society*, is about that complexity. It is a collection of original papers by theoreticians and researchers from the United States, Europe, and the United Kingdom who have spent their careers studying constructive or prosocial behavior and destructive or aggressive/antisocial behavior. Some chapters are original theoretical contributions, others are reviews of research, and still others are research reports. This book provides an overview of some of the most significant work in the field, including topics such as the development of moral behavior, the role of empathy in development, factors that mediate the development of stability of prosocial and antisocial/aggressive behavior, effective parenting, the role of guilt and shame in constructive and destructive behavior, the effects of viewing violence, theories of cognitive factors in aggressive behavior, overviews of prevention programs, the role of emotional expression in reducing anger and aggression, and factors that contribute to war. The book will be useful for those who want an overview of current work in the field of aggression and prosocial behavior, such as professors teaching advanced undergraduate classes and graduate classes, and for those working in the field of research and prevention. The book not only provides a grounding in many of the important issues involved in understanding prosocial and antisocial behavior, but it also serves as a springboard for future research.

A unique strength of the book is its focus on the interrelationship of prosocial to antisocial/aggressive behavior. For instance, some of the topics considered include the relationship of empathy to aggression, the relationship of guilt and shame to prosocial and antisocial behavior, the role of the expression of emotion in both prosocial and antisocial behavior, school as a promoter of prosocial and antisocial behavior, and intervention programs aimed at promoting prosocial development that have a concomitant effect on reducing antisocial behavior.

OVERVIEW OF TOPICS

The *New Webster's Dictionary* (1984) defines *constructive* as, among other things, "intended to be helpful" (p 218). "Destructive" is "having a tendency to destroy; ruinous; deprecating" (p. 272). These definitions give the authors in this book wide latitude in the research that they describe.

Most of the authors who focus on destructive behavior examine psychological (expressed verbally and through emotional expressions) and physical aggression. Definitions of aggression vary in the field of psychology. Feshbach (1971) defined *aggression* broadly as "any behavioral sequence that results in injury to or destruction of an animal, human, or inanimate object" (p. 283). Parke and Slaby (1983) considered only acts against humans as aggression: "behavior that is aimed at harming or injuring another person or persons" (p. 550). *Antisocial behavior* is defined by Loeber (1990) as "behavior that inflicts physical or mental harm or property loss or damage on others" (p. 6).

No definition of aggression is entirely satisfying. For instance, Parke and Slaby, congruent with many others in the field, emphasize behavior whose aim or intention is to harm. Yet how important is the concept of aim or intention? Consider a robbery during which the perpetrator harms someone who tries to stop him from safely getting away. The robber's primary intention is not to inflict harm. Is this still aggressive? Or consider the actions of some corporations that lead to a callous disregard for human life to maximize profits (e.g., Hamilton & Sanders, 1999). Could their actions be considered aggressive? Coie and Dodge (1998) have pointed out that even defining infliction of harm is problematic. Would it include giving a student a low grade? Breaking up with a girlfriend? Protecting oneself? Sexist language? What is considered "aggressive" depends partly on one's point of view and on who gets to define reality (Muehlenhard & Kimes, 1999).

The authors in this book deal with the ambiguity and subjectivity of the construct by being clear about how they operationalize aggression in their own research or the research they review. They address a broad spectrum of topics related to aggression and other destructive behaviors. Edward Zigler and Sally J. Styfco (chapter 11) discuss research related to delinquency in adolescence. Lea Pulkkinen (chapter 8) and Gian Vittorio Caprara, Claudio Barbaranelli, and Concetta P. Pastorelli (chapter 9) examine stability in aggression, using peer and teacher ratings and self-report. Pulkkinen examines ways in which patterns of these early ratings predict criminality (arrests) and other problem behavior (e.g., drinking). Inger M. Endresen and Dan Olweus (chapter 7) use a self-report measure to measure bullying behavior. Paulo Albiero and Alida LoCoco (chapter 10) also use peer nominations, teacher ratings, and self-report to measure both prosocial and aggressive behavior. Moving from the individual to the global level, Robert A. Hinde (chapter 4) analyzes war as an example of aggression.

Many forms of constructive, prosocial behavior are considered in the book, including compliance with social norms (Paul Mussen & Nancy Eisenberg, chapter 5), the self-regulation of negative emotions (L. Rowell Huesmann & Meredith A. Reynolds, chapter 12; June Price Tangney, chapter 6), dealing with conflict without inflicting psychological or physical harm (Myrna B. Shure, chapter 13), engaging in altruistic or other prosocial acts such as helping, sharing, comforting, and volunteering (Tangney; Mussen & Eisenberg), and expressing positive emotions, such as empathy and sympathy (Albiero & LoCoco; Martin L. Hoffman, chapter 3; Tangney; Endresen & Olweus). Mussen and Eisenberg discuss acts that address broad social injustice, such as working to save victims of the holocaust and participating in civil rights activities, as well as interpersonal acts.

Empathy is a particular concern. There exist many conceptions of what empathy is (Bohart & Greenberg, 1997; Eisenberg & Fabes, 1990; Eisenberg & Strayer, 1987). However what they all have in common is that empathy includes some kind of "fellow feeling" for others, or sensing or knowing what others are going through. Definitions may or may not include an active concern for helping those in distress. In the current volume Endresen and Olweus conceive of empathy as involving both fellow feeling and a concern for helping the other, whereas Hoffman and Albiero and LoCoco focus more on the component of feeling, in particular having an emotional reaction relevant to the other's experience.

Three aspects of constructive and destructive behavior are examined in this book: (a) developmental pathways and the emergence of relatively stable individual differences; (b) possible causes of different developmental pathways and situational factors influencing constructive and destructive behavior; and (c) purposeful and programmatic attempts to reduce destructive and increase constructive pathways and behavior.

Developmental Pathways and Individual Differences

Some authors examine the roots and sequence in the development of constructive and destructive behavior. Hoffman, for example, theoretically traces stages in the development of empathy from an infant's mimicry, to a child in middle childhood's true understanding and experiencing of others' emotions. Albiero and LoCoco and Endresen and Olweus empirically trace the development of empathy as well as examine individual differences.

Several chapters (Pulkkinen and Caprara et al.) provide evidence suggesting that pathways toward destructive or constructive behavior begin early in life—at least by the early elementary grades, if not before. Our authors' findings support and extend the research of other scholars who have found that aggression (Coie & Dodge, 1998) and prosocial behavior (Eisenberg & Fabes, 1998) are moderately stable over childhood. Pulkkinen and Caprara et al. present further evidence on the stability of aggression and prosocial behavior and clarify when they begin to stabilize. These authors also provide evidence on the stability of prosocial behavior.

Our authors go beyond assessing stability, endeavoring to explain findings of stability in the context of a variety of conceptual frameworks. Pulkkinen focuses on the development of skills, whereas Caprara et al. introduce the notion that reputation may play a role in stability. Deborah Stipek (chapter 14) proposes that even consistency in academic achievement in school—which is positively associated with constructive and negatively associated with destructive behavior—might be explained in part by educational practices that maintain the status quo in students' relative performance.

It has been traditionally believed that females are more likely to be prosocial and empathic than are males. However, research findings have been inconsistent (Eisenberg & Fabes, 1998). Although Albiero and LoCoco and Endresen and Olweus provide further evidence that girls are more empathic than boys, Endresen and Olweus provide a more complicated picture. They find, for example, that gender differences are affected by the gender of the target of empathy as much as by the gender of the empathizer. With respect to prosocial behavior, both Pulkkinen and Caprara et al. find that girls are rated as more prosocial than are boys.

Recent literature reviews have also questioned the heretofore little debated assumption that males are more aggressive than females (Coie & Dodge, 1998; Geen, 1998). These scholars suggest that gender difference may be more in how aggression is expressed, with males expressing aggression more physically and females through interpersonal relationships, such as ostracism of those whom they do not like. This raises the issue of how aggression is defined. Caprara et al. define aggression using a rating scale that includes both physical aggression (hitting and biting) and verbal aggression (insulting). Using this measure, Caprara et al. find that boys rate themselves as more aggressive than girls. Additionally, teachers and peers also rate boys as more aggressive. Clearly, definition of aggression matters, and the issue of gender differences is not yet settled.

Causes

Although some scholars in the field review evidence for genetic components to prosocial (Eisenberg & Fabes, 1998) and antisocial and aggressive (Coie & Dodge, 1998; Geen, 1998) behaviors, there is substantial room for environmental effects. This book is primarily about malleability. Although a few of the authors identify early predictors of constructive and destructive behavior, the goal is to identify influences that can be manipulated. Every chapter has implications, summarized in the final chapter, for promoting constructive developmental pathways or putting into reverse destructive trajectories

Authors consider causes that are external to the individual—in the family (Jonathan Bloom-Feshbach & Sally Bloom-Feshbach, chapter 15; Hoffman; Mussen & Eisenberg; Shure), schools (Stipek), the media (Leonard D. Eron, chapter 2), and the broader society (e.g., norms, beliefs, values: Hinde; Eron; Huesmann & Reynolds). They also examine internal psychological mediators that are themselves influenced by external agents—such as attachment (Robert B. Cairns & Beverly D. Cairns, chapter 1; Bloom-Feshbach & Bloom-Feshbach); empathy (Tangney; Alberio & LoCoco) and other emotional experiences (e.g., guilt and shame: Hoffman; Mussen & Eisenberg; Tangney); expressions (e.g., catharsis; Bloom-Feshbach & Bloom-Feshbach; Arthur Bohart, chapter 16); scripts (Eron; Huesmann & Reynolds; Hoffman); and social problem-solving skills (Shure). We elaborate below on their treatment of variables in the environment and individuals' skills and understandings that might be manipulated to promote constructive and reduce destructive behavior.

External Influences

The family is clearly key to the development of constructive or destructive pathways. Two chapters, Bloom-Feshbach and Bloom-Feshbach and Cairns and Cairns, consider the role of attachment between caretaker and child and its potential effects on aggression. The effect of parental disciplining styles on the development of empathy, prosocial behavior, and the inhibition of aggression is considered theoretically by Hoffman and empirically by Mussen and Eisenberg. The authors describe a number of parenting practices that are associated with the development of prosocial behavior—including providing warm, supportive environments; pointing out the effects of the child's behavior on others; explaining and reasoning rather than punishing; and modeling prosocial behavior. They consider the direct effects of such practices, as well as the indirect effects through the arousal of perspective taking and empathy. Huesmann and Reynolds and Eron also mention the role of parents as models of prosocial versus aggressive behavior.

The role of school contexts are addressed by two authors. Stipek discusses the impact of school practices that can discourage a child's effort and performance in school, and thus the development of destructive developmental pathways. Zigler and Styfco focus on the potential of early childhood educational programs to set children on constructive rather than destructive developmental pathways.

At a broader level, Huesmann and Reynolds and Eron discuss the impact of normative beliefs about aggression. They point out that one's culture, subculture, social group, and family all have normative beliefs about how to interpret and respond to events. Norms can legitimize aggression as a response to provocation. Focusing on exposure to media, Eron suggests that realistic violence may have more influence because it normalizes violence, thus promoting the view that it is acceptable. Hinde makes the case that war is not an act of individual aggression, but rather a reflection of societal norms regarding duty and patriotism.

Internal Psychological Mediators

Several authors consider ways in which emotions, especially those associated with empathy, mediate constructive and destructive behavior. Empathy has long been an interest of the developmental psychologist, but it has recently been popularized by Goleman (1995) and others, who identify empathy as one of the skills of "emotional intelligence."

Interest in empathy is based primarily on an assumption that empathic people ought to be more caring and less willing to harm others. Research has, accordingly, examined associations between empathy and prosocial behavior and aggression. Most studies suggest that these relationships are complex and often involve other emotions, particularly guilt. Tangney, for example, summarizes her body of research suggesting that the individual's proneness to experiencing guilt (feeling bad about a deed) enhances empathy and promotes prosocial behavior. Shame (feeling bad about one's whole self), in contrast, is associated with a focus on the self and negative behaviors, such as defensiveness and withdrawal. Hoffman elaborates on the connection between guilt and empathy, adding that parents create guilt by directing a child's empathic attention to the effects of his or her transgressions.

Although some studies suggest that empathy does not always inhibit aggression or lead to prosocial behavior (Eisenberg & Fabes, 1998), Albiero and LoCoco and Endresen and Olweus discuss and elaborate on findings that do suggest some relationship. Tangney examines the relationship of empathy to prosocial behavior and aggression, mediated by its relationship to guilt and shame. Hoffman presents a theoretical account of how empathy should promote prosocial behavior and inhibit aggression, and Mussen and Eisenberg describe research relevant to parenting practices that seem to facilitate a relationship between empathy and the development of prosocial behavior.

Cognitive as well as emotional mediators of constructive and destructive behavior are also considered in this volume. Hoffman and Huesmann and Reynolds discuss the development of cognitive scripts for prosocial behavior and aggression. Eron, for example, suggests that children's observations of aggression are incorporated into aggressive scripts, which are then activated in situations with relevant stimuli. Eron comments also on other cognitive processes that moderate aggressive reactions, such as fantasy and cognitive desensitization. Huesmann and Reynolds note that destructive behavior occurs despite social condemnation because information about unacceptable behavior is filtered through children's own cognitive processes and may be internalized or dismissed. Several authors consider cognitive problem-solving skills. Shure, for example, discusses perspective taking and problem-solving skills as factors in controlling impulses to act aggressively.

Prevention and Intervention

Examination of factors affecting constructive and destructive behavior provide important practical information that can be used to guide efforts to increase constructive and reduce destructive behavior. For example, chapters discussing parenting practices and other societal influences (e.g., the media) suggest direct and indirect (e.g., through emotional or cognitive mediators) strategies for prevention and possible remediation.

Our authors discuss also interventions for those individuals who are on a negative trajectory. Programs discussed by Huesmann and Reynolds, for example, have attempted to modify how children think and reason about socially provocative situations, biases in how they interpret others' behavior, cognitive scripts, and to increase empathy and perspective taking.

Family and School Settings

Some of the interventions involve parents and teachers. Shure describes a training program she developed with George Spivack that is designed to help children develop effective, nonaggressive social problem-solving strategies. Zigler and Styfco review evidence on the effects of early childhood intervention programs for children placed at risk as a strategy for preventing the development of antisocial, delinquent, and criminal behavior. Huesmann and Reynolds review a number of prevention approaches to aggression that are aimed at changing children's perceptions (e.g., of the reasons for the target child's intentions) and attitudes (e.g., toward violence), as well as changing the contexts in which children develop. Stipek proposes ways in which school practices could be modified to support school achievement for children at risk of developing both self- and other-destructive behaviors.

The tone of these chapters is guarded optimism. All of the chapters suggest promising strategies for assisting children to stay on or get on to a constructive pathway, but none of the authors suggest that the interventions they describe are a panacea.

Clinical Contexts

Several of the authors discuss theory and research related to catharsis, a clinical practice that has been proposed as a strategy for preventing aggressive acts. Traditionally those who have favored catharsis have held a "hydraulic" view of emotions and drives. Both emotions and drives are seen as having energy-like qualities. If they are not discharged through expression, they build up and then either cause psychological distress or explode into harmful or destructive expression. Some advocates of catharsis promote the expression of negative emotions in substitute harmless contexts and form, such as punching pillows with rubber batons. Another proposed strategy is to vicariously drain off negative emotions by observing violence in movies, television, and drama.

The anticatharsis forces, led primarily by those originally in the behavioral tradition, have argued that expressing emotions and drives does not drain them off but instead reinforces and strengthens aggressive habits. Watching violent movies or television or engaging in fantasy aggression should therefore be avoided because these tasks build aggressive habits and strengthen rather than diminish the likelihood of acting aggressively.

The issue has been most prominently studied in the question of vicarious catharsis: whether violence on television is beneficial or harmful, with the bulk of current opinion falling on the anticatharsis side that violence in the media stimulates or teaches violence rather than reduces it (Coie & Dodge, 1998; Geen, 1998; Eron). However, both Bloom-Feshbach and Bloom-Feshbach and Bohart argue that the direct expression of emotion under the proper conditions can be beneficial. They contend, as Feshbach (Feshbach, 1964; Feshbach & Singer, 1971) noted a number of years ago, catharsis is most likely not an either–or issue. Perhaps a better question is, When does expression stimulate and when does it reduce destructive behavior?

CONCLUSION

The contributions in this volume identify many of the factors involved in the promotion of constructive and prosocial behavior and the control and reduction of destructive and antisocial/aggressive behavior. In domains as vast and as complicated as these, it would be difficult to bring together in one volume perspectives on all possible components. Several components are somewhat neglected here. With the exception of a brief discussion of genetics by Cairns and Cairns, biological and genetic factors are not covered, although there is evidence that heritability, hormones, neurotransmitters, disorders such as attention deficit hyperactivity disorder, and environmental toxins contribute to antisocial/aggressive behavior (Coie & Dodge, 1998). There is also evidence that genetics and biology contribute to prosocial behavior (Eisenberg & Fabes, 1998). Several social–environmental factors are covered in the volume, such as parenting, the media, and the role of cultural norms and institutions. However, other factors, such as poverty, neighborhood violence, and racism, are not included, although they also play a role in destructive behavior (Coie & Dodge, 1998).

Nonetheless, a wide variety of factors are considered. It can be seen that there will neither be any one "cause" of prosocial or aggressive behavior, nor will any one intervention be the solution. By taking a look at many of the factors involved, this volume contributes to a further understanding of how to prevent not only school shootings like those in Littleton, Colorado, but also the many other acts of violence that continually happen: brutality toward gay men and lesbians, gang violence, police brutality, and war. Further, as several authors note, we should not merely focus on the prevention of antisocial/ aggressive behavior, but instead on the promotion of behavior designed to enhance other people's lives. The complexity involved is humbling, and in one way could be discouraging. However, the more we learn the better able we will be to make constructive change occur piece by piece. We expect that this volume will make a contribution to promoting such change.

REFERENCES

Anonymous. (1984). *New Webster's Dictionary of the English Language*. Delair Publishing.

Bohart, A., & Greenberg, L. S. (1997). Empathy and psychotherapy: An introductory overview. In A. Bohart & L. Greenberg (Eds.), *Empathy reconsidered* (pp. 4–31). Washington, DC: American Psychological Association.

Coie, J. D., & Dodge, K. A. (1998). Aggression and antisocial behavior. In N. Eisenberg (Vol. Ed.) & W. Damon (Ed.-in-Chief), *Handbook of child psychology (5th ed.): Vol. 3. Social, emotional, and personality development* (pp. 779–862). New York: Wiley.

Eisenberg, N., & Fabes, R. A. (1990). Empathy: Conceptualization, assessment, and relation to prosocial behavior. *Motivation and Emotion, 14*, 131–149.

Eisenberg, N., & Fabes, R. A. (1998). Prosocial development. In N. Eisenberg (Vol. Ed.) & W. Damon (Ed.-in-Chief), *Handbook of child psychology (5th ed.): Vol. 3. Social, emotional, and personality development* (pp. 701–778). New York: Wiley.

Eisenberg, N., & Strayer, J. (Eds.). (1987). *Empathy and its development.* Cambridge, England: Cambridge University Press.

Feshbach, S. (1971). Dynamics and morality of violence and aggression: Some psychological considerations. *American Psychologist, 26*, 281–292.

Feshbach, S. (1964). The function of aggression and the regulation of aggressive drive. *Psychological Review, 71*, 257–272.

Feshbach, S., & Singer, R. (1971). *Television and aggression.* San Francisco: Jossey-Bass.

Geen, R. G. (1998). Aggression and antisocial behavior. In D. T. Gilbert, S. T. Fiske, & G. Lindzey (Eds.), *The handbook of social psychology* (4th ed., Vol. II, pp. 317–356). New York: McGraw-Hill.

Goleman, D. (1995). *Emotional intelligence.* New York: Bantam.

Hamilton, V. L., & Sanders, J. (1999). The second face of evil: Wrongdoing in and by the corporation. *Personality and Social Psychology Review, 3*, 222–233.

Loeber, R. (1990). Development and risk factors of juvenile antisocial behavior and delinquency. *Clinical Psychology Review, 10*, 1–41.

Muehlenhard, C. L., & Kimes, L. A. (1999). The social construction of violence: The case of sexual and domestic violence. *Personality and Social Psychology Review, 3*, 234–245.

Parke, R. D., & Slaby, R. G. (1983). The development of aggression. In P. Mussen (Series Ed.) & E. M. Hetherington (Ed.), *Handbook of child psychology: Vol. 4. Socialization, personality, and social development* (pp. 547–641). New York: Wiley.

I

THEORY

The four chapters in this part are theoretical contributions to the understanding of constructive and destructive behavior and their interrelationship. Three chapters (Cairns and Cairns, Eron, and Hoffman) are full-fledged research-based theoretical elaborations. One chapter (Hinde) is a brief theoretical comment presenting a unique perspective on the nature of war.

ROBERT R. CAIRNS AND BEVERLY D. CAIRNS

From their interactional, contextual perspective, Robert B. Cairns and Beverly D. Cairns discuss several current topics in psychology. First, they focus on genetics. In recent years the idea that genetics plays an important role in behavior in general, and in prosocial and antisocial behavior in particular, has become influential (e.g., Kagan, 1998; Rowe, 1997). Cairns and Cairns, however, argue that the idea that something has a genetic basis is often misinterpreted to mean that therefore it is stable and impervious to circumstances. From an interactional perspective, genes are in interaction with environments, and the same genotype could manifest itself positively or negatively, depending on experience. Furthermore, the manifestation of genes can change over time, depending on circumstances.

Second, they discuss attachment (see Thompson, 1998). Cairns and Cairns suggest that the meaning of attachment behavior is not fixed. First, insecure attachments do not inevitably lead to negative outcomes; this depends on other contextual variables. Second attachments themselves are not stable entities but grow and change over time. Therefore, simple linear correlations between early attachments and later outcomes are not to be expected.

Cairns and Cairns also argue that aggression has evolved because it can have adaptive consequences. They suggest that aggression and attachment (i.e., affiliation) co-exist, and both can play a role in fostering effective functioning. They note that attachment and aggression play complementary roles in promoting social synchrony while preserving individual autonomy. Therefore, from their point of view it is no surprise that research is now finding that many aggressive boys may also possess good social skills and may be popular (e.g., Rodkin, Farmer, Pearl, & Van Acker, 2000) and capable of forming close relationships. Nor would it be a surprise that some aggressive individuals may have high self-esteem (Baumeister & Campbell, 1999; Staub, 1999).

These findings have important implications for intervention, given that many interventions are based on the idea that aggressive boys need to learn social skills and need to have their self-esteem raised. They suggest, among other things, that aggressive behavior may be socially supported and reinforced if it is exhibited by boys who are otherwise popular. This will fit, as we shall see, with research findings to be reviewed in Part II, implying that boys who exhibit empathy may learn that this is not socially adaptive. In other words, it may be that the social context in part reinforces boys being tough. If that is the case, training in social skills and even in empathy may not be sufficient to alter aggressive behavior if it is being maintained by social reinforcement. Certainly this is a topic that merits thorough empirical investigation.

LEONARD D. ERON

Leonard D. Eron presents a theoretical–empirical contribution on the role of "seeing is believing" in the genesis and promotion of aggressive behavior. The issue of aggression in the media remains a timely topic. The two shooters at Columbine High School in Littleton, Colorado, Dylan Klebold and Eric Harris, were apparently fans of a violent interactive computer game. Eron has been on the forefront of the study of violence in the media, and in this chapter he gives a research-based theoretical overview of how observing or fantasizing about violence may teach or stimulate it. In so doing, Eron argues that at least certain kinds of fantasy violence act as rehearsals for the potential for real violence rather than serving as control functions, as had been postulated by others. Eron's work in this regard raises serious questions about the kinds of fantasy violence children engage in through the use of interactive media, such as video games. Eron concludes by describing several factors that contribute to aggression, such as cognitive and emotional desensitization.

Eron uses a cognitive information-processing model, developed by Huesmann (see Huesmann and Reynolds, chapter 12,) that emphasizes the concepts of scripts and of social norms. In an information-processing perspective, observing aggressive models in the home and on television strengthens internal scripts that promote aggression. Aggressive scripts are triggered by a combination of situation and norms to precipitate aggressive behavior. Eron's view is compatible with our speculation in the Introduction that if aggression is supported by social norms and portrayed favorably in the media, it may not be sufficient to simply train children in social skills.

The cognitive perspective presented by Eron is compatible with other perspectives offered by Bandura (1986, 1999), Berkowitz (1990), and Dodge (1986), all of whom emphasize cognitive and social-information–processing factors as important causes of aggressive behavior.

MARTIN L. HOFFMAN

Various skills or talents are as or more important in adjustment than traditional intellectual ability. Among the most important of these is empathy. Empathy is therefore widely researched (Eisenberg & Fabes, 1990); Eisenberg & Strayer, 1987). In this volume Martin L. Hoffman uses the concept of cognitive scripts to present an original, comprehensive theory of how the development of empathy forms the basis for the development of morality and prosocial behavior. In so doing he also struggles with the thorny issues of how empathy-based moral reasoning cannot always resolve all dilemmas and may not always lead to caring outcomes. He describes the potential situations in which people may fail to be empathic (particularly situations in which one does not reach beyond those one knows, or those to whom one feels similar, to empathize with others who are in an "outgroup," or who one perceives as different) In so doing, Hoffman presents an important theory of the development of moral and prosocial behavior and in addition begins to theoretically delineate important qualifications as to why empathy does not always and inevitably lead to caring behavior.

ROBERT A. HINDE

Recently an emerging topic has been the study of "evil" (Miller, 1999). *Evil* refers to extremes of antisocial aggressive behavior, such as torture and the committing of atrocities. Many of the examples of evil behavior occur during war. How are humans capable of wiping out whole populations of those they disagree with? In his chapter Robert A. Hinde offers a unique perspective on war.

The causes of war are often sought in the individual nature of human beings, focusing on individuals' genetics, childhood histories, and in general the kinds of factors that make individuals aggressive. Hinde argues to the contrary that the factors that drive individual aggression are not typically the ones that drive the behavior of individuals in war. He argues instead that war is a societal institution and needs to be understood at that level. Hinde emphasizes how societal institutions support war by characterizing outgroups in terms of negative stereotypes and through language. He also discusses the role of social norms and of cultural institutions such as the military–industrial complex.

Others have commented on some of the factors Hinde mentions. For instance, Bandura (1999) has written on the use of sanitizing language, dehumanization of the targets of aggression, diffused responsibility, and moral disengagement as contributors to violence. Staub (1999), Bandura (1999), and Baumeister and Campbell (1999) have all commented on the tendency of people to see their aggressive acts as positively motivated by higher social purposes—what Baumeister and Campbell have termed "idealistic evil" (p. 210), Muehlenhard and Kimes (1999) noted how who controls the definition of language controls what is viewed as violence. For instance, for many years it was definitional impossible for a man to rape his wife.

What is unique about Hinde's perspective is that it frames all of these factors within a larger cultural context. Although Hinde's chapter does not cover all the potential causes and complications of what causes war, its value is in presenting a unique alternative perspective. This perspective is in keeping with a theme running through all the chapters in this part—emphasizing the role of sociocultural and ecological factors in the promotion and sustaining of violence. Even Hoffman, who focuses largely on the development of the individual's moreal sense, points out the tendency of humans to empathize more with those with whom they identify (i.e., members of their "ingroups") and to therefore be less empathic with members of outgroups. This suggests that it may be easy to engage in stereotyping and denigrating of those whom we see as different from us. In this regard, Hoffman suggests that we need to make a deliberate effort to empathize with those who differ from us, a point congruent with Hinde's suggestion for what can be done to prevent war. Furthermore, as we have already mentioned, to effectively intervene it will not be enough simply to intervene at the individual level. Interventions will have to also address the larger sociocultural context (National Research Council, 1995; Burt, Resnick, & Novick, 1998; Richel & Beckerk-Lausen, 1997).

REFERENCES

Bandura. A. (1986). *Social foundations of thought and action: A social cognitive theory.* Englewood Cliffs, NJ: Prentice Hall.

Bandura, A. (1999). Moral disengagement in the perpetration of inhumanities. *Personality and Social Psychology Review, 3*, 193–209.

Baumeister, R. F., & Campbell, W. K. (1999). The intrinsic appeal of evil: Sadism, sensational thrills, and threatened egotism. *Personality and Social Psychology Review, 3*, 210–221.

Berkowitz, L. (1990). On the formation and regulation of anger and aggression: A cognitive–neoassociationistic analysis. *American Psychologist, 45*, 494–503.

Burt, M. R. Resnick, G., & Novick, E. R. (1998). *Building supportive communities for at-risk adolescents: It takes more than services.* Washington, DC: American Psychological Association.

Dodge, K. A. (19985). A social information processing model of social competence in children. In M. Perlmutter (Ed.), *The Minnesota Symposium on Child Psychology* (Vol. 18, pp. 77–125), Hillsdale, NJ: Erlbaum.

Eisenberg, N., & Fabes, R. A. (1990). Empathy: Conceptualization, assessment, and relation to prosocial behavior. *Motivation and Emotion, 14*, 131–149.

Eisenberg, N., & Strayer, J. (Eds.). (1987). *Empathy and its development.* Cambridge, England: Cambridge University Press.

Kagan, J. (1998). Biology and the child. In N. Eisenberg (Vol. Ed.) & W. Damon (series Ed.), *Handbook of child psychology: Vol. 3. Social, emotional, and personality development* (5th ed., pp. 177–235). New York: Wiley.

Miller, A. G. (Ed.). (1999). Special issue: Perspectives on evil and violence. *Personality and Social Psychology Review, 3,* 176–275.

Muehlenhard, C. L., & Kimes, L. A. (1999). The social construction of violence: The case of sexual and domestic violence. *Personality and Social psychology Review, 3,* 234–245.

National Research Council. (Ed.). (1995). *Losing generations: Adolescents in high-risk settings.* Washington, DC: American Psychological Association.

Richel, A. V., & Becker-Lausen, E. (1997). *Keeping children from harm's way: How national policy affects psychological development.* Washington, DC: American Psychological Association.

Rodkin, P. C., Farmer, T. W., Pearl. R., & Van Acker, R. (2000). Heterogeneity of popular boys: Antisocial and prosocial configurations; *Developmental Psychology, 36,* 14–24.

Rowe, D. C. (1997). Genetics, temperament, and personality. In R. Hogan, J. Johnson, & S. Briggs (Eds.), *Handbook of personality psychology* (pp. 369–386). New York: Academic Press.

Staub, E. (1999). The roots of evil: Social conditions, culture, personality, and basic human needs. *Personality and Social Psychology Review, 3,* 179–192.

Thompson, R. A. (1998). Early sociopersonality development. In N. Eisenberg (Vol. Ed.) & W. Damon (Series Ed.), *Handbook of child psychology: Vol. 3, Social, emotional, and personality development* (5th ed., pp. 25–104). New York: Wiley.

1

AGGRESSION AND ATTACHMENT: THE FOLLY OF SEPARATISM

ROBERT B. CAIRNS AND BEVERLEY D. CAIRNS

A generation of brash and bright students in psychology returned from World War II more than 50 years ago and became engaged in a different kind of warfare, one involving ideas rather than nuclear devices. These graduate students found two competing theoretical models that vied for attention and commitment. One was neo-behaviorism, the learning model that had gained hegemony in experimental psychology and expanded its dominance to most areas of academic psychology by mid-century. The other was psychoanalysis, whose implications for psychotherapy, assessment, and development gained a commanding position in psychiatry and clinical psychology in the postwar period.

But the postwar engagements were, for the most part, quiet conflicts. More intratheory confrontations than between-theory confrontations occurred because psychoanalysis and behaviorism typically were occupied with different phenomena and methods. Accordingly, the two great metatheories of the 20th century have rarely been found on a collision course; they usually sail past each other without awareness or acknowledgment. There has been, however, some overlap where the two models offered contrasting explanations for the same phenomena. In these instances, confrontation was inevitable. One area of overlap has involved negative interpersonal actions, subsumed by the concept of aggression. Another overlap area has involved the development of intimate interpersonal relations—domains subsumed by the concept of *dependency* in social learning theory and *attachment* in neo-analytic object relation theory.

In light of the continuing interest and controversy about the essential phenomena to which the concepts of dependency and attachment refer, it seems appropriate to take stock of their current status and the relations between them. To adumbrate a primary conclusion of this chapter, we propose that the partitioning of negative and positive interpersonal behaviors into separate processes and different explanatory models has outlived its usefulness. Empirical findings from longitudinal and comparative studies provide guides on how traditional domain-specific accounts may be reorganized and understood on the common plane of development.

AGGRESSION AND CATHARSIS

The mid-century psychoanalytic perspective emphasized the intra-organismic dynamics of aggressive expression, including the regulatory roles of emotional, empathetic, and cognitive factors. One counterintuitive implication was the proposal that the action-specific aggressive energy could be diminished by vicarious experiences and actions, a proposition consistent with the general catharsis proposal of classical psychoanalysis (e.g., Fenichel, 1945). Conversely, behavioral approaches focused on the environmental conditions responsible for stimulating, consolidating, and learning aggressive actions and motives. Could these "inside" and "outside" views on aggression be resolved in a way that captured the best features of both?

In a brilliant research program that spanned four decades, Seymour and Norma Feshbach accepted the challenge (see S. Feshbach, 1955, 1956, 1964, 1971, 1976, 1984; N. Feshbach [e.g., Feshbach & Feshbach, 1969; Feshbach, Singer, & Feshbach, 1963], and colleagues [e.g., Feshbach & Singer, 1971; Murray & Feshbach, 1978]). Among other things, they demonstrated the critical functions of emotional regulation, fantasy, and empathy in anger elicitation and expression. This personality-based position was initially contrasted with the behavioral proposal that all depictions of aggression—regardless of context or individual status—led to increases in aggression through imitation, modeling, and learned stimulus–response sequences. The Feshbachs found that the outcome observed—an increase or decrease in aggression—depended on the individual's initial level of anger, the time and timing of manipulations, the contexts of measurement, the role of fantasy, and what was measured during and following the manipulation. They scored a major victory by initiating a new research agenda for the next generation. Their substantive legacy includes contemporary research themes of emotional regulation, affect development, and the constructive aspects of development. Their methodological legacy for developmental, social, and personality researchers is of equal importance. Experimental research designs that attempted to isolate single variable–single outcome effects—independent of the emotional and cognitive status of individual participants—became increasingly suspect.

Another contest between behavioral and psychoanalytic theory was brewing in the postwar period—namely, how might the origins and maintenance of close social relationships be explained? Is the foundation of the mother–infant relationship best described through the operation of innate, immanent forces that strive for expression or through the operation of learning and secondary drive mechanisms? On the side of learning, behaviorist models of social relations proposed that a "dependency" drive arose as an outcome of early mother–child relations and guided the nature and quality of subsequent interactions (Gewirtz, 1967; Sears, Whiting, Nowlis, & Sears, 1953). In instances in which the child's striving for attention and affection were neglected or rebuffed, conditions of dependency–anxiety were established whereby future relations would be tenuous or easily fractured (Bandura & Walters, 1959; Cairns, 1961). On the side of inherent forces, psychoanalyst John Bowlby emphasized the immanent need for security, and the devastating outcomes of any failure of maternal care and bonding during the formative years of infancy (Bowlby, 1952, 1958, 1969, 1973). This "object-relations theory" kept intact the traditional emphases of psychoanalysis on psychopathology and the enduring impact of early infant experiences while extending the motivational system beyond psychosexual impulses.

Unlike the catharsis–stimulation debate—which gave way to an integrative account of aggressive processes—the attachment dispute was a virtual rout. Attachment theory—and psychoanalysis—seems to have won hands down. One reason was the discovery of a simple and robust natural phenomenon; namely, human infants late in the first year of life typically become distressed and disrupted when separated from their principal caretaker and calm down when their caretaker returns (Ainsworth, 1963; Schaffer & Emerson, 1964). Because the phenomenon was observed across cultures (Kagan, 1976) and across mammalian species (Cairns, 1966a), it qualified for being a species-typical, near-universal phenomena that was directly linked to development. This observation was interpreted as providing strong support for the psychoanalytic assumption that an intense, "passionate," and specific mother–infant bond was established in the first year of life. Subsequently, the assessment of this phenomenon was institutionalized in the "Strange Situation" procedure (Ainsworth, Blehar, Waters, & Wall, 1978), although the phenomenon was so robust that it could be readily assessed by various observational (Fleener & Cairns, 1970) and interview (Schaffer & Emerson, 1964) procedures.

What was expected to be a face-off between the main protagonists of the attachment–dependency debate led to a full-scale behaviorist retreat. The pioneering social learning theorist who had championed the dependency concept in the first place conceded the shortcomings of the behavioral account (Sears, 1972). In contrast, Ainsworth (1972) stood her ground for the correctness of Bowlby's neoanalytic attachment theory. Over the next few years there was a rapid disappearance of the concept of dependency and its focus on learning mechanisms. The retreat of dependency was not wholly due to words, however, because the social learning model had been fatally injured by the failure to replicate key earlier findings on dependency (i.e., Cairns, 1972; Radke Yarrow, Campbell, & Burton, 1968).

So what has happened to the tension between psychoanalytic and behavioral theories that was so palpable in the first half of the first century? There seems to have been a general agreement that molar models of social behavior and personality had become stalled, and greater specificity seemed called for in theoretical construction and explanation. Accordingly, domain-specific accounts (i.e., attachment, aggression, altruism) have been displaced by the molar theories offered by behaviorism and psychoanalysis. It is almost true to say that the domains of destructive, aggressive behaviors were ceded to modern behaviorism (i.e., social–cognitive learning), and the domains of close social relations were assigned to modern psychoanalysis (i.e., attachment theory). Although this categorization is too broad to be fully accurate—among other things, there has been a recent rise of biological, genetic, and social network analyses applied to both domains—there seems to have been a broad division of responsibility.

These mid-century conflicts are germane to this chapter for four reasons:

1. The tug-of-war between models of negative destructive behaviors and constructive, positive ones is long-standing. Among other considerations, negative acts, behaviors, and beliefs are more easily and reliably measured than positive, constructive, and adaptive behaviors and beliefs (Boucher & Osgood, 1969; Cairns & Lewis, 1962; Levine, Leitenberg, & Richter, 1964). Even measures of attachment strength—which seems at first blush to be the prototypic positive relationship—use negative states (discriminative crying, separation disruption and relief on mother–infant reunion).

2. The separation of aggression–attachment into separate theoretical and methodological domains has become deeply entrenched, and it is hard to conceive of the concepts as fundamentally linked. That is a pity, because the two dispositions

could ultimately be shown to support each other in achieving adaptation and behavior organization.

3. Theorists as diverse as Lewin (1935), Sears et al. (1953), and Schneirla (1966) have observed that there are dangers in proposing qualitatively different explanations for seemingly different acts. There is not only the potential loss of parsimony; the search for general principles may be terminated prematurely.

4. The results of longitudinal and intergenerational studies conducted over the ensuing 40 years invite a holistic model that can transcend these earlier domain-specific explanations of aggression and attachment. These long-term studies provide fresh information on the nature of individual change and continuity over the life span and the nature of changes across generations.

In summary, longitudinal–intergenerational information now available on individual social development provides an empirical basis for re-examining the common adaptation processes underlying both attachment and aggression.

A DRIVE FOR SYSTEM

On the criteria for evaluating scientific theories, philosopher W. V. Quine (1981) wrote,

> A good scientific theory is under tension from two opposing forces: the drive for evidence and the drive for system. . . . If either of these drives were unchecked by the other, it would issue in something unworthy of the name of scientific theory: in the one case a mere record of observations, and in the other a myth without foundation (p. 31).

In the evolution of the domain-specific models of attachment and aggression, some findings that could check the model building appear to have been ignored to enhance their apparent inclusiveness. But as Lewin (1935) observed, this is a hazardous strategy because it is an error in science to hold that "the exception makes the rule." On the contrary, one rigorously documented exception should be able to force basic revisions in the model, or bury it.

ATTACHMENT AND LEARNING

Attachment theory has enjoyed enormous popularity over the past three decades as a model of initial relationship development (Ainsworth, 1972;

Bowlby, 1969, 1973). The assessment procedures developed by Ainsworth and her colleagues have become the "gold standard" for describing the quality of the mother–infant relationship (Ainsworth et al., 1978). When social learning theory abandoned dependency and, more generally, the phenomena of attachment, it retreated at exactly the time when careful accounts of the learning mechanisms of attachment seemed called for. Researchers on attachment became focused on descriptions of the stability of categories of early-formed relationships and their continuity over the life course. Advances in descriptions involved (a) the identification of a fourth category of mother–infant reunion activity and (b) the creation of an "adult attachment" interview that was designed to assess the nature, quality, and coherence of the attachment of adults. In contrast with studies of attachment in nonhumans, scant attention has been given to learning mechanisms and the dynamics of developmental change.

Animal behaviorists early discovered that social attachment to the mother or principal caregiver was indeed immanent and innate. That provides confirmation for a basic assumption in attachment theory. However, comparative studies also showed that social attachments are eminently learnable, extendible, context dependent, and inevitably modified over development (Cairns, 1966a, 1966b, Cairns & Johnson, 1965; Cairns & Werboff, 1967; Mason & Kinney, 1974). These phenomena are consistent with the proposition that the phenomena are basic in social behavior evolution. If the mother dies, or the mammalian infant is otherwise abandoned, its survival depends on rapidly establishing a new attachment to a maternal surrogate. Moreover, attachments form in the absence of positive feedback; punishment and abuse do not preclude the formation of social attachment in nonhuman infants.

Few parallel human mother–infant experiments have been conducted on the dynamics, extendibility, and modification of attachment phenomena. Given the commitment of attachment theory to the significance of behavioral evolution, it is puzzling that the discipline has failed to vigorously extend experimental analyses of attachment findings from nonhumans. In the few instances in which parallel studies of humans have been conducted, the research has replicated in human infants the findings observed in nonhuman mammalian infants. For instance, it has been demonstrated that new, strong attachments can be rapidly formed in infants and young children (Cairns, 1979; Fleener, 1967, 1973; Rheingold, 1959, 1969; Rheingold & Bayley, 1959). Moreover, these new relationships can mimic or rival in strength those observed in the infant–biological mother relationship. Sound inconceivable? To the contrary, this outcome would make sense from an evolutionary–psychobiological framework in which early attachment is necessarily synchronized with the survival needs of infants and the evolutionary preparedness of their mothers. But if mothers were to reject, abandon, or die, infants could not survive without some kind of fail-safe mechanism that would permit the rapid realignment of a new relationship. Although the results to date have yielded robust and seemingly incontrovertible findings, they have been infrequently pursued and are rarely cited in discussions of human attachment. Why is this so?

One possibility is that such research is deemed to be unethical, in that it would involve tampering with an innate disposition of the child and mother. Although that proposal might be consistent with a fundamental tenet of attachment theory, it defies everyday observations on the natural rapid emergence of new relationships to other people (e.g., baby sitters, aunts, siblings, caretakers) and specific things (e.g., a blanket, a teddy bear, a stuffed bunny, a pillow). These attachment phenomena of everyday life are readily induced and manipulated under laboratory conditions, and their stability, functions, and similarities to the mother–infant attachment objectively determined. To the extent that the results of experiments and close observations over time identify the dynamic processes of change and realignment, they might challenge basic assumptions of attachment theory on how social relationships are fixed in early experience.

Available findings now implicate biological mechanisms as partners with social experiences in the formation and change of early relationships. The findings also implicate the role of learning mechanisms at several stages of ontogeny in promoting the preservation and modification of attachment patterns. These processes—psychobiological and learning—operate in consort to bring about short-term social attachment and long-term social adaptation. Both emphases are required for a holistic analysis of social development. Failure to examine systematically the dynamic processes of social accommodation may create, in (Quine 1981, p. 31) Quine's words, "a myth without foundation."

AGGRESSION AND BIOLOGY

Nowadays, it cannot be said that attachment phenomena reflect, in part, the operation of inherent psychobiological and genetic mechanisms. The role of learning has been suspect, even denigrated, in attachment. The reverse seems to hold for modern social learning–cognitive accounts of aggression. Although virtually all systematic accounts of aggressive phenomena in humans leave open the possibility of biological factors, this opening is rarely the first choice of social development models (although it has sometimes been used as a last resort). When social learning and social–cognitive processes fail to explain—or when prevention trials fall short—an appeal can always be made to an irreversible genetic disposition or an intractable neurobiological deficit. Although it has seemed easy to accept the innate proposition in accounts of attachment, it is difficult to do so in accounts of aggressive behavior.

AGGRESSION AND GENETICS

It is broadly accepted in animal behavior that aggressive patterns inevitably emerge in ontogeny in the absence of specific learning experiences. In the instances in which the role of learning experiences for the first emergence of aggressive patterns has been investigated, the results are unambiguous. Aggressive patterns arise in the absence of specific training experiences in "learning to fight." Rearing animals alone, in social isolation, without the benefit of play-fighting or other presumably necessary antecedents, has proved to be an effective social manipulation to create highly reactive and aggressive animals, from mice to monkeys.

In addition, the role of inherent factors has been repeatedly underscored using attempts to modify aggressive behavior by genetic and neurobiological manipulation. Genetic influences on the social behaviors of nonhuman mammals are ubiquitous, powerful, and readily detected. But demonstrations that aggressive behaviors are influenced by biology constitute only part of the story. Developmental findings have shown how social behaviors help organize biological processes (Cairns, 1973, 1976, 1996). Specifically, these studies show the following:

- Genetic effects for aggressive behaviors are highly malleable over the course of development.
- Genetic influences on aggressive behavior are more dynamic, easily achieved, and open to rapid manipulation than has been recognized in current models of social evolution and behavior genetics.
- Developmental timing has a significant impact on the nature of the genetic effects observed in aggressive behaviors.

These empirical results are consistent with the view that social behaviors are among the first features to be influenced by genetic selection as well as by environmental experience. Social actions have distinctive properties in adaptation because they organize the space between the organism and the environment and promote rapid, selective, and novel accommodations. A simple answer to the innate-learned question for aggressive behavior is now available from animal models. Aggressive patterns are indisputably inherent, but once established in development, they are highly malleable by forces within and without the individual.

If genes are significant in behavior evolution, their operation should be general enough to extend to the human condition. Yet direct linkages are required in an extrapolation to human beings. Over the past two decades, a number of studies have been conducted on the role of genetics in criminal and antisocial aggressive behaviors. Unlike genetic–neurobiological animal studies, research with humans has been limited for the most part to the study of naturally occurring genetic phenomena. This has been the basis for within- and between-family comparisons and, more precisely, for comparisons among monozygotic (MZ) twins, same-sex dizygotic (DZ) twins, same-sex siblings, and unrelated persons of the same sex. All things being equal, it is assumed that the greater the commonalty in genetic background, the greater should be the aggressive behavior similarities. Accordingly, MZ and DZ twins should be more similar to each other than they are to same-sex siblings and nonsiblings, and MZ twins will be more similar than DZ twins.

But what if all things are not equal, and residual social differences exist beyond genetics in MZ and DZ twins? For example, identical twins may be more likely than fraternal twins to establish mutual behavioral dependencies and closer shared identities. These outcomes would be mediated, say, by wearing the same clothes, joining the same friendship networks, or being mistaken for the other twin. On the last point, it is a rare identical twin who has not taken the place of the other twin to amuse and confuse friends, teachers, or dates. Given that shared psychological identities may exist in the eyes of others—whether planned or accidental—it is no small wonder there are greater behavioral similarities among identical twins, genetics notwithstanding. Yet little systematic research has been conducted on how distinctive interactions among twins and the creation of shared identities affect the level of behavioral similarities in MZ and DZ pairs. Moreover, the developmental trajectories of MZ twins suggest that fresh behavioral differences may emerge at critical points in the life trajectory, such as when the twins become married to dissimilar spouses (personal communication, K. Whitfield, March 1999). Until such data become available, the nature of the joint contributions of genetics and development to twin similarities will remain intriguing, although speculative.

AGGRESSION AND NEUROBIOLOGY

Unlike behavioral investigators, neurobiological researchers readily accept the possibility of a direct and immediate neurotransmitter–aggression connection. The debate in neuroscience these days seems to center on which transmitter and which neurobiological pathway is most important, rather than whether they are implicated.

Neurogenetic investigations have been recently propelled by significant advances in the techniques of molecular genetic analysis. Molecular geneticist David Goldman (1996) provides a succinct account of the procedures now available and a summary of the early research results. With the development of automated sequencing methods and rapid procedures for scanning for genetic variants, the direct scanning of candidate genes has now become a practical and productive enterprise. When used in conjunction with other methodologies that have different advantages and limitations, the procedures provide convergent evidence with respect to the neurogenesis of aggressive behavior.

These procedures provide evidence consistent with the serotonin–impulsivity–violent suicide observations reported by Asberg and colleagues in Sweden (e.g., Asberg, Traksman, & Thoren, 1976). Linnoila and Virkkunen, with colleagues in Helsinki and Bethesda, Maryland, reported similar findings for Finnish impulsive violent offenders, suicide risks, and early onset male alcoholics (e.g., Linnoila et al., 1983; Nielson et al., 1994; Virkkunen & Linnoila, 1996). The common feature they describe is impulsivity, not violence, fire-setting, suicidal behavior, or alcoholism per se.

AGGRESSION AND DEVELOPMENT

Developmental psychobiological investigations have followed a different strategy, beginning with the assumption that interactions help organize neurobiological structures as much as the reverse. Social interactions, including aggressive behaviors, occur at the interface between organismic and environmental sources of influence (Cairns, Gariépy, & Hood, 1990; Gariépy, Lewis, & Cairns, 1996). The work begins with the assumption that social actions are multidetermined and dynamic over time, hence the detailed study of behavior should come first rather than last. The developmental perspective promotes a focus on the plasticity of the biology of the organism and its environment. This research indicates that the effects of genetic background and neurobiology on aggressive behavior can be modified, neutralized, or reversed by experiences.

Developmental research on neurobiological relations to aggressive behavior indicates that neurotransmitters operate in collaboration and are bidirectionally influenced by experiences, contexts, and relationships. Hence it seems unlikely that the behavioral outcomes of aggression and violence will be mediated in a single site or by the operation of a single neurobiological agent, whether serotonin, dopamine, or gamma amino butyric acid (GABA). Individuals behave in dynamic settings as integrated, holistic beings, not as gene machines or biochemical reactors. Unraveling these relations is not simply a problem for the integrative study of aggression; rather, it speaks to a broader need to understand the functional integration of neurobiological systems with social interactions of all types, including attachment.

THE FOLLY OF SEPARATISM

It should be clear by now that we do not believe that it is a good idea to assign attachment and aggression to separate and mutually exclusive explanatory bins or to keep learning and biology dissociated in developmental accounts. The categorical assignments and the domain-specific models they support have been responsible for covering up some robust empirical findings which, if acknowledged, could clarify the nature of interactional development. Below are broadly replicated findings that have cut across both domains and have been ignored in the "drive for system."

THE FICKLENESS OF FRIENDSHIPS

Popular myths notwithstanding, most intimate adolescent friendships of childhood and adolescence are dynamic, unstable, and fickle (Cairns & Cairns, 1994; Neckerman, 1996). The best friend of today can become the foe of tomorrow, or vice versa. But instability of friendships does not diminish their importance or function in personal development. In fact, the "unreliability" can ensure variability of influences and the evolution over adolescence of relationships consistent with other features of the individual's preferences and life. The broader issues raised by fickleness concern the utility of interpersonal constancy. In these adolescent experiences, it would appear that it is usually more functional to switch than stay. Indeed, failure to switch friendships when the interests, goals, and beliefs of the members diverge may lead to chronic conflicts in the relationship and in the self.

What are those conditions that make continued commitment between two people adaptive and functional despite developmental changes? Enduring relationships are likely to occur when individuals change together and adopt the goals that may be integrated with those of the other person. The foregoing suggests a developmental proposal on adolescent relationships; namely, a stable friendship in adolescence is not a passive thing but a dynamic process that requires active changes by both members of the relationship. Hence friendships between adolescents must change to remain stable, and the changes must somehow be coordinated. To the extent that the people involved share similar social backgrounds, athletic or musical talents, and interpersonal skills, the changes that each undergo are themselves likely to be coordinated. But if the friendship is based on characteristics that are ephemeral or likely to be sharply modified in development, the foundation for mutual support may become eroded.

In this regard, "best friends" among teenagers and the intense emotional commitment associated with them are not likely to endure, despite the hopes of the people involved. Nor, over the long run of development, may it be functional for such adolescent relationships to remain constant. Their immediate service could be to facilitate social and personal growth by providing avenues for change in each person through the support of fresh adaptations in behaviors and beliefs. For this function to be served, the relationship must be intense and involve high levels of mutual trust, and each individual should believe that the relationship is highly durable. The last requirement appears, in most instances, to represent a necessary fiction so the other two criteria may be met. In the course of development, there may be a selective evolution across relationships in order to arrive at behavior patterns and beliefs distinctive for each person.

AGGRESSION AND REJECTION

Until recently, it was broadly assumed that aggressive children were rejected children. Although that belief is doubtless still held by many people in the sciences and society, most contemporary investigators now reject it. The evidence simply has failed to support the aggression–rejection proposition. Clearly, highly aggressive boys tend to have as many close, reciprocated friendships as nonaggressive boys. The difference lies in what the friends are like and how many each boy has. As one might expect, aggressive children tend to have friends who share their propensity toward aggressive, antisocial behavior. When they get together, to terrorize teachers and other students, they are not particularly liked by the classmates they dominate or by the teachers they challenge. If anything, the social groups or gangs established by truly aggressive youth are more stable over time and more tightly woven than cliques and groups formed by nonaggressive youth. But these friendships and social support groups do not mean that aggressive youth are any better off because of their stable friendships. To the contrary, both individuals and the gangs with which they are associated can exacerbate problems at home, at school, in the community, and in the judicial system (Cairns, Cadwallader, Estell, & Neckerman, 1997).

These outcomes figure into the attachment–aggression relationship in some noteworthy ways. First, the findings challenge the assumption that aggressive youth are limited to shallow, unstable relationships. Second, the findings are inconsistent with the idea that an insecure early mother–infant attachment cascades directly into a failure to form close relationships and, subsequently, peer rejection leads to further aggression. Finally, the findings are consistent with the principle of interactional synchrony, whereby one's close relationships are assumed to provide mutual support and direction for interchanges. Accordingly, the development of aggressive strategies grows out of close affiliations and relationships, not because of their absence. In effect, the data are consistent with the idea that analyses should focus on what is present rather than what is absent or missing. In studies of the affiliations of aggressive youth, there is strong evidence of considerable support for their aggressive behaviors, typically by peers and often by parents.

DEPENDENCY AND AGGRESSION

In one of the first major investigations of social learning, Sears and his colleagues (1953) found that the aggression and affiliative actions were positively correlated in young children. Those preschool children who were most aggressive were also the most affiliative. Sears and his collaborators took their counterintuitive finding in stride, attributing the outcome to differences among children in activity level: The more active the child, the more likely he or she would be observed in any behavior pattern, whether positive or negative. Once activity level was removed, the correlation became insignificant.

But once the confound was corrected, why did not the correlation between aggression and affiliation become negative? The fact that it did not seems to contradict common sense. The research findings in several domains suggest aggression and attachment are not necessarily orthogonal in nature, as common sense would have it. On the contrary, the available data indicate that there may be basic commonalties in developmental functions and dynamics.

ATTACHMENT AND PUNISHMENT

We have focused almost exclusively on experimental and longitudinal studies of human development up to this point. That is customary in a field that has viewed animal behavior findings with suspicion. But it seems reasonable to expect fundamental genetic and neurobiological phenomena to be productively studied in nonhuman mammals. As it turns out, examination of the relations between attachment and aggression in animals has helped clarify the dynamic relations across these interactional patterns.

Early investigations in rhesus monkeys found that social attachment is not necessarily inhibited or extinguished by aggression and punishment. This was persuasively shown by Harlow and his co-workers (Arling & Harlow, 1967; Seay, Alexander, & Harlow, 1964). Rhesus monkeys that are reared in isolation, even in the constant company of a cloth surrogate, exhibit "strange" social behavior at early maturity; they are socially and sexually inept. Even in those cases in which previously isolated females have been impregnated by a male and bear offspring, they typically behave in an entirely nonmotherly manner toward their young. According to work done at the Wisconsin Primate Laboratory, motherless mothers were inadequate mothers; those studied either abused their offspring or were indifferent to and ignored them. The investigators felt that few of the infants would have survived if intervention measures had not been taken by the laboratory staff. In one instance,

> the mother passively accepted the baby to the breast by Day 3 [after birth], and attempts to remove and hand feed the baby were abandoned on Day 4 since such efforts provoked violent attacks directed against her infant. These attacks included crushing the infant's head and body against the floor . . . and jumping up and down with her full weight on the infant. (Seay et al., 1964, p. 347)

To determine what effect such rearing experiences had on the social preferences of surviving infants, Sackett (1967) permitted them to approach and remain with one of three different individuals, one of whom was the infant's punitive mother. Comparisons were made between infants who were normally reared, those reared on a cloth surrogate, and those reared by a punitive "motherless monkey" mother. Surprisingly, of the various groups tested, the punitively reared animals showed the strongest preferences for spending time in the area of the mother.

In a related experimental study, Rosenblum and Harlow (1963) devised a cloth cylinder that would irrationally punish its infant. During the first 5 1/2 months of life, the baby rhesus monkeys were blasted with compressed air approximately every 30 minutes if they were clinging to the surrogate. The animals reared with the punitive model spent more time on their surrogate than same-age animals spent on a standard, nonpunitive surrogate.

How might we account for such infant masochism? One possible interpretation is suggested by the detailed observations that Seay et al. (1964) made of one of the more punitive mothers. As the preceding description indicates, some of the more violent attacks occurred when attempts were made to remove the infant or when the infant attempted to separate itself from the mother. The infant found that an effective way to minimize such treatment was to cling to the central or dorsal surface of the mother's body. The "punitive" behavior thus might simply constitute a particular reaction by the adult to which the infant's own responses must adapt. Sackett (1967) reported that the offspring of motherless monkeys were subjected to extreme aggression only during the first 2–3 months of life. "After this time overt hostility by the mothers rarely occurred because the infants seemed to avoid attacks by the mothers" (p. 365).

These observations and others like them were made under special conditions of environmental restriction (Cairns, 1966a; Cairns & Johnson, 1965). Neither the young nor the "mothers" were permitted to escape, and alternative objects were not available that would support the performance of the young animals' response patterns. Quite a different outcome is obtained when experiments are conducted under less restrictive conditions. In the natural or seminatural setting, continued punishment is typically associated with physical separation and diminution of the filial bond (Altmann, 1960). Unfortunately, no attempts have been made to rear a single infant simultaneously with a "good" and a "bad" mother—that is, one that accepts and another that rebuffs the approaches of the young. It would be remarkable indeed if the more tolerant one failed to become the event around which the infant's behavior was organized. Observations of herd animals suggest that rebuffs by other potential mothers maintain the coherence of the relationship between an infant and its biological mother. The young animal does not become "attached" to the punishing female.

In summary, both punitive and positive conditions may increase the level of the infant's social attachment. In some rearing situations, punishment has the paradoxical effect of increasing the preference of the young animal for the punisher. When the punishment organizes the young animal's activity toward the "other," it helps consolidate the relationship. This appears to be a special case of the general phenomenon that the degree of preference that an infant shows for a person or object reflects the extent to which that infant's behavior is organized around it. Nonhuman attachment can be strengthened by kindness or by coercion.

PUPPY LOVE AND BEYOND

Other research findings illustrate the hazards of relationships maintained beyond their time or with the wrong individual. It has been shown that "puppy love"—cross-specific attachments among immature canines 25–28 days of age—can be established rapidly when they are separated from their mothers. From an evolutionary perspective, the rapidity makes sense. If adaptation did not proceed rapidly, then it might not succeed at all. The pups would perish.

Experimental attempts to plot the course of puppies' attachment to a surrogate illustrate the rapidity. In a representative study (Cairns & Werboff, 1967), 4-week-old puppies were taken from their mothers and reared alone with an adult rabbit. Checks were made during the first 24 hours of pairing and at staggered intervals thereafter. In a predecessor to the Strange Situation, the primary test simply involved brief removal, then replacement, of the rabbit. If during removal the pup showed frantic yelping and running around the compartment and immediate quieting when the rabbit was returned, it was assumed that the surrogate had acquired significant social control properties. In brief, the pup had developed an "attachment" for the surrogate. Within only 2–4 hours of cohabitation with the rabbit, the pups became extremely upset when separated from the new companion. Subsequent social preference tests indicated the development of virtual puppy love—experimental pups even preferred a rabbit over another puppy, whereas control pups preferred other pups.

But that is only part of the story. To focus on just the early success of cross-specific adoptions can be terribly misleading. Longitudinal observations demonstrated that the early affectional relationship did not guarantee life-time bliss. The findings showed just the opposite. Within 5 weeks, immature puppies become young, frisky dogs, whereas adult rabbits do not change phys-ically. If unchecked, the warm and fuzzy actions of puppies when at 4 weeks of age—sleeping on top of the bunny and suckling its fur—would become intolerable for the surrogate over the next month. Under usual rearing con-ditions, punishment by the mother normally serves to redirect puppies away from herself, ensuring both her safety and integrity while stimulating auton-omy and independence in the pups. The marvelous synchrony and dynamic nature of the accommodations generated by co-evolution may be obscured in one-shot, cross-sectional observations.

The lesson is that early attachment behavior—including puppy love—does not necessarily preclude the development of aggressive and hurtful inter-changes. The puppies became engaged in destructive exchanges when inherent patterns that would be normally checked and redirected by parents were permitted to persist. In these special conditions, there were only victims, no aggressors. Therein may be an insight about the natural synchronies and constructive redirection that facilitates adaptive social development in mam-malian species, including humans. Dynamic realignment of actions and rela-tionships over time is necessary to ensure successful adaptation for both young and parents.

ON ADAPTATION

The possibility that aggressive and affiliative patterns have common adaptive functions has been often overlooked in modern discussions. The view that aggressive acts are by definition dysfunctional tends to close doors on research when further information is required. While at first blush the investigation of adaptive functions of aggression may be a curious pursuit, the inquiry may help one understand why negative actions are so ubiquitous in individual development and evolution.

FUNCTIONS OF AGGRESSION

Interactional Functions

In most interchanges, a tug-of-war exists between maintaining the integrity of one's own behavior patterns and thoughts while simultaneously synchronizing them with the behavior patterns and thoughts of others. That interpersonal synchrony occurs—virtually without effort and outside consciousness from infancy through adulthood—is something of a miracle. In the absence of role hierarchies and other structures, inevitable tensions arise within interpersonal units—mother and infant, a schoolmate pair, collegial collaboration—in determining whose actions are to be modified and whose will prevail. When the tensions become great as compromises fail and/or overt conflicts arise, the interaction/collaboration may dissolve because of dysynchrony. In the case of infants, children, and adolescents, in which escape is not possible, the use of negative or coercive feedback is a common mechanism to modify the behavior of others. A closely related function of negative actions is to remove threats to one's self or one's concept of oneself.

Survival Functions

With development and maturation, the protective functions of aggressive acts extend beyond psychological considerations and include protection of one's physical self, and one's living space and possessions. How these protective functions operate are relative to such basic parameters as species, age, gender, and ecology. Beyond the specific and species-typical considerations, there are some general principles that provide a surprisingly close fit to human beings. For instance, the right to use force to protect oneself, one's home, and one's possessions against intruders is one of the primary justifications for aggression accepted by law. The protection of one's physical self against harm—and by extension, one's family and their physical well-being and access to resources—helps ensure behavioral and psychological integrity.

Evolutionary Functions

Protection of offspring constitutes a special case that combines certain features of physical protection and possession protection and addresses the basic problem of how species reproduce themselves and maintain continuity across generations. Protection of one's offspring, and one's distinctive genetic material, may be an evolutionary extension of the protection of one's self (Wilson, 1975). However, sociobiologists have also raised key questions on the certainty of parentage. Among mammalian species, there is necessarily less ambiguity in the neonatal period and infancy with respect to infants' motherhood than to their fatherhood. Accordingly, the function of physical protection of young offspring typically is the responsibility of mothers in nonhuman mammals (e.g., Green , 1978).

Social Functions

One of the primary lessons of social group organization is the unifying effect of identifying a common enemy or an outgroup. Sherif and Sherif

(1953), in their study of how to organize children into subgroups with deep loyalties, found that the creation of outgroups or common enemies was an especially effective device. Having specific outgroups—or enemies of the nation—helped unify not only the youth, but also served to consolidate broader public support, with eventually disastrous consequences. It may be the case that the same principle underlying the maintenance of personal integrity helps account for the use of negative acts and aggression to consolidate and maintain the integrity of social groups. On this count, the most egregious and extended acts of violence in modern history have occurred in religious conflicts.

In light of the multiple functions of aggression, perhaps the classic question of Konrad Lorenz (1966) should have been "Why not aggression?" rather than "Why aggression?" Because of the attractiveness of negative and aggressive acts there exists a broad network of practices and controls that are built into the very fabric of conventional society.

FUNCTIONS OF ATTACHMENT

Unlike aggression, the happy functions of attachment may seem self-evident and beyond dispute. It is generally accepted that mother–infant social attachment is nature's way of ensuring the survival of young mammals who cannot make it without maternal warmth, nourishment, and protection. Another function is the establishment of mental schemas—working models—that predict and guide the development of future social relationships. The initial three functions—warmth, nourishment, and protection—have been broadly supported by findings with animals and humans. However, the idea that the first relationship is predictable of all future ones is a hypothesis that remains open for investigation.

Mother Love

The primary functions of attachment noted above refer to the needs of infants and young children. The notion that social attachment is a reciprocal affair, with equal contributions by the infant and the mother, are happy assumptions about the nature of the onset of early relationships. But is love for one's mother the same as the mother's love for her infant? Obviously both are precious. The question must be asked because there are large differences in timing, and the needs of mothers clearly differ from needs of offspring. For instance, human mothers normally experience the onset of strong positive social attachment immediately at birth and before. In contrast, human infants fail to show the onset of discriminative attachment patterns until much later—ages 9–12 months. Parallel timing phenomena have been observed in studies of nonhuman mammalian attachment, with mothers showing different patterns of attachment at onset and diminution than their infants.

All this suggests that attachment phenomena may represent overlapping but different processes for mothers and infants. In nonhuman mothers, attachment and associated suckling by infants usually dampen fertility so that the mother does not become prematurely pregnant with new offspring. Psychobiological and endocrine changes in the mother are linked to morphological, physiological, mobility, and behavioral changes in the offspring. When infantile physiological and behavioral dependence diminish, maternal attachment behaviors also wane. Among most nonhuman mammals, the reproductive cycle is permitted to recur only after the young become nutritionally and behaviorally capable. This is associated with diminished maternal protection, less disruption when separated from the older offspring, and increased rejection.

In brief, mother love and infant love reflect overlapping but different needs. The differences reflect the capabilities and needs that are distinctive to infants, and the physiological and social conditions that are distinctive to mothers. In infants, the onset of attachment is less linked to chronological age since parturition than to milestones of infant development (e.g., temperature regulation, nutritional patterns, perceptual development, locomotor development). Accordingly, attachment onset occurs at 9–12 months in humans and is coordinated with the onset of locomotion and perceptual–cognitive development in infants. The disjunction between maternal and infant attachment occurs because the adult's behavioral, cognitive, and emotional systems are more mature and better organized at birth than the infant's, at precisely the time that external support is required for survival.

This transition does not mean that parents become less attached to their older children, adolescents, and young adults. To the contrary, parental commitment to older offspring may be manifested in multiple ways; including the supervision, monitoring, and protection of vulnerable youth; parental sharing of time and resources; and parental participation in helping make expectations become reality for children.

Infant Love

It is beyond the scope of this chapter to dwell on the similarities and differences between the attachment patterns of infants, toddlers, children, adolescents, and adults. That methodological and theoretical debate is ongoing. There seems to be acceptance of the proposition that the changes occur in both quality and form of the relationship, but it is unclear whether a single term should be used to cover all forms of close relationship, regardless of age (see, e.g., Fox, 1995).

In this regard, the child's attachment to parents can coexist with new close relationships in childhood, adolescence, and adulthood. Changes in quality of the relationship with parents can occur independently of—or may be linked to—changes in these relationships. For instance, changes in quality may occur when friends or spouses promote greater distance and independence from one's parents, or vice versa. As noted above, the friendships and romantic engagements of childhood and adolescence are typically short-lived, regardless of the nature of early familial attachments. Whether these childhood–adolescent patterns are carried forward seem to reflect the individual's prior experiences, continuing attitudes about fickleness and promiscuity, and contextual opportunities and constraints. The larger point is that relations with parents and peers are not static; they reflect the dynamic conditions and contexts that prevail in both settings.

Prediction and Change

A primary issue of attachment concerns the persistence of individual differences in the propensity to form social relations. This has been viewed as one of the "pillars" of attachment theory; namely, the ability to predict from infancy the quality of relationships formed in subsequent stages of the life course. Does parent–infant attachment persist over the life course, and does it form the substrate for subsequent relations? The evidence from longitudinal study with respect to these individual-difference propositions is mixed at best—it is another area where the doors of research must remain open.

Beyond this dispute on the predictability of individual differences in attachment classification, there is strong evidence for the carryover effects of early social experiences into subsequent relationships. On the positive side, people tend to prefer to be around, affiliate with, and marry others of their own nationality, ethnic group, religion, and region. On the dark side, the preference for the familiar supports social exclusion, prejudice, and discrimination. In the 20th century, demagogues have manipulated this preferential tendency so as to dehumanize or "cleanse" entire segments of the population.

One positive outcome of research on early relationships is that neophobic and ethnic biases may be diminished by early experiences. But if relational disjunction occurs at subsequent developmental stages, the gains achieved by early experience diminish or wash out. Early experience aside, cross-group relationships can be first established in adolescence and maturity with the same happy diminution of class and ethnic prejudice. The capacity for basic attitudinal change persists throughout life; it is not limited to the early formative stages of childhood.

DIFFERENT CATEGORIES, COMMON PRINCIPLES

Adopting static, domain-specific accounts of aggression and attachment prevented mid-century theoretical warfare in psychology, but at a cost.

The cost was to adopt a narrow view of social phenomena and thereby obscure their common principles and functions. Behavioral biologists took a different strategy and tried to pick up some pieces of the puzzle that psychology left separate and detached. To their credit, behavioral zoology and sociobiology explicitly recognized the primacy of social behavior and social organization, along with the dilemma it created for the classical evolutionary model. This recognition, in turn, led to the formulation of a modern evolutionary model around the concept of inclusive genetic fitness (Hamilton, 1964; Wilson, 1975).

Although the modern synthesis may have solved a large theoretical dilemma in behavioral biology, it has left virtually untouched a related and equally critical problem in psychology. The problem refers to the seemingly inevitable tension between individual psychobiological integration and behavioral autonomy versus social synchrony and interchange reciprocity. How is it possible for people to be synchronized and supportive in their actions without giving up individual autonomy and internal integration, or vice versa?

Integration at both levels occurs seemingly without effort, from birth to maturity to death. Human beings, in particular, enjoy both high levels of social synchrony and individual autonomy. From birth onward, humans manage to serve two different masters simultaneously—one under the skin, and the other in the social ecology. Specifically,

- Effective individual adaptation demands adequate levels of within-person synchrony across psychobiological, cognitive, emotional, and behavioral systems. Feedback loops within and across systems are required to coordinate internal synchrony to permit rapid mobilization, stable maintenance, or restorative quiescence or rest. Without such coordinated internal feedback loops, there would be chaos in biology and in behavior, along with an inability to think coherently and direct one's own behavior. Such within-organism integration occurs in multiple ways; it is a prerequisite for autonomy in behavior and cognition.
- Effective social adaptation requires high levels of synchrony in action, biology, emotion, and cognition between two or more persons. Such interactional synchrony is vital for the maintenance of basic exchanges fundamental to individual survival and basic evolutionary adaptations, including sexual reproduction, parent–infant caregiving, and mutual protection and defense. It is also required for the creation and maintenance of communities, complex cultures, and the preservation and transmission of information across people and time.

By cataloguing attachment and aggression as separate or opposed propensities, motives, or psychological structures, we may have, by default, obscured common strategic roles played by these interactional patterns in social development. Over time, they appear to play complementary roles in preserving individual autonomy while promoting social synchrony. Given inevitable developmental changes in capabilities and coordination, the strategies become available at different stages of ontogeny to promote social adaptation. This is because not all forms of interpersonal synchrony are possible, feasible, or desirable.

In this regard, even infants must have interpersonal tools to minimize disruption of intrapersonal and interpersonal organization. The phenomena of attachment—approaching familiar people, reciprocating actions, crying when the major scaffolds of behavior and security are removed—indicate that very young humans can promote the restoration of order within and without. As they grow older and infantile tactics wane in effectiveness, other interpersonal strategies emerge. A first line of defense, regardless of age, is to remove oneself from intrusive, disynchronous social interchanges. Withdrawal can be physical or psychological. Other, more direct attempts can be made to terminate or redirect acts of others. These invasive responses can be labeled *punishment*, *aggression*, *protest*, or *retribution*, depending on the relationship and circumstance. Which strategy is adopted, and with whom, is determined partly by its success or failure in prior exchanges and partly by its social cost.

The interactional phenomena subsumed by the labels *aggression* and *attachment* also share basic characteristics in development, despite obvious differences in form and expression. These include

- the involvement of immanent psychobiological processes that universally emerge in development;
- the demonstration of predictable yet distinctive trajectories of establishment;
- changes in form and expression over time that are fitted in experience to specific persons, relationships, and contexts;
- the consolidation and maintenance of these modifications through dynamic learning processes, yet subject to fresh reorganization as contexts and capacities change;
- shared conformity to the interactional principles of synchrony, reciprocity, and complementarity; and
- at least one common aim—to cause changes in external conditions and bring them into alignment with internal needs and goals.

The interactional patterns are also complementary in development. The controlling strategies of attachment in infancy give way in time to more active techniques, including those labeled *aggressive* and *punitive*.

Focus on the universality, common functions, and shared principles of these interactional systems does not mean that they cannot go awry. For instance, inappropriate reliance on attachment strategies beyond their time or their chronic dysfunction in infancy can signal problems for individual development. Similarly, the frequent and indiscriminate deployment of aggressive strategies and hostile affect by people, regardless of age, is a bad sign for their current and future adjustment. That said, psychopathology and intervention research has been loaded with excess baggage by the failure to recognize that constructive and destructive strategies can coexist in behavior organization of individuals. Understanding the functions and dynamics of interactions—even those that have unhealthy consequences for the self and others—could be the first step toward effective intervention and change.

CONCLUDING COMMENTS

Psychology has pigeonholed and marginalized essential social phenomena and so has fumbled a large opportunity for societal relevance. We also noted that the negative tilt in developmental theory and research has deflected the discipline from areas in which its distinctive contributions should be at the leading edge of interdisciplinary research and thinking. Beyond the critique, we have highlighted recent empirical and theoretical advances critical to understanding the development and functions of social interactions. These advances point to the interrelations between the strategies that are required to construct integrated, autonomous lives while simultaneously promoting synchronous and adaptive relationships.

Does this reorientation have concrete implications for social applications or national priorities? We believe it does. Among other things, it suggests a new focus on productive adaptive patterns of aggressive children and adolescents. To create enduring change in adaptive patterns, it implies greater attention should be given to the presence of events that guide and enhance functioning than to what is missing (Cairns & Cairns, 1998; Feshbach & Adelman, 1974; Feshbach & Price, 1984). A happy by-product is that such a reorientation promotes—especially for high-risk youth—new levels of mastery and fresh means for finding meaning in their lives.

REFERENCES

Ainsworth, M. D. S. (1963). The development of infant-mother interaction among the Ganda. In B. M. Foss (Ed.), *Determinants of infant behavior: II* 67–104. New York: Wiley.

Ainsworth, M. D. S. (1972). Attachment and dependency: A comparison. In J. L. Gewirtz (Ed.), *Attachment and dependency* 97–137. New York: Wiley.

Ainsworth, M. D. S., Blehar, M., Waters, E., & Wall, S. (1978). *Patterns of attachment: A psychological study of the strange situation.* Hillsdale, NJ: Lawrence Erlbaum.

Altmann, M. (1960). The role of juvenile elk and moose in the social dynamics of their species. *Zoologica, 45,* 35–39.

Arling, G. L., & Harlow, H. P. (1967). Effects of social deprivation on maternal behavior of rhesus monkeys. *Journal of Comparative and Physiological Psychology, 64,* 371–377.

Asberg, M., Traksman, L., & Thoren, P. (1976). 5-HIAA in the cerebrospinal fluid: A biochemical suicide predictor? *Archives of General Psychiatry, 33,* 1193–1197.

Bandura, A., & Walters, R. H. (1959). *Adolescent aggression.* New York: Ronald Press.

Boucher, J., & Osgood, C. E. (1969). The Pollyanna hypothesis. *Journal of Verbal Learning and Verbal Behavior, 8,* 1–8.

Bowlby, J. (1952). *Maternal care and mental health* (2nd ed.). Geneva: World Health Organization.

Bowlby, J. (1958). The nature of the child's tie to his mother. *International Journal of Psychoanalysis, 39,* 350–373.

Bowlby, J. (1969). *Attachment and loss. Vol. 1: Attachment.* New York: Basic Books.

Bowlby, J. (1973). *Attachment and loss. Vol. 2: Separation.* New York: Basic Books.

Cairns, R. B. (1961). The influence of dependency inhibition on the effectiveness of social approval. *Journal of Personality, 29,* 466–488.

Cairns, R. B. (1966a). Attachment behavior of mammals. *Psychological Review, 72,* 409–426.

Cairns, R. B. (1966b). Development, maintenance, and extinction of social attachment behavior in sheep. *Journal of Comparative and Physiological Psychology, 62,* 298–306.

Cairns, R. B. (1972). Attachment and dependency: A psychobiological and social learning synthesis. In J. L. Gewirtz (Ed.), *Attachment and dependency* 29–80. New York: Wiley.

Cairns, R. B. (1972). Fighting and punishment from a developmental perspective. In J. K. Cole & D. D. Jensen (Eds.), *Nebraska Symposium on Motivation* 59–124. Lincoln: University of Nebraska Press.

Cairns, R. B. (1976). The ontogeny and phylogeny of social interactions. In M. Hahn & E. C. Simmel (Eds.), *Evolution of communicative behaviors.* 115–139 New York: Academic Press.

Cairns, R. B. (1979). *Social development: The origins and plasticity of social interchanges.* San Francisco: Freeman.

Cairns, R. B. (1996). Aggression from a developmental perspective: Genes, environments, and interactions. In M. Rutter (Ed.), *Genetics of criminal and anti-*

social behavior (Ciba Foundation Symposium No. 194, pp. 45–60). London: John Wiley & Sons.

Cairns, R. B., Cadwallader, T., Estell, D., & Neckerman, H. J. (1997). Groups to gangs: Developmental and criminological perspectives and implications for prevention. In D. M. Stoff, J. D. Maser, & J. Breiling (Eds.), *Handbook of antisocial behavior* (pp. 194–204). New York: Wiley.

Cairns, R. B., & Cairns, B. D. (1994). *Lifelines and risks: Pathways of youth in our time.* New York: Cambridge University Press.

Cairns, R. B., & Cairns, B. D. (1998). *Prevention through engagement: "Diamonds in the lights."* Unpublished manuscript, University of North Carolina at Chapel Hill.

Cairns, R. B., Gariépy, J.-L., & Hood, K. E. (1990). Development, microevolution, and social behavior. *Psychological Review, 97,* 49–65.

Cairns, R. B., & Johnson, D. L. (1965). The development of interspecies social preferences. *Psychonomic Science, 2,* 337–338.

Cairns, R. B., & Lewis, M. (1962). Dependency and the reinforcement value of a verbal stimulus. *Journal of Consulting Psychology, 26,* 1–8.

Cairns, R. B., & Werboff, J. (1967). Behavior development in the dog: An interspecific analysis. *Science, 158,* 1070–1072.

Fenichel, O. (1945). *The psychoanalytic theory of neurosis.* New York: W. W. Norton.

Feshbach, N., & Feshbach, S. (1969). The relationship between empathy and aggression in two age groups. *Developmental Psychology, 1,* 102–107.

Feshbach, S. (1955). The drive-reducing function of fantasy behavior. *Journal of Abnormal and Social Psychology, 50,* 3–11.

Feshbach, S. (1956). The catharsis hypothesis and some consequences of interaction with aggressive and neutral play objects. *Journal of Personality, 24,* 449–462.

Feshbach, S. (1964). The function of aggression and the regulation of aggressive drive. *Psychological Review, 7,* 257–272.

Feshbach, S. (1971). Dynamics and morality of violence and aggression: Some psychological considerations. *American Psychologist, 26,* 281–292.

Feshbach, S. (1976). The role of fantasy in the response to television. *Journal of Society Issues, 32,* 71–85.

Feshbach, S. (1984). The catharsis hypothesis, aggressive drive, and the reduction of aggression. *Aggressive Behavior, 10,* 91–101.

Feshbach, S., & Adelman, H. (1974). Remediation of learning problems among the disadvantaged. *Journal of Educational Psychology, 66,* 16–28.

Feshbach, S., & Price, J. (1984). Cognitive competencies and aggressive behavior: A developmental study. *Aggressive Behavior, 10,* 185–200.

Feshbach, S., & Singer, R. D. (1971). *Television and aggression: An experimental field study.* San Francisco: Jossey-Bass.

Feshbach, S., Singer, R., & Feshbach, N. (1963). Effects of anger arousal and similarity upon the attribution of hostility to pictorial stimuli. *Journal of Consulting Psychology, 27,* 248–252.

Fleener, D. E. (1967). *Attachment formation in humans.* Doctoral dissertation, Indiana University, 1967. Ann Arbor, MI: University Microfilms No. 6872-12.

Fleener, D. E. (1973). Experimental production of infant-maternal attachment behaviors. *Proceedings, 81st Annual Convention, American Psychological Association, 8,* 57–58.

Fleener, D. E., & Cairns, R. B. (1970). Attachment behavior in human infants: Discriminative vocalizations on maternal separation. *Developmental Psychology, 2,* 215–223.

Fox, N. A. (1995). Of the way we were: Adult memories about attachment experiences and their role in determining infant parent relationships: A commentary on van IJzendoorn. *Psychological Bulletin, 117,* 404–410.

Gariépy, J.-L., Lewis, M. H., & Cairns, R. B. (1996). Genes, neurobiology, and aggression: Time frames and functions of social behavior in adaptation. In D. M. Stoff & R. B. Cairns (Eds.), *Aggression and violence: Genetic, neurobiological, and biosocial perspectives* (pp. 41–64). Mahwah, NJ: Lawrence Erlbaum.

Gewirtz, J. L. (1967). Deprivation and satiation of social stimuli as determinants of their reinforcing efficacy. In J. P. Hill (Ed.), *Minnesota symposium on child psychology* (Vol. 1, 3–56). Minneapolis: University of Minnesota Press.

Goldman, D. (1996). The search for alleles contributing to self–destructive and aggressive behaviors. In D. M. Stoff & R. B. Cairns (Eds.), *Aggression and violence: Genetic, neurobiological, and biosocial perspectives* 23–40. Mahwah, NJ: Lawrence Erlbaum.

Green, J. A. (1978). Experiential determinants of postpartum aggression in mice. *Journal of Comparative and Physiological Psychology, 92,* 1179–1187.

Hamilton, W. D. (1964). The genetical evolution of social behavior. *Journal of Theoretical Biology, 7,* 1–52.

Kagan, J. (1976). Emergent themes in human development. *American Scientist, 64,* 186–196.

Levine, M., Leitenberg, H., & Richter, M. (1964). The blank trials law: The equivalence of positive reinforcement and nonreinforcement. *Psychological Review, 71,* 94–103.

Lewin, K. (1935). *A dynamic theory of personality.* New York: McGraw-Hill.

Linnoila, M., Virkkunen, M., Schenin, M., Nuntila, A., Rimon, R., & Goodwin, F. K. (1983). Low cerebrospinal fluid 5-hydroxyindoeacetic acid concentration differentiates impulsive from non-impulsive violent behavior. *Life Sciences, 33,* 2609–2614.

Lorenz, K. Z. (1966). *On aggression.* New York: Harcourt, Brace, & World.

Mason, W. A., & Kinney, M. D. (1974). Redirection of filial attachments in rhesus monkeys: Dogs as mother surrogates. *Science, 183,* 1209–1211.

Murray, J., & Feshbach, S. (1978). Let's not throw the baby out with the bathwater: The catharsis hypothesis revisited. *Journal of Personality, 46,* 462–473.

Neckerman, H. J. (1996). The stability of social groups in childhood and adolescence: The role of the classroom social environment. *Social Development, 5,* 131–145.

Nielson, D. A., Goldman, D., Virkkunen, M., Tokola, R., Rawling, R., & Linnola, M. (1994). Suicidality and 5-hydroxyindolacetic acid concentration associated with a tryptophan hydroxylase polymorphism. *Archives of General Psychiatry, 51,* 34–38.

Quine, W. V. (1981). *Theories and things.* Cambridge, MA: Belknap Press.

Radke Yarrow, M., Campbell, J. D., & Burton, R. V. (1968). *Child rearing: An inquiry in research and methods.* San Francisco: Jossey-Bass.

Rheingold, H. L. (1959). The modification of social responsiveness in institutional babies. *Monographs of the Society for Research in Child Development, 21*(2; Whole No. 63).

Rheingold, H. L. (1969). The social and socializing infant. In D. A. Goslin (Ed.), *Handbook of socialization theory and research* 779–790. Chicago: Rand McNally.

Rheingold, H. L., & Bayley, N. (1959). The later effects of an experimental modification of mother. *Child Development, 30,* 363–372.

Rosenblum, L. A., & Harlow, H. F. (1963). Approach-avoidance conflict in the mother-surrogate situation. *Psychological Reports, 12,* 83–85.

Sackett, G. P. (1967). Some persistent effects of different rearing conditions on preadult social behavior of monkeys. *Journal of Comparative and Physiological Psychology,64,* 363–365.

Schaffer, H. R., & Emerson, P. F. (1964). The development of social attachments in infancy. *Monographs of the Society for Research in Child Development, 29*(3, Whole No. 94).

Schneirla, T. C. (1966). Behavioral development and comparative psychology. *Quarterly Review of Biology, 41,* 283–302.

Sears, R. R. (1972). Attachment, dependency, and frustration. In J. L. Gewirtz (Ed.), *Attachment and dependency* 1–27. New York: Wiley.

Sears, R. R., Whiting, J. W. M., Nowlis, V., & Sears, P. S. (1953). Some child-rearing antecedents of aggressive and dependency in young children. *Genetic Psychology Monographs, 47,* 135–234.

Seay, B., Alexander, B. K., & Harlow, H. (1964). Maternal behavior of socially deprived rhesus monkeys. *Journal of Abnormal and Social Psychology, 69,* 345–354.

Sherif, M., & Sherif, C. W. (1953). Groups in harmony and tension. New York: Harper.

Virkkunen, M., & Linnoila, M. (1996). Serotonin and glucose metabolism in impulsively violent alcoholic offenders. In D. M. Stoff & R. B. Cairns (Eds.), *Aggression and violence: Genetic, neurobiological, and biosocial perspectives* 87–99. Mahwah, NJ: Lawrence Erlbaum.

Wilson, E. O. (1975). *Sociobiology: The new synthesis.* Cambridge, MA: Harvard University Press.

2

SEEING IS BELIEVING: HOW VIEWING VIOLENCE ALTERS ATTITUDES AND AGGRESSIVE BEHAVIOR

L. D. ERON

It is well known that certain kinds of exposure to violence (e.g., photographs of guns, violent sequences on television, witnessing of interpersonal violence in the home) predict subsequent aggression, in both the short- and long-term. In this chapter I review earlier behavioral explanations and then various factors that mediate the relation between exposure to violence-related material and later aggressive behavior.

A BEHAVIORAL EXPLANATION

When psychologists first wrote about predictions of violence (Bandura, Ross, & Ross, 1961; Berkowitz, 1962; Eron, 1961, 1963) they explained them by invoking associative learning, classical conditioning, and reinforcement theories. For example, Bandura (1973) proposed that aggressive behavior is learned and maintained through experience either directly or vicariously. Aggression is learned, like any other new behavior, by the application of rewards and punishments on its first appearance and subsequent occurrences. Berkowitz and LePage (1967) explained in their findings that there was a greater frequency and intensity of aggressive behavior when a weapon was in sight and maintained that guns served as classically conditioned stimuli to aggressive responses. Eron and his colleagues argued that aggressive behaviors are learned as a result of socializing agents (e.g., parents, teachers, and peers) serving as role models who reward or punish certain behaviors (Eron, Banta, Walder, & Laulicht, 1961), and also by watching violent models on television (Eron, 1963).

In the 1960s and early 1970s, researchers paid little attention to how observation of aggressive stimuli influences the observers' subsequent behavior. Toward the end of this period, aggression researchers began to develop cognitive explanations of the effects of observing violence (Farber, 1963; Feigenbaum & Feldman, 1963; Gregg & Simon, 1967 ; Neisser, 1967). This shift to a focus on cognitive mediators represented a significant departure from traditional learning theory. Bandura (1977) played a major role in this transition. He hypothesized that a complex interaction of cognitive processes determines whether observed behavior is modeled. These processes include attention to the observed interaction, retention of it in memory, reproduction of the sequence in imagination, and motivation to perform the behavior. Later, Bandura (1986) postulated that in addition to modeling the observed behavior, children also adopted the evaluative standards used by the models, and had to have some confidence that they could live up to them (self-efficacy) before engaging in them.

Influenced by Bandura's explanation of modeling, Berkowitz (1984) later dismissed classical conditioning as a theoretical model to explain his results. According to Berkowitz, viewing aggression on television or the sight of a gun activates other related thoughts, which in turn influence subsequent evaluation of social interactions. Thus, viewing violence on television or elsewhere primes other thoughts, which are related semantically to the original reaction, thereby increasing the possibility that they will come to mind and influence aggressive responding. This concept of cognitive priming helps explain why very often the aggressive behavior observed on television, for example, need not be exactly replicated in the subsequent violent behavior of the observer. Many studies have demonstrated the phenomenon that violence viewed on television primes subsequent aggression of various forms on the part of the viewer (Berkowitz & Rogers, 1986). The same effect has been demonstrated using music videos (Hansen & Hansen, 1990).

Cognitive theories of aggressive behavior have influenced my own thinking as well. On analyzing the results from the first stage of the longitudinal research, when participants were 8 years old (Eron, Walder, & Lefkowitz, 1971), I was faced with unexpected findings. My prediction, based on Hullian theory, that youngsters who were punished by their parents for aggressive behavior would not tend to engage in such behaviors, held true only for a small group of boys who were closely identified with their fathers. All other participants who were punished for aggression tended to become more aggressive. This result would not have been predicted from Hullian theory, as explicated by Miller (1941). Instead, for most participants, the punishment seemed to instigate rather than inhibit aggressive behavior. It seemed that the occurrence of intense punishment subsequent to the act was less important than the cognitive "spin" the youngster used to interpret the parent's action. The "identified" child (i.e., a child identified with the father) was likely to consider the punishment as justified because of his own misbehavior and administered because the parent wanted him to be a good person, like the father. The "unidentified" youngster (i.e., not identified with the father) was likely to interpret the punishment as unjustified and as a demonstration of the way adults go about solving interpersonal problems. Thus, this youngster would model the punitive behavior. This interpretation is consonant with Bandura's (1986) contention that social behavior is under the control of internal self-regulating processes. What is important is the cognitive evaluation of events taking place in the child's environment, how the child interprets these events, and how competent he or she feels about responding in various ways (self-efficacy).

INFORMATION-PROCESSING EXPLANATION

More recently, explicitly cognitive theories based on information processing have been invoked to explain the findings of both laboratory and field research that have consistently demonstrated this link between observation of violent behavior and the subsequent expression of such behavior by the observer. According to Dodge (Crick & Dodge, 1994; Dodge, 1980), deficient information processing causes the youngster to perceive hostility in others when no hostility is present. This hostile bias leads to deficient social problem solving and ultimately to aggression.

Huesmann (1988; Huesmann & Eron, 1984) also viewed the child as a processor of information who develops programs called *scripts* to guide social behavior (Abelson, 1976). He further proposed that by observing television violence many children learn scripts for complex aggressive behavior and develop normative beliefs and attitudes that support the use of aggression. According to Huesmann, social behavior is controlled to a great extent by cognitive scripts, schemas, and strategies that have been stored in memory and are used as guides for behavior. These strategies must be encoded, rehearsed, stored, and retrieved in much the same way as the strategies for intellectual efforts. These strategies might be closely associated with specific cues in the encoding context or might be abstractions, not connected to specific cues. Encoding is the "formation of a representation of an external stimulus in the memory system" (Kintsch, 1977, p. 485). Accordingly, an aggressive strategy must be (a) encoded, (b) retained in memory, and (c) retrieved at a later time in order to influence the child's behavior.

A number of situational and interpersonal factors can influence each process. To encode an aggressive response, a child must attend to the behavior and must not reject it as completely inappropriate. To maintain the encoded strategy in memory, the child must rehearse it. Through "elaborative" rehearsal, the child may develop abstract representations of the aggressive strategies. Finally, to retrieve and use the strategy, the child must be able to access it in memory. According to the "encoding specificity principle," the presence of cues that were present at encoding time facilitates retrieval.

MEDIATORS BETWEEN VIOLENCE VIEWING AND VIOLENT BEHAVIOR

Normative Belief

The reason that the above processes can influence the occurrence and maintenance of aggressive behavior, in that the observer, especially the young observer, has certain beliefs and attitudes that are often fostered by his or her experiences within the family, in the neighborhood, at school, and with television. Most of the evidence for this contention comes from television research, but there have been studies of other venues with similar findings. Children growing up observing violence around them behave more violently (e.g. Guerra, Huesmann, Tolan, VanAcker, & Eron, 1995), and children whose parents aggress against them physically are more likely to aggress physically against their own children later in life (Eron, 1987; Widom, 1989). Growing up in an aggressive environment encourages the development of violent behavior because of the opportunities it provides for learning from observation and adopting attitudes and norms of violence.

The more salient an aggressive behavior is to a child, the more likely the behavior is to be encoded and maintained in memory. The more realistic it appears to be, the more salient it is. Early on, Seymour Feshbach (1972) emphasized that realism is a determinant of imitation. A later investigation by Rowell Huesmann, myself, and our colleagues confirmed that the occurrence of aggression is greater in children who believe that violence is representative of real life (Huesmann, Eron, Lefkowitz, & Walder, 1984). In fact, normative beliefs about aggression (beliefs about what behaviors are appropriate in which situations) have been found to mediate the relation between observation of media violence and aggressive behavior.

Huesmann and Guerra (1997) used a reliable and well validated measure of an individual's normative beliefs about the acceptability or unacceptability of a behavior, rather than a measure of consensual social norms (Thiebaut & Kelley, 1959). They showed that approval of aggression increased over time in a large sample of elementary school children living in economically disadvantaged urban neighborhoods. As children grew older they increasingly embraced aggression as a way of solving social problems and acquiring material possessions. This increase in approval, unfortunately, predicted increases in aggressive behavior.

In a parallel study, the strongest correlate of aggressive behavior was children's normative beliefs about the appropriateness of aggression. Furthermore, poor children (as measured by subsidized lunch status) were more likely to accept aggressive behavior. In addition, children who had more accepting beliefs behaved more aggressively (Eron, Guerra, & Huesmann, 1997).

Children growing up in impoverished environments will likely adopt normative beliefs legitimizing violence as a means of gaining status, material rewards, or simply coping with the fear of victimization. Eli Anderson (1990), the social ethnographer, reported that a "code of violence" often prevails among youth in impoverished areas. According to this code, aggression and violence come to be seen as appropriate ways to deal with numerous types of social interactions. Children in impoverished communities, where violence is epidemic, may learn normative beliefs by observing their role models' aggression, by direct tuition from peers, and by instrumental learning (Guerra, Huesmann, & Hanish, 1994; Huesmann & Guerra, 1997. These beliefs, in turn, promote aggressive behavior (Huesmann, Guerra, Miller, & Zelli, 1992).

There are at least three ways in which normative beliefs may affect children's perception of others' behavior. The more they approve of aggression, the more likely they may be to perceive hostility in others, even if no hostility is present (hostile bias). Second, normative beliefs about the acceptability of aggression may cue the retrieval of aggressive scripts for social behavior. And finally, if normative beliefs affect the likelihood of inappropriate behavior, children with more aggressive normative beliefs would be less likely to reject aggressive behaviors once they have thought of them. It is therefore easy to understand how continual observation of characters and plots on television can inculcate social beliefs in young children. Indeed, it has been shown that in young adults the presence of such beliefs is correlated with the extent of television viewing (Huesmann & Guerra, 1997; Huesmann & Miller, 1994). Furthermore, similar results were found in a 15-year follow-up of 758 children originally assessed in 1977. When these children were in the first and third grades, the pattern of correlation was consistent with the hypothesis that normative beliefs in aggression, as well as continual fantasizing about aggression, mediate the long-term effects of exposure to media violence (Huesmann, Moise, Podolski, & Eron, 1996).

Use of Fantasy

This brings us to the next cognitive mediator between the viewing of violence and violent behavior: fantasy about such behavior. From an information-processing perspective, fantasizing about behavior is a form of rehearsal. Thus, the more a child fantasizes about aggressing, the more ready the child will be to retrieve aggressive strategies and carry out aggressive behaviors. Of course, the more children behave aggressively or observe others behaving aggressively, the more material they obtain for their aggressive fantasy. Thus, the cycle continues.

Data from the 22-year follow-up study illustrate this cycle. My colleagues and I interviewed the oldest child of 82 participants in the final wave of that study and asked them about their aggressive fantasies. Even though the participants had never been asked such a question, the data provided interesting results. Children's aggressive fantasy correlated highly (.40) with their parent's (the original participant's) peer-nominated aggression 22-years earlier. Apparently, the cognitive processes associated with aggression are stable, not only within a participant's life span, but also across generations within a family. In fact, if one accepts aggressive fantasy as an indirect measure of child aggression, the cross-generational stability of aggression from parent at age 8 to child at age 8 (as represented in a structural model) is as high as the within-subject stability from age 8 to age 30 (.50). It is my conviction that this cross-generational stability can be explained by learning processes (Eron, 1987). However, this does not rule out a genetic/biological explanation, and it is likely that heredity and environment interact to produce this generational consistency (Cloniger & Gottesman 1987).

Furthermore, the findings from the cross-national longitudinal study (Huesman & Eron, 1986) support using children's aggressive fantasy as a measure of their aggressive behavior, suggesting that aggressive fantasy serves as a cognitive rehearsal for aggressive behavior. These data come from 800 primary school children in the Chicago area. The children were interviewed and tested three times at one-year intervals from 1977 to 1979. At the beginning of the study, half of the children were first graders and the other half were third graders. The study was replicated with samples of more than 200 children each in Finland, Israel, and Poland and more than 300 children in Australia.

Two scales from the Children's Fantasy Inventory (Rosenfeld, Huesmann, Eron, & Torney-Purta, 1982) were used to measure the rehearsal of aggressive behavior in all of these samples. One scale measured the child's negative, antisocial aggressive fantasy; the other measured the more heroic but still aggressive fantasy. Each scale score is derived from a number of self-report items measuring the child's daydreams, night dreams, and imaginary play. There were consistent positive correlations in every country between aggressive or heroic fantasy and peer-nominated aggression. The children who reported more aggressive fantasies were more aggressive. Such a finding is consistent with the theory that fantasizing about aggression serves as cognitive rehearsal of aggressive acts.

The data also implicate television in the aggression–fantasy cycle. The more children watched television and identified with the characters, the more they fantasized about aggression. The measure of identification with television characters assessed the extent to which children believe they are like the characters. Longitudinal regressions were calculated in each country in an attempt to ascertain the causal ordering between aggressive fantasy and aggressive behavior. All of these regressions, in every country, indicated nearly equal effects of fantasy on aggression and of aggression on fantasy. These results are consistent with the model that aggressive behavior stimulates aggressive fantasy, which in turn serves as a rehearsal for later aggression. The more children believe they are like an aggressive character, the more aggressive they are. The more realistic they believe the program to be, the more aggressive they are.

The direct positive relation found between aggressive fantasy and the extent of aggressive behavior has important implications concerning the use of fantasy to reduce aggression. It is sheer folly for parents or therapists to encourage their children or clients to engage in fantasy rehearsal of aggressive problem solving in the mistaken assumption that if you work it out in fantasy you do not have to work it out in behavior. Such rehearsal often leads to acting out the very behavior one is trying to prevent. Simple principles derived from memory studies suggest that the more one rehearses an item, the more one is apt to remember it and therefore use it in problem solving. Similarly, the more a sequence or script is practiced, the more likely is it to be acted out, especially when the actor believes it is appropriate. And the more it is observed and is rehearsed, whether in fantasy or overt behavior, the more appropriate and normative it appears to be. If it becomes more normative, it is likely to be retrieved, and therefore used in solving problems. Fantasy constitutes practice for real life. It is not a substitute or compensation for it. Of course, it is possible that fantasy may be used constructively in therapy to find more socially appropriate solutions to the problems presented by the patient (Eron & Lund, 1996).

COGNITIVE DESENSITIZATION

As mentioned above, a substantial body of data indicates that media violence influences beliefs and attitudes about violence. The more televised violence a child watches, the more accepting the child is of aggressive behavior (Dominick & Greenberg, 1972; Drabman & Thomas, 1974; Thomas & Drabman, 1975). This cognitive desensitization then makes children's own aggression more acceptable to them. Equally important, the more television a person watches, the more suspicious that person becomes, and the greater the expectancy of being involved in real violence, what Gerbner called the "mean world syndrome" (Gerbner & Gross, 1980). Such hostile attributional biases promote aggressive interactions with others (Crick & Dodge, 1994).

Several years ago my colleagues and I conducted a study that both reinforces the importance of attitudes and suggests ways to reduce the effects of media violence on children (Huesmann, Eron, Klein, Brice, & Fisher, 1983). In this study, my colleagues and I randomly assigned high violence viewing children to an experimental attitude change treatment or to a control group. The children's attitudes were changed, and they came to believe that media violence was unreal and represented inappropriate ways to solve problems. Several months later, after being reassessed, these children had become less aggressive than the control group children.

EMOTIONAL DESENSITIZATION

One might designate the changes in attitudes brought about by frequent violence viewing as a cognitive desensitization to violence. There is some evidence that a real emotional desensitization can occur. In one quasi-experimental field study (Cline, Croft, & Courrier, 1973), boys who regularly watched a large amount of television displayed less physiological arousal in response to new scenes of violence than did control participants. Although these results have apparently been difficult to replicate in the field, similar laboratory studies of changes in skin conductance in response to violence were discovered by Thomas, Horton, Lippincott, and Drabman (1977). It should not be surprising that emotional and physiological responses to scenes of violence habituate, as do responses to other stimuli. The arousal that is naturally stimulated by observing violent behaviors is unpleasant for most people and therefore inhibits aggressive actions (Halpern, 1975; Winn, 1977). Once this arousal habituates, however, aggression is no longer inhibited.

COGNITIVE JUSTIFICATION PROCESSES

Another psychological explanation for the link between aggressive behavior and violence viewing involves the need to justify one's own aggressive behavior. The justification hypothesis posits that people who are aggressive like to watch violent television because they can then justify their own behavior as being normal (Huesmann, 1982). It involves the observational learning of attitudes, but it operates differently from the process described above. According to this theory, television violence viewing not only stimulates the child's aggressiveness, but it is also a result of the child's aggressiveness. A child's own aggressive behaviors normally elicit guilt, but this guilt is relieved if the same child views violent behavior on television. Thus, the child who has behaved aggressively watches violent television shows to justify his or her own aggressiveness.

CONCLUSION

Reported research findings, both my own and those of other researchers, clearly indicate that seeing aggression all around fosters the belief that aggressive behavior is appropriate. Perhaps if a parent, relative, teacher, therapist, or peer repeatedly reassures a child that life is not really that way, the effect of viewing violence or violent behavior can be diminished. Helping children learn that there are better ways to solve interpersonal problems might also be constructive. Without this positive guidance, children who view violence are likely to believe that aggressive behavior is normative and appropriate, and thus behave aggressively when the appropriate cues are present in the environment.

REFERENCES

Abelson, R. P. (1976). Script processing in attitude formation and decision making. In J. S. Carroll & J. W. Payne (Eds.), *Cognition and social behavior* (pp. 33–46). Hillsdale, NJ: Erlbaum.

Anderson, E. J. (1990). *Streetwise: Race, class, and change in an urban community*. Chicago: University of Chicago Press.

Bandura, A. (1973). *Aggression: A social learning analysis*. Englewood Cliffs, NJ: Prentice-Hall.

Bandura, A. (1977). *Social learning theory*. Englewood Cliffs, NJ: Prentice-Hall.

Bandura, A. (1986). Social foundations of thought and action: A social cognitive theory. Englewood Cliffs, NJ: Prentice-Hall.

Bandura, A., Ross, D., & Ross, S. A. (1961). Transmission of aggression through imitation of aggressive models. *Journal of Abnormal Social Psychology, 63*, 575–582.

Berkowitz, L. (1962). *Aggression: A social psychology analysis*. New York: McGraw Hill.

Berkowitz, L. (1984). Some effects of thoughts on anti- and prosocial influences of media events: A cognitive–neoassociation analysis. *Psychological Bulletin, 95*(3), 410–427.

Berkowitz, L., & LePage, A. (1967). Weapons as aggression eliciting stimuli. *Journal of Personality and Social Psychology, 7,* 202–207.

Berkowitz, L., & Rogers, K. H. (1986). A priming effect analysis of media influences—. In J. Bryant (Eds.), *Perspectives on media effects* (pp. 57–82). Hillsdale, NJ: Erlbaum.

Cline, V. B., Croft, R. G., & Courrier, S. (1973). Desensitization of children to television violence. *Journal of Personality and Social Psychology, 27,* 360–365.

Cloninger, C. R., & Gottesman, A. (1987). Genetic and environmental factors in antisocial behavior disorders. In S. A. Mednick, T. E. Moffitt, & S. A. Stack (Eds.), *The causes of crime: New biological approaches* (pp. 92–109). New York: Cambridge University Press.

Crick, N. R., & Dodge, K. A. (1994). A review and reformulation of social information processing mechanisms in children's adjustment. *Psychological Bulletin, 115,* 74–101.

Dodge, K. A. (1980). Social cognition and children's aggressive behavior. *Child Development, 53,* 620–635.

Dominick, J. R., & Greenberg, B. S. (1972). Attitudes toward violence: The interaction of television exposure, family attitudes, and social class. In G. A. Comstock & E. A. Rubinstein (Eds.), *Television and social behavior* (Vol. 3, pp. 314–335). Washington, DC: U.S. Government Printing Office.

Drabman, R. S., & Thomas, M. H. (1974). Does media violence increase children's toleration of real-life aggression? *Developmental Psychology, 10,* 418–421.

Eron, J. B., & Lund, T. W. (1996). *Narrative solutions in brief therapy.* New York: Guilford Press.

Eron, L. D. (1961). Application of role and learning theories to the study of the development of aggression in children. *Psychological Reports, 9* (Suppl. 2-V9), 291–334.

Eron, L. D. (1963). The relationship of TV viewing habits and aggressive behavior in children. *Journal of Abnormal and Social Psychology, 67,* 193–196.

Eron, L. D. (1987). The development of aggressive behavior from the perspective of a developing behaviorist. *American Psychologist, 42,* 435–442.

Eron, L. D., Banta, T. J., Walder, L. O., & Laulicht, J. H. (1961). A comparison of data obtained from mothers and fathers on child rearing practices and their relation to child aggression. *Child Development, 9,* 291–334.

Eron, L. D., Guerra, N. G., & Huesmann, L. R. (1997). Poverty and aggression—. In S. Feshbach & J. Zagrodska (Eds.), *Biological and sociological perspectives on aggression* (pp. 139–154). New York: Plenum Press.

Eron, L. D., Walder, L. O., & Lefkowitz, M. M. (1971). *The learning of aggression in children.* Boston: Little Brown.

Farber, I. E. (1963). The things people say to themselves. *American Psychologist, 18,* 185–197.

Feigenbaum, E. A., & Feldman, J. (1963). *Computers and thought*. New York: McGraw-Hill.

Feshbach, S. (1972). Reality and fantasy in filmed violence—. In J. Murray, E. Rubinstein, & G. Comstock (Eds.), *Television and social behavior* (Vol. 2, pp. 318–345). Washington, DC: U.S. Department of Health, Education and Welfare.

Gerbner, G., & Gross, L. P. (1980). The violent face of television and its lessons. In E. L. Palmer & A. Dorr (Eds.), *Children and the faces of television: Teaching, violence, selling* (pp. 149–162). New York: Academic Press.

Gregg, L. W., & Simon, H. A. (1967). Process models and stochastic theories of simple concept formation. *Journal of Mathematical Psychology, 4,* 246–276.

Guerra, N. G., Huesmann, L. R., & Hanish, L. (1994). The role of normative beliefs in children's social behavior–. In N. Eisenberg (Ed.), *Review of personality and social psychology, development and social psychology: The interface* (pp. 140–158). London: Sage.

Guerra, N., Huesmann, L. R., Tolan, P., VanAcker, R., & Eron, L. D. (1995). Stressful events and individual beliefs as correlates of economic disadvantage and aggression. *Journal of Consulting and Clinical Psychology, 63,* 518–528.

Halpern, W. I. (1975). Turned-on toddlers. *Journal of Communication, 25,* 66–70.

Hansen, C. H., & Hansen, R. D. (1990). The influence of sex and violence on the appeal of rock music videos. *Communication Research, 17,* 212–234.

Huesmann, L. R. (1982). Television violence and aggressive behavior–. In D. Pearl, L. Bouthilet, & J. Lazar (Eds.), *Television and behavior: Ten years of programs and implications for the 80's* (pp. 126–137). Washington, DC: U.S. Government Printing Office.

Huesmann, L. R.(1988). An information processing model for the development of aggression. *Aggressive Behavior, 14,* 13–24.

Huesmann, L. R., & Eron, L. D. (1984). Cognitive processes and the persistence of aggressive behavior. *Aggressive Behavior, 10,* 243–251.

Huesmann, L. R., & Eron, L. D. (1986). *Television and the aggressive child: A cross natural comparison*. Hillsdale, N.J.: Erlbaum.

Huesmann, L. R., Eron, L. D., Brice, P., Klein, R., & Fisher, P. (1983). Mitigating the imitation of aggressive behaviors by changing children's attitudes about media violence. *Journal of Personality and Social Psychology, 44,* 899–910.

Huesmann, L. R., Eron, L. D., Lefkowitz, M. M., & Walder, L. O. (1984). The stability of aggression over time and generations. *Developmental Psychology, 20*(6), 1120–1134.

Huesmann, L. R., & Guerra, N. G. (1997). Normative beliefs and the development of aggressive behavior. *Journal of Personality and Social Psychology, 72,* 408–419.

Huesmann, L. R., Guerra, N. G., Miller, L., & Zelli, A. (1992). The role of social norms in the development of aggression–. In H. Zumckly & A. Fraczek (Eds.), *Socialization and aggression* (pp. 139–151). New York: Springer-Verlag.

Huesmann, L. R., & Miller, L. S. (1994). Long-term effects of repeated exposure to media violence in childhood. In L.R. Huesmann (Ed.), *Aggressive behavior: Current perspectives* (pp. 153–186). New York: Plenum.

Huesmann, L. R., Moise, J., Podolski, C., & Eron, L. D. (1996, July). The roles of normative beliefs and fantasy rehearsal in mediating the observational learning of aggression. Paper presented at American Psychological Society, San Francisco CA.

Kintsch, W. (1977). *Memory and cognition.* New York: Wiley.

Miller, N. E. (1941). The frustration–aggression hypothesis. *Psychological Review, 48,* 337–342.

Neisser, U. (1967). *Cognitive psychology.* New York: Appleton.

Rosenfeld, E., Huesmann, L. R., Eron, L. D., & Torney-Purta, J. V. (1982). Measuring patterns of fantasy behavior in children. *Journal of Personality and Social Psychology, 42,* 247–266.

Thiebaut, J. W., & Kelley, H. H. (1959). *The social psychology of groups.* New York: Wiley.

Thomas, M. H., & Drabman, R. S. (1975). Toleration of real-life aggression as a function of exposure to televised violence and age of subject. *Merrill-Palmer Quarterly, 21,* 227–232.

Thomas, M. H., Horton, R. W., Lippincott, E. C., & Drabman, R. S. (1977). Desensitization to portrayals of real-life aggression as a function of television violence. *Journal of Personality and Social Psychology, 35,* 450–458.

Widom, C. S. (1989). Does violence beget violence? A critical examination of the literature. *Psychological Bulletin, 106*(1), 3–28.

Winn, M. (1977). *The plug-in-drug.* New York: Viking Press.

3

TOWARD A COMPREHENSIVE EMPATHY-BASED THEORY OF PROSOCIAL MORAL DEVELOPMENT

MARTIN L. HOFFMAN

Contemporary theories of prosocial moral development tend to focus solely on one dimension—behavioral (helping), cognitive (moral reasoning), or emotional–motivational (empathy, guilt). I have written on the emotional–motivational dimension, as well as the interaction of emotion and cognition in moral socialization and the development of empathy and guilt. Here, I update my previous work and present a condensed although comprehensive theory of prosocial moral development.[1] In this chapter I focus on empathy's contribution to moral emotion, motivation, and behavior, but I also highlight cognition. I cover five types of moral encounters that encompass the prosocial moral domain, defined in terms of the consequences of one's actions for others: bystander, transgression, virtual transgression, multiple claimant, and caring versus justice. These types share an

---

[1]A full treatment can be found in Hoffman, 2000.

empathic motive base—each features empathic distress and the derived motives of sympathetic distress, empathic anger, empathic feeling of injustice, guilt. Each type is described below.

MORAL ENCOUNTER TYPE 1: WITNESSING DISTRESS AS A BYSTANDER

Bystanders are people who witness someone in pain, danger, or distress (physical, emotional, economic). The moral question is whether or not they are motivated to help. The bystander role is a prototypic opportunity to experience empathy for another's distress and related emotions.

There is much evidence to support the notion that empathic distress is a prosocial motive: It is associated with and precedes helping behavior. Like other motives, its intensity diminishes, and bystanders feel better if they help and feel worse if they do not (Hoffman 1978, 2000). *Empathy* is defined here as a feeling that fits someone else's condition more than one's own. This feeling may or may not exactly match that of the other person. The fact that such a match is not required has advantages that will become apparent later in the chapter. Because prosocial action involves helping someone in distress, I focus on empathic distress.

Arousal of Empathic Distress

There are five *arousal modes*, or ways in which empathic distress can be aroused. Three of the five are primitive, automatic, and involuntary. The first, *mimicry*, has two steps: The observer spontaneously imitates the victim's facial, vocal, or postural expressions of feeling, resulting in changes in the observer's facial and postural musculature. These facial changes trigger the brain, which, through afferent feedback, produces feelings that resemble the victim's. The second mode is *classical conditioning*: observers acquire empathic distress as a conditioned response by witnessing someone in distress while at the same time having their own independent experience of distress. In the third mode, *direct association*, cues in the victim's situation remind the observer of similar past experiences and evoke feelings fitting the victim's situation. The remaining empathy-arousing modes involve higher order cognition. In one mode, *mediated association*, language communicates a victim's emotional state and connects the victim's situation to personal past experiences. In the final arousal mode, *role-taking*, the observer feels something of the victim's distress by imagining how he or she would feel in the same situation (self-focus) or imagining how the victim feels based on knowledge about the victim or about how others like the victim (same age, sex, culture) would feel in the same situation (other focus), or both. Because this role-taking is cognitively demanding, it is often deliberate but can be spontaneous, in children as well as in adults (Wilson & Cantor, 1985).

The importance of multiple modes of empathic arousal is that they enable observers to respond empathically to whatever distress cues are available. Cues from the victim's face, voice, or posture can be picked up through mimicry; situational cues can be processed through conditioning or association. If the victim expresses distress verbally or in writing or some-one else describes her situation, observers can be empathically aroused through mediated association or role-taking.[2] Empathic distress is thus a multidetermined, reliable human response. This fits well with the argument that it became part of human nature through natural selection (Hoffman, 1981) and the finding that it may have a hereditary component (Zahn-Waxler, Robinson, Emde, & Plomin, 1992).

Mature observers who can engage in higher order thinking are aware of their empathic feelings. They feel distressed but know that the distress is a response to the other's misfortune and their perception of how the other feels. They thus have a cognitive sense of themselves and others as separate beings with independent inner states, personal identities, and life condi-tions. They have a sense of how they (and others) would feel in the victim's situation, and they know that the victim's outward behavior (facial expres-sion) may not fully reflect how he feels inside. Finally, they make sponta-neous inferences about the cause of the victim's plight, using whatever information they have.

Development of Empathy

When can children empathize in this metacognitive way? Strayer (1993) found that 7-year-olds who watched a film attributed their own feel-ing to a character's feeling or situation, a rudimentary form of metacognitive empathy (which is lacking in 5-year-olds). Younger children could be em-pathically aroused without this awareness. These findings suggest that empa-thy develops along with children's acquiring a cognitive sense of themselves and others. I describe below five developmental levels of empathic distress that I hypothesize are based on children's ability to differentiate themselves from others.

1. *Global empathic distress—reactive newborn cry.* The cry in re-sponse to the sound of another's cry by an alert, content newborn is not a reaction to a noxious stimulus, nor is it just imitation. It is vigorous, intense, and identical to sponta-neous cries of infants in actual distress (Sagi & Hoffman,

---

[2]The involuntary modes can prevent "egoistic drift" that can occur when observers engage in self-focused role-taking.

1976). It must therefore be considered an early, global empathic distress. It disappears with the dawning awareness of self and other as separate beings. By 6 months infants only cry in response to prolonged cries, and they look sad and pucker up their lips before crying (Hay, Nash, & Pedersen, 1981).

2. *Egocentric empathic distress.* By 11–12 months, infants do the same thing, but they also whimper and silently watch the victim (Radke-Yarrow & Zahn-Waxler, 1984.) Some infants are more active, but their actions are designed to reduce their own distress. I observed a 1-year-old, for example, who saw a friend fall and cry, stare at her friend, begin to cry, and then put her thumb in her mouth and bury her head in her mother's lap, just as she does when she hurts herself.

A parsimonious explanation is that the observing infant behaves the same way in both situations because she is unclear about the difference between something happening to the other and to herself. This interpretation is compatible with Stern's (1985) claim that even 7-month-olds have a sense of controlling their actions and being coherent, physically bounded continuous entities. Stern's "core self" is based on the integration of sensations from muscles, tendons, and joints. It is an "experiential, proprioception-based self, not the representational, reflective self that emerges around the middle of the second year" (p. 7). I propose further that it is a fragile self, whose boundaries can break down when its constituent bodily sensations are mingled with bodily sensations resulting from automatic empathic distress (from mimicry, conditioning, or association). This breakdown of barriers could explain the 6-month-old's looking sad, whimpering, and bursting into tears, as well as our 1-year-old's confusion about the origin of her empathic distress. In any case, the response to one's own and other's distress is similar, so I call it "egocentric" empathic distress: an egocentric motive (to reduce own distress) but also prosocial (contingent on another's distress).

3. *Quasi-egocentric empathic distress.* Within a few months the observing infant's whimpering, staring, and crying begin to wane and are replaced by helpful advances such as patting, touching, kissing, hugging, reassuring, advising, and getting others to help the victim (Radke-Yarrow & Zahn-Waxler, 1984). These acts show that the infant clearly knows that the other is in pain or discomfort but is still egocentric enough to use helping strategies he or she finds comforting. Thus a 14-month-old colleague's child responded to a crying friend with

a sad look, then gently took the friend's hand and brought him to his own mother, even though the friend's mother was present. This quasi-egocentric act shows both empathic distress as prosocial motive and confusion between his and the other's desires.

4. *Veridical empathy for another's feeling.* In the second year of life, infants become aware that others have inner states (thoughts, feelings, and desires) independent of their own. They can now empathize more accurately with others' feelings and desires and help them more effectively. A 2-year-old I know brought his own teddy bear to comfort a crying friend. When that action did not work, he paused, ran to the next room, and returned with the friend's bear. The friend hugged his bear and stopped crying. This behavior suggests the transition to veridical empathy, which may occur when children are cognitively ready to learn from corrective feedback following their "quasi-egocentric" mistakes.

    This is only the beginning of the development process. Learning to fully empathize with others is a lifelong task. By 8 years, children learn that conflicting emotions can coexist in a person (Gnepp, 1989); by 16, they may refrain from helping because they know it can put a victim at a social disadvantage (Midlarsky & Hannah, 1985). Adults know their empathic distress can sometimes be more intense than the victim's (she has adjusted to the problem or it means less to her). Therapists may delay expressing empathic grief over the death of a friend because it might inhibit the patient's expressing negative feeling about the person who died.

5. *Empathic distress beyond the situation.* We might infer from gender and ethnic identity research that children's sense of themselves as coherent, continuous, and stable beings is hazy until about 6–9 years. This suggests that soon after age 9 children know that others have identities that affect their reactions to the immediate situation, although interference from situational and expressive cues may keep children from using this knowledge to infer another's current state. There is little research, but Gnepp and Gould's (1985) finding supports this understanding in 7–10-year-old children. They described a child's prior experience (bitten by a gerbil, rewarded for an excellent dive) and then asked their subjects to predict the child's emotional reaction in a related subsequent event (his turn to feed the class gerbil). Half the second graders and most of the fifth graders correctly used the prior information. This suggests that at roughly 7–10 years is when knowledge of

others' separate lives and past experiences begins to affect empathic responses.

Following this development, children should be able to empathize with someone who is chronically ill, emotionally deprived, or hopelessly poor, regardless of his immediate behavior. If he seems sad at a particular time, knowing that his life circumstances generally provoke sadness should intensify the observer's empathic distress. If he appears happy, the observer may not respond to his happy expression with empathic joy, but rather may believe that his sad life circumstance is a more compelling index of his well-being and respond with empathic sadness or a mixture of joy and sadness. Mature empathy is thus a response to a network of cues, including another's behavior and expression and everything known about him.

Sympathetic Distress

In advancing from global to quasi-egocentric empathy, children's empathic distress is qualitatively transformed into a more reciprocal concern for victims. Children still feel empathic distress but also sympathetic distress, or compassion. From then on, developmentally, empathic distress includes a sympathetic component: Children want to help because they feel sorry for the victim, not just to relieve their own empathic distress. [3] Sympathetic distress may therefore be the child's first truly prosocial motive.

This shift can be observed in children's progression from comforting themselves to comforting victims. Anecdotes suggest an in-between stage. For example, a 1-year-old, who previously sucked his thumb and pulled his ear when he was distressed also sucked his thumb and pulled his father's ear when his father looked sad. Another example is shown in a child whose first prosocial act alternated between gently touching a distressed peer and gently touching himself. Researchers found that mirror self-image recognition at 18 months predicted sympathetic distress and prosocial behavior at 24 months, which supports the hypothesis that self–other differentiation contributes to sympathetic distress (Bischoff-Kohler, 1991; Zahn-Waxler et al., 1992).

Cognitively Expanded Bystander Model

Cognitive processes enable humans to form images, represent events, and imagine themselves in another's place. And because represented events can evoke emotions (Fiske, 1982; Hoffman, 1985), empathy can be aroused by imagining victims, as in reading about their misfortunes, arguing about economic or political issues, or making moral judgments about hypothetical

---

[3]Children may never help just to relieve their own empathic distress, as there are easier ways to do this.

dilemmas. Consider, for example, a 13-year-old male research subject who responded to the question "Why is it wrong to steal from a store?" as follows:

> Because the people who own the store work hard for their money, and they deserve to be able to spend it for their family. It's not fair; they sacrifice a lot and they make plans, and then they lost it all because somebody who didn't work for it goes in and takes it (Hoffman, 1982).

This boy turned an abstract, Kohlberg-style moral question into an empathy-relevant one by imagining a victim's inner thoughts and states (motivation, expectation and future plans, and disappointment).

Causal Attribution and Empathic Emotions

Most people make spontaneous judgments about the cause of events (Weiner, 1985) and probably do this when observing someone in distress. Depending on the attribution, empathic distress may be reduced or transformed into other empathic emotions. It is reduced when victims are blamed for their condition. Blaming victims, with or without a factual base (jogging in dangerous places, staying with abusive husbands, having promiscuous sex), can neutralize bystanders' empathic distress and thus can reduce guilt and feeling of responsibility or make them feel indifference or even contempt for victims. Staub (1996) suggested that distancing may occur because it is extremely difficult to see others suffer when one can do nothing about it.

Empathic distress is transformed into sympathetic distress if the cause is believed to be beyond the victim's control (accident, illness; Weiner, Graham, Stern, & Lawson, 1982) or when the cause is unclear. If someone other than the victim is judged to be the cause, empathic distress may be transformed into empathic anger—empathy with the victim's anger or if the victim is sad rather than angry, a dual feeling of empathic distress for the victim's pain and anger at the culprit. It is hard to distinguish empathic anger (when unaccompanied by empathic distress for the victim) from direct anger, because the behavioral outcomes are similar. Examples would be a 17-month-old who watched his brother get a flu shot and tried to hit the doctor or a highly aggressive toddler who learned to channel his aggression so well that by age 6 he expressed more empathic anger than did his peers (Cummings, Hollenbeck, Iannotti, Radke-Yarrow, & Zahn-Waxler, 1986). Six-year-olds express empathic anger, but they cannot differentiate between anger- and sadness-evoking situations (Levine, 1995). The similar reactions suggest the need to study how empathic and direct anger interrelate.[4]

---

[4] A person who (due to socialization) cannot feel direct anger may feel empathic anger, especially with a victim who is hurt but not angry.

People also make character attributions based on victims' reputation or stereotypes of their group. These attributions may decrease empathy when victims are viewed as bad, immoral, or lazy, and thus deserving of their fate. But if victims are viewed as good, one may not only empathize with their personal distress but also view them as victims of injustice (non-reciprocity of deeds and outcomes), which can transform empathic distress into an empathic feeling of injustice (Hoffman, 1987, 1991).

Prosocial Motivation and Guilt in Bystanders

Empathic distress has long been known to arouse a bystander motive to reduce victims' distress (Eisenberg & Miller, 1987). Furthermore, empathic helpers focus on the ultimate consequences for victims, not themselves; they remain distressed if their efforts fail even for legitimate reasons (Batson & Weeks, 1996). There is no assurance that empathic observers will help; powerful egoistic motives (fear, avoiding involvement) may intervene. But observers who do not help may feel guilt over inaction.

Blaming the self for inaction transforms empathic distress into guilt—not for causing the victim's distress, but for allowing it to continue. There is scattered anecdotal evidence that guilt over inaction motivates prosocial behavior. White 1960s civil rights activists said that they would have felt guilty if they had done nothing, because that would have allowed the victimization of Southern Black people to continue (Keniston, 1968). A German who saved Jews from Nazis said "unless we helped, they would be killed. I could not stand that thought. I never would have forgiven myself" (Oliner & Oliner, 1988, p. 168). One of my undergraduate students reported, "The woman kept hitting her kid. I felt I'd feel bad if I did nothing. So I got my keys and entertained him. He responded. The mother then acted better. I felt real good."

Even when bystanders help, they may feel guilt over hesitating because the victim suffered in the interim. This means that bystanders may always feel some guilt unless they act immediately.

Empathic Anger as a Prosocial Motive

There is no research, only anecdotes, on empathic anger as a prosocial motive, which is surprising given its social importance as the "guardian of justice" (Mill, 1861/1979). It seems likely, because anger "mobilizes energy and makes one capable of defending oneself with vigor" (Izard, 1977, p. 333), that empathic anger mobilizes energy to defend victims. Anecdotal evidence can be seen in the following quotations: "I think there was a double feeling: compassion for Jews and anger toward the Germans" (Oliner & Oliner, 1988, p. 118). "And when they started taking Jewish people, that really lit my fire . . . I couldn't stand it anymore. I really became full of hate because they took innocent people—especially when they took little kids" (Oliner & Oliner, 1988, p. 143). "The pictures of starving children in Ethiopia are heart wrenching, but feeling sad is not enough. We send a check, the pictures disappear from television screens, and soon we forget that millions are dying. Instead we should feel outraged that in a world of plenty hunger still exists. Outrage produces action" (*New York Times*, Feb. 7, 1985)

Individual Differences and Socialization

Abused and conduct-disordered children often show little empathy (Cohen & Strayer, 1996; Main & George, 1985). Children who are securely attached show, on average, more empathy than children who are not (Waters, Wippman, & Sroufe, 1979). Empathy is also relatively high among children whose parents are empathic and use socialization methods that encourage sympathetic helping and discourage actions likely to hurt others (Eisenberg, Fabes, Carlo, Troyer, Speet, Karbon, R. Switzer, 1992). These socialization methods figure heavily in the transgression model, which follows.

MORAL ENCOUNTER TYPE 2: TRANSGRESSION

Transgressions are situations in which one harms someone or considers acting in a way that might cause harm. Transgressions may be provoked, intentional, accidental, by-products of conflict, or violations of another's legitimate expectations. The moral issue is whether one is motivated to avoid the harmful act or feels guilty and acts prosocially afterward. The transgression model is prototypic for a moral encounter involving empathy-based guilt.

Although empathy-arousing processes described above may produce prosocial moral motives in bystanders, they may not work when children harm or are about to act in a way that might harm someone. In the latter case, emotions (anger) may blind them to the harm done and override any empathic tendencies. External agents are then needed.

Examples of Transgressions

Accidents

When children are aware of the harm they have done, feel empathic distress and guilt, and engage in reparative action, intervention is not needed. Intervention is needed when children are unaware of the harm done or ignore or laugh at the victim's distress.

Intentional Harm

Most adults do not harm others intentionally except in self-defense, retaliation, or when misperceiving their intentions. The same is true of children, who also harm others through innocent pranks (throwing stones at school windows) and for no apparent reason. Consider, for example, a 5-year-old who sulked over a scolding. When her younger sister tried to comfort her by offering a toy; she said "go away, I don't like you," whereupon her sister ran away, buried her head in the couch, and sobbed. Such situations may require adult intervention.

Conflicts

Peer conflicts, mainly over possessions (toys, candy, the swings or slide, a jump rope), are a big challenge to the promotion of moral development and socialization, because of their high frequency and children's emotionality (Hay, 1984). For example, Child A says that it is his turn to play and grabs a toy from Child B, who grabs it back. They fight until Child A pushes Child B away, grabs the toy and runs, leaving Child B crying. If Child A is empathic and comforts Child B, no intervention is needed. Intervention is needed if Child A ignores Child B's cries or Child B chases and hits Child A, because powerful egoistic, angry emotions may keep each child from attending to both his own behavior and the other's distress, which is necessary for empathic distress and accepting blame. People try to avoid blame anyway, as it is self-deprecatory, painful, and associated with punishment. Intervention may thus be needed to put empathy- and especially guilt- arousing processes in motion and to prevent someone from getting hurt.

Discipline, Guilt, and Moral Socialization

I have long argued that the foundation for guilt and moral internalization, which is necessary for combating egoistic needs in conflict situations, occurs in discipline encounters at home when children harm someone. Whether the transgression is accidental, intentional, or conflict related, and whether the victim is a parent or peer, it is only in discipline encounters that adults help children make connections among their motives, actions, and their harmful consequences for others. When children inflict harm, intervention is needed if they are unaware of the harm done or if they ignore or laugh at the victim's distress. No intervention is necessary when children are aware of the harm they have done, feel empathic distress and guilt, and attempt to make reparations. After three decades of research (from Hoffman, 1963, to Krevans & Gibbs, 1996), it appears that the most effective parental discipline methods for producing guilt and moral internalization are *inductions*, which point up the harmful consequences of children's acts for others while arousing empathy for the victim.

To explain the underlying processes of inductions, I made an information-processing analysis of the cognitive and emotional changes in children between discipline encounters (Hoffman, 1983). I present here a revised analysis, using generalized event representations, or "scripts." Scripts are useful because (a) even young children form them to organize experience and memory and to guide actions (Nelson, 1993); (b) like other representations, they become more complex with age through successive use; and (c) most important, they can be charged with emotion and thus acquire motive properties. Scripts of behavioral interaction sequences, charged with prosocial moral emotion (empathic distress, sympathetic distress, guilt) may thus provide the affective–cognitive–behavioral units of people's prosocial moral motivational structure. My analysis follows:

1. Inductions, like other discipline methods, communicate disapproval of children's harmful acts but also call attention to both the victim's distress and the child's role in causing it. Making victim's distress salient activates empathy-arousal modes: mimicry if children see the victim, role-taking if they are asked to imagine how they would feel in her place, and mediated association if relevant past experiences are mentioned. Children may then feel empathic distress for the victim's pain, hurt feelings, and suffering beyond the situation. When they process the information about their causal role, the resulting self-blame transforms their empathic distress into transgression guilt (Hoffman 1970, 1982). This kind of parental disapproval adds a sense of committing an infraction by causing harm.

2. After several repetitions of transgression followed by induction, empathic distress, and empathy-based guilt, children form a Transgression->Induction->Guilt script, which is emotionally charged (empathic distress, guilt), giving it motive properties. The full script may include reparative acts by the child, the parent's and victim's positive responses to them, and the child's resulting empathic relief and guilt reduction, which reinforce the reparative acts' connection to guilt (Hoffman, 2000). These acts are not discussed here to maintain the focus on guilt.

3. Over the years children successively assimilate into their Transgression->Induction->Guilt scripts the information contained in thousands of inductions—enough to transform them into increasingly complex, generalized structures of

emotionally charged knowledge about the effects of their actions on others. [5] Early scripts consist of kinesthetic representations of one's harmful acts (due to sensations from muscles, tendons, joints), images of the victim's pain and parents' discipline behaviors, and associated empathy and guilt. With age, they become less kinesthetic–imagistic and more semantic, propositional, and principle-like (one must not hurt others), while retaining the empathy and guilt feelings.

4. These generalized scripts result from children's active semantic integration of induction content and the connections they make to their own action and the victim's condition. Children's own internal mental and emotional processes are thus salient, and the scripts are experienced as their own constructions and part of their internal motive system, despite having an external origin. The internalization process is enhanced by the tendency of "episodic" details (parent's presence) to fade from memory (Nelson, 1993; Tulving, 1972).

5. The process described above may explain how early encounters between a child's egoistic motives and parental demands (discipline encounters) are transformed into encounters between his egoistic motives and his internalized prosocial motives (moral encounters). From early on, inductions give discipline encounters an increasingly moral-encounter component, which eventually takes over. Parental intervention becomes less necessary, as children "internalize" the motive to consider others even in conflict situations. The scripts, now Transgression->Guilt scripts, are activated directly by children's awareness of doing harm, and the associated guilt feels like it comes from within.

6. Guilt's value as a prosocial motive would be limited if it only operated after the fact. Transgression->Guilt scripts, however, like other representations, can be activated in advance by relevant stimuli (children's anticipatory thoughts and images of harmful effects of their planned action on others). The script's associated guilt, felt as "anticipatory guilt," can then serve as motive against the act. To feel anticipatory guilt and act on it has cognitive and behavior-control prerequisites: being able, under fire, to consider other perspectives and connect intentions, acts, and consequences that have not occurred, and to control impulses.

---

[5]"Thousands" is based on Wright's (1967) finding that 2–10 year-olds experienced parental influence attempts every 6–9 minutes (about 50 a day or 15,000 a year!) and evidence that middle-class parents use "reasoning" half the time (Chapman & Zahn-Waxler, 1982; Ross, Tessla, Kenyon, & Lollis, 1990; Smetana, 1989).

The Context of Discipline

For discipline to be effective, as described above, it needs to occur in an ongoing relationship. Only securely attached toddlers will be receptive to parental inductions (Hoffman, 1988; Londerville & Main, 1981). A good relationship is not enough, however, and at times the emotionality of situations in which children harm others calls for power assertion (force, threats, commands). Although power assertion arouses emotions (fear, anger) and acts (gaze aversion, withdrawal) that disrupt cognitive processing and undermine inductions and guilt arousal (Hoffman 1963)—some power assertion may be needed to get a child to stop, pay attention, and process inductive information. How much is needed varies: A mild directive may do if the child is simply unaware ("Don't you see you hurt Mary? Don't pull her hair"). But highly charged conflicts may require physically removing and calming a child before verbalizing inductions or holding him firmly and insisting he listen. Another factor is temperament: Less power assertion is needed to get fearful children to attend to inductions and resist temptation (Kochanska, 1995), and the same may be true of empathic children.

Guilt, Induction, and Prosocial Behavior

Many studies provide evidence to support the validity of the connections among induction, empathy, guilt and prosocial action, described in this chapter. Baumeister, Stillwell, and Heatherton (1994) report in their review that empathy-based guilt motivates prosocial acts (apology, reparation, generalized helping). A study by Krevans and Gibbs (1996) supports our particular hypothesis that empathic distress mediates induction's contribution to prosocial action. Previous findings relating induction to empathy and prosocial action were replicated in this study, but induction's relation to prosocial behavior disappeared when empathy was controlled. Our guilt-as-mediator hypothesis received post-hoc support: Guilt correlated positively with prosocial behavior in high-empathy children and with empathy in children whose parents favored induction. There is also experimental support for induction's contribution to prosocial action and for empathy's mediating role (Kuczynski, 1983; Sawin & Parke, 1980).

MORAL ENCOUNTER TYPE 3: VIRTUAL TRANSGRESSIONS

Once acquired, Transgression->Guilt scripts can be activated and trigger guilt feelings when individuals think that they have transgressed, even if they have not. I refer to this as *virtual guilt* and to the presumed harmful act as *virtual transgression*. This assumption is not new. *Webster's Ninth*

Collegiate Dictionary (1985, p. 542) defined *guilt* as "feelings of culpability, especially for imagined offenses." Early instances are 15–20-month-old infants who, on finding their mothers looking sad or sobbing for no apparent reason, looked sad (empathic distress) and then approached and tried to comfort the mother (Zahn-Waxler, Radke-Yarrow, & King, 1979). Half the time they seemed to accept blame ("I sorry, Mommy, did I do something wrong?"). This may only be imitation, but because the same children obtained high projective guilt scores five years later (Cummings et al., 1986), it could be a forerunner of a type of guilt inherent in close relationships.

Relationship Guilt

Close relationships have considerable value, but they also have a price. Baumeister, Stillwell, and Heatherton (1995) asked adults to describe a recent instance in which they felt guilty. The largest categories were neglecting a partner and failing to live up to an interpersonal obligation. As Tangney and Fischer (1995, p. 134) pointed out, close relationships provide endless opportunities for hurting one's partner, "from unintended slights, thoughtless remarks, and forgotten appointments, to more serious betrayals of confidence, bald-faced lies, and crushing infidelities," that is, endless opportunities for feeling transgression guilt.

Close relationships also provide endless opportunities for blaming oneself when innocent, because relationship partners can become so interdependent that their feelings and moods depend heavily on the feelings, moods, and actions of the other. More important, each knows the other is dependent on him or her. Indeed, owing to countless interactions, each becomes aware of new and unpredictable ways of unintentionally and unknowingly distressing his or her partner. As a result, each develops a keen sensitivity to the possible impact of her words and deeds on the other. It may thus seem reasonable, when one's partner is sad or unhappy and the cause is unclear, to blame oneself as well as to feel empathic distress. There are many ways to harm others that are unique to close relationships (breaking promises, neglecting obligations, not being attentive enough). Feeling guilty over a partner's distress may thus be endemic to close relationships. I call it *relationship guilt* because it is generated more by the relationship than by a particular act.

Relationship guilt may be involved in the infant guilt described earlier. Infants cry, and mothers run to take care of them. Infants get injured or become ill, and mothers respond with vocal, facial, or bodily expressions of pain or sorrow. Infants crawl, walk, and talk for the first time, and mothers express delight. These maternal responses, and their implicit statement of how important the children are, may create in infants feelings of omnipotence toward mothers. As a result, long before infants develop a "theory of mind" that enables them to infer the impact of their actions, they may connect their actions to changes in mothers' moods through simple association. Accordingly, an ambiguous stimulus, (the mother's sad expression or sobbing without a clear cause), together with infants' undeveloped sense of agency (their fuzzy awareness of causing or not causing things to happen), and their physical proximity, may lead to guilt: "Mommy is sad; it must be something I did."

Infant guilt is far simpler than mature relationship guilt. Mature relationships involve peers and are multifaceted, not simple nurturer–nurturee dimensioned. And mature relationship guilt is not due to an undeveloped sense of agency but instead to learning from experience about subtle ways of hurting others and one's limited memory of past interactions that might explain the other's state. In sum, it is caused by a complex web of interactions in which partners are certain of their importance to the other but are unclear about the cause of the other's distress at a given time.

A student of mine felt

> really down one day. My boyfriend was near crying and asked "What did I do?" I said "it's not your fault." He asked again. I said "it's not your fault." He said "then why are you so down?" I said "I don't know, but it's not your fault." He said "I must have done something."

After suicides, relationship partners may feel guilty ("I should have known he was depressed"; "If only I had (or had not) . . .").

 Relationship guilt, of course, has prosocial effects. It makes people less likely to hurt or disappoint and motivates them to attend and express positive feelings toward their partners.

Responsibility Guilt

Feeling responsible for others, which develops with age and maturity, often makes one feel guilty. Parents whose child has a fatal disease may be convinced, despite all evidence to the contrary, that they could have prevented it (Chodoff, Frieman, & Hamburg, 1964). A person can feel responsible for harming someone in an accident even though she tried to avoid it, logic says she was not to blame, and witnesses say it was the victim's fault. Guilt can be acute in jobs involving responsibility for others' lives when things go wrong despite one's best efforts. Consider, for example, the words of a police sergeant who watched two of his men standing next to him get shot by a sniper who no one knew was there:

> I was the one making decisions [to lead his men down the street] . . . It was my responsibility . . . He got hit, I didn't . . . I brought him to that door . . . Maybe if I was slower or faster . . . if I had been on the right

side instead of the left . . . Did I do something wrong? Was there any other way I could have handled it? . . . I was responsible . . . Maybe we could have hit the door a second earlier. (Lindsay-Hartz, De Rivera, & Mascolo, 1995, p. 277).

What happens in responsibility guilt is one empathizes with the victim and engages in "counter-factual thinking" (Sanna & Turley, 1996). One reviews the situation mentally, realizes one could have acted differently and prevented the bad outcome, then switches from "I could have" to "I should have," and feels guilty.

Developmental Guilt

In individualistic societies, one can feel guilty as a result of growing up and pursuing personal goals that involve leaving home and separating from one's parents, achieving, and being affluent.

Separation Guilt

Clinicians describe patients who are excited about leaving home but feel empathic distress and guilt whenever they think about it because it will pain their parents (Modell, 1963). For example, a friend's separation guilt made him turn down a top university for a local college (a decision he now regrets). His mother's saying she would not stand in his way, although she would be unhappy if he left, did not help. Children may of course sense a parent's anxiety over their leaving even when it is less explicit.

Achievement Guilt

When teachers begin grading children on their performance relative to others, high performers soon realize that their own achievements come at a cost to others, and thus can make others feel inadequate. Consider a talented child who draws a picture that engenders adult approval; his peers look on dejectedly. Adolescents may feel guilty if they are the only one in the peer group to go to college because they think it lowers others' self-esteem (although it could of course give them vicarious pride: "one of us made it"). There is no research on guilt over achievement, but a reason given for the "fear of success" syndrome found in 1970s research (Horner, 1974) was that one person's success can make others feel like failures.

Affluence Guilt

Older children and adolescents are sensitive to lifestyle differences based on affluence, and being affluent is a potential source of guilt (Hoffman, 1989). It seems that some 1960s social activists transformed their empathic distress over society's disadvantaged into guilt over affluence when they became aware of the vast discrepancy between their good life and others' meager existence. They may have experienced "guilt by association" when they perceived their own social class as culpable (Keniston, 1968). A congressional intern expressed this clearly when asked why many middle-class youth were "turned off" by the very system that gave them so many advantages and opportunities:

> They feel guilty because, while they are enjoying this highest standard of living, American Indians are starving and black ghettoes are overrun by rats . . . This goes on while they eat steak every day . . . Their sense of moral indignation can't stand this; and they realize that the blame rests on the shoulders of their class. (*New Republic*, November 28, 1970, p. 11).

Guilt over affluence relates to survivor guilt (Hoffman, 1989). It happens in adults, but I classify it as developmental guilt because it is more likely to occur in adolescents, and when it does occur it can play a significant role in their prosocial moral development.

MORAL ENCOUNTER TYPE 4: MULTIPLE CLAIMANTS

Sometimes bystanders must choose which victims to help. Obvious examples are in situations in which people are drowning or are caught in burning buildings. Multiple moral claimants also pose a dilemma in such situations as writing letters of recommendation for a favorite student. The student expects support, colleagues expect candid replies, and unknown candidates hope for the job. Such dilemmas involve "caring," and one's motive to act may be empathy or a more general caring principle (we are our brother's keeper).

The moral philosophical issue is who should one help? The scientific question is who does one help? Evolutionary biology's answer is simple: One helps those with whom one shares the most genes (Hamilton, 1971). Psychology's answer seems more complex, although it is ultimately not very different. With single claimants one empathizes with anyone in distress. With multiple claimants, one may empathize with them all but to a greater degree with those he knows and cares about (Costin & Jones, 1992): who share his race, gender, or personality profile (Feshbach & Roe, 1968; Klein, 1971; Krebs, 1970): and whose plight fits his own enduring concerns (Houston, 1990). [6] Principled people making life-and-death choices can transcend these biases.

---

[6]By "empathize to a greater degree," I mean one's threshold for empathic distress is lower for these victims than for others.

The dilemma of bystanders in multiple victim contexts is powerfully illustrated below.

> When asked how many of the Jewish people they helped were strangers, over 90% of the rescuers said at least one. Their universalist view of ethical obligations sometimes put them in a tragic situation. When they could only choose one person to save, they struggled to find a guiding criterion. Should it be the doctor, judge, or poor uneducated person whose life promised little more than survival? The child, the aged, or frail? This "playing God" with people's lives left its mark: choice itself violated the principle of universal responsibility, and guilt feelings continue to plague them as they reflect on the choices they made. (edited quotation from Oliner & Oliner, 1988, p. 170)

These remarks show the agony of choosing among moral claimants in extreme situations, and the guilt experienced by principled people who despite their sacrifices may nevertheless feel culpable because of the victims they could not help.

MORAL ENCOUNTER TYPE 5: CARING VERSUS JUSTICE

Empathy's link to caring is clear. This is not true of its link to justice, which is concerned with society's criteria for administering punishments (criminal justice) and allocating resources (distributive justice). Although I focus on distributive justice in this section, empathy's relevance to criminal justice should be noted. It seems likely that the intensity of people's empathic distress for victims and anger at perpetrators of a crime influences their beliefs about the appropriate punishment for that crime. Also that people's empathy is affected by the age, gender, and class of the victims and perpetrators (empathic distress for a lower-class culprit viewed as a victim of society).

Distributive justice in contemporary Western society demands that resources be allocated primarily according to merit (output, competence, effort) and, to some extent, need. Empathy's link to "need" is clear: Poverty is painful and people may respond to the poor with empathic distress. This may reflect empathy and "caring," but it may also reflect need-based justice (people *deserve* to have food and shelter). This is a fine distinction, and conflict between caring and need is apt to be rare.

Empathy's link to "effort" is reflected in the individual's explanation for why stealing is wrong, cited earlier. That response may also explain the link between empathy and need based on effort. People are distressed by unrewarded effort. They empathize with that distress because they believe that their own hard work should be rewarded and feel unjustly victimized when it is not. They might of course just empathize with the victim's loss ("caring"). This is another fine distinction, and conflict between caring and effort is probably unusual.

Empathy's links to output- and competence-based merit are more problematic because these factors reveal little about people's feelings. The following arguments for a link can be made: (a) If output and competence require hard work and expectations of reward, then the argument given above for effort applies; (b) if a high producer is poorly rewarded, we may view him as victim of deed–outcome nonreciprocity and have empathic feelings of injustice; (c) a link to empathy is suggested by the idea that rewarding output–competence motivates people to produce more, which "trickles down" to the poor. But these links are circuitous, and it is expected that empathy will lead to a preference for need or effort. There is no research on effort, but empathically aroused children and adults apparently do prefer need over output (Damon, 1977; Montada, Schmitt, & Dalbert 1986; Wender, 1986).

It follows that output–competence differs fundamentally from caring and may often be involved in caring-versus-justice dilemmas. Consider the letter-of-recommendation example. The conflict so far is a caring dilemma: the writer could empathize with each moral claimant, imagine their distress if she writes a favorable or a candid letter, and feel appropriate anticipatory guilt for any who are disadvantaged by her choice. She might base her decision on what would cause her the least guilt, which claimant's distress would be the greatest, or whether empathy for her student should simply override all other concerns.

But there are justice issues, too. The academic system places high value on scholarly output and competence, and its integrity rests on recommendations based on candid assessments of job applicants. The caring-versus-justice dilemma becomes acute when letter writers believe that their student may not be the most competent candidate. If they candidly reveal the student's weaknesses, in keeping with "justice," they violate "caring" and may feel empathic guilt over betraying the student. If empathy prevails, and they emphasize the student's strengths and downplay his weaknesses, they violate "justice" and may feel guilt.

Within academia, similar issues are involved in promotion, tenure, and related decisions. Consider a situation in which an esteemed faculty member died and his wife, a part-time adjunct instructor with below-average teacher ratings, was being considered for a renewal of her contract. Caring and need would seem to dictate renewing her contract, which some faculty advocated. Other faculty argued that it would be immoral to renew her contract because it was inconsiderate of the students (caring) or because the university should hire only the best people (justice).

INTEGRATION OF THE MORAL ENCOUNTERS

If these five types of moral encounters encompass the prosocial moral domain, their sharing an empathic base speaks to empathy's importance and augurs well for a comprehensive theory. The theory's cornerstone is the bystander–transgression model combination: (a) the "bystander" model generates a stage scheme for empathic–sympathetic distress, empathic anger and feeling of injustice, and guilt over inaction; (b) "transgression" adds socialization and moral internalization; (c) the two models intersect in discipline encounters; Children contribute an empathic capability, which is activated by inductions and transformed into transgression guilt; (d) transgression guilt becomes independent of its discipline–encounter origin and can be evoked autonomously, along with empathic distress, not only when children harm someone, but also when they think they did—as we saw in relationship, responsibility, and separation guilt and in guilt over affluence.

The bystander–transgression combination thus provides a core set of interrelated processes that apply in all prosocial moral encounters. To complete the theory requires filling in the self-blame attributions that activate Transgression->Guilt scripts in each type of encounter and the conditions that produce these attributions (close relationships, responsibility, separation, multiple claimants).

LIMITATIONS OF EMPATHIC MORALITY

Empathic morality is limited by its dependence on intensity, salience of distress cues, and the relationship between observer and victim (Hoffman, 1984). For example, although we expect more salient distress cues to produce more intense empathic arousal, highly salient distress cues can be aversive enough to transform observers' empathic distress into intense feelings of personal distress. This *empathic over-arousal* can move observers out of the empathic mode and preoccupy them with their own distress (Hoffman, 1978). This process is illustrated in a study by Strayer (1993) in which 5–3-year-olds were shown film clips of distressed children (child unjustly punished by parent, disabled child climbing stairs, child forcibly separated from family). The more the child was distressed, the higher the observers' empathic distress and focus on the child. However, when the intensity of their empathic distress equaled the victim's, their focus shifted to themselves. A similar shift in focus away from the victim was reported by Bandura and Rosenthal (1966). Adult participants who were administered a drug to increase their empathic distress while witnessing someone being shocked reduced their distress by thinking distracting thoughts and attending to the lab.

People are more vulnerable to overarousal when they feel unable to reduce victims' distress. In one study high-empathy nursing students were so empathetically overaroused when they started working in the wards that they found being with terminally ill patients too painful and avoided them in favor of other patients. The nurses changed their behavior once they realized that they could make a difference (Stotland, Matthews, Sherman, Hansson, & Richardson, 1978; Williams, 1989). Competence is also implicated by the finding of less empathic overarousal in children whose parents taught them coping strategies for handling anxiety (Eisenberg, Fabes, Schaller, Carlo, & Miller, 1991).

We are not yet certain that overarousal is a serious problem. It may actually increase helping in people committed to a helping relationship, such as therapists and parents (Hoffman, 2000). Even if overarousal is an occasional problem, empathic morality seems to apply well in bystander, transgressor, and virtual-transgressor encounters. It may be limited in multiple-claimant and caring-versus-justice encounters, however, because of empathy's bias in favor of (a) victims familiar and similar to the actor, as noted earlier, and also (b) victims who are present, due to the empathy-arousing modes that require situational and personal cues (conditioning, association, mimicry). The two biases interact, as familiarity and proximity often go together.

Empathic bias may not be a big problem in small homogeneous "primary group" societies or in bystander, transgressor, and virtual-transgressor situations with one victim. There may even be a hidden virtue: If we empathized with everyone in distress and tried to help them all equally, society might quickly come to a halt. In this light, bias and overarousal may be empathy's ultimate self-regulating, self-preserving mechanisms.

Still, empathic bias may pose serious problems in multicultural societies, in which multiple-claimant and caring-versus-justice conflicts are frequent. It can lead to extreme empathy within groups and hostility (empathic anger?) between groups. Reducing empathic bias should thus be a high priority for society. I have suggested elsewhere interventions for reducing it and increasing empathic distress, guilt, and other empathic affects (Hoffman, 1984, 1993, 2000), some of which have been combined with other methods (Gibbs, 1993) to reduce male adolescent violence. Included are socialization and moral education methods that focus attention on the consequences of one's actions for others' immediate and long-term well-being. These methods encourage people to look beyond the situation when considering the effects of their actions and also highlight commonalties across ethnic groups—such as induction, role-taking, multiple empathizing (for example, the letter writer could empathize with other job applicants by imagining that his own child is one of them).

In addition, bias (and overarousal) can be reduced when empathy is "embedded" in congruent moral principles (mainly caring, need, effort), because the principles' cognitive dimension can give empathy structure and stability (Hoffman, 1987, 2000). The quote from Oliner and Oliner (1988) suggests the value of a universal caring ethic that builds on empathy but transcends its bias. Although not everyone can live by such an ethic, a critical mass of people who can may be needed to keep society civil.

REFERENCES

Bandura, A., & Rosenthal, T. L. (1966). Vicarious classical conditioning as a function of arousal level. *Journal of Personality and Social Psychology, 3,* 54–62.

Batson, C. D., & Weeks, J. L. (1996). Mood effects of unsuccessful helping: Another test of the empathy-altruism hypothesis. *Personality and Social Psychology Bulletin, 22,* 148–157.

Baumeister, R. F., Stillwell, A. M., & Heatherton, T. F. (1994). Guilt: An interpersonal approach. *Psychological Bulletin, 115,* 243–267.

Baumeister, R. F., Stillwell, A. M., & Heatherton, T. F. (1995). Interpersonal aspects of guilt. In J. P. Tangney & K. W. Fischer (Eds.), *Self-conscious emotions: Shame, guilt, embarrassment, and pride* (pp. 255–273). New York: Guilford Press.

Bischoff-Kohler, D. (1991). The development of empathy in infants. In M. Lamb & M. Keller (Eds.), *Infant development: Perspectives from German-speaking countries* (pp. 245–273). Hillsdale, NJ: Erlbaum.

Chapman, M., & Zahn-Waxler, C. (1982). Young children's compliance and noncompliance to parental discipline in a natural setting. *International Journal of Behavior Development, 5,* 81–94.

Chodoff, P., Friedman, S., & Hamburg, D. (1964). Stress, defenses and coping behavior: Observations of parents and children with malignant disease. *American Journal of Psychiatry, 120,* 742–749.

Cohen, D., & Strayer, J. (1996). Empathy in conduct-disordered and comparison youth. *Developmental Psychology, 32,* 988–998.

Costin, S. C., & Jones, C. J. (1992). Friendship as a facilitator of emotional responsiveness and prosocial interventions among young children. *Developmental Psychology, 28,* 941–947

Cummings, E. M., Hollenbeck, B., Iannotti, R., Radke-Yarrow, M., & Zahn-Waxler, C. (1986). Early organization of altruism and aggression: Developmental patterns and individual differences. In C. Zahn-Waxler, E.M. Cummings, & R. Iannotti (Eds.), *Altruism and aggression: Biological and social origins* (pp. 165–188). New York: Cambridge University Press.

Damon, W. (1977). *The social world of the child.* San Francisco: Jossey-Bass.

Eisenberg, N., Fabes, R. A., Carlo, G., Troyer, D., Speer, A. L., Karbon, M., & Switzer, G. (1992). The relations of maternal practices to children's vicarious emotional responsiveness. *Child Development, 63,* 583–602.

Eisenberg, N., Fabes, R. A., Schaller, M., Carlo, G., & Miller, P. A. (1991). Parental characteristics and practices, and children's emotional responding. *Child Development, 62*, 1393–1408.

Eisenberg, N., & Miller, P. (1987). Relation of empathy to prosocial behavior. *Psychological Bulletin, 101*, 91–119.

Feshbach, N. D., & Roe, K. (1968). Empathy in six- and seven-year olds. *Child Development, 39*, 133–145.

Fiske, S. F. (1982). Schema-triggered affect: Applications to social perception. In M. S. Clark & S. T. Fiske (Eds.), *Affect and cognition: The 17th Annual Carnegie Symposium on Cognition* (pp. 55–78). Hillsdale, NJ: Erlbaum.

Gibbs, J. C. (1993). Moral–cognitive interventions. In A. P. Goldstein & C. R. Huff (Eds.), *The gang intervention handbook*, (pp. 159–185). Champaign, IL: Research Press.

Gnepp, J. C. (1989). Children's use of personal information to understand other people's feelings. In C. Saarni & P. L. Harris (Eds.), *Children's understanding of emotion* (pp. 151–177). New York: Cambridge University Press.

Gnepp, J., & Gould, M. E. (1985). The development of personalized inferences: Understanding other people's emotional reactions in light of their prior experiences. *Child Development, 56*, 1455–1464.

Hamilton, W. D. (1971). Selection of selfish and altruistic behavior in some extreme models. In J. F. Eisenberg & W. F. Sillon (Eds.), *Man and beast: Comparative social behavior*. Washinton, D. C.: Smithsonian Institute Press.

Hay, D. (1984). Social conflict in early childhood. *Annals of Child Development, 1*, 1–44.

Hay, D. F., Nash, A., & Pedersen, J. (1981). Responses of six-month-olds to the distress of peers. *Child Development, 52*, 1071–1075

Hoffman, M. L. (1963). Parent discipline and the child's consideration for others. *Child Development, 34*, 573–588.

Hoffman, M. L. (1970). Conscience, personality, and socialization techniques. *Human Development, 13*, 90–126.

Hoffman, M. L. (1978). Empathy, its development and prosocial implications. *Nebraska Symposium on Motivation, 25*, 169–218.

Hoffman, M. L. (1981). Is altruism part of human nature? *Journal of Personality and Social Psychology, 40*, 121–137.

Hoffman, M. L. (1982). Development of prosocial motivation: Empathy and guilt. In N. Eisenberg-Berg (Ed.), *Development of prosocial behavior* (pp. 281–313). New York: Academic Press.

Hoffman, M. L. (1983). Affective and cognitive processes in moral internalization: An information processing approach. In E. T. Higgins, D. Ruble, & W. Hartup (Eds.), *Social cognition and social development: A socio-cultural perspective* (pp. 236–274). New York: Cambridge University Press.

Hoffman, M. L. (1984) Empathy, its limitations, and its role in a comprehensive moral theory. In J. Gewirtz & W. Kurtines (Eds.), *Morality, moral development, and moral behavior* (pp. 283–302). New York: Wiley.

Hoffman, M. L. (1985). Affect, motivation, and cognition. In E. T. Higgins & R. M. Sorrentino (Eds.), *Handbook of motivation and cognition: Foundations of social behavior* (pp. 244–280). New York: Guilford Press.

Hoffman, M. L. (1987). The contribution of empathy to justice and moral judgment. In N. Eisenberg & J. Strayer (Eds.), *Empathy and its development* (pp. 47–80). New York: Cambridge University Press.

Hoffman, M. L. (1988). Moral development. In M. Lamb & M. Bornstein (Eds.), *Developmental psychology: An advanced textbook* (2nd ed., pp. 497–548). Hillsdale, NJ: Erlbaum.

Hoffman, M. L. (1989). Empathy and prosocial activism. In N. Eisenberg, J. Reykowski, & E. Staub (Eds.), *Social and moral values: Individual and societal perspectives* (pp. 65–86). Hillsdale, NJ: Erlbaum.

Hoffman, M. L. (1990). Empathy and justice motivation. *Motivation and Emotion, 4*, 151–172.

Hoffman, M. L. (1991). Toward an integration: Commentary. *Human Development, 34*, 105–110.

Hoffman, M. L. (1993). Empathy, social cognition, moral education. In A. Garrod (Ed.), *Approaches to moral development: New research and emerging themes* (pp. 157–179). New York: Teachers College Press.

Hoffman, M. L. (2000). *Empathy and moral development: Implications for caring and justice*. New York: Cambridge University Press.

Horner, M. S. (1974). Sex differences in achievement motivation and performance in competitive and non-competitive situations. Ann Arbor, MI, University Microfilms.

Houston, D. A. (1990). Empathy and the self: Cognitive and emotional influences on the evaluation of negative affect in others. *Journal of Personality and Social Psychology, 59*, 859–871.

Izard, C. (1977). *Human emotions*. New York: Plenum Press.

Keniston, K. (1968). *Young radicals*. New York: Harcourt.

Klein, R. (1971). Some factors influencing empathy in six- and seven-year-old children varying in ethnic background (Doctoral dissertation, University of California, Los Angeles, 1970). *Dissertation Abstracts International, 31*, 3960A. (University Microfilms No. 71-3862)

Kochanska, G. (1995). Children's temperament, mother's discipline, and security of attachment: Multiple pathways to emerging internalization. *Child Development, 66*, 597–615.

Krebs, D. L. (1970). Empathy and altruism. *Journal of Personality and Social Psychology, 32*, 1124–1146.

Krevans, J., & Gibbs, J. C. (1996). Parents' use of inductive discipline: Relations to children's empathy and prosocial behavior. *Child Development, 67*, 3263–3277.

Kuczynski, L. (1983). Reasoning, prohibitions, and motivations for compliance. *Developmental Psychology, 19*, 126–134.

Levine, L. J. (1995). Young children's understanding of the causes of anger and sadness. *Child Development, 66*, 697–709.

Lindsay-Hartz, J., De Rivera, J., & Mascolo, M. F. (1995). Differentiating guilt and shame and their effects on motivation. In J. Tangney & K. Fischer (Eds.), *Self-conscious emotions: Shame, guilt, embarrassment, and pride* (pp. 274–299). New York: Guilford Press.

Londerville, S., & Main, M. (1981). Security of attachment, compliance, and maternal training methods in the second year of life. *Developmental Psychology, 17*, 289–299.

Main, M., & George, C. (1985). Response of abused and disadvantaged toddlers to distress in Agemates. *Developmental Psychology, 21*, 407–412.

Midlarsky, E., & Hannah, M. E. (1985). Competence, reticence, and helping by children and adolescents. *Developmental Psychology, 21*, 534–541.

Mill, J. S. (1979). *Utilitarianism.* Cambridge, MA: Hackett. (Original work published 1861)

Modell, A. H. (1963). On having the right to a life: An aspect of the superego's development. *International Journal of Psychoanalysis, 46*, 323–331.

Montada, L., Schmitt, M., & Dalbert, C. (1986). Thinking about justice and dealing with one's privileges: A study on existential guilt. In H. W. Bierhoff, R. Cohen, & J. Greenberg (Eds.), *Justice in social relations* (pp. 125–144). New York: Plenum Press.

Nelson, K. (1993). The psychological and social origins of autobiographical memory. *Psychological Science, 4*, 7–14.

New Republic. (November 28, 1970). Bridging the generation gap: Editor's summary of Rep. Morris K. Udall's (D. Ariz.) discussion with his "interns," pp. 11-14.

Oliner, S. P., & Oliner, P. M. (1988). *The altruistic personality.* New York: Free Press.

Radke-Yarrow, M., & Zahn-Waxler, C. (1984). Roots, motives, and patterns in children's prosocial behavior. In E. Staub, D. Bar-Tal, J. Karylowski, & J. Reykowski (Eds.), *Development and maintenance of prosocial behavior* (pp. 81–99). New York: Plenum.

Ross, H., Tesla, C., Kenyon, B., & Lollis, S. (1990). Maternal intervention in toddler peer conflict: The socialization of principles of justice. *Developmental Psychology, 26*, 994–1003.

Sagi, A. R., Hoffman, M. L. (1976). Empathic distress in the newborn. *Developmental Psychology, 12*, 175-176.

Sanna, L. J., & Turley, K. J. (1996). Antecedents to spontaneous counter-factual thinking. *Personality and Social Psychology Bulletin, 22*, 906–919.

Sawin, D. B., & Parke, R. D. (1980). Empathy and fear as mediators of resistance-to-deviation in children. *Merrill-Palmer Quarterly, 26*, 123–134.

Smetana, J. G. (1989). Toddler's social interactions in the context of moral and conventional transgression in the home. *Developmental Psychology, 25*, 499–508.

Staub, E. (1996). Responsibility, helping, aggression, and evil. *Psychological Inquiry*, *7*, 252.

Stern, D. (1985). *The interpersonal world of the infant*. New York: Basic.

Stotland, E., Matthews, K., Sherman, S., Hansson, R., & Richardson, B. (1978). *Empathy, fantasy, and helping*. Beverly Hills, CA: Sage.

Strayer, J. (1993). Children's concordant emotions and cognitions in response to observed emotions. *Child Development, 64*, 188–201.

Tangney, J., & Fischer, K. (1995). *Self-conscious emotions: Shame, guilt, embarrassment, and pride*. New York: Guilford Press.

Thompson, R., & Hoffman, M. L. (1980). Empathy and the development of guilt in children. *Developmental Psychology, 16*, 155–156.

Tulving, E. (1972). Episodic and semantic memory. In E. Tulving & W. Donaldson (Eds.), *Organization of memory* (pp. 301–403). New York: Academic Press.

Waters, E., Wippman, J., & Sroufe, L. A. (1979). Attachment, positive affect, and competence in the peer group. *Child Development, 50*, 821–829.

Webster's Ninth New Collegiate Dictionary. (1985). Springfirld, MA: Merriam-Webster.

Weiner, B. (1985). "Spontaneous" causal thinking. *Psychological Bulletin, 97*, 74–84.

Weiner, B., Graham, S., Stern, P., & Lawson, M. E. (1982). Using affective cues to infer causal thoughts. *Developmental Psychology, 18*, 278–286.

Wender, I. (1986). Children's use of justice principles in allocation situations. In H. Bierhoff, R. Cohen, & J. Greenberg (Eds.), *Justice in social relations* (pp. 249–266). New York: Plenum.

Williams, C. (1989). Empathy and burnout in male and female helping professionals. *Research in Nursing and Health, 12*, 169–178.

Wilson, B. J., & Cantor, J. (1985). *Journal of Experimental Child Psychology, 39*, 284–299.

Wright, H. F. (1967). *Recording and analyzing child behavior*. New York Harper & Row.

Zahn-Waxler, C., Radke-Yarrow, M., & King, R. (1979). Childrearing and children's prosocial initiations toward victims of distress. *Child Development, 50*, 319–330.

Zahn-Waxler, C., Robinson, J. L., Emde, N. E., & Plomin, R. (1992). Development of empathy in twins. *Developmental Psychology, 28*, 1038–1047.

4

INSTITUTIONALIZED AGGRESSION: CULTURAL AND INDIVIDUAL FACTORS THAT SUPPORT WAR

ROBERT A. HINDE

World War II was less difficult for me than it was for many others. Yet it took me many years to accept the deaths of my brother and many of my friends and to forget the horrors that had happened. Twenty years later, in the midst of the Vietnam War era, I woke up. No one who has ever been in a war could possibly want another, and I began to wonder why on earth they happen at all. What I knew about individual aggression did not seem to account for it. My own service experience as an Royal Air Force pilot, the reports that I had read about World War II and the Korean War, and the reflections of friends all convinced me that war does not happen simply because men are aggressive. Men fight in war because they are coerced, because they are made to feel that it is their duty to fight. I came to believe that it is not human aggression that leads to war, but the institution of war that causes aggression. Men who kill in war are rarely motivated by the factors that lead to individual aggressive acts. Indeed, when they do behave aggressively (as at My Lai), their behavior is not likely to be condoned.

This chapter owes much to the contributors to two conferences, only some of whom have been named here. The first (Hinde, 1991) was supported by the Catherine T. MacArthur Foundation of Chicago and the second (Hinde & Watson, 1995) by the Carnegie Corporation of New York and the John D. and Catherine T. MacArthur Foundation.

It seems to me that if we are to understand why war occurs, we must examine it as an institution—an institution with constituent roles for generals, soldiers, politicians, doctors, nurses, transport workers, munitions workers, air raid wardens, propagandists, broadcasters, and so on. World War II engulfed whole populations, assigning each individual his or her own role with its attendant rights and duties. My brother, a medic badly wounded in an open boat after a submarine attack, dispensed to others dressings that he might have used to save himself. My father carried on as a general practitioner, answering every call through the blackout, and my medically qualified elder sister joined him, taking his partner's place. Another sister helped to decode intercepted enemy radio signals, while my mother patrolled the streets as the bombs were falling. In each case they acted because they felt it was their duty to do so. Our entire family, like many others, became completely immersed in the war. Of course, duty was not the only issue. Some volunteered for service because of the attendant glamour and honor, but those illusions were just another product of the institution of war.

If war is seen as an institution with numerous roles, each with its own rights and duties, then what supports it? In identifying the forces that maintain and support war, it is possible to examine and perhaps undermine it as an institution.

The ways in which we continually support the notion of war seem to fall into three categories. First, we can observe them in our everyday lives. Our casual speech is filled with war metaphors. We speak of "keeping our heads down," "outflanking our rivals," and "holding our fire." It may seem trivial, but this way of speaking contributes to the idea of war as acceptable, possible, and normal. We have tried to rid our speech of sexism, why not treat "warism" in the same way? The euphemisms that we use when actually talking about war take away its horrors and make it seem honorable. We talk of "the fallen," of "our glorious dead," making their suffering acceptable, while forgetting that they cannot enjoy their lives, their friends, they can no longer love or be loved as we can (Fussell, 1975).

Although there have been honorable exceptions, most books about war also sanitize the suffering. They tend to follow the fortunes of the survivors and rarely dwell on the casualties. They speak of victory more than defeat, of the action more than boredom and frustration, of courage more than the terror gnawing at the entrails. The young become familiar with the apparatus of war and grow to believe that war is a normal part of adult life. In 1974, UNESCO recommended that member states should foster education for peace, but this has been almost totally disregarded, with the exception of Finland and, to some extent, Canada. Male chauvinism is another contributing factor. Others have seen war as an opportunity to confirm and assert their virility (e.g. Mosse, 1995). By nature or by nurture, women are more peace-oriented than men, and of course they seldom participate in decisions relevant to war.

Many of those who have gone to war have been seduced by propaganda that paints a glorious picture of their role in it. The difference between the expectations of the new recruit and the realities encountered in battle has often been devastating (Brodie, 1990). But once the battle is over, memories of the horror can be less durable than those of the comradeship and the contrast with civilian life.

There are many pervasive cultural factors that support the institution of war. For instance, the Judeo–Christian religions are not distinguished for promoting peace, and the same can be said of Muslim fundamentalism. The Old Testament reports bloody battles in which the Hebrews are depicted as fighting for their religion, and the Book of Revelation refers continually to war and death. Although the early Christians were pacifists, the conversion of the Roman Emperor Constantine in the 4th century was instrumental in causing Christians to accommodate to war. Christians, with notable individual exceptions, some of whom became martyrs, have tended to support and even initiate belligerence by their native countries. The concept of Saint Augustine's "just war" has helped maintain the tradition of war across the centuries. The Christian symbol of death on the cross has been equated with death in war, making the latter acceptable. A widely distributed poster in World War I showed Christ on the cross with a soldier peacefully dead at his feet, a barely visible and neatly sanitized bullet hole in his forehead (Sykes, 1991). Hitler used the religious vocabulary of sacrifice in appeals to the German people to tolerate losses for the sake of the German *Volk* (Stern, 1975).

In a perceptive analysis of individuals who have been involved in more recent wars, Watson (1995) has shown how violence can become acceptable when it is represented and understood as an essential aspect of religious duty:

> The expression of violence in a religious idiom legitimizes war and shifts it from the realm of the "ordinary" on to a higher plane of moral existence. . . . When a past struggle is presented in mythical form, defined by ancient religious law and overlaid by religious symbolism, it provides a powerful model for future generations. (p. 176)

Some countries have a long record of belligerence; others, like Switzerland, have a history of neutrality. Although national attitudes toward war must be associated with conditions perceived as conducive to the country's welfare, they imply a shared perspective among the citizens. Some historians have regarded nationalism as a form of political loyalty that does not differ in any fundamental way from loyalty to a clan or tribe (Hinsley, 1973). Feshbach's work has shown the superficiality of this view. He demonstrated that *patriotism*, or love of one's country, and *nationalism*, or feelings of superiority over other nations, are related but different phenomena. An experiment conducted in the Cold War era in the United States showed that individuals who had high scores on a nationalism scale tended to be hawkish about nuclear weapons but less willing to risk their lives for their country than those who had high scores on patriotism, who tended to be much less hawkish (Feshbach, 1990; Kosterman & Feshbach, 1989).

In another study, highly patriotic individuals tended to have a strong early attachment to their fathers. In Japan, such individuals had a strong attachment to both their fathers and mothers (Feshbach, 1991).

Other research has revealed different sources of patriotism and nationalism. Individuals possess propensities to associate with those who are similar in certain ways to themselves. Because individuals attempt to see the world in a coherent way (and it is reasonable to suppose that those who see the world in a coherent way are better able to deal with it), an individual with similar attitudes and beliefs to oneself can be attractive simply because the similarity validates one's own beliefs. The attractiveness of such similarity is stronger when the beliefs are otherwise unverifiable, as with religious beliefs. Such tendencies to perceive favorably others who are similar to the self may be augmented by an unconscious perception of them as kin (Johnson, 1986, 1989), activating biological mechanisms of kin selection (Wilson, 1975). But even more powerful forces are intrinsic to the processes of socialization in which group membership is emphasized. Unfortunately, group loyalty tends to be associated with a tendency to denigrate those outside of the group—hence the association between patriotism and nationalism. Cultural values, magnified out of proportion by propaganda, promote patriotism by equating it with family loyalty, using such phrases as "fatherland," "mother country," and "brothers-in-arms" (Feshbach, 1990). In nationalism the "Other" is presented as evil, dangerous, and even as subhuman (Wahlstrom, 1987). The success of this tactic depends on the fear of strangers that appears in the first year or two of life and is maintained in some degree thereafter, and it depends on the tendency of group members to exaggerate the differences between their own group and others while emphasizing the superiority of their own.

Derogatory images of the enemy tend to have considerable resilience (Tetlock et al., 1989). This is especially the case when enmity has been long-standing. An example is provided by the Greeks and Turks in Cyprus. Nationalistic constructions of the past in school textbooks and elsewhere emphasize past armed confrontations, create dehumanized images of the other side, and glorify their own heroes. Two Museums of National Struggle, on either side of the divided capital of Nicosia, present opposing views of history and encourage a diachronic transference of pain across the generations so that past sufferings lead to notions of revenge and retribution, perpetuating the conflict (Papadakis, 1995).

There is a potent lesson from history here. The Warring States period in China was a time of strife and turmoil. Lewis (1995) has recorded how militaristic images persisted in Chinese literature for many centuries into a period when the only wars were on distant frontiers with hostile nomads. These images later served as a model for secret societies, forming the basis for bloody rebellions.

Propaganda also has other uses. It minimizes the horrors of war and exaggerates the consequences of defeat or victory. It is worthwhile to examine how it uses very basic human propensities: fear of strangers, group tendencies including cooperation and loyalty to the group, aggression, and the desire to feel in control.

The third category of forces that maintain war as an institution is perhaps the most powerful, although I shall mention it only briefly here. Eisenhower (1961) referred to it as the "military–industrial complex," but perhaps "military–industrial–scientific complex" would be more appropriate. Each element in this triad supports the others. Each has enormous complexity, but each has a relatively simple basis in pan-cultural human propensities, notably the ambitiousness and assertiveness of individuals who develop loyalties to the group in which they work but who turn a blind eye to the long-term consequences. It is abundantly clear that a great deal of the blame for the suffering in the world must ultimately be laid at the door of arms dealers and their supporters in governments (Brzoska, 1995).

The destructive bombing of Hiroshima and Nagasaki did little to diminish the incidence of war over the world as a whole. We have survived a good many decades without another world war, but there has been suffering in countless lesser wars—Korea, Vietnam, Angola, the former Yugoslavia, and Rwanda, to mention only a few. The conflicts form a continuum from those in which war itself clearly fomented aggression, to those in which individual aggression may have enhanced the intensity of the war.

If the analysis in this chapter is accepted, it is clear that every effort must be made to undermine the institution of war. Nobody wants a uniform world in which cultural diversity is eliminated. But if we are to have such diversity, we must respect values other than our own. In this century the British have been forced to recognize that a colonial culture is simply not acceptable. Citizens of the United States must recognize that even though their material well-being is envied, their values are mistrusted throughout much of the world. It is not necessarily the case that their form of society, however well it works in the United States, is necessarily the best for every country in the world. I cannot do better than to use Feshbach's (1995) words to describe one of the most fundamental issues that must be tackled if we are to undermine the institution of war and build a world where diversity is respected: We must

> utilize education and social action to sharpen the difference between patriotic and nationalistic attitudes and values. It is important that it be recognized and accepted that one can be strongly attached to one's nation without believing in national superiority or supporting national dominance. (p. 163)

REFERENCES

Brodie, M. (1990). A world worth fighting for. East Wittering, England: Gooday.

Brzoska, M. (1995). The arms trade. In R. A. Hinde & H. Watson (Eds.), *War: A cruel necessity?* (pp. 224–237). London: Tauris.

Eisenhower, D. (1961). Public papers of the Presidents of the United States: Dwight D. Eisenhower, 1960–1961. Washington, DC:

Feshbach, S. (1990). Psychology, human violence, and the search for peace: Issues in science and social values. *Journal of Social Issues, 76,* 183–198.

Feshbach, S. (1991). Attachment processes in adult political ideology: Patriotism and nationalism. In J. L. Gewirtz & M. Kurtines (Eds.) *Intersections with attachment* (pp. 207–226). Hillsdale, NJ: Erlbaum.

Feshbach, S. (1995). Patriotism and nationalism: Two components of national identity with different implications for peace and war. In R. A. Hinde & H. Watson (Eds.), *War: A cruel necessity?* (pp. 153–164). London: Tauris.

Fussell, P. (1975). *The Great War and modern memory.* London: Oxford University Press.

Hinde, R. A. (Ed.) (1991). *The institution of war.* Basingstoke: Macmillan.

Hinde, R. A., & Watson, H. (Eds.) (1995). *War: A cruel necessity?* London: Tauris.

Hinsley, F. H. (1973). *Nationalism and the international system.* London: Hodder & Stoughton.

Johnson, G. R. (1986). Kin selection, socialisation, and patriotism. *Politics and the Life Sciences, 4,* 127–154.

Johnson, G. R. (1989). The role of kin recognition mechanics in patriotic socialisation: further reflections. *Politics and the Life Sciences, 8,* 62–69.

Kosterman, R., & Feshbach, S. (1989). Towards a measure of patriotic and nationalistic attitudes. *Political Psychology, 10,* 257–274.

Lewis, M. E. (1995). The warring state in China as an institution and idea. In R. A. Hinde & H. Watson (Eds.), *War: A cruel necessity?* (pp. 13–23). London: Tauris.

Mosse, G. (1995). The knights of the sky and the myth of the war experience. In R. A. Hinde & H. Watson (Eds.), *War: A cruel necessity?* (pp. 132–142). London: Tauris.

Papadakis, Y. (1995). Nationalist imaginings of war in Cyprus. In R. A. Hinde & H. Watson (Eds.), *War: A cruel necessity?* (pp. 54–68). London: Tauris.

Stern, J. P. (1975). *Hitler: The Fuhrer and the people.* London: Fontana.

Sykes, S. (1991). Sacrifice and the ideology of war. In R. A. Hinde (Ed.), *The institution of war* (pp. 87–98). Basingstoke: Macmillan.

Tetlock, P. E. (1989). Methodological themes and variations. In P. E. Tetlock, J. L. Husbands, R. Jervis, P. C. Stern, & C. Tilly (Eds.), *Behavior, society, and nuclear war* (Vol. 1). New York: Oxford University Press.

Wahlstrom, R. (1987). The image of the enemy as a psychological antecedent of warfare. In J. M. Ramirez, R. A. Hinde, & J. Groebel (Eds.), *Essays on violence*. Seville, Spain: Publicaciones de la Universidad de Sevilla.

Watson, H. (1995). War and religion: An unholy alliance. In R. A. Hinde & H. Watson (Eds.), *War: A cruel necessity?* (pp. 165–180). London: Tauris.

Wilson, E. O. (1975). *Sociobiology*. Cambridge, MA: Harvard University Press.

II

EMPIRICAL FINDINGS

In this part authors consider empirical findings on the development of prosocial and antisocial behavior and on their interrelationship.

PAUL MUSSEN AND NANCY EISENBERG

Paul Mussen and Nancy Eisenberg present a comprehensive overview of research on parenting and its relationship to the development of prosocial behavior. Their research review provides support for the ideas presented by Hoffman in part I. These authors describe a number of parenting practices that are associated with the development of prosocial behavior—including providing warm, supportive environments, pointing out the effects of the child's behavior on others, explaining and reasoning rather than punishing, and modeling prosocial behavior. They consider the direct effects of such practices, as well as the indirect effects through the arousal of perspective taking and empathy.

JUNE PRICE TANGNEY

Hoffman argues that guilt relates to prosocial behavior. June Price Tangney presents research that supports this hypothesis but additionally clarifies the role of both shame and guilt in constructive and destructive behavior. She notes that the two closely related emotions of shame and guilt have important, different relationships to empathy and aggressive behavior. Tangney's research shows that guilt and shame operate differently. Guilt is a prosocial emotion, where as shame is more destructive in its consequences.

Although not directly addressed, Tangney's research indirectly deals with self-concept issues as well. She describes *guilt* as a feeling about what one has done whereas *shame* is a negative feeling about oneself. Guilt focuses on behavior and its consequences, shame on the value of the self. In this regard, there has been considerable debate over the role of self-esteem in antisocial behavior, with some arguing that high self-esteem ought to prevent aggression. However, Baumeister and Campbell (1999) and Staub (1999) have argued that high self-esteem is often associated with aggressive behavior, and bullies are often high in self-esteem. However, both Staub and Baumeister note that what matters is not so much how high self-esteem is but rather how self-esteem is structured. If it is structured on power and dominance of others (Staub, 1999), it will be associated with a greater likelihood of aggression. If it is unstable (Baumeister & Campbell, 1999), it is also more likely to be associated with aggression. Tangney's findings that shame leads to antisocial behavior and low empathy are congruent with this. Tangney suggests that shame-prone individuals are more likely to have instability in self-esteem, and thus it makes sense that they may be more likely to be aggressive. Clarifying further the relationship between self-esteem and related emotions such as shame and guilt, and aggression and prosocial behavior, remains one of the most intriguing research areas.

INGER M. ENDRESEN AND DAN OLWEUS; AND PAOLO ALBIERO AND ALIDA LO COCO

The next two chapters deal with the nature of empathy, its development, and its relationship to prosocial and aggressive behavior. Both are reports of research studies. Inger M. Endresen and Dan Olweus and Paolo Albiero and Alida Lo Coco study the development of empathy and reach somewhat different conclusions. Although all authors suggest that empathy develops, Endresen and Olweus find that boys become less empathic toward other boys with age, whereas girls in general become more empathic. On the other hand, Albiero and Lo Coco find a general trend for both boys and girls to become more empathic. In part, this may be a function of how they operationally define empathy. Endresen and Olweus use a self-report measure; whereas Albiero and Lo Coco use a measure in which children report their feelings while watching a story. Empathy is the degree of match between the feelings the child is having and the feelings of the main character in the story.

These two chapters taken together reveal the complexity in studying empathy. Endresen and Olweus, for instance, with their self-report measure of empathic behavior, may be getting more at how individuals perceive themselves as actually functioning empathically in everyday life, whereas Albiero and Lo Coco may be more measuring children's developing capacity for empathy. The findings of these two sets of researchers also suggest the need to take a more differentiated look at empathy—not as a generalized capacity but as a function of target. Endresen and Olweus note differences as a function of who is being empathized with—boys or girls—and Albiero and Lo Coco discover differences based on what emotions are being empathized with. Both also examine the interrelationships of empathy to antisocial aggression behavior and to prosocial behavior. Both find relationships, but once again, there are complexities.

Of particular current interest are Endresen and Olweus's findings with respect to the relationship of empathy to bullying. Endresen and Olweus find that empathy does not directly mediate bullying behavior but may indirectly mediate it through affecting attitudes toward bullying. Since the Columbine High School shootings there has been much focus on bullying. The two Columbine shooters were presumably retaliating for the verbal bullying and mistreatment they had received at the hands of other, more popular high school students. Recent research has supported the omnipresence of bullying in schools and the passivity of teachers and peers in its face (Farmington, 1993; Olweus, 1993; Staub, 1999). Other research has shown that at least some bullies are indeed popular and high in self-esteem (Coie

& Dodge, 1998; Olweus, 1993; Rodkin, Farmer, Pearl, & Van Acker, 2000). Clearly, bullying then becomes an important source of social stress potentially leading to aggression, especially because bullies themselves are more likely to grow up to be aggressive (Staub, 1999), and rejected children may also grow up to be aggressive (Coie &Dodge, 1998). The odd combination of social popularity and antisocial/aggressive behavior supports the complexity that Cairns and Cairns refer to in chapter 1.

In light of this, two of the findings of Endresen and Olweus are disturbing. First, they find that empathy does not directly affect bullying. This suggests the possibility that a child could have some degree of empathic capacity and still be a bully. This would fit with findings that some bullies are socially popular. This also fits with the contention of Cairns and Cairns that aggressive children are not necessarily shallow in terms of their social relationships. What it does suggest is the possibility that bullies may not use their empathic capacities with members of outgroups, a possibility suggested by Hoffman in his Chapter 3. This also fits with contentions by Hinde (Chapter 4), Bandura (1999), Staub (1999), Baumeister and Campbell (1999), and many others that a major mechanism of aggression is to negatively stereotype and devalue those against whom one is aggressing (i.e., to not reach out to them empathically).

Second, boys, at least by self-report, become less empathic toward other boys with age. This seems to contradict a general belief that we tend to be more empathic with those similar to us. Endresen and Olweus speculate that this may have to do with being socialized into the male role, where one is supposed to be "tough." This also fits with the findings that bullies can be popular. Research on popularity has found that although some children rated by their peers as popular can be described as cooperative, sociable, friendly, helpful, and sensitive (Rubin, Bukowski, & Parker, 1998), other studies suggest that popular boys often are belligerent, ridicule others, and defy authority (Adler & Adler, 1998). Furthermore, boys who are "nice" may get labeled as effeminate (Adler & Adler, 1998; Eder, Evans, & Parker, 1995) and thereby be rejected.

Although Albiero and Lo Coco report that boys' capacities for empathy may increase with age, the Endresen and Olweus findings, especially in light of the popularity of tough and aggressive boys, suggests that there may be social pressures on boys to mask or hide their empathic capacities. Furthermore, it suggests that to be seen as effeminate is socially disadvantageous. It is interesting that Dylan Klebold and Eric Harris, the two boys in the Columbine shootings, were labeled as "fags" by some of the socially popular boys in their school. These findings thus may also contribute to understanding gay-bashing.

Is it difficult for boys to be empathic because of fears that they will be seen as less masculine? This is an important and fruitful research direction. Is the masculine socialization experience such that it increases the probability of rejection of anything stereotypically associated with being effeminate (e.g., sensitivity, empathy, or being gay)? How is it that society supports aggressive boys as socially popular, thereby sending a contradictory message? For instance, if society values boys who are aggressive, the message is, in effect, that some aggression is okay. The fact that aggressive boys may get important social rewards needs further research, and one wonders how this provides models to socially rejected boys for aggressive behavior. In fact, one might speculate that aggressive boys who are not socially popular may even be ineffectively modeling successful aggressive boys. This is an important area for further research and dovetails with our discussion in the introduction to part I that focusing on individual change without addressing sociocultural factors that help promote and maintain antisocial/aggressive behavior will likely prove to be of only modest success.

LEA PULKKINEN; AND GIAN VITTORIO CAPRARA, CLAUDIO BARBARANELLI, AND CONCETTA PASTORELLI

An enduring topic in psychology is the stability of behavior. This becomes especially important with behavior that society wants to foster (prosocial behavior) and behavior that society wants to discourage (aggressive behavior). Depending on how stable it is, when behavior stabilizes, and the mechanisms of stability, intervention at various points becomes more or less likely. Additionally, the type of intervention depends on the mechanisms of stability and change. In this part, two chapters deal with the stability of constructive and destructive behavior: Lea Pulkkinen, and Gian Vittorio Caprara, Claudio Barbaranelli, and Concetta Pastorelli. For Pulkkinen, stability is measured by looking at correlations over time, from childhood into adulthood. For Caprara et al., stability is operationalized in terms of the intercorrelations of different raters' views of how much a child exhibits prosocial or antisocial behavior, or both. Although a child may exhibit antisocial behavior as early as age 8, which persists into adulthood (Pulkkinen), children's behavior is nonetheless more unstable earlier than later in adolescence (Caprara et al., supporting the view of many that early intervention is more profitable than intervention in adulthood once the offender has already become a chronic one (Huesmann & Reynolds, chapter 12).

There is other research supporting the conclusions of Caprara et al. and Pulkkinen about the relative stability of aggressive behavior (see Coie & Dodge, 1998; Olweus, 1979). However many questions remain. Among them concern the mechanisms of stability. There are a number of candidates for stability: genes, personality traits, and cognitive schemas and scripts (see Eron, chapter 2, Huesmann & Reynolds, chapter 12), among others. However, Cairns and Cairns (chapter 1) have cautioned against the idea that just because something is genetic means it is stable over time. And both Caprara et al. and Pulkkinen propose alternative models of stability to that of the trait concept, one emphasizing skills (Pulkkinen) and the other emphasizing the power of interpersonal factors, reputation, and self-fulfilling prophecy in the form of the self-concept that the child eventually internalizes from other (Caprara et al.). Following up on Caprara et al.'s findings that children's self-images begin to internalize some of the appraisals of them by others as aggressive, but that aggressive children also feel justified from within themselves about their aggression, we point out that there is other work that suggests that staying power of self-concepts, once formed, due to needs for self-verification (Swann, 1985). Additionally, Caprara et al.'s suggestion that aggressive children feel justified in their aggression fits with suggestions that self-justification is one of the major mechanisms supporting aggressive behavior (Bandura, 1999; Baumeister & Campbell, 1999; Staub, 1999).

Discovering more about the mechanisms of stability, the mechanisms of change, and just how malleable are behaviors, skills, traits, self-images, and reputations all await further research but are crucial topics if we hope to be able to modify antisocial/aggressive behavior in a productive direction

REFERENCES

Adler, P. A., & Alder. P. (1998). *Peer power: Preadolescent culture and identity*. New Brunswick, NJ: Rutgers University Press.

Bandura, A. (1999). Moral disengagement in the perpetration of inhumanities. *Personality and Social Psychology Review, 3*, 193–209.

Baumeister, R. F., & Campbell, W. K. (1999). The intrinsic appeal of evil: Sadism, sensational thrills, and threatened egotism. *Personality and Social Psychology Review, 3*, 210–221.

Eder, D., Evans, C. C., & Parker, S. (1995). *School talk: Gender and adolescent culture*. New Brunswick, NJ: Rutgers University Press.

Farrington, D. (1993). Understanding and preventing bullying. *Crime and Justice, 17*, 381–458.

Olweus, D. (1979). Stability of aggressive reaction patterns in males: A review. *Psychological Bulletin, 86*, 852–875.

Rodkin, P. C., Farmer, T. W., Pearl, R., & Van Acker, R. (2000). Heterogeneity of popular boys: Antisocial and prosocial configuration. *Developmental Psychology, 36*, 14–24.

Rubin, K. H., Bukowski, W. M., & Parker, J. G. (1998). Peer interactions, relationships and groups. In N. Eisenberg (Vol. Ed.) & W. Damon (Series Ed.), *Handbook of child psychology; Vol. 3. Social, emotional, and personality development* (5th ed., pp. 619–700). New York: Wiley.

Staub, E. (1999). The roots of evil: Social conditions, culture, personality, and basic human needs. *Personality and Social Psychology Review, 3,* 179–192.

Swann, W. B., Jr. (1985). Self-verification: Bringing social reality into harmony with the self. In Suls & A. G. Greenwald (Eds.), *Social psychological perspectives on the self* (Vol. 2, pp. 33–66). Hillsdale, NJ: Erlbaum.

5

PROSOCIAL DEVELOPMENT IN CONTEXT

PAUL MUSSEN AND NANCY EISENBERG

In 1995, the University Art Museum in Berkeley, California, featured the art exhibit "The New Child, British Art and the Origins of Modern Childhood (1730 to 1830)." The art in this exhibit was produced during the Romantic Period, when assertion of the self, reason, humane values, and the beauties of nature were major themes. One painting, done in 1841 by William Mulready, depicted a romantic setting of trees, cliffs, and rocks, and two elegantly dressed women standing behind a handsome 7- or 8-year-old boy, who is delivering something—probably money—into the outstretched hand of one of three seated Indian beggars. One of the women, likely the boy's mother, is whispering in the child's ear, no doubt, encouraging him. The painting appeared to be artistic propaganda for the burgeoning British charity movement of that time. But equally striking for psychologists and educators interested in prosocial behavior is the title of the picture, which is almost a sermon: "Train up a child in the way he should go; and when he is old he will not depart from it." (It may be assumed that in the days before

Work on this chapter was supported by grants from the National Science Foundation (DBS-9208375) and the National Institutes of Mental Health (1 R01 HH55052 and K05 M801321) to Nancy Eisenberg.

the feminist movement, the use of "he" in the title is the generic term for "child.") Each clause of the title relates to a separate important social psychological issue: (a) the early acquisition of moral behavior and (b) the continuity or long-term stability of this behavior. We intend to deal with both issues in this chapter—with an emphasis on the constructive or positive domain of behavior.

The first clause and the contents of the painting clearly refer to parental training as the major determinant of children's prosocial behavior. The painter recognized that such responses are products of training rather than simple, natural consequences of development, and he even seemed to have some insight into how such training should be conducted. Our view is consistent with that of the painter: We assume that socializers' practices and behaviors are an important influence on children's prosocial development.

For the past 20 to 25 years, many developmental psychologists have centered their attention on what parental practices promote and strengthen the development of prosocial behavior. In this chapter, we briefly review the findings of many relevant studies.

The findings discussed come from studies of different types or manifestations of prosocial behavior as well as different age groups and are based on diverse theoretical perspectives and methods of investigation. Most studies of prosocial behavior concentrate on one or two types of such behavior, such as helping, sharing, or comforting; a few deal with more dramatic modes of prosocial behavior such as trying to save victims of the Holocaust, volunteering in crisis centers, or participating in the civil rights movement. The prosocial responses studied, and the criteria used to assess them, may not be conceptually independent and may substantively overlap. For example, sharing, one species of prosocial action, sometimes involves an attempt to comfort someone else, which is another kind of prosocial response. It may also involve caring or sympathy, which are other-oriented emotional responses.

The ages of the participants in the studies range from infancy to adulthood, and the research methods used vary tremendously. In some studies prosocial behavior is measured by observations of children in naturalistic, real-life settings, such as schools, playgrounds, and the home. In other studies, ratings or responses to sociometric questions given to peers or teachers provide the criteria for evaluation, and in still others, children's responses in experimental, contrived situations are the bases of evaluation. Data on parental practices may be derived from direct observations of parent—child interaction, from interviews, from questionnaires, or from parental accounts of their handling of disciplinary problems. Just as the measures of prosociality used in different studies may overlap, so may the assessments of parental behavior. An investigator studying explanation (induction) as a disciplinary technique may also be assessing parental modeling of consideration, another potentially significant antecedent variable. Yet in spite of the tremendous variations in research foci, in the populations studied, and in methods used, some relatively convincing generalizations have emerged.

Before turning our attention to specific conclusions, it is worthwhile to emphasize two conditions that seem basic to almost all of them. The first is that, not surprisingly, the practices that promote prosocial behavior seem to be most effective if they are embedded in warm, nurturant, and supportive environments—the opposite of the conditions related to violence, aggression, and destruction among children (see Eisenberg & Fabes, 1998; Hoffman, 1983). If socializers are basically rejecting or neglecting, their attempts to use these practices are not likely to be effective (e.g., Dlugokinski & Firestone, 1974; Yarrow, Scott, & Waxler, 1973). The second point is that empathy and sympathy are the bases of much prosocial responding, although prosocial actions are often enacted simply due to habit or custom, to obtain rewards, or to avoid criticism or punishment. So the effective techniques to be discussed are, in many cases, empathy-arousing techniques that help children to understand the perspectives of others.

Clearly, *prosocial behavior*—voluntary behavior intended to benefit another—can be performed for a variety of reasons, some moral and some not. In general, we would expect the development of prosocial behavior based on the internalization of moral principles or based on empathy and sympathy to reflect individual tendencies that are relatively enduring over time. If children are motivated to help merely for practical reasons (to obtain rewards or to avoid censure), they are not likely to assist in contexts in which these motivations are not present. In contrast, children's moral beliefs and their tendencies to experience empathy and sympathy probably have some stability—that is, they would be manifest in a variety of contexts and would endure over time (e.g., Eisenberg, Carlo, Murphy, & Van Court, 1995; Eisenberg, Miller, Shell, McNalley, & Shea, 1991).

By *empathy*, we mean an emotional reaction based on the comprehension of another's emotional state or condition that is identical or similar to that state. (Eisenberg & Fabes, 1998). Empathy involves both cognitive and emotional elements (Feshbach, 1987; Hoffman, 1982). Thus, a boy who is sad when he views a sad peer is empathizing. *Sympathy* is an emotional response to another's emotional state, one in which the individual does not feel the same emotion as the distressed or needy individual but still feels concern or sorrow for the other person. Sympathy may stem either from empathy or from cognitively based processes such as perspective taking or drawing on information stored in memory that helps the child understand how the other person is feeling or the consequences of the situation.

In the review that follows, we first discuss child-rearing practices likely to induce empathy and sympathy and then describe other techniques that, without emphasizing empathy, have proven effective in increasing children's prosocial behavior. Our view is that socializers' practices and behaviors influence children's prosocial behavior and that socializers' influence often is mediated by affective processes (e.g., empathy, sympathy, guilt), although the internalization of moral values also may be a mediating factor. However, not all parents use practices that promote prosocial behavior, and we cannot assume that the positive effects of even optimal parental practices will persist if the child encounters adverse conditions. Therefore, we also are concerned with the promotion of prosocial behavior by agents of socialization outside the home, such as school teachers and peers. They may act either to help maintain well-developed prosocial tendencies or to raise the level of such tendencies among children who have not acquired strong prosocial proclivities in their families.

EMPATHY-INDUCING SOCIALIZATION TECHNIQUES

Inductive Procedures

Inductions involve the use of reasoning by socializers to try to influence children's behavior. For example, socializers may point out another's emotional reactions (e.g., "See, you made Johnny feel bad") or may highlight other consequences of the child's behavior or moral rules. Hoffman (1970b, 1983, chapter 3 in this volume) suggested that inductions promote moral development because they induce an optimal level of arousal for learning (i.e., enough to capture the child's attention but not enough to disrupt learning). Inductions also focus the children's attention on the consequences of their behavior for others, thereby capitalizing on children's capacity for empathy and guilt. Also, inductions are not likely to be viewed as arbitrary by children and, consequently, may produce relatively little resistance. Hoffman further suggested that over time, inductive messages are experienced by the child as internalized because the child plays an active role in processing the information embedded in an induction (which is encoded and integrated with information from other inductions) and the focus is on the child's behavior and its consequences rather than on the parent as disciplinarian. Thus, over time children are likely to remember the causal link between their actions and consequences for others rather than the parent's external pressure or the specific disciplinary incident.

There are several types of inductions, such as those that appeal to justice and perspective taking ("How do you think Ann felt when you hit her?"), to the consequences of the child's behavior for another, either to peer or parent (e.g., "What you did upset me") or to legitimate authorities ("You are supposed to follow the teacher's rules about sharing toys"), or that provide matter-of-fact, nonmoralistic information ("If you move the chairs over, you could both see the video"; Henry, 1980; Hoffman, 1970a).

Hoffman and Saltzstein differentiated between inductions regarding peers and those involving the parent. Middle-class mothers' use of both kinds of inductions was related to seventh graders' sociometric ratings of classmates' consideration for others, particularly for girls (although some findings were for the combined sample). Furthermore, parents' use of inductions regarding the parent were related to girls' level of consideration of others.

In another study, mothers' attempts to encourage perspective taking when interacting with their two-year-olds (e.g., "Why do you think John is so sad?") were found to be associated with the children's observed prosocial behavior toward adults (findings for prosocial behavior toward peers were in the same direction but not significant; Iannotti, Cummings, Pierrehumbert, Milano, & Zahn-Waxler, 1992). However, maternal encouragement of understanding others' perspectives was not related to children's prosocial behavior toward peers at age 5. In another study, maternal use of inductions emphasizing how another feels was related to maternal ratings of preschoolers' general helpfulness (Stanhope, Bell, & Parker-Cohen, 1987).

Miller, Eisenberg, Fabes, Shell, and Gular (1989) studied inductions regarding only peers (including how the child would feel in a victim's place). Inductions were related to children's sad reactions to viewing others in distress and, when delivered by mothers with affect intensity, to low levels of facial distress (believed to be associated with egoistic rather than with other-oriented motivation).

Other investigators who do not specify the type of induction used report findings consistent with these, although the degree of the association varies considerably with sex, age, or socioeconomic status of the children, as well as with the specific measure of prosocial responding. For example, fifth and eighth graders' reports of parental use of induction (type unspecified) were related to the generosity of their donations to charity, peer ratings of kindness and consideration, self-report of other-oriented values, and concepts of kindness reflecting an emphasis on intentionality and self-sacrifice (Dlugokinski & Firestone, 1974). Feshbach (1975) found that maternal inductions (type unspecified, combined with positive reinforcement) were positively correlated with 6-and 8-year-old boys' (but not girls') generosity.

A dramatic extensive study of rescuers of Jews in Nazi Germany—a study to which we will refer several times in this chapter—provides further support for the hypothesis that parental use of induction enhances children's use of prosocial behavior. In this study by Oliner and Oliner (1988), rescuers were compared with a control group of nonrescuers who were in the same Nazi-controlled locations at the same time. The rescuers, many of whom literally risked their lives to save Holocaust victims, reported that their parents used reasoning as discipline more than did the parents of the nonrescuers.

In contrast, other researchers have found little evidence of a relation between unspecified types of induction and children's prosocial behavior or sympathy (e.g., Janssens & Gerris, 1992; Mullis, Smith, & Vollmers, 1983;

Trommsdorff, 1991). Nonetheless, most investigators have found at least some support for a relation between prosocial behavior or sympathy and inductions focused on peers or others' feelings (Hoffman & Saltzstein, 1967; Stanhope et al., 1987; also see Iannotti et al., 1992).

The emotional intensity associated with an induction appears to influence the effects of inductions. Consistent with some of Miller et al.'s findings reported above, Zahn-Waxler, Radke-Yarrow, and King >(1979) found that maternal use of effectively charged explanations, particularly those including moralizing, was related to very young children's prosocial behavior. Toddlers (one- to two-year-olds) whose mothers used emotionally charged, empathy-eliciting explanations in disciplining them—for example, strong, sharply expressed statements like, "Don't you see you've hurt Margaret? You mustn't bite anyone"—tried to repair their transgressions and expressed concern with their victims more than did toddlers who met with inductions delivered without emotion or with simple verbal prohibitions, such as "Stop that." Perhaps explanations delivered without affect were not effective because the toddlers were unlikely to attend or to think that their mothers meant what they said. It is important to note, however, that parental inductions delivered in situations involving relatively high degrees of anger, particularly inductions that sometimes are guilt-inducing, seem to be associated with low levels of prosocial reactions by preschoolers to their parent (Denham, Renwick-DeBardi, & Hewes, 1994). In the Yarrow et al. study, the mothers who used empathy-eliciting techniques were generally rated by observers as higher in empathy and nurturance than the mothers who used other kinds of disciplinary techniques.

There also is initial evidence that different types of inductions may be associated with different moral orientations, that is, children's ways of thinking about moral issues. Hoffman (1970b) found that children oriented toward conventional principles without regard to extenuating circumstances—that is, children who were rigid and justified moral actions primarily in terms like "it's against the law"—had fathers who reported using inductions about harm to the parent. Humanistic children—that is, those who stressed human needs as the underlying reason for compliance with rules and considered extenuating circumstances—reported that their mothers used more matter-of-fact inductions pointing up the pragmatic requirements of the situation. Parents of both groups of children used more inductions than did the parents of children who were oriented toward external punishment in their moral judgments. We see similar results in a study of the use of induction by mothers of high school girls (Karylowski, 1982). The girls' prosocial behavior was based either on anticipated effects on their own feeling of moral satisfaction and pride (endocentrism) or on the consequences of prosocial action for others (exocentrism). The study showed that the mothers of endocentric girls were less likely to use other-oriented inductions than were mothers of exocentric girls.

As one would expect, the effectiveness of inductions for promoting prosocial behavior varies as a function of the other practices used by parents and the child's socialization history. Inductions appear to be most effective if used by socializers who typically do not use power-assertive (punitive) techniques (Hoffman, 1963; also see Dekovic & Janssens, 1992) and have used inductions in the past (Dlugokinski & Firestone, 1974). Moreover, inductions seem to be most effective if combined with demands for responsible behavior. In one study, mothers' and fathers' use of inductions (as reported by Dutch children), combined with parental demands for mature behavior and low power assertion, was associated with level of children's self-reported empathy, which in turn was linked to teachers' reports of the children's prosocial behavior (Janssens & Gerris, 1992).

Similarly, in her classic studies, Baumrind (1967, 1971, 1973, 1989, 1995) found "authoritative" parenting most effective in strengthening children's positive development. Authoritative parents are warm, loving, responsive, supportive, and make substantial use of explanation and discussion in guiding and disciplining their children. At ages 4 and 9, children of authoritative parents showed greater social responsibility, friendliness, and cooperativeness than did the children reared by authoritarian, punitive, or permissive parents.

In summary, the empirical findings on the relation of inductions to children's prosocial behavior vary considerably across studies, perhaps due to differences in measures of type of induction and prosocial behavior. Nonetheless, inductions that are focused on the victim or point out the consequences of children's actions seem to be linked to some degree with children's prosocial behavior and children's moral orientation. Moreover, inductive discipline appears to have the most beneficial effects if combined with support, authoritative parenting practices and, at least for young children, if delivered with affective force. Unfortunately, there is little research on paternal use of inductive discipline.

Some other dimensions of inductions have not been examined systematically. For example, Staub (1979) suggested that inductions pointing out the positive consequences of desirable behavior may be more effective than inductions pointing out the negative consequences of the child's behavior. Supporting this suggestion are the findings of an experimental study: children who were told that someone else would feel happy if they helped them were more likely to assist than were children who were told that someone would be sad if they did not help (McGrath, Wilson, & Frassetto, 1995). Moreover, the comprehensibility and tone of inductions may be critical. Grusec and Goodnow (1994) suggested that the internalization of parental messages depends on children's accurate understanding of the message (including its content, the rules implied in the message, and the parent's intentions and investment in the message) and their acceptance of the message. Children may or may not perceive the intended message, depending on its clarity, redundancy, and consistency, as well as its appropriateness for the child's developmental level. It is hypothesized that the child will be more likely to accept the message if he or she perceives it as appropriate. As Hoffman suggested (1983), the message must be motivating (e.g., arousing empathy or insecurity) and encourage the child to believe that the values are his or her own rather than externally imposed. Furthermore, parental responsiveness or past willingness to grant the child's wishes may enhance the child's willingness to comply with the parent's wishes (Grusec & Goodhow, 1994).

Victim-Oriented Discipline

Several researchers have studied victim-oriented discipline, which usually involves inductions and additional parental practices. For example, Hoffman (1975) operationalized *victim-oriented discipline* as parental displays of concern for the victim, such as encouraging children's attempts at reparation or apologies for doing harm. Fifth graders whose parents reported victim-oriented discipline were relatively high in same-sex peer nominations of prosocial behaviors such as caring about others.

Similarly, de Veer and Janssens (1994) defined victim-oriented discipline as discipline that stresses the position of the victim, including references to the material and personal consequences of the child's action for the victim, as well as parental attempts to encourage the child to repair the damage or to apologize. They found that the relation of such discipline to children's guilt (i.e., expression of concern over harm to another or concern with principles of justice when discussing hypothetical transgressions) was mediated by the relation of victim-oriented discipline to children's interpersonal understanding. Victim-oriented discipline appeared to enhance the level of children's interpersonal understanding (e.g., perspective taking), which was associated with higher guilt (also see de Veer & Janssens, 1994).

Preachings

It is almost inevitable that parents preach to their children about caring, helping, and cooperating. Is such preaching effective? Judging from pertinent research data, the answer is that it depends on the kind of preaching and the context. The rescuers of the Jews from the Holocaust noted their parents' frequent discussions about caring and universal ethical standards, characteristics that were often reflected in the rescuers' own value system (Oliner & Oliner, 1988). Other studies of adult altruists yield similar findings (e.g., Rosenhan, 1970).

Laboratory studies also generally are consistent with the conclusion that preaching can have the desired effects (e.g., increase the amount of prizes children are willing to share) if it engages children's empathy and sympathy by highlighting the needy state of potential beneficiaries of altruistic behavior (Burleson & Fennelly, 1981; Dlugokinski & Firestone, 1974; Dressel & Midlarsky, 1978; Eisenberg-Berg & Geisheker, 1979; Ladd, Lange, & Stremmel, 1983; Perry, Bussey, & Freiberg, 1981; Smith, 1983; Smith, Leinbach, Stewart, & Blackwell, 1983). Typical empathy-inducing preachings include statements such as, "They [poor children] would be so happy and excited if they could buy food and toys . . . " (Eisenberg-Berg & Geisheker, 1979, p. 170). The effects of empathy-inducing preachings also resulted in increased prosocial behavior a week later and have generalized to new prosocial behaviors (Smith, 1983). Of course, empathic preachings may not always be effective (e.g., McGrath & Power, 1990; Staub, 1971). They may work best if children feel that they have a choice about whether to assist or not and if the focus is on the positive outcomes of prosocial behavior (e.g., a peer or adult feeling happy) rather than negative consequences of not helping (e.g., others feeling sad; McGrath et al., 1995).

In contrast to empathy-inducing preachings, simply exposing children to preaching about norms such as "We should help poor people" has not proven particularly effective in promoting children's prosocial behavior (Bryan, Redfield, & Mader, 1971; Bryan & Walbek, 1970). Normative preachings can induce generosity if the preaching is very strong in its emphasis on the importance of helping (Anderson & Perlman, 1973) or if the preacher is an adult such as a teacher who is likely to have direct power over the children (Eisenberg-Berg & Geisheker, 1979). In general, however, adults' preachings that include empathy-inducing content seem to be most effective.

Modeling

The parent who reasons with a child, uses induction, and elicits empathy is not only disciplining the child, but also providing a model of caring, sympathy, and perspective-taking that the child can imitate. Indeed, there is compelling evidence from both experimental and clinical studies that modeling and identification with nurturant caregivers foster the development of prosocial behavior. For example, preschool boys who perceived their fathers as models of generosity and compassion, (as evidenced in their doll play) shared more winnings in an experimental situation than did boys who did not view their fathers in this way (Rutherford & Mussen, 1968). Other researchers have found that children imitate the prosocial (or selfish) actions modeled by an adult (see Eisenberg & Fabes, 1998). This is most likely to happen if the model is also appropriately nurturant (Weissbrod, 1976; Yarrow, Scott, & Waxler, 1973), albeit not if an adult is nurturant no matter how the child behaves (e.g., Grusec, 1971; Weissbrod, 1976, 1980; see Eisenberg & Fabes, 1998, for a more detailed review).

In the study of rescuers of Jews, rescuers reported having much closer family relationships with parents who modeled caring behavior and communicated—and perhaps preached—caring values and an inclusive definition of the concept of "we" and "us." They

> implicitly or explicitly communicate the obligation to help others in the spirit of generosity without concern for external rewards or reciprocity. . . . Because of their solid family relationships, such children tended to internalize their parents' values, increasingly incorporating standards for personal integrity and care within their own value systems. (Oliner & Oliner, 1988, p. 250)

In other interview studies, dedicated civil rights workers—those who participated in the civil rights movement on a sustained basis and at considerable personal sacrifice—when compared with more casual workers, gave more evidence of identification with nurturant parents. These parents had been excellent models of prosocial behavior, concerned with the welfare of others and frequently working for altruistic causes and discussing altruism with their children (Rosenhan, 1970). Similarly, volunteers at a crisis counseling agency who maintained their commitment rather than quitting were somewhat more likely to report that their parents were nurturant and altruistic (Clary & Miller, 1986). In a recent study, African American and Latin American adolescents chosen by community leaders as exemplars of caring behavior were more likely than their peers to incorporate aspects of parental representations in their self-descriptions (e.g., discussed what their mothers were like or expected of them; Hart & Fegley, 1995). These findings on adolescent and adult altruists suggest that early modeling can be a highly significant factor in the internalization and enduring quality of prosocial motivation. However, given the self-report, retrospective nature of much of the data, additional research with longitudinal studies would be very useful for demonstrating causal relations.

PROVISION OF OPPORTUNITIES FOR PROSOCIAL BEHAVIOR AND ASSIGNMENT OF RESPONSIBILITY

Children's prosocial behavior appears to be enhanced by engaging in such behavior, particularly if children do not feel forced to do so. For example, cross-cultural (Whiting & Whiting, 1975), experimental (Staub, 1979), and correlational (Rehberg & Richman, 1989; Richman, Berry, Bittle, & Himan, 1988) studies within American culture show that early assignment of responsibility stimulates prosocial responding. Children reared in cultures in which they are assigned responsibilities for taking care of siblings or contributing to the family economy (e.g., helping with agricultural pursuits) early are more helpful and supportive of peers and family members than are children in other cultures (Whiting & Whiting, 1975). Analogously, American boys and girls who are assigned various sorts of responsibilities in an experimental setting are more likely to behave altruistically with peers than children in control groups. For example, Staub (1979) found that children (particularly girls) who taught younger children, made toys for poor hospitalized children, or wrote letters to hospitalized children were later more likely to be helpful or generous in other situations. Moreover, there is some evidence that adolescents' and young adults' participation in voluntary community service is related to greater feelings of commitment to helping others (Yates & Youniss, 1995) and to the attitude that society has the obligation to meet the needs of others (although there was no increase in feelings of personal responsibility; Hamilton & Fenzel, 1988; Rutter & Newmann, 1989).

The effects of practice on helping or other prosocial activities vary with age and characteristics of the child. Eisenberg, Cialdini, McCreath, and Shell (1987, 1989) found that inducing children to donate through suggestion rather than coercion in one context was associated with more helping a couple of days later. However, this effect was found only for children in mid-elementary school or older (rather than for kindergartners) and was stronger for children who reported that they valued consistency in behavior than for those who did not (also see Eisenberg, Cialdini et al., 1987).

One explanation for these findings is that involvement in prosocial activities changes the degree to which children view themselves as prosocial, and that children's self-concepts are important guides for subsequent behavior. Young children who do not have a firm understanding of the enduring nature of personality, and children who are less concerned with consistency in behavior, would not be expected to behave in ways consistent with a self-perception explanation. If a child does not value consistency in behavior, there is little motivation to behave in a manner consistent with one's prior behavior and self-perceptions in regard to prosocial behavior.

Supportive of a self-concept explanation of prosocial behavior are the findings that children who engaged in an initial donating task and who also valued consistency were less likely to attribute hedonistic motives to themselves for prosocial actions approximately 2 months later, when compared with children exposed to the initial helping experience but who did not value consistency (Eisenberg, Cialdini, et al., 1987). Moreover, children viewed by teachers as generally consistent in their behavior (which may stem from children's valuing of consistency) also are reported to be helpful (Rotenberg & Pilipenko, 1983/1984). However, researchers who have examined the self-perception explanation with adults have not obtained clear support for its importance in explaining the effects of an initial prosocial experience on subsequent behavior (see Beaman, Cole, Preston, Klentz, & Stablay, 1983; Dillard, 1991).

Regardless of the role of perception of oneself as altruistic, it is probable that opportunities to engage in prosocial behaviors allow children to discover that they have the skills to help and that engaging in prosocial behavior can be interesting and rewarding in a variety of ways. Engaging in prosocial behavior may result in empathic rewards (e.g., feelings of vicarious happiness), feelings of competence to help, and social approval. In brief, it is likely that inducing rather than forcing children to assist others enhances prosocial responding in the future for a variety of reasons.

PUNITIVE DISCIPLINE AND PUNISHMENTS

In general, punitive parenting practices have been found to be either unrelated to or negatively correlated with individual differences in children's prosocial behavior (Bar-Tal, Nadler, & Blechman, 1980; Dekovic & Janssens, 1992; Dlugokinski & Firestone, 1974; Feshbach, 1978; Iannotti et al., 1992; Janssens & Gerris, 1992; Mussen, Rutherford, Harris, & Keasey, 1970 ; Zahn-Waxler et al., 1979). Moreover, children who are physically abused tend to be low in empathy and prosocial behavior (e.g., Howes & Eldredge, 1985; Main & George, 1985; see also Miller & Eisenberg, 1988). Punitive, especially abusive, parents provide a hostile model for the child and are unlikely to create an optimal context for learning. Moreover, Hoffman (1970a) argued that children are likely to attribute prosocial behavior induced by power-assertive techniques to external motives such as fear of detection or punishment (Dix & Grusec, 1983; Smith, Gelfand, Hartmann, & Partlow, 1979); thus, children who are disciplined primarily by punishment are unlikely to develop a prosocial self-concept or prosocial values and motives.

Although harsh, punitive parenting generally does not foster prosocial behavior and personal responsibility, occasional use of punishment in a measured and rational manner by supportive, authoritative parents may have no negative effects on children's prosocial behavior (Baumrind, 1971). Rescuers of Jews in Nazi Europe reported that when they received punishments from their parents, these punishments were linked to specific behaviors rather than used gratuitously; moreover, punishment was not the parents' usual mode of discipline (Oliner & Oliner, 1988).

REINFORCEMENT

Principles of social learning theory often are applied intuitively by parents. Parents who observe their children acting in prosocial ways sometimes reward them with praise or in some other way. Use of such praise has been correlated with prosocial behavior in the home and experimental studies (e.g., Bryan et al., 1971; Eisenberg et al., 1993; Gelfand, Hartmann, Cromer, Smith, & Page, 1975 ; Grusec & Redler, 1980; Rushton & Teachman, 1978; see also Eisenberg & Fabes, 1998).

Some types of praise appear to be more effective than others at fostering prosocial behavior. As attribution theorists would predict, praise that attributes the children's positive behavior to their dispositional kindness or intrinsic motives (e.g., because they enjoy helping others) seems to be more effective than praise involving simply labeling of the act as positive, for example, "That was a nice thing to do" (Grusec & Redler, 1980; Mills & Grusec, 1989). In one study, an experimenter said, "I guess you shared because you're the kind of person who likes to help other people" to some of the 7- to 10-year-olds who donated to a charity for poor children some prizes they had won. In subsequent sessions, these children donated more generously than children who, after donating in the first session, were told simply, "You shared quite a bit" (Grusec, Kuczynski, Rushton, & Simutis, 1978). Moreover, children provided with attributional praise are more helpful or generous even weeks later than are other children (Grusec et al., 1978; Grusec & Redler, 1980; Holte, Jamruszka, Gustafson, Beaman, & Camp, 1984; cf. Eisenberg, Cialdini, McCreath, & Shell, 1987,1989), whereas research findings regarding the generalizability and long-term effects of simple nonattributional praise are mixed (Eisenberg, Wolchik, Goldberg, & Engel, 1992; Grusec & Redler, 1980; Rushton & Teachman, 1978). The provision of internal attributions is believed to foster a prosocial self-image, which then results in enhanced prosocial behavior (Grusec & Redler, 1980). However, support for this explanation is mixed (Holte et al., 1984; Mills & Grusec, 1989).

The effects of concrete (e.g., material) rewards for prosocial behavior appear to differ from those of social rewards. Although concrete rewards may foster prosocial behavior in a particular context, the long-term effects of concrete rewards may be to inhibit or undermine prosocial development. Researchers have argued that concrete rewards deter the development of intrinsic motivation (Lepper, 1983) and may induce children to attribute their prosocial actions to external motivation. Thus, third graders promised tangible rewards if the younger children they tutored did well were less likely to engage voluntarily in teaching subsequently than were tutors who were not promised rewards for this activity (Szynal-Brown & Morgan, 1983). Children who were promised rewards that were not contingent on the pupil's learning were in between the aforementioned two groups in regard to volunteer teaching but did not differ significantly from either. Furthermore, children given material rewards for helping subsequently engaged in less prosocial behavior when they were alone than did children not given rewards, particularly for children whose mothers valued the use of rewards (Fabes, Fultz, Eisenberg, May-Plumlee, & Christopher, 1989). Moreover, mothers who reported that they felt relatively positive about using rewards rated their children as less prosocial than did mothers who were less enthusiastic about the use of rewards.

Undoubtedly the contexts of rewards (and punishments) need to be considered. A reward from a warm, nurturant parent may have a more marked effect on the child's prosocial orientation than simple rewards by a generally aloof or rejecting parent. However, there is little research on this topic. Naturalistic investigations of the factors that influence whether the effects of praise are substantial and lasting in everyday life are needed.

EXTRAFAMILIAL INFLUENCES

Let us return to the child in the painting described at the beginning of this chapter, imagining that a real child is being depicted. We may infer that in "training him up," his economically advantaged, upper-class parents have exposed him to most of the practices conducive to the enhancement of prosocial behavior. He has experienced empathy-arousing reactions to his transgressions; inductive, reasoning explanations rather than power assertion in discipline; modeling of prosocial actions and perhaps assignment of responsibilities for others; preachings likely to elicit empathy with those in need of help; and praise for prosocial actions. All of this is likely to have occurred in an authoritative, nurturant, supportive familial context.

The findings that we have summarized clearly have applied social utilitarian implications; that is, they suggest practices by which caregivers may influence and discipline their children to become more prosocial, caring, and altruistic, thus benefiting society at large and enhancing the level of the general welfare. Fortunately, many caregivers intuitively—or by virtue of their training, education, and guidance—apply these practices.

But many parents or other caregivers in our society who live under conditions of poverty, stress, familial dysfunction, prejudice, discrimination, or abuse are not as likely to use these prosocial-fostering procedures. Perhaps in the future parent training programs will reach into familial milieu where they are badly needed. However, as things stand at present, those most in need of help in learning how to promote children's prosocial behavior are probably least likely to get it.

If children fail to acquire strong prosocial dispositions and responses at home, can they acquire them from other agents of socialization, for example, from peers and teachers? Can these socialization agents provide experiences that strengthen poorly developed prosocial tendencies? Or, reversing this perspective, can constructive prosocial behavior that is the product of positive parental practices be reversed by experiences in school or other situations outside the home? Will children who are "trained up" in their homes to be sympathetic and prosocial ipso facto be altruistic subsequently?

Remember the second clause of the title of Mulready's painting: "And when he is old he will not deviate from it," "it" meaning the path of righteous behavior. In the case of the child in the painting, the painter's statement may be valid. He was obviously a child of the gentry class so it is likely that the values, attitudes, and responses he acquired at home would be reinforced in other settings. For one thing, children of his class were likely to remain at home for tutoring—probably by tutors who shared the orientations of the children's parents—or went to school with other children from similar backgrounds whose families shared values, perspectives, and many patterns of behavior. As adults, their most significant interactions would also be with people of the same background so they could expect social support for their prosocial orientations and activities. For these reasons there is likely to be continuity between their earlier (childhood) and later behaviors.

But in our complex and diversified society, most people are exposed to numerous socialization inputs; some experiences outside the family reinforce what is acquired at home, whereas others may counteract or undermine predispositions formed early in life. In their book *Some Do Care*, Colby and Damon (1992) reported an intensive study of 12 people of diverse backgrounds who have devoted their lives to altruistic activities, often in the face of great obstacles. Underlying their dedicated, consistent prosocial orientations and work were early-acquired, positive attitudes toward others and internalized prosocial motivations plus—and this is a big plus—subsequent strong support from other significant figures in their lives.

Clearly some individuals maintain prosocial proclivities established during childhood. Recall that adult altruists such as rescuers of Jews from the Holocaust and dedicated civil rights workers had close relationships with parents who modeled and preached altruism, social responsibility, and general humane values. In addition, longitudinal studies at the Institute of Human Development at Berkeley as well as those conducted by Jack and Jeanne Block (cited in Feld, 1994) uncovered significant relations between certain positive childhood personality characteristics—presumably the products of early child rearing—and humane, liberal attitudes in adulthood (Mussen, 1982).

Yet, it is to be expected that many individuals' initial levels of prosociality change as their life experiences and situations change. What happens to an 8-year-old middle-class girl who is responding well to her parents' positive child-rearing practices when her father loses his job and the family moves to a neighborhood in which destructive, violent behavior is prevalent? Is she likely to maintain the prosocial behavior patterns that she acquired at home? What happens to the prosocial proclivities of a child whose intact family somehow becomes dysfunctional, and a parent becomes neglectful, rejecting and hostile? There doubtlessly are many more examples of changes in milieu and experiences that nullify or at least reduce the positive consequences of early training. In brief, certain caregiver practices initiate or stimulate the development of prosocial orientations, motivations, and actions in childhood, but their long-term effects are hardly assured and may in fact be limited. (Perhaps Mulready should have placed a question mark at the end of his painting's title.)

In the final analysis, it must be recognized that adults' prosocial orientations and activities are the products of many interacting critical antecedents. Early child-rearing practices are only one of these. It follows that the enhancement of the general welfare and the betterment of society require that extrafamilial agents of socialization become engaged in training for and extending prosocial values and responses. The school is obviously a socialization agent with the potential to do this, and in fact it has been demonstrated that schools can serve in this way by introducing creative programs and activities into their curricula. This can be done without reduced emphasis on the so-called "basics."

Consider, for example, the seminal work by Seymour and Norma Feshbach who developed and implemented a school program designed to raise the level of children's empathy. The program involved classroom activities conducted with small groups, including role-playing and discussions of alternative solutions to dilemmas and conflicts. There were three 45-minute sessions of these activities per week over a period of 10 weeks. The striking significant outcomes of the program give compelling evidence that school can be the setting for effective prosocial training. Compared with control groups, children in the empathy training conditions subsequently manifested more cooperation, helping, and generosity (Feshbach & Feshbach, 1982, 1983, 1986).

Following the Feshbachs' pioneering work, a number of school programs focused on prosocial development have been initiated. One of these, the Child Development Project centered in Oakland, California, involves a complex, comprehensive plan of teaching strategies, activities, and parental and community involvement (Solomon, Watson, Delucchi, Schaps, & Battistich, 1988; Watson, Solomon, Battistich, Schaps, & Solomon, 1989). As part of the program, teachers were trained to develop and maintain positive personal relationships with their students and to use a child-centered approach to classroom management. Inductive discipline and student participation in rule-setting were emphasized, and components of the program were designed to promote social understanding, highlight prosocial values, and provide opportunities for helping activities, although these were viewed as playing a more limited, supportive role in the program (Battistich, Watson, Solomon, Schaps, & Solomon, 1991).

With implementation of the program for five years (kindergarten through fourth grade), students in the program classrooms, compared with those in control classes, generally scored higher on measures of prosocial behavior. The pattern persisted when both teachers' general competence and students' participation in cooperative activities were controlled, suggesting that program effects on children's prosocial behavior were not due simply to differences in teacher-initiated cooperative interactions or to more efficiently organized and managed classrooms (Solomon et al., 1988). Moreover, there was some evidence that the impact of the program was greatest for the first year it was introduced (in kindergarten); children enrolled in the program (but not the children in the control group) were highest in prosocial behavior and harmony in kindergarten.

The degree to which the effects of the program generalized beyond the immediate classroom environment was unclear (Battistich et al., 1991). However, teachers in the program had limited experience in implementing the program, so the effects of the program might be more sustained if the teachers had more time to develop their techniques and fully integrate the program into the ongoing routine of the classroom. Moreover, in a second longitudinal test of the program, there was evidence that it increased children's prosocial reasoning somewhat and their conflict resolution skills (including consideration of others' needs and a reliance on the use of compromise and sharing; Solomon, Battistich, & Watson, 1993).

Unfortunately, most of the few school intervention programs have been implemented in schools with predominantly advantaged students, although the Child Development Project currently is being extended to six American cities representing a wide range of demographic characteristics (see Battistich, Solomon, Watson, & Schaps, 1997). Moreover, there is little evidence that teachers actively promote or reinforce prosocial behavior in their everyday activities (Caplan & Hay, 1989; Eisenberg et al., 1981), although data pertaining to this issue are very limited. Nonetheless, it is likely that there are warm, prosocial teachers who, perhaps inadvertently, foster prosocial behavior in their students (Yarrow et al., 1973). The quality of teachers' relationships with their students does seem to matter; in one study, children classified as securely attached to their current and previous preschool teachers were rated as more sensitive and empathic with unfamiliar peers than were children with insecure relationships with their contemporary teachers (Howes, Matheson, & Hamilton, 1994). Contemporary teacher—child relations predicted behavior with peers better than contemporary maternal attachment relations or child care history. Thus, even if teachers do not intentionally promote prosocial development, their interactions with students may have a significant positive influence on the development of children's prosocial behavior.

Operating on the premise that raising the level of prosocial motivation and behavior depends on continued and repeated reinforcement, investigators need to analyze carefully the potential of the role of other agents of socialization—including friends, social clubs, youth organizations, religious groups, informal peer associations, even gangs—and turn up the rheostat on research on their impacts on prosocial development. Relatively little is known about the role of peers and youth organizations in prosocial development (see Eisenberg & Fabes, 1998). With creative thought and planning, activities that would enhance empathy and prosocial actions can be introduced into the agendas of such formal and informal institutions. Moreover, there would be the potential for large benefits if the moguls of the media, particularly television, could be persuaded to give more attention to how they can contribute to the enhancement of constructive thinking and behavior.

CONCLUSION

Without minimizing the complexity of the problem and the difficulties of strengthening children's tendencies toward prosocial behavior, we believe that the studies reviewed in this chapter provide a sufficient empirical foundation for some recommendations on social planning and policy. First, much can be accomplished in parent education programs by encouraging the use of techniques such as induction and modeling that researchers have shown to be successful in facilitating the early development of prosocial behavior. Second, it appears that school-based intervention programs have the potential to produce significant positive effects on children's prosocial development, although there is a critical need to develop and test programs that can be readily adapted and used in many school settings without extensive and costly training of teachers.

REFERENCES

Anderson, J. A., & Perlman, D. (1973). Effects of an adult's preaching and responsibility for hypocritical behavior on children's altruism. *Proceedings, 81st Annual Convention, American Psychological Association*, 291–292.

Bar-Tal, D., Nadler, A., & Blechman, N. (1980). The relationship between Israeli children's helping behavior and their perception on parents' socialization practices. *Journal of Social Psychology, 111,* 159–167.

Battistich, V., Solomon, D., Watson, M., & Schaps, E. (1997). Caring school communities. *Educational Psychologist, 32,* 137–151.

Battistich, V., Watson, M., Solomon, D., Schaps, E., & Solomon, J. (1991). The Child Development Project: A comprehensive program for the development of prosocial character. In W. M. Kurtines & J. L. Gewirtz (Eds.), *Handbook of moral behavior and development. Vol. 3. Application* (pp. 1–34). New York: Erlbaum.

Baumrind, D. (1967). Child care practices anteceding three patterns of preschool behavior. *Genetic Psychological Monographs, 75,* 43–88.

Baumrind, D. (1971). Current patterns of parental authority. *Developmental Psychology Monographs, 4,* 1–33

Baumrind, D. (1973). The development of instrument competence through socialization. In A. D. Pick (Ed.), *Minnesota Symposia on Child Psychology* (Vol. 7, pp. 3–46) Minneapolis: University of Minnesota Press.

Baumrind, D. (1989). Rearing competent children. In W. Damon (Ed.), *Child development today and tomorrow* (pp. 349–378). San Francisco: Jossey-Bass.

Baumrind, D. (1995). *Child maltreatment and optimal caregiving in social contexts.* New York: Garland.

Beaman, A. L., Cole, C., Preston, M., Klentz, B., & Steblay, N. M. (1983). Fifteen years of foot-in-the-door research. *Personality and Social Psychology Bulletin, 9,* 181–196.

Bryan, J. H., Redfield, J., & Mader, S. (1971). Words and deeds about altruism and the subsequent reinforcement power of the model. *Child Development, 42,* 1501–1508.

Bryan, J. H., & Walbek, N. H. (1970a). The impact of words and deeds concering altruism upon children. *Child Development, 41,* 747–757.

Burleson, B. R., & Fennelly, D. A. (1981). The effects of persuasive appeal form and cognitive complexity on children's sharing behavior. *Child Study Journal, 11,* 75–90.

Caplan, M. Z., & Hay, D. F. (1989). Preschoolers' responses to peers' distress and beliefs about bystander intervention. *Journal of Child Psychology and Psychiatry, 30,* 231–242.

Colby, A., & Damon, W. (1992). *Some do care: Contemporary lives of moral commitment.* Toronto: Free Press.

Clary, E. G., & Miller, J. (1986). Socialization and situational influences on sustained altruism. *Child Development, 57,* 1358–1369.

Dekovic, M., & Janssens, J. M. A. M. (1992). Parents' child-rearing style and children's sociometric status. *Developmental Psychology, 28,* 925–932.

Denham, S. A., Renwick-DeBardi, S., & Hewes, S. (1994). Emotional communication between mothers and preschoolers: Relations with emotional competence. *Merrill-Palmer Quarterly, 40,* 488–508.

de Veer, A. J. E., & Janssens, J. M. A. M. (1994). Victim-orientated discipline, interpersonal understanding, and guilt. *Journal of Moral Education, 23,* 165–182.

Dillard, J. P. (1991). The current status of research on sequential-request compliance techniques. *Personality and Social Psychology Bulletin, 17,* 283–288.

Dix, T., & Grusec, J. E. (1983). Parental influence techniques: An attributional analysis. *Child Development, 54,* 645–652.

Dlugokinski, E. L, & Firestone, I. J. (1974). Other centeredness and susceptibility to charitable appeals: Effects of perceived discipline. *Developmental Psychology, 10,* 21–28.

Dressel, S., & Midlarsky, E. (1978). The effects of model's exhortations, demands, and practices on children's donation behavior. *Journal of Genetic Psychology, 132,* 211–223.

Eisenberg, N., Cameron, E., Tryon, K., & Dodez, R. (1981). Socialization of prosocial behavior in the preschool classroom. *Developmental Psychology, 17,* 773–782.

Eisenberg, N., Carlo, G., Murphy, B., & Van Court, P. (1995). Prosocial development in late adolescence: A longitudinal study. *Child Development, 66,* 1179–1197.

Eisenberg, N., Cialdini, R., McCreath, H., & Shell, R. (1987). Consistency-based compliance: When and why do children become vulnerable? *Journal of Personality and Social Psychology, 52,* 1174–1181.

Eisenberg, N., Cialdini, R. B., McCreath, H., & Shell, R. (1989). Consistency-based compliance in children: When and why do consistency procedures have immediate effects? *Journal of Behavioral Development, 12,* 351–367.

Eisenberg, N., & Fabes, R. A. (1998). Prosocial development. In W. Damon (Series Ed.) & N. Eisenberg (Vol. Ed.), *Handbook of child psychology: Vol. 3. Social, emotional, and personality development* (5th ed., pp. 701–778). New York: Wiley.

Eisenberg, N., Fabes, R. A., Carlo, G., Speer, A. L., Switzer, G., Karbon, M., & Troyer, D. (1993). The relations of empathy-related emotions and maternal practices to children's comforting behavior. *Journal of Experimental Child Psychology, 55,* 131–150.

Eisenberg, N., Miller, P. A., Shell, R., McNalley, S., & Shea, C. (1991). Prosocial development in adolescence: A longitudinal study. *Developmental Psychology, 27,* 849–857.

Eisenberg, N., Wolchik, S., Goldberg, L., & Engel, I. (1992). Parental values, reinforcement, and young children's prosocial behavior: A longitudinal study. *Journal of Genetic Psychology, 153,* 19–36.

Eisenberg-Berg, N., & Geisheker, E. (1979). Content of preachings and power of the model/preacher: The effect on children's generosity. *Developmental Psychology, 15,* 168–175.

Fabes, R. A., Fultz, J., Eisenberg, N., May-Plumlee, T., & Christopher, F. S. (1989). The effects of reward on children's prosocial motivation: A socialization study. *Developmental Psychology, 25,* 509–515.

Feld, P. (1994). *A prospective longitudinal study of personality and political orientation.* Unpublished doctoral dissertation, University of California, Berkeley.

Feshbach, N. D. (1975). The relationship of child-rearing factors to children's aggression, empathy, and related positive and negative behaviors. In J. DeWit & W. W. Hartup (Eds.), *Determinants and origins of aggressive behavior* (pp. 426–436). The Hague, Netherlands: Mouton.

Feshbach, N. D. (1978). Studies of empathic behavior in children. In B. A. Maher (Ed.), *Progress in experimental personality research* (Vol. 8, pp. 1–47). New York: Academic Press.

Feshbach, N. D. (1987). Parental empathy and child adjustment/maladjustment. In N. Eisenberg & J. Strayer (Eds.), *Empathy and its development* (pp. 271–291). New York: Cambridge University Press.

Feshbach, N. D., & Feshbach, S. (1982). Empathy training and the regulation of aggression: Potentialities and limitations. *Academic Psychology Bulletin, 4,* 399–413.

Feshbach, N. D., & Feshbach, S. (1983). *Learning to care: Classroom activities for social and affective development.* Glenview, IL: Scott, Foresman.

Feshbach, S., & Feshbach, N. D. (1986). Aggression and altruism: A personality perspective. In C. Zahn-Waxler, E. M. Cummings, & R. Iannotti (Eds.), *Altruism and aggression: Biological and social origins* (pp. 189–217). Cambridge, England: Cambridge University Press.

Gelfand, D. M., Hartmann, D. P., Cromer, C. C., Smith, C. L., & Page, B. C. (1975). The effects of instructional prompts and praise on children's donation rates. *Child Development, 46,* 980–983.

Grusec, J. E. (1971). Power and the internalization of self denial. *Child Development, 42,* 93–105.

Grusec, J. E. (1983). The internalization of altruistic dispositions: A cognitive analysis. In E. T. Higgins, D. N. Ruble, & W. W. Hartup (Eds.), *Social cognition and social development: A sociocultural perspective* (pp. 275–293). Cambridge, MA: Cambridge University Press.

Grusec, J. E., & Goodnow, J. J. (1994). Impact of parental discipline methods on the child's internalization of values: A reconceptualization of current points of view. *Developmental Psychology, 30,* 4–19.

Grusec, J. E., Kuczynski, L., Rushton, J. P., & Simutis, Z. M. (1978). Modeling, direction instruction, and attributions: Effects on altruism. *Developmental Psychology, 14,* 51–57.

Grusec, J. E., & Redler, E. (1980). Attribution, reinforcement, and altruism: A developmental analysis. *Developmental Psychology, 16,* 525–534.

Hamilton, S. F., & Fenzel, L. M. (1988). The impact of volunteer experience on adolescent social development: Evidence of program effects. *Journal of Adolescent Research, 3,* 65–80.

Hart, D., & Fegley, S. (1995). Altruism and caring in adolescence: Relations to self-understanding and social judgment. *Child Development, 66,* 1346–1359.

Henry, R. M. (1980). A theoretical and empirical analysis of 'reasoning' in the socialization of young children. *Human Development, 23,* 105–125.

Hoffman, M. L. (1963). Parent discipline and the child's consideration for others. *Child Development, 34,* 573–588.

Hoffman, M. L. (1970a). Conscience, personality, and socialization techniques. *Human Development, 13,* 90–126.

Hoffman, M. L. (1970b). Moral development. In P. H. Mussen (Ed.), *Carmichael's manual of child development* (Vol. 2, pp. 261–359). New York: Wiley.

Hoffman, M. L. (1975a). Altruistic behavior and the parent–child relationship. *Journal of Personality and Social Psychology, 31,* 937–943.

Hoffman, M. L. (1982). Development of prosocial motivation: Empathy and guilt. In N. Eisenberg (Ed.), *The development of prosocial behavior* (pp. 281–313). New York: Academic Press.

Hoffman, M. L. (1983). Affective and cognitive processes in moral internalization. In E. T. Higgins, D. N. Ruble, & W. W. Hartup (Eds.), *Social cognition and social development: A sociocultural perspective* (pp. 236–274). Cambridge, MA: Cambridge University Press.

Hoffman, M. L., & Saltzstein, H. D. (1967). Parent discipline and the child's moral development. *Journal of Personality and Social Psychology, 5*, 45–57.

Holte, C. S., Jamruszka, V., Gustafson, J., Beaman, A. L, & Camp, G. C. (1984). Influence of children's positive self-perceptions on donating behavior in naturalistic settings. *Journal of School Psychology, 22*, 145–153.

Howes, C., & Eldredge, R. (1985). Responses of abused, neglected, and non-maltreated children to the behaviors of their peers. *Journal of Applied Developmental Psychology, 6*, 261–270.

Howes, C., Matheson, C. C., & Hamilton, C. E. (1994). Maternal, teacher, and child care history correlates of children's relationships with peers. *Child Development, 65*, 264–273.

Iannotti, R. J., Cummings, E. M., Pierrehumbert, B., Milano, M. J., & Zahn-Waxler, C. (1992). Parental influences on prosocial behavior and empathy in early childhood. In J. M. A. M. Janssens & J. R. M. Gerris (Eds.), *Child rearing: Influence on prosocial and moral development* (pp. 77–100). Amsterdam, The Netherlands: Swets & Zeitlinger.

Janssens, J. M. A. M., & Gerris, J. R. M. (1992). Child rearing, empathy and prosocial development. In J. M. A. M. Janssens & J. R. M. Gerris (Eds.), *Child rearing: Influence on prosocial and moral development* (pp. 57–75). Amsterdam, The Netherlands: Swets & Zeitlinger.

Karylowski, J. (1982). Doing good to feel good v. doing good to make others feel good: Some child-rearing antecedents. *School Psychology International, 3*, 149–156.

Ladd, G. W., Lange, G., & Stremmel, A. (1983). Personal and situational influences on children's helping behavior: Factors that mediate helping. *Child Development, 54*, 488–501.

Lepper, M. R. (1983). Social-control processes and the internalization of social values: An attributional perspective. In E. T. Higgins, D. N. Ruble, & W. W. Hartup (Eds.), *Social cognition and social development: A sociocultural perspective* (pp. 294–330). Cambridge, England: Cambridge University Press.

Main, M., & George, C. (1985). Responses of abused and disadvantaged toddlers to distress in agemates: A study in the day care setting. *Developmental Psychology, 21*, 407–412.

McGrath, M. P., & Power, T. G. (1990). The effects of reasoning and choice on children's prosocial behavior. *International Journal of Behavioral Development, 13*, 345–353.

McGrath, M. P., Wilson, S. R., & Frassetto, S. J. (1995). Why some forms of induction are better than others at encouraging prosocial behavior. *Merrill-Palmer Quarterly, 41*, 347–360.

Miller, P., & Eisenberg, N. (1988). The relation of empathy to aggression and externalizing/antisocial behavior. *Psychological Bulletin, 103*, 324–344.

Miller, P. A., Eisenberg, N., Fabes, R. A., Shell, R., & Gular, S. (1989). Socialization of empathic and sympathetic responding. In N. Eisenberg (Ed.),

The development of empathy and related vicarious responses. New directions in child development (pp. 65–83). San Francisco: Jossey-Bass.

Mills, R. S. L., & Grusec, J. (1989). Cognitive, affective, and behavioral consequences of praising altruism. *Merrill-Palmer Quarterly, 35,* 299–326.

Mullis, R. L., Smith, D. W., & Vollmers, K. E. (1983). Prosocial behaviors in young children and parental guidance. *Child Study Journal, 13,* 13–21.

Mussen, P. (1982). Parenting, prosocial behavior, and political attitudes. In L. W. Hoffman, R. Gandelman, & H. R. Schiffman (Eds.), *Parent: Its causes and consequences* (pp. 111–121). Hillsdale: NJ: Erlbaum.

Mussen, P., Rutherford, E., Harris, S., & Keasey, C. (1970). Honesty and altruism among preadolescents. *Developmental Psychology, 3,* 169–194.

Oliner, S. P., & Oliner, P. M. (1988). *The altruistic personality: Rescuers of Jews in Nazi Europe.* New York: Free Press.

Perry, D. G., Bussey, K., & Freiberg, K. (1981). Impact of adults' appeals for sharing on the development of altruistic dispositions in children. *Journal of Experimental Child Psychology, 32,* 127–138.

Rehberg, H. R., & Richman, C. L. (1989). Prosocial behavior in preschool children: A look at the interaction of race, gender, and family composition. *International Journal of Behavioral Development, 12,* 385–401.

Richman, C. L., Berry, C., Bittle, M., & Himan, M. (1988). Factors related to helping behavior in preschool-age children. *Journal of Applied Developmental Psychology, 9,* 151–165.

Rosenhan, D. L. (1970). The natural socialization of altruistic autonomy. In J. Macaulay & L. Berkowitz (Eds.), *Altruism and helping behavior* (pp. 251–268). New York: Academic Press.

Rotenberg, K. J., & Pilipenko, T. A. (1983/1984). Mutuality, temporal consistency, and helpfulness in children's trust in peers. *Social Cognition, 2,* 235–255.

Rushton, J. P., & Teachman, G. (1978). The effects of positive reinforcement, attributions, and punishment on model induced altruism in children. *Personality and Social Psychology Bulletin, 4,* 322–325.

Rutherford, E., & Mussen, P. (1968). Generosity in nursery school boys. *Child Development, 39,* 755–765.

Rutter, R. A., & Newmann, F. M. (1989). The potential of community service to enhance civic responsibility. *Social Education, 53,* 371–374.

Smith, C. L. (1983). Exhortations, rehearsal, and children's prosocial behavior. *Academic Psychology Bulletin, 5,* 261–271.

Smith, C. L., Gelfand, D. M., Hartmann, D. P., & Partlow, M. E. Y. (1979). Children's causal attributions regarding help giving. *Child Development, 50,* 203–210.

Smith, C. L., Leinbach, M. D., Stewart, B. J., & Blackwell, J. M. (1983). Affective perspective-taking, exhortations, and children's prosocial behavior. In D. L. Bridgeman (Ed.), *The nature of prosocial development* (pp. 113–137). New York: Academic Press.

Solomon, D., Battistich, & Watson, M. (1993, March). *A longitudinal investigation of the effects of a school intervention program on children's social development*. Paper presented at the biennial meeting of the Society for Research in Child Development. New Orleans.

Solomon, D., Watson, M. S., Delucchi, K. L., Schaps, E., & Battistich, V. (1988). Enhancing children's prosocial behavior in the classroom. *American Educational Research Journal, 25*, 527–554.

Stanhope, L., Bell, R. Q., & Parker-Cohen, N. Y. (1987). Temperament and helping behavior in preschool children. *Developmental Psychology, 23*, 347–353.

Staub, E. (1971). The use of role playing and induction in children's learning of helping and sharing behavior. *Child Development, 42*, 805–817.

Staub, E. (1979). *Positive social behavior and morality: Vol. 2: Socialization and development*. New York: Academic Press.

Szynal-Brown, C., & Morgan, R. R. (1983). The effects of reward on tutor's behaviors in a cross-age tutoring context. *Journal of Experimental Child Psychology, 36*, 196–208.

Trommsdorff, G. (1991). Child-rearing and children's empathy. *Perceptual Motor Skills, 72*, 387–390.

Watson, M., Solomon, D., Battistich, V., Schaps, E., & Solomon, J. (1989). The Child Development Project: Combining traditional and developmental approaches to values education. In L. Nucci (Ed.), *Moral development and character education: A dialogue* (pp. 51–92). Berkeley, CA: McCutchan.

Weissbrod, C. S. (1976). Noncontingent warmth induction, cognitive style, and children's imitative donation and rescue effort behaviors. *Journal of Personality and Social Psychology, 34*, 274–281.

Weissbrod, C. S. (1980). The impact of warmth and instruction on donation. *Child Development, 51*, 279–281.

Whiting, B. B., & Whiting, J. W. M. (1975). *Children of six cultures: A psychocultural analysis*. Cambridge, MA: Harvard University Press.

Yarrow, M. R., Scott, P. M., & Waxler, C. Z. (1973). Learning concern for others. *Developmental Psychology, 8*, 240–260.

Yates, M., & Youniss, J. (1995, March). *A developmental perspective on community service in adolescence*. Paper presented at the biennial meeting of the Society for Research in Child Development, Indianapolis.

Zahn-Waxler, C., Radke-Yarrow, M., & King, R. A. (1979). Child rearing and children's prosocial initiations toward victims of distress. *Child Development, 50*, 319–330.

6

CONSTRUCTIVE AND DESTRUCTIVE ASPECTS OF SHAME AND GUILT

JUNE PRICE TANGNEY

Is the human capacity to experience shame and guilt a blessing or a curse? These emotions each involve, in one form or another, painful self-reflection coupled with negative self-directed affect. For whom, under what conditions, and in what form do such negative moral emotions serve constructive as opposed to destructive functions?

In this chapter, I summarize a program of research indicating that shame and guilt are distinct affective experiences with very different implications for adjustment at both the individual and interpersonal level. Taken together, my research indicates that feelings of shame often give rise to a range of potentially destructive motivations, defenses, interpersonal behaviors, and psychological symptoms. In contrast, guilt appears to be the "quintessential" moral emotion, serving numerous constructive, "relationship-enhancing functions" without many of the burdens and costs inherent in feelings of shame. In a very real sense, negatively balanced "moral" emotions, such as shame and guilt, highlight the best and worst sides of human emotional experience.

Portions of this chapter were adapted from Tangney (1995a). Much of the research summarized here was supported by the National Institute for Child Health and Human Development (Grant R01HD27171) and by a Faculty Research Grant from George Mason University. I wish to thank the many graduate and undergraduate students who have worked tirelessly on this research and the research participants who graciously shared their time and thoughts.

127

ARE SHAME AND GUILT DISTINCT EMOTIONS?

Many psychologists mention shame and guilt in the same breath, as "moral emotions" that inhibit socially undesirable behavior and foster moral conduct (e.g., Damon, 1988; Eisenberg, 1986; Harris, 1989; Schulman & Mekler, 1985). Although shame and guilt are assumed to serve adaptive functions at the societal level, clinicians have long identified these emotions as potentially problematic for the individual. Shame and guilt have been implicated as factors contributing to many types of psychological disorders, including depression, anxiety, obsessional neuroses, bipolar illness, schizophrenia, masochism, substance abuse, and eating disorders (Bradshaw, 1988; Fossum & Mason, 1986; Freud, 1909/1955, 1917/1957, 1924/1961; Goldberg, 1991; Kohut, 1971; A. P. Morrison, 1989; N. K. Morrison, 1987; Potter-Efron, 1989; Rodin, Silberstein, & Striegel-Moore, 1985). Often, clinicians use the term *guilt* as a catch-all phrase to refer to aspects of both emotions. In recent years, there has been a growing interest in shame in the popular and clinical literature, with a corresponding de-emphasis on guilt (Bradshaw, 1988; Cook, 1988, 1991; Fossum & Mason, 1986; Goldberg, 1991; Kaufman, 1985, 1989; Miller, 1985; Nathanson, 1987; Scheff, 1987). But here, too, by de-emphasizing guilt, little attention is paid to the difference between these two closely related emotions.

When people do make a distinction between shame and guilt, they often refer to differences in the content or structure of events eliciting these emotions. The assumption is that certain kinds of situations lead to shame, whereas other kinds of situations lead to guilt. For example, there is a long-standing notion that shame is a more "public" emotion than guilt, arising from public exposure and disapproval, whereas guilt represents a more "private" experience arising from self-generated pangs of conscience. This public–private distinction, popularized by mid-century social scientists (Ausubel, 1955; Benedict, 1946), remains an often-cited basis for discriminating between shame and guilt. Gehm and Scherer (1988) clearly articulated this view, speculating that

> shame is usually dependent on the public exposure of one's frailty or failing, whereas guilt may be something that remains a secret with us, no one else knowing of our breach of social norms or of our responsibility for an immoral act. (p. 74)

Surprisingly, virtually no empirical research evaluated the validity of this public–private distinction until recently. To my knowledge, my study of children and adults' narrative accounts of personal shame, guilt, and pride experiences represents the first systematic analysis of "audiences" to these emotion-eliciting events (Tangney, Marschall, Rosenberg, Barlow, & Wagner, 1994). The results clearly challenge the public versus private distinction. Among both children and adults, shame and guilt were most likely to be experienced in the presence of others, but a substantial number of respondents (17.2% of children and 16.5% of adults) reported experiencing shame when alone. More important, solitary shame was about as prevalent as solitary guilt. In addition, although adults reported that on average somewhat more people were present during shame- than guilt-eliciting situations, the number of people involved in these events and (most to the point) the frequency with which others were aware of the respondents' behavior did not vary as a function of shame and guilt. Similarly, in an independent study of adults' narrative accounts of personal shame, guilt, and embarrassment experiences (Tangney, Miller, Flicker, & Barlow, 1996), there was no evidence that shame was the more "public" emotion. In fact, in this study shame was somewhat more likely (18.2%) than guilt (10.4%) to occur when not in the presence of others.

If shame and guilt do not differ in terms of the degree of public exposure, do they differ in terms of the types of the transgressions or failures that elicit them? Not very much, as it turns out. Analyses of narrative accounts of personal shame and guilt experiences provided by children and adults indicate that there are very few, if any, "classic" shame-inducing or guilt-inducing situations (Tangney, 1992; Tangney et al., 1994). Most types of events (e.g., lying, cheating, stealing, failing to help another, disobeying parents) were cited by some people in connection with feelings of shame and by other people in connection with guilt. Unlike moral transgressions, which are equally likely to elicit shame or guilt, there was some evidence that nonmoral failures and shortcomings (e.g., socially inappropriate behavior or dress) may be more likely to elicit shame. Even so, failures in work, school, or sport settings and violations of social conventions were cited by a significant number of children and adults in connection with guilt.

How do shame and guilt differ, if not in terms of the types of situations that elicit them? In her landmark book *Shame and Guilt in Neurosis*, Helen Block Lewis (1971) presented a radically different, and now highly influential, conceptualization of shame and guilt, centering on differences in the role of the self in these experiences:

> The experience of shame is directly about the self, which is the focus of evaluation. In guilt, the self is not the central object of negative evaluation, but rather the thing done or undone is the focus. In guilt, the self is negatively evaluated in connection with something but is not itself the focus of the experience. (p. 30)

According to Lewis, this differential emphasis on self ("*I* did that horrible thing") versus behavior ("I *did* that horrible *thing*") gives rise to very different phenomenological experiences. Shame is an acutely painful emotion typically accompanied by a sense of shrinking or of "being small," and by a sense of worthlessness and powerlessness. Shamed people also feel exposed. Although shame does not necessarily involve an actual observing audience present to witness one's shortcomings, there is often the imagery of how one's defective self would appear to others. Lewis described a split in self-functioning in which the self is both agent and object of observation and disapproval. An observing self witnesses and denigrates the focal self as unworthy and reprehensible. Finally, shame often leads to a desire to escape or to hide—to sink into the floor and disappear.

In contrast, guilt is generally a less painful and devastating experience than shame. Guilt's primary concern is with a particular behavior, somewhat apart from the self, so it does not affect one's core identity. Feelings of guilt can be painful, nonetheless. Guilt involves a sense of tension, remorse, and regret over the "bad thing done." People in the midst of a guilt experience often report a nagging focus or pre-occupation with the transgression—thinking of it over and over, wishing they had behaved differently or could somehow undo the deed.

There is now impressive empirical support for this distinction between shame and guilt from research using a range of methods—including qualitative case study analyses (Lewis, 1971; Lindsay-Hartz, 1984; Lindsay-Hartz, DeRivera, & Mascolo, 1995), content analyses of shame and guilt narratives (Ferguson, Stegge, & Damhuis, 1990; Tangney, 1992; Tangney et al., 1994), participants' quantitative ratings of personal shame and guilt experiences (e.g., Ferguson, Stegge, & Damhuis, 1991; Tangney, 1993; Tangney, Miller, et al., 1996; Wicker, Payne, & Morgan, 1983; Wallbott & Scherer, 1995), and analyses of participants' counterfactual thinking (Niedenthal, Tangney, & Gavanski, 1994). For example, in two independent studies, I asked young adults to describe a personal shame experience and a personal guilt experience, and then rate these experiences along a number of phenomenological dimensions (Tangney, 1993; Tangney, Miller, et al., 1996). The results across the two studies were remarkably consistent. Compared with guilt, shame experiences were rated as significantly more painful and intense. When shamed, people felt physically smaller and more inferior to others. Shame experiences were more likely to involve a sense of exposure and a preoccupation with others' opinions. And when feeling shame, people were more compelled to hide and less inclined to admit what they had done. These and many other studies underscore that shame and guilt are distinct emotional experiences, differing along cognitive, affective, and motivational dimensions, as described by Lewis (1971).

DISPOSITIONAL TENDENCIES TO EXPERIENCE SHAME AND GUILT

I have been discussing differences in the states of shame and guilt (i.e., differences in the phenomenologies of situation-specific experiences of shame and guilt). In my work, I am also concerned with the traits or dispositions "proneness to shame" and "proneness to guilt." Most people have the capacity to experience both shame and guilt at various points in their lives, but it appears that in similar negative situations, some people are more likely to respond with guilt (about a specific behavior), whereas others are more likely to respond with shame (about the entire self). That is, there are stable individual differences in the degree to which people are prone to shame or guilt (Harder, 1995; Harder, Cutler, & Rockart, 1992; Harder & Lewis, 1987; Lewis, 1971; Tangney, 1990, 1991, 1992, 1995a, 1995b; Tangney, Burggraf, & Wagner, 1995; Tangney, Wagner, & Gramzow, 1992). These moral affective styles appear to be well established by at least middle childhood (Burggraf & Tangney, 1990; Tangney, Wagner, Fletcher, & Gramzow, 1991). And these individual differences in proneness to shame and proneness to guilt have been differentially related to a broad range of intrapersonal and interpersonal adjustment characteristics.

A number of methods have been developed in recent years to assess individual differences in shame-proneness and guilt-proneness (Harder & Lewis, 1987; Hoblitzelle, 1987; Tangney, 1990; Tangney, Burggraf, Hamme, & Domingos, 1988; Tangney, Burggraf, & Wagner, 1995; Tangney, Wagner, & Gramzow, 1992; see Tangney, in press, for a discussion of the pros and cons of various measurement strategies). In my scenario-based paper-and-pencil measures (e.g., the TOSCA for adults, the TOSCA–A for adolescents, and the TOSCA–C for children), respondents are presented with a range of situations that they are likely to encounter in day-to-day life, followed by responses that capture phenomenological aspects of shame, guilt, and other theoretically relevant experiences (e.g., externalization, detachment, pride in self, pride in behavior). Respondents are asked to imagine themselves in each situation and then rate their likelihood of reacting in each of the manners indicated. For example, in the adult TOSCA, participants are asked to imagine the following scenario: "You make a big mistake on an important project at work. People were depending on you, and your boss criticizes you." Participants then rate their likelihood of reacting with a shame response ("You would feel like you wanted to hide"), a guilt response ("You would think, I should have recognized the problem and done a better job"), and so forth. Across the various scenarios, the responses capture affective, cognitive, and motivational features associated with shame and guilt, respectively, as described in the theoretical, phenomenological, and empirical literature. It is important to note that these are not forced-choice measures. Respondents are asked to rate, on a 5-point scale, each of the responses. This allows for the possibility that some respondents may experience shame, guilt, both, or neither emotion in connection with a given situation.

Previous research supports the reliability and validity of these measures of shame and guilt. For example, in a recent cross-sectional developmental study (Tangney, Wagner, Barlow, Marschall, & Gramzow, 1996), internal consistency (Cronbach's alpha) estimates of reliability for the TOSCA shame scales were .74 for adults (TOSCA), .74 for college students (TOSCA), .77 for adolescents (TOSCA–A), and .78 for children (TOSCA–C). The internal consistency estimates for the TOSCA guilt scales were .61 for adults (TOSCA), .69 for college students (TOSCA), .81 for adolescents (TOSCA–A), and .83 for children (TOSCA–C). These estimates of internal consistency are generally high, given that the alpha coefficient tends to underestimate reliability due to the situation variance introduced by this scenario approach. (In other words, the items of a given scale share common variance due to the psychological construct of interest, but each item also includes unique variance associated with its own scenario.)

Of the three measures, the TOSCA for adults has been used most extensively. Previous studies offer strong support for the validity of the adult shame and guilt scales in terms of their differential relationship to indices of psychopathology (Gramzow & Tangney, 1992; Tangney, Burggraf, & Wagner, 1994; Tangney, Wagner, & Gramzow, 1992), aspects of interpersonal functioning (Tangney, 1993, 1994; Tangney, Wagner, Fletcher, & Gramzow, 1992), and family functioning (Hamme, 1990; Tangney, Wagner, Fletcher, & Gramzow, 1991). Similarly, a large-scale study of fifth-grade children provided strong evidence for the reliability and validity of the shame and guilt scales from the TOSCA–C (Tangney, Wagner, Burggraf, Gramzow, & Fletcher, 1991; Tangney, Wagner, Fletcher, & Gramzow, 1991). My analyses of the TOSCA–A show comparable evidence for the validity of the adolescent shame and guilt scales, as indicated by their relationship to indices of anger, empathy, and psychological symptoms.

The substantive results from these studies are consistent and compelling. Together, data from a broad range of studies—studies of children, adolescents, college students, and adults from many walks of life—show that proneness to guilt (about specific behaviors) is a fairly adaptive affective style or disposition, especially in the interpersonal realm. In contrast, proneness to shame appears to be a substantial liability, in terms of both individual and interpersonal adjustment (see Tangney, 1995b; Tangney, Burggraf, & Wagner, 1995, for reviews). In the next sections, I describe results from several representative studies to illustrate some of the key findings regarding the dispositional capacity for empathy, dispositional hostility and anger, and people's characteristic anger management strategies.

EMPATHY

The first set of findings concern interpersonal empathy. The findings across numerous studies using diverse measures of shame, guilt and empathy clearly converge: Shame-prone people are not empathic people (Tangney,

1991, 1994, 1995b). And this is significant because, as underscored by the ground-breaking work of Norma Feshbach (1975a, 1975b; Feshbach & Feshbach, 1969) and the many who have followed her, empathy is the "good" moral affective capacity or experience. There's a vast empirical literature indicating that empathy facilitates altruistic, helping behavior (Eisenberg, 1986; Feshbach, 1975b, 1978, 1987; Feshbach & Feshbach, 1986; for a review, see Eisenberg & Miller, 1987), that it fosters warm, close interpersonal relationships, and that it inhibits interpersonal aggression (Eisenberg, 1986; Feshbach, 1975b, 1984, 1987; Feshbach & Feshbach, 1969, 1982, 1986; for a review, see Miller & Eisenberg, 1988). In addition, empathy has been identified as an essential component of numerous valued social processes, including positive parent–child relationships (Feshbach, 1987), effective client–therapist interactions (Rogers, 1975), and individuals' application of moral principles to real-life interpersonal situations (Hoffman, 1987).

Current conceptualizations of empathy emphasize and integrate both cognitive and affective components of empathic responsiveness (Davis, 1980, 1983; Eisenberg, 1986; Feshbach, 1975a). For example, Feshbach (1975a) defined *empathy* as a "shared emotional response between an observer and stimulus person," a response that requires three interrelated skills or capacities: (a) the cognitive ability to take another person's perspective (role-taking or perspective-taking), (b) the cognitive ability to discriminate or to read accurately cues regarding another person's particular emotional experience (affective cue discrimination), and (c) the affective capacity to personally experience a range of emotions (because empathy involves the sharing of another's affective experience in one form or another).

Feshbach and Lipian (1987) developed the Empathy Scale for Adults, a 59-item paper-and-pencil measure adapted from the Parent/Partner Empathy Scale (Feshbach & Caskey, 1987). The measure yields subscales tapping each of the components of empathy described by Feshbach (1975a): Cognitive Empathy (assessing a role-taking or perspective-taking ability— for example, "I try to see things through the eyes of others"), Affective Cue Discrimination (assessing the ability to perceive others' affective states accurately—for example, "I pick up changes in other people's moods that most others miss"), and Emotional Responsiveness (assessing the ability to experience a range of affect—for example, "I find it difficult to hold back tears at weddings").

My colleagues and I included Feshbach and Lipian's (1987) Empathy Scale for Adults and the TOSCA measure of shame-proneness and guilt-proneness (Tangney, Wagner, & Gramzow, 1989) in several recent studies of college undergraduates (Ns = 182, 252, and 244, respectively).

The results from these three samples replicate findings from several earlier studies (Tangney, 1991) in which the Feshbach and Lipian (1987)

Empathy measure and the Self-Conscious Affect and Attribution Inventory (SCAAI; Tangney et al., 1988), the forerunner of the TOSCA, were used. As shown in Table 6.1, a dispositional tendency to experience shame was generally negligibly or negatively correlated with indices of both cognitive and emotional empathy. In contrast, proneness to guilt was positively correlated with a capacity for empathy, especially when considering the Cognitive Empathy and Emotional Arousal dimensions.

These results were even more clear-cut when considering the part correlations, where shame was factored out from guilt, and vice versa. Across numerous studies, I have found a substantial positive correlation between shame-proneness and guilt-proneness (about .42–.48 among college students and adults). This covariation between measures of shame and guilt no doubt reflects the fact that these emotions share a number of common features (e.g., both are dysphoric affects, both involve internal attributions of one sort or another) and that these emotions can co-occur with respect to the same situation. In isolating the unique variance of shame and guilt, respectively, I am focusing on individual differences in a tendency to experience "shame-free" guilt and "guilt-free" shame. As clearly shown in Table 6.1 under guilt residuals, people who are prone to experience feelings of guilt about specific behaviors, uncomplicated by feelings of shame about the self, have a well-developed capacity for other-oriented empathy. In contrast, shame residuals were consistently negatively correlated with indices of both cognitive and emotional empathy.

TABLE 6.1
Relationship of Empathy to Shame-proneness and Guilt-proneness

Empathy Dimensions	N	Bivariate Correlations		Part Correlations	
		Shame	Guilt	Shame Residuals	Guilt Residuals
Cognitive empathy	182	−.08	.24***	−.20**	.31***
	252	−.01	.26***	−.16*	.30***
	244	−.04	.25***	−.14*	.28***
Affective cue discrimination	182	−.09	.13	−.16*	.20**
	252	−.09	.03	−.13*	.10
	244	−.13*	.18**	−.20***	.24***
Emotional arousal	182	.11	.22**	.02	.19*
	252	−.01	.19**	−.13*	.23***
	244	−.10	.18**	−.17**	.22***

*p < .05. **p < .01. ***p < .001.

These findings are consistent with the notion that there is a special link between guilt and empathy (e.g., Eisenberg, 1986; Hoffman, 1982; Zahn-Waxler & Robinson, 1995). By its very nature, guilt steers one in the direction of other-oriented empathic concern (Tangney, 1991, 1995b). In focusing on an offending behavior (as opposed to an offensive self), the person experiencing guilt avoids the egocentric, self-absorbed, self-focus of shame. Rather, in focusing on the specific behavior, one's attention is naturally drawn to the consequences of that behavior for a distressed other, thereby further promoting a continued other-oriented empathic connection.

In contrast, feelings of shame are incompatible with other-oriented empathy reactions in several respects (Tangney, 1991, 1995b). First, shame is typically a very painful emotion that involves a marked self-focus. This preoccupation with the self is likely to draw one's focus away from a distressed other back to the self—in effect, precluding or interrupting other-oriented feelings of empathy. The shamed person is less likely to be concerned with the hurt that was caused and more likely to be consumed with thoughts and concerns about the self—"I am such a horrible person (for having hurt you)." In fact, rather than promoting other-oriented empathic concern, the acute self-focus of shame appears to foster self-oriented personal distress responses (Tangney, 1991, 1995b).

Second, because shame is such a painful emotion, it often motivates a range of defensive maneuvers, each of which may further interfere with feelings of empathy. On one hand, feelings of shame often motivate a desire to withdraw or hide from shame-related situations (Lindsay-Hartz, 1984; Tangney, 1993; Tangney, Miller, Flicker, & Barlow, 1996; Wicker et al., 1983). On the other hand, feelings of shame can motivate feelings of anger—in particular, a hostile, humiliated fury.

SHAME AND ANGER

Lewis (1971) first noted a link between shame and anger (or humiliated fury) in her clinical case studies. In shame, according to Lewis, hostility is initially directed toward the self. But because shame also involves the imagery of a disapproving other, this hostility is easily redirected outward toward others who may be held in part responsible for the shame feeling. This sort of redirected hostility likely serves a defensive function. In redirecting anger outside the self, shamed individuals may be attempting to regain a sense of agency and control, which is so often impaired in the shame experience.

Consistent with this notion, across a range of studies, I have repeatedly found that individuals prone to the ugly feeling of shame also are prone to feelings of outwardly directed anger and hostility (Tangney, 1995b;

Tangney, Wagner, Fletcher, & Gramzow, 1992; Tangney, Wagner, Barlow, Marschall, & Gramzow, 1996). For example, in a study of young adults, the tendency to experience shame was significantly positively correlated with measures of trait anger and indices of indirect hostility, irritability, resentment, and suspicion. In contrast, proneness to "shame-free" guilt (i.e., independent of the variance shared with shame) was negatively or negligibly correlated with these indices of anger and hostility (Tangney, Wagner, Fletcher, & Gramzow, 1992). Similarly, in a study of 363 fifth-grade children (Tangney, Wagner, Burggraf, Gramzow, & Fletcher, 1991), shame-proneness was positively correlated both with boys' self-reports of anger and teacher reports of aggression, whereas guilt was negatively correlated with self reports of anger. Among girls, proneness to shame was also positively correlated with self-reports of anger.

Shame-prone individuals are not only more prone to anger, in general, than their non-shame-prone peers. Once angered, they are also more likely to manage their anger in a destructive fashion. In a recent cross-sectional developmental study involving 302 children (grades 4–6), 427 adolescents (grades 7–11), 176 college students, and 194 adult travelers passing through a large urban airport (Tangney, Wagner, Barlow, Marschall, & Gramzow, 1996), shame was clearly related to maladaptive and nonconstructive responses to anger, across individuals of all ages (8 years through adulthood), consistent with Scheff's (1987, 1995) and Retzinger's (1987) descriptions of the "shame-rage spiral." Shame-proneness was consistently related to malevolent intentions; direct, indirect, and displaced aggression; self-directed hostility; and projected, negative long-term consequences of everyday episodes of anger. In contrast, guilt was generally associated with constructive means of handling anger, including constructive intentions, attempts to take direct corrective action and to discuss the matter with the target of the anger in a nonhostile fashion, cognitive reappraisals of the target's role in the anger situation, and positive long-term consequences.

FEELINGS OF SHAME AND GUILT IN THE MOMENT: IMPLICATIONS FOR INTERPERSONAL BEHAVIOR

So far, I have been considering the implications of shame-prone and guilt-prone dispositions or traits—that is, individual differences in the tendency to experience shame (or guilt) across a range of situations. In interpreting these results, I have been hypothesizing about the effects of situation-specific feelings of shame on, for example, the ability to empathize, the likelihood of becoming angry, and subsequent means of managing that anger. But so far the data have been at the trait or dispositional level. This sort of correlational data at the level of dispositions is open to all sorts of alternative explanations—some other third variable, for example. Recently,

I have begun to take a more direct look at feelings of shame in specific situations and their implications for interpersonal behavior, using three approaches.

Autobiographical Narratives of Shame and Guilt Experiences

The first line of research centers on people's autobiographical accounts of specific shame and guilt experiences. I asked substantial samples of both children and adults to describe a recent personal experience of shame and guilt (Tangney et al., 1994) and then coded these accounts along a range of theoretically relevant dimensions. (These dimensions captured a number of processes relevant to empathy. The coding scheme did not consider issues associated with anger.) One area of interest concerned people's interpersonal focus when describing these personal shame and guilt experiences. Here I found systematic differences in the nature of respondents' interpersonal concerns as they described their personal failures, misdeeds, and transgressions. Among adults, especially, shame experiences were more likely to involve a concern with others' evaluations of the self, whereas guilt experiences were more likely to involve a concern with one's effect on others. This difference in "egocentric" versus "other-oriented" concerns is not that surprising in light of Lewis's (1971) observation that shame involves a focus on the self, whereas guilt involves a focus on a specific behavior. A shamed person who is focusing on negative self-evaluations would naturally be drawn to a concern over others' evaluations of the self, as well. In contrast, a person experiencing guilt who is already relatively "de-centered"— focusing on a negative behavior somewhat apart from the self—is more likely to recognize (and become concerned with) the effects of that behavior on others.

Perhaps more important, when people described guilt-inducing events, they conveyed more other-oriented empathy than when describing shame-inducing events (Tangney et al., 1994). In other words, when considering situation-specific episodes of shame and guilt, coding indices of empathy in these specific situations, I found the same differential link of shame and guilt to empathy as observed in the dispositional studies considering individual differences in proneness to shame, guilt and empathy (Tangney, 1991, 1995b).

Experimental Studies: Inducing Feelings of Shame

The second line of research focusing on shame "states" is a series of laboratory experiments where my colleagues and I induce feelings of shame in participants randomly assigned to a "shame condition" and then examine the effects of the shame induction on empathy, altruism, covert aggression, and so forth. The first in this series of studies was completed in 1996 by Donna

Marschall (as part of her master's thesis). Marschall induced feelings of shame by providing participants with false-negative feedback on a purported intelligence test. After making a fairly public estimate of their test scores, participants in the shame condition were told they scored substantially lower than they had guessed by an experimenter who exchanged shocked, surprised, and then dubious looks with an assistant. (The experiment was immediately followed with extensive "process" debriefing procedures, conducted by carefully trained and closely supervised senior research assistants.)

Marschall found that people induced to feel shame subsequently reported less empathy for a disabled student in an apparently unrelated task immediately afterward. Interestingly, this effect was particularly pronounced among low shame-prone individuals. Consistent with results from my dispositional studies (Tangney, 1991, 1995b), shame-prone individuals were unempathic across the board, regardless of whether they were shamed in the laboratory or not. But among their less shame-prone peers—who show a fair capacity for empathy in general—the shame induction appears to "short-circuit" participants' empathic responsiveness.

I am currently in the midst of a second experimental study, examining the effects of a shame induction on subsequent covert aggression (malicious gossip). Again, the aim is to extend initial findings regarding the interpersonal implications of shame-prone and guilt-prone dispositions, looking for parallel patterns of results at the level of situations.

Real-Life Episodes of Anger: Shame- Versus Non-Shame-Related Events

Finally, my colleagues and I have been examining the implications of situation-specific feelings of shame and guilt in a recent study of about 200 young adult romantically involved couples and a parallel study of about 100 adolescents and their parents. The focus of these studies is on specific real-life episodes of anger. The aim is to delineate factors (situational and dispositional) that foster constructive as opposed to destructive responses to anger in everyday contexts. To this end, I have conducted extensive interviews with the couples and families concerning recent episodes of shared anger. For example, in the couples' study (Tangney, Barlow, Borenstein, & Marschall, in preparation), my colleagues and I first met with the couple together and asked them to identify (but not discuss) two recent events involving anger—one in which the boyfriend had angered the girlfriend and one in which the girlfriend had angered the boyfriend. The couple was then separated and interviewed independently concerning their perceptions, thoughts, and behaviors during the event.

The couples described a broad range of anger-eliciting events. These events varied along a number of dimensions, but one factor of particular interest was whether the event (the offense) caused the victim to feel shame.

Victims were asked if the event had involved "a loss of pride, self-esteem, or personal worth." (I used this as a layperson's description of situation-specific shame, having found that people tend to bristle at the word *shame*.) Thus, the couples' anger events were sorted into two categories, depending on whether the events involved feelings of shame on the part of the victim.

My colleagues and I are still in the midst of coding and analyzing these interviews, but the first set of results from the couples' study strongly support the link between shame and maladaptive responses to anger. First, victims of the shame-related anger events were significantly more angry than victims in the non-shame-related events. Second, shamed victims were more likely to report malevolent and fractious intentions. That is, they tended to be oriented toward getting back at their partner and letting off steam, rather than trying to fix the situation. Third, shamed victims responded to their anger differently from non-shamed victims—they behaved differently. Here, I observed some interesting sex differences. Shamed boyfriends showed a tendency to respond with a range of direct and indirect forms of aggression—behaviors intended to cause harm in one way or another to the perpetrating girlfriend. These shamed boyfriends also were prone to a ruminative anger (thinking about the situation over and over, becoming more and more angry). Whereas shamed boyfriends showed a tendency to lash out at their girlfriends, shamed girlfriends showed a tendency to engage in displaced aggression (aggression displaced onto people and things other than the boyfriend), as well as self-directed hostility. Fourth, and not surprisingly, shamed victims did not feel very good about the way they handled their anger. Shamed girlfriends reported that they felt more embarrassed, anxious, sad, shamed, and surprised about how they handled their anger. (There was also a trend for shamed girlfriends to feel proud—perhaps because of the restraint many showed in these situations.) The aggressive shamed boyfriends reported that they felt dominant, sad, and ashamed about how they handled their anger.

Fifth, these apparently maladaptive expressions of anger did not result in any positive behavior on the part of the shame-inducing perpetrators (especially according to the victims' accounts). Perpetrator's responses to the aggressive retaliation of shamed victims centered on anger, resentment, defiance, and denial—rather than, for example, on apologies and attempts to fix the situation.

Finally, I asked the couples about the long-term consequences of the entire anger episode—considering the event itself, the victim's responses, and the perpetrator's reactions. In no case did the shame-related anger episodes result in more beneficial consequences than the non-shame-related episodes. The consensus was that the situations involving shamed boyfriends were the most destructive, particularly from the girlfriends' perspective. (This makes a great deal of sense, considering the shamed boyfriends' tendency toward overt aggression.) The couples identified the situations involving shamed girlfriends as less problematic. (This is where the girlfriends were prone to engage in displaced and self-directed aggression.) Here, there was a trend for the girlfriends themselves to note negative long-term consequences for the relationship. Boyfriends, not surprisingly, were oblivious.

In sum, these findings regarding situation-specific feelings of shame in the midst of couples' real-life episodes of anger converge nicely with the results from the dispositional studies linking trait shame with trait anger and characteristic maladaptive responses to anger. These data provide a powerful empirical example of the shame-rage spiral described by Lewis (1971) and Scheff (1987), where (a) victim shame leads to feelings of rage, then to (b) destructive retaliation, which then (c) sets into motion partner anger and resentment, as well as (d) expressions of blame and retaliation in kind, which is then (e) likely to further shame the victim, and so forth without any constructive resolution in sight.

CONCLUSION

This portrayal of the implications of shame in everyday life is pretty grim. Shame and guilt are generally regarded as key "moral emotions" that serve important adaptive functions for both the individual and society. Results from a range of empirical studies drawing on diverse samples and methods, however, underscore that shame and guilt may not be equally "moral" or adaptive emotions. Guilt does appear to serve a number of critical relationship-enhancing functions (Baumeister, Stillwell, & Heatherton, 1994, 1995; Tangney, 1991, 1995b). But in many respects, shame seems to represent the darker side of "moral affect." The potentially destructive nature of shame is perhaps most clearly seen in its link to irrational, defensive, retaliative anger, as vividly illustrated in the study of couples' everyday episodes of anger.

Is there a way out—for individuals, couples, families, or nations—embroiled in the "interminable quarrel" of the "shame–rage spiral" (Scheff, 1987)? My guess is that an important path toward resolution, a key to breaking the shame–rage cycle, lies in other-oriented empathy. To the degree that clinicians can help people re-orient toward the other, to decenter from the problematic self-focus of shame, such destructive dynamics can be interrupted.

REFERENCES

Ausubel, D. P. (1955). Relationships between shame and guilt in the socializing process. *Psychological Review, 62,* 378–390.

Baumeister, R. F., Stillwell, A. M., & Heatherton, T. F. (1994). Guilt: An interpersonal approach. *Psychological Bulletin, 115,* 243–267.

Baumeister, R. F., Stillwell, A. M., & Heatherton, T. F. (1995). Interpersonal aspects of guilt: Evidence from narrative studies. In J. P. Tangney & K. W. Fischer (Eds.), *Self-conscious emotions: Shame, guilt, embarrassment, and pride* (pp. 255–273). New York: Guilford Press.

Benedict, R. (1946). *The chrysanthemum and the sword.* Boston: Houghton-Mifflin.

Bradshaw, J. (1988). *Healing the shame that binds you.* Deerfield Beach, FL: Health Communications.

Burggraf, S. A., & Tangney, J. P. (1990, June). *Shame-proneness, guilt-proneness, and attributional style related to children's depression.* Poster presented at the meeting of the American Psychological Society, Dallas.

Cook, D. R. (1988, August). *The measurement of shame: The Internalized Shame Scale.* Paper presented at the annual meeting of the American Psychological Association, Atlanta.

Cook, D. R. (1991). Shame, attachment, and addictions: Implications for family therapists. *Contemporary Family Therapy, 13,* 405–419.

Damon, W. (1988). The moral child: Nurturing children's natural moral growth. New York: Free Press.

Davis, M. H. (1980). A multidimensional approach to individual differences in empathy. *JSAS Catalog of Selected Documents in Psychology, 10,* 85.

Davis, M. H. (1983). Measuring individual differences in empathy: For a multidimensional approach. *Journal of Personality and Social Psychology, 44,* 113–126.

Eisenberg, N. (1986). *Altruistic cognition, emotion, and behavior.* Hillsdale, NJ: Erlbaum.

Eisenberg, N., & Miller, P. A. (1987). Empathy, sympathy and altruism: Empirical and conceptual links. In N. Eisenberg & J. Strayer (Eds.), *Empathy and its development* (pp. 292–316). New York: Cambridge University Press.

Ferguson, T. J., Stegge, H., & Damhuis, I. (1990, March). *Spontaneous and elicited guilt and shame experiences in elementary school-age children.* Poster presented at the annual meeting of the Southwestern Society for Research in Human Development, Dallas.

Ferguson, T. J., Stegge, H., & Damhuis, I. (1991). Children's understanding of guilt and shame. *Child Development, 62,* 827–839.

Feshbach, N. D. (1975a). Empathy in children: Some theoretical and empirical considerations. *Counseling Psychologist, 5,* 25–30.

Feshbach, N. D. (1975b). The relationship of child-rearing factors to children's aggression, empathy, and related positive and negative behaviors. In J. deWit & W. W. Hartup (Eds.), *Determinants and origins of aggressive behavior.* The Hague, Netherlands: Mouton.

Feshbach, N. D. (1978). Studies of empathic behavior in children. In B. A. Maher (Ed.), *Progress in experimental personality research* (Vol. 8, pp. 1–47). New York: Academic Press.

Feshbach, N. D. (1984). Empathy, empathy training and the regulation of aggression in elementary school children. In R. M. Kaplan, V. J. Konecni, &

R. Novoco (Eds.), *Aggression in children and youth*. The Hague, Netherlands: Martinus Nijhoff.

Feshbach, N. D. (1987). Parental empathy and child adjustment/maladjustment. In N. Eisenberg & J. Strayer (Eds.), *Empathy and its development* (pp. 271–291). New York: Cambridge University Press.

Feshbach, N. D., & Caskey, N. (1987). *Feshbach Parent/Partner Empathy Scale*. Los Angeles: University of California.

Feshbach, N. D., & Feshbach, S. (1969). The relationship between empathy and aggression in two age groups. *Developmental Psychology, 1*, 102–107.

Feshbach, N. D., & Feshbach, S. (1982). Empathy training and the regulation of aggression: Potentialities and limitations. *Academic Psychology Bulletin, 4*, 399–413.

Feshbach, N. D., & Feshbach, S. (1986). Aggression and altruism: A personality perspective. In C. Zahn-Waxler, E. M. Cummings, & R. Iannotti (Eds.), *Altruism and aggression: Biological and social origins* (pp. 189–217). Cambridge, England: Cambridge University Press.

Feshbach, N. D., & Lipian, M. (1987). *The Empathy Scale for Adults*. Los Angeles: University of California.

Fossum, M. A., & Mason, M. J. (1986). *Facing shame: Families in recovery*. New York: W. W. Norton.

Freud, S. (1955). Notes upon a case of obsessional neurosis. In J. Strachey (Ed. & Trans.), *The standard edition of the complete psychological works of Sigmund Freud* (Vol. 10, pp. 155–318). London: Hogarth Press. (Original work published 1909)

Freud, S. (1957). Mourning and melancholia. In J. Strachey (Ed. & Trans.), *The standard edition of the complete psychological works of Sigmund Freud* (Vol. 14, pp. 243–258). London: Hogarth Press. (Original work published 1917)

Freud, S. (1961). The economic problem of masochism. In J. Strachey (Ed. & Trans.), *The standard edition of the complete psychological works of Sigmund Freud* (Vol. 19, pp. 159–170). London: Hogarth Press. (Original work published 1924)

Gehm, T. L., & Scherer, K. R. (1988). Relating situation evaluation to emotion differentiation: Nonmetric analysis of cross-cultural questionnaire data. In K. R. Scherer (Ed.), *Facets of emotion: Recent research* (pp. 61–77). Hillsdale, NJ: Erlbaum.

Goldberg, C. (1991). *Understanding shame*. Northvale, NJ: Jason Aronson.

Gramzow, R., & Tangney, J. P. (1992). Proneness to shame and the narcissistic personality. *Personality and Social Psychology Bulletin, 18*, 369–376.

Hamme, H. (1990). *Family correlates of proneness to shame and proneness to guilt*. Unpublished dissertation, Bryn Mawr College.

Harder, D. W. (1995). Shame and guilt assessment and relationships of shame and guilt proneness to psychopathology. In J. P. Tangney & K. W. Fischer (Eds.), *Self-conscious emotions: Shame, guilt, embarrassment, and pride* (pp. 368–392). New York: Guilford Press.

Harder, D. W., Cutler, L., & Rockart, L. (1992). Assessment of shame and guilt and their relationship to psychopathology. *Journal of Personality Assessment, 59,* 584–604.

Harder, D. W., & Lewis, S. J. (1987). The assessment of shame and guilt. In J. N. Butcher & C. D. Spielberger (Eds.), *Advances in personality assessment* (Vol. 6, pp. 89–114). Hillsdale, NJ: Erlbaum.

Harris, P. L. (1989). Children and emotion: The development of psychological understanding. New York: Basil Blackwell.

Hoblitzelle, W. (1987). Attempts to measure and differentiate shame and guilt: The relation between shame and depression. In H. B. Lewis (Ed.), *The role of shame in symptom formation* (pp. 207–235). Hillsdale, NJ: Erlbaum.

Hoffman, M. L. (1982). Development of prosocial motivation: Empathy and guilt. In N. Eisenberg-Berg (Ed.), *Development of prosocial behavior* (pp. 281–313). New York: Academic Press.

Hoffman, M. L. (1987). The contribution of empathy to justice and moral judgement. In N. Eisenberg & J. Strayer (Eds.), *Empathy and its development* (pp. 47–80). New York: Cambridge University Press.

Kaufman, G. (1985). *Shame: The power of caring.* Cambridge, MA: Schenkman.

Kaufman, G. (1989). The psychology of shame: Theory and treatment of shame-based syndromes. New York: Springer.

Kohut, H. (1971). *The analysis of the self.* New York: International Universities Press.

Lewis, H. B. (1971). *Shame and guilt in neurosis.* New York: International Universities Press.

Lindsay-Hartz, J. (1984). Contrasting experiences of shame and guilt. *American Behavioral Scientist, 27,* 689–704.

Lindsay-Hartz, J., De Rivera, J., & Mascolo, M. (1995). Differentiating shame and guilt and their effects on motivation. In J. P. Tangney & K. W. Fischer (Eds.), *Self-conscious emotions: Shame, guilt, embarrassment, and pride* (pp. 274–300). New York: Guilford Press.

Marschall, D. E. (1996). *Effects of induced shame on subsequent empathy and altruistic behavior.* Unpublished master's thesis, George Mason University, Fairfax, VA.

Miller, P. A., & Eisenberg, N. (1988). The relation of empathy to aggressive and externalizing/antisocial behavior. *Psychological Bulletin, 103,* 324–344.

Miller, S. (1985). *The shame experience.* Hillsdale, NJ: Erlbaum.

Morrison, A. P. (1989). *Shame: The underside of narcissism.* Hillsdale, NJ: Analytic Press.

Morrison, N. K. (1987). The role of shame in schizophrenia. In H. B. Lewis (Ed.), *The role of shame in symptom formation* (pp. 51–87). Hillsdale, NJ: Erlbaum.

Nathanson, D. L. (Ed.). (1987). *The many faces of shame.* New York: Guilford Press.

Niedenthal, P., Tangney, J. P., & Gavanski, I. (1994). "If only I weren't" versus "If only I hadn't": Distinguishing shame and guilt in counterfactual thinking. *Journal of Personality and Social Psychology, 67,* 585–595.

Potter-Efron, R. T. (1989). Shame, guilt and alcoholism: Treatment issues in clinical practice. New York: Haworth Press.

Retzinger, S. R. (1987). Resentment and laughter: Video studies of the shame-rage spiral. In H. B. Lewis (Ed.), *The role of shame in symptom formation* (pp. 151–181). Hillsdale, NJ: Erlbaum.

Rodin, J., Silberstein, L., & Striegel-Moore, R. (1985). Women and weight: A normative discontent. In T. B. Sondregger (Ed.), *Psychology and gender: Nebraska symposium on motivation, 1984.* Lincoln: University of Nebraska Press.

Rogers, C. R. (1975). The necessary and sufficient conditions of therapeutic personality change. *Journal of Consulting Psychology, 21*, 95–103.

Scheff, T. J. (1987). The shame-rage spiral: A case study of an interminable quarrel. In H. B. Lewis (Ed.), *The role of shame in symptom formation* (pp. 109–149). Hillsdale, NJ: Erlbaum.

Scheff, T. J. (1995). Conflict in family systems: The role of shame. In J. P. Tangney & K. W. Fischer (Eds.), *Self-conscious emotions: Shame, guilt, embarrassment, and pride* (pp. 393–412). New York: Guilford Press.

Schulman, M., & Mekler, E. (1985). *Bringing up a moral child.* New York: Addison-Wesley.

Tangney, J. P. (1990). Assessing individual differences in proneness to shame and guilt: Development of the self-conscious affect and attribution inventory. *Journal of Personality and Social Psychology, 59*, 102–111.

Tangney, J. P. (1991). Moral affect: The good, the bad, and the ugly. *Journal of Personality and Social Psychology, 61*, 598–607.

Tangney, J. P. (1992). Situational determinants of shame and guilt in young adulthood. *Personality and Social Psychology Bulletin, 18*, 199–206.

Tangney, J. P. (1993). Shame and guilt. In C. G. Costello (Ed.), *Symptoms of depression* (pp. 161–180). New York: John Wiley.

Tangney, J. P. (1994). The mixed legacy of the super-ego: Adaptive and maladaptive aspects of shame and guilt. In J. M. Masling & R. F. Bornstein, (Eds.), *Empirical perspectives on object relations theory* (pp. 1–28). Washington, DC: American Psychological Association.

Tangney, J. P. (1995a). Recent empirical advances in the study of shame and guilt. *American Behavioral Scientist, 38*, 1132–1145.

Tangney, J. P. (1995b). Shame and guilt in interpersonal relationships. In J. P. Tangney & K. W. Fischer (Eds.), *Self-conscious emotions: Shame, guilt, embarrassment, and pride* (pp. 114–139). New York: Guilford Press.

Tangney, J. P., Barlow, D. H., Borenstein, J., & Marschall, D. (in preparation). *Couples in conflict: Implications of shame for the (mis)management of anger in intimate relationships.* Manuscript in preparation.

Tangney, J. P., Burggraf, S. A., Hamme, H., & Domingos, B. (1988, March). *Assessing individual differences in proneness to shame and guilt: The self-conscious affect and attribution inventory.* Poster presented at the meetings of the Eastern Psychological Association, Buffalo, NY.

Tangney, J. P., Burggraf, S. A., & Wagner, P. E. (1995). Shame-proneness, guilt-proneness, and psychological symptoms. In J. P. Tangney & K.W. Fischer (Eds.), *Self-conscious emotions: Shame, guilt, embarrassment, and pride* (pp. 343–367). New York: Guilford Press.

Tangney, J. P., Marschall, D. E., Rosenberg, K., Barlow, D. H., & Wagner, P. E. (1994). Children's and adults' autobiographical accounts of shame, guilt and pride experiences: An analysis of situational determinants and interpersonal concerns. Manuscript submitted for publication.

Tangney, J. P., Miller, R. S., Flicker, L., & Barlow, D. H. (1996). Are shame, guilt and embarrassment distinct emotions? *Journal of Personality and Social Psychology, 70,* 1256–1269.

Tangney, J. P., Wagner, P. E., & Barlow, D. H. (in preparation). *The relation of shame and guilt to empathy: An intergenerational study.* Manuscript in preparation.

Tangney, J. P., Wagner, P. E., Barlow, D. H., Marschall, D. E., & Gramzow, R. (1996). The relation of shame and guilt to constructive vs. destructive responses to anger across the life-span. *Journal of Personality and Social Psychology, 70,* 797–809.

Tangney, J. P., Wagner, P. E., Burggraf, S. A., Gramzow, R., & Fletcher, C. (1991, June). *Children's shame-proneness, but not guilt-proneness, is related to emotional and behavioral maladjustment.* Poster presented at the meetings of the American Psychological Society, Washington DC.

Tangney, J. P., Wagner, P. E., Fletcher, C., & Gramzow, R. (1991, April). Intergenerational continuities and discontinuities in proneness to shame and proneness to guilt. In J. P. Tangney (Chair), *Socialization of emotion in the family.* Symposium conducted at the meetings of the Society for Research in Child Development, Seattle.

Tangney, J. P., Wagner, P. E., Fletcher, C., & Gramzow, R. (1992). Shamed into anger? The relation of shame and guilt to anger and self-reported aggression. *Journal of Personality and Social Psychology, 62,* 669–675.

Tangney, J. P., Wagner, P., & Gramzow, R. (1989). *The Test of Self-Conscious Affect.* Fairfax, VA: George Mason University.

Tangney, J. P., Wagner, P., & Gramzow, R. (1992). Proneness to shame, proneness to guilt, and psychopathology. *Journal of Abnormal Psychology, 103,* 469–478.

Wallbott, H. G., & Scherer, K. R. (1995). Cultural determinants in experiencing shame and guilt. In J. P. Tangney & K. W. Fischer (Eds.), *Self-conscious emotions: Shame, guilt, embarrassment, and pride* (pp. 465–487). New York: Guilford Press.

Wicker, F. W., Payne, G. C., & Morgan, R. D. (1983). Participant descriptions of guilt and shame. *Motivation and Emotion, 7,* 25–39.

Zahn-Waxler, C., & Robinson, J. (1995). Empathy and guilt: Early origins of feelings of responsibility. In J. P. Tangney & K. W. Fischer (Eds.), *Self-conscious emotions: Shame, guilt, embarrassment, and pride* (pp. 143–173). New York: Guilford Press.

7

SELF-REPORTED EMPATHY IN NORWEGIAN ADOLESCENTS: SEX DIFFERENCES, AGE TRENDS, AND RELATIONSHIP TO BULLYING

INGER M. ENDRESEN AND DAN OLWEUS

Empathy or *empathic responsiveness* concerns the reactions of one individual to the experience of another: "a vicarious emotional response to the perceived emotional experience of others" (Mehrabian & Epstein, 1972, p. 525). Barnett (1987) offers a similar, somewhat more elaborate definition: "empathy denotes the vicarious experiencing of an emotion that is congruent with, but not necessarily identical to, the emotion of another individual" (p. 146). In this chapter we review a study that examined sex differences and age trends in empathic responsiveness.

It is common to differentiate between two emotional or affective facets of empathy: empathic concern and personal/empathic distress (Davis, 1983; Lennon & Eisenberg, 1987). Lennon and Eisenberg's (1987) concept of *personal distress* occurs when an individual's vicarious experience of emotion is

Those parts of this chapter that deal with age trends and sex differences in empathic responsiveness are to a considerable degree based on Olweus and Endresen (1998). Adapted with permission. The research program reported on in this chapter was supported by grants from the Ministry of Families and Children's Affairs, the Johann Jacobs Foundation and, in earlier phases, from the Ministry of Education to Dan Olweus, which are gratefully acknowledged.

experienced as a sense of self-concern; the focus of the emotion is on the self rather than on the other. This aspect of empathy is often seen as at least partially related to individuals' own negative arousal and feelings of anxiety, personal unease, and discomfort in reaction to the emotions of others (e.g., Davis, 1983). In *empathic* or *sympathetic concern*, on the other hand, the focus is on the other rather than the self, and there is generally not an exact match between the other's and one's own emotion. These two facets or aspects of empathy may have different developmental courses (Lennon & Eisenberg, 1987) and behavioral consequences (Eisenberg, Carlo, Murphy, & Van Court, 1995; Strayer, 1993). In designing the study reported on in this chapter, we considered it important to pay attention to both aspects of empathic responsiveness.

Cognitive and affective development are likely to influence the nature and extent of empathic responsiveness. Accordingly, the appropriateness of a particular method for the measurement of empathy depends in part on the maturity of the child or youth. These developmental changes make it difficult to ensure that the same constructs are measured when empathic responsiveness is studied in different age groups. The diversity of methods that have been applied in various studies also may account for some of the conflicting results that have been reported with regard to developmental trends in empathic responsiveness (Lennon & Eisenberg, 1987).

Self-report questionnaires are often the preferred method of data collection in studies of school-age children and adolescents. They are easy to administer in large groups, and it is possible to specify responses reflecting different facets of empathy. One objection to this method is the possibility of faulty self-presentation due to social desirability bias. Still, it has not been convincingly shown that this bias is truly a problem with such methods (Bryant, 1982; Mehrabian & Epstein, 1972), and measures relatively free from such bias, like physiological indicators, clearly have other limitations. In any case, our goal in this chapter is not to evaluate different methods, and we will restrict our further discussion to studies based on self-report methods.

Results derived from research with questionnaires indicate that empathic responsiveness tends to increase with age, at least up to the mid-elementary school level, and in general, girls seem to be more empathic than boys (Eisenberg & Lennon, 1983; Feshbach, 1982; Lennon & Eisenberg, 1987). However, results with regard to age trends in school-age children and adolescents are far from conclusive. Some studies indicate a decreasing level of empathic responsiveness (Saklofske & Eysenck, 1983), whereas others show stable or increasing levels (Adams, Schvaneveldt, & Jenson, 1979; Eysenck, Easting, & Pearson, 1984) with varying patterns for boys and girls. Lennon and Eisenberg (1987) demonstrated that empathy seems to increase in the elementary school years, whereas no consistent age-related trends have been identified for participants older than about age 11. The common limitations in the studies reviewed seem to be that different facets of empathy have not been well differentiated and that the number of participants included in several of the studies is small.

One major issue in our study was effect of the sex of the stimulus object. The importance of this concept in research on empathy was suggested in an early study by Feshbach and Roe (1968). Using the now well-known Feshbach and Roe Affective Situation Test for Empathy (FASTE) with slide-sequence stories, they found that 6–7-year-old boys were more empathic with boys than with girls, whereas the converse was true with girls. A study conducted by Bryant in 1982 confirmed and extended these findings. Bryant, using a slightly modified version of the Mehrabian and Epstein (1972) empathy questionnaire and three age groups (Grades 1, 4, and 7), found that both age trends and the magnitude of the sex differences were clearly dependent on the sex of the stimulus object. By using a subset of parallel self-report items with same-sex versus cross-sex stimulus objects, it was shown that the girls' empathic responsiveness to their own sex increased with age, whereas the boys' responsiveness to other boys decreased. In contrast, the trends with regard to the opposite sex were similar (and nonlinear) for boys and girls, with a decrease from Grades 1 to 4 and an increase from Grades 4 to 7. In the study reported in this chapter, we examined possible effects of the sex of stimulus object in somewhat older age groups than those included in the Bryant study.

We will now turn to the second focus of our study, the relationship between empathic responsiveness and aggressive behavior. Empathic concern and distress have been assumed to contribute to the inhibition of aggressive, negative, or externalizing behavior (Davis, 1996; Feshbach & Feshbach, 1986; Miller & Eisenberg, 1988). However, the main motive for inhibition or reduction of such behavior may be different, depending on the dominating emotional reaction. Reduction of one's own negative arousal is assumed to be the key motivating factor when high personal/emphatic distress dominates, whereas empathic concern is more related to altruistic concern for the well-being of the other person and genuine prosocial behavior (Eisenberg & McNally, 1993).

The assumption that empathic responsiveness can contribute to the inhibition of aggressive behavior is supported by a meta-analysis performed by Miller and Eisenberg (1988). They based their analysis on results from nine studies examining the relation between empathy (as measured by self-report questionnaires) and aggression (measured in several ways, including self-reports). The authors concluded that the dominating pattern was a negative association between empathy and aggression. However, the relationship was relatively weak, with an average correlation of -.18. In addition, in most of these studies differentiation between facets of empathic responsiveness was lacking, leaving open the question about the relative contribution of empathic concern versus empathic distress to this relationship.

An exception in this regard is a recent study reported by Davis (1996). In this study of college students, empathic concern was negatively related to self-reports of antagonistic hostility (assaults and verbal hostility), but the associations reached significance only in the female sample. Personal distress, on the other hand, was significantly and positively related to various hostility measures (resentment and suspicion, presumably tapping neurotic hostility), especially in the male sample. Even if complex, the results from this study suggest that it is the tendency to respond with empathic concern, rather than personal distress, that may have an inhibitory effect on aggressive behavior.

The first aim of our study was, then, to examine sex differences and age trends in self-reported empathic responsiveness in four large representative samples of youths, with modal ages ranging from 13 to 16 years. We used scales reflecting empathic concern for boys and girls in distress, respectively, as well as personal distress, and we examined the effects of both same-sex and cross-sex stimulus objects.

A second aim was to explore the associations between the empathy scales and aggressive behavior tendencies measured by self-reports of bullying behavior and a positive attitude toward such behavior. In this context, we were also interested in exploring whether a possible empathy–aggression relationship could be, wholly or in part, "accounted for" by assuming that such an attitude toward bullying serves a mediating function between (dispositional) empathy and (dispositional) aggressive behavior.

THE STUDY

The data used in this study were collected as a part of a large-scale cohort–longitudinal project "The school as a context for social development" under the direction of the second author. The overriding focus of the project was on bully–victim problems in school and, in particular, on the effects of a school-based intervention program against such problems (e.g., Olweus, 1991, 1993, 1994). A total of 2,286 students, 1,093 girls and 1,193 boys, in Grades 6–9 (modal ages 13–16 years) participated in the study (see Olweus & Endresen, 1998, for more details).

We used two self-report questionnaires. The Empathic Responsiveness questionnaire, developed by Olweus, includes 12 items (see Exhibit 7.1) Each item has six response alternatives, from *does not apply at all* (scored as 1) to *applies exactly* (scored as 6). A high score indicates high empathic responsiveness. As in Bryant's modification (1982) of the Mehrabian and Epsteinscale, two sets of four items used identical wordings, except that the stimulus object was a boy in one set and a girl in the other. One of these (parallel) items was taken from the Bryant questionnaire. As in the Bryant study, some of the items focused on relatively strong emotional distress reac-

EXHIBIT 7.1
Items and Scales of Empathy Questionnaire

Girl-as-Stimulus Empathic Concern scale
1. When I see a girl who is hurt, I wish to help her.
6. Seeing a girl who is sad makes me want to comfort her.
7. Seeing a girl who can't find anyone to be with makes me feel sorry for her.

Boy-as-Stimulus Empathic Concern scale
9. When I see a boy who is hurt, I wish to help him.
3. Seeing a boy who is sad makes me want to comfort him.
11. Seeing a boy who can't find anyone to be with makes me feel sorry for him.

Empathic Distress scale
2. It often makes me distressed when I see something sad on TV.
5. Sometimes I feel a bit distressed when I read or hear about something sad.
8. When I see a boy who is distressed I sometimes feel like crying.
10. When I see a girl who is distressed I sometimes feel like crying.

Remaining items
4. I feel very sorry for a student who is being bullied by others.
12. I want to help and comfort a student who is distressed.

Note. Item numbers reflect order of presentation; however, the statements were interspersed with items from other scales.

tions such as crying. However, the present questionnaire included a smaller proportion of such items (only two items as compared with eight in the Bryant study), because crying is presumably considered a somewhat inappropriate reaction by many boys. Two other items focused on the respondent's own distress when seeing, reading, or hearing about sad things.

Based on results from principal component analyses (see Olweus & Endresen, 1998), conceptual considerations, and prior research, three subscales were formed. The Empathic Distress scale consists of four items reflecting feelings of distress (items 2, 5, 8, 10) when exposed to others in distress or when hearing or seeing something sad. The other two subscales reflect sympathetic reactions toward girls (items 1, 6, 7) and boys (items 3, 9, 11) in distress, respectively (see Exhibit 7.1). They were named Girl-as-Stimulus Empathic Concern scale and Boy-as-Stimulus Empathic Concern scale, abbreviated as Girl-as-Stimulus and Boy-as-Stimulus in this chapter. A total score of Empathic Responsiveness, comprising all 12 items, was also computed.

The internal consistency of the scales was high. Chronbach's alpha was .92 for the Total Scale of Empathic Responsiveness, .79 for Empathic Distress, .85 for Boy-as-Stimulus, and .83 for Girl-as-Stimulus.

Two subscales taken from the Olweus Bully/Victim Questionnaire (Olweus, 1989, 1996) were used to assess bullying. One of the subscales includes five items reflecting a positive–negative attitude to bullying—Positive Attitude to Bullying (e.g., "Do you think you could join in bullying a student whom you don't like?"). The second scale comprises four items reflecting participation in bullying behavior—Bullying Others (e.g., "How often have you taken part in bullying another student(s) at school this term?"). Alpha scores for both of these scales was .80.

FINDINGS

Sex and Grade Differences

Sex and grade differences for the total scale and the subscale reflecting empathic distress were assessed with 2 (sex) × 4 (grade) analyses of variance (ANOVAs). The analyses for the Total Scale of Empathic Responsiveness yielded a highly significant effect of sex [$F(1, 2,258) = 573.87, p < .001$], and an interaction effect for sex × grade [$F(3, 2,258) = 6.76, p < .001$]. Girls had clearly higher scores than boys. The effect size value for the total sample, expressed as Cohen's d ($d = X1 - X2/s$, where $X1$ and $X2$ are mean values for the sexes on the Total Scale of Empathic Responsiveness, and s is the pooled standard deviation; see Cohen, 1977), was large, 1.00 (usually, effect size values above .80 are regarded as large; see Cohen, 1977). The interaction effect reflected an increase with grade for girls and a slight decrease for boys. Trend analyses were performed for each sex separately with one-way ANOVAs; a significant linear trend was present in the girl sample [$F(3, 1,089) = 7.30, p < .005$], whereas the decrease for boys did not reach significance.

To make the sex effect findings more concrete, we also examined the relative number of boys and girls at the upper and lower ends of the combined distribution of empathy scores (the approximately 5% highest scoring and lowest scoring participants for the Total Scale of Empathic Responsiveness). It is often at the extreme ends of a characteristic or behavioral dimension that sex (and other) differences may be of particular relevance or societal interest. The proportions of boys and girls were strikingly different. For the whole sample, almost 95% of the participants in the lowest part of the distribution (low in empathy) were boys, whereas 88% in the highest part were girls. For the higher grades, the differences were even more pronounced, with 97% boys at the low-empathy end and 95% girls in the high-empathy part of the distribution. The corresponding values for the lower grades were 76% girls in the high-empathy group and 95% boys at the low-empathy end.

For the Empathic Distress scale there was again a highly significant effect of sex [$F(1, 2,258) = 569.42, p < .001$], significant but weak or relatively weak effects of grade [$F(3, 2{,}258) = 2.75, p < .05$] and the grade $\times$ sex interaction [$F(3, 2{,}258) = 11.26, p < .001$]. The interaction effect mainly reflected the difference in grade/age trends for girls and boys: an increasing linear trend for girls [$F(3, 1{,}089) = 8.82, p < .0001$] and a slowly decreasing linear trend for boys [$F(3, 1{,}189) = 4.42, p < .005$].

Effects of Sex of Stimulus Object

The effects of sex of stimulus object was examined with repeated-measures ANOVA: The Girl-as-Stimulus (Empathic Concern) scale and the Boy-as-Stimulus scale were dependent variables, sex and grade were between-subject factors, and sex of the stimulus was a within-subject factor.

The between-subject analyses yielded results that were in general agreement with the already reported findings, with strong effects of sex of respondent and much weaker effects of grade and the grade $\times$ sex interaction. With regard to the within-subject analyses, there was a strong main effect of sex of stimulus factor [$F(1, 2{,}259) = 588.8, p < .001$]. Also, a number of other effects involving sex of stimulus object were significant or highly significant [for grade $\times$ sex of stimulus, $F(3, 2{,}259) = 3.4, p < .05$; for sex $\times$ sex of stimulus, $F(1, 2{,}259) = 30.4, p < .001$; for grade $\times$ sex $\times$ sex of stimulus, $F(3, 2{,}259) = 39.1, p < .001$]. These findings reflect that, on average, both boys and girls were most empathic when a girl (in distress) was the stimulus. However, the effect of sex of stimulus varied for the two sexes (sex $\times$ sex of stimulus) and to some degree with grade (grade $\times$ sex of stimulus) and with the interaction between sex of respondent and grade (grade $\times$ sex $\times$ sex of stimulus).

These somewhat complex results can be best understood by reference to Figure 7.1. Here it can be seen that there were three roughly parallel, increasing grade trends (two of them significant and one near-significant in one-way trend analyses): for girls in regard to both girls and boys as stimulus objects and for boys with reference to girls as stimuli. The deviating, linearly decreasing trend was associated with boys with respect to boys as stimulus objects. It is also evident from Figure 7.1 that the difference in empathy toward girl and boy stimuli increased with age for the boys, and it narrowed for the girls.

Empathic Responsiveness and Bullying Behavior

The (Pearson) correlations among the empathy scales and the Positive Attitude to Bullying and Bullying Others scales are shown in Table 7.1, for the total sample and separately for the two sexes and grade levels (low and high grades comprise Grades 6 and 7 and Grades 8 and 9, respectively). Positive Attitude to Bullying and Bullying Others were significantly associated (in a negative direction) with the various scales reflecting empathic

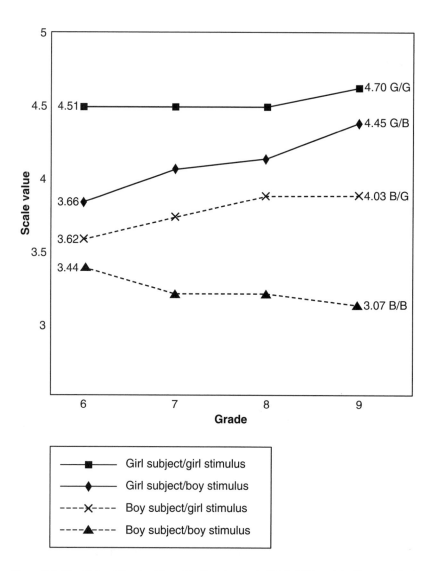

Figure 7.1. The Girl-as-Stimulus Empathic Concern scale (G/G, B/G) and the Boy-as-Stimulus Empathic Concern Scale (G/B, B/B) as a function of sex, grade, and sex of stimulus object.

Note. From "The Importance of Sex-of-Stimulus Object: Age Trends and Sex Differences in Empathic Responsiveness," by D. Olweus & I. M. Endresen, 1998, *Social Development, 7,* p. 380. Copyright 1998 by Blackwell Publishers. Reprinted with permission.

concern; for boys and girls alike, the correlations were substantial for the attitude scale and considerably lower (but still significant) for the scale reflecting bullying behavior. In addition, the attitude scale evinced weaker correlations with the Empathic Distress scale than with the scales of empathic concern, and the correlations between the Bullying Others scale and Empathic Distress were nonsignificant and close to zero.

TABLE 7.1.

Correlations among the Empathy scales and the Bullying scales.
Correlations are shown for the total samples of boys and girls
and for low and high grades separately.

	Positive Attitude to Bullying			Bullying Others		
	Total	Low	High	Total	Low	High
Girls						
Empathy Scales						
Total scale	−.41**	−.44**	−.40**	−.15**	−.11**	−.18*
Girl-as-Stimulus	−.42**	−.43**	−.40**	−.17**	−.15**	−.19*
Boy-as-Stimulus	−.34**	−.34**	−.35**	−.11**	−.04	−.15*
Empathic Distress	−.25**	−.28**	−.21**	−.06	−.03	−.07
Positive Attitude to Bullying	—	—	—	.46*	.42**	.51**
Boys						
Empathy Scales						
Total scale	−.40**	−.36**	−.45**	−.15**	−.15*	−.15*
Girl-as-Stimulus	−.24**	−.22*	−.27*	−.07	−.08	−.05
Boy-as-Stimulus	−.42**	−.41**	−.42**	−.19**	−.17*	−.21*
Empathic Distress	−.20**	−.16*	−.24*	−.02	−.04	−.02
Positive Attitude to Bullying	—	—	—	.48**	.49**	.47**

Note. Low grades = Grades 6–7; High Grades = Grades 8–9.

* = p < .05. ** = p < .01, two-tailed.

The correlation between the scales measuring bullying behavior and attitude to bullying was .51 in the total sample, and varied between .42 and .51 when the sample was broken down by sex and grade.

This pattern of correlations between empathic concern, attitude to bullying, and bullying behavior suggests the possibility that the participants' attitude to bullying may mediate an "effect" of (dispositional) empathic concern on bullying behavior. To examine this possibility in more detail, we conducted a number of regression analyses. Bullying Others served as the dependent variable, Positive Attitude to Bullying was entered at the first step in the analyses (as a predictor variable), and the empathy measures (one scale in each analysis) at the second step. These analyses were done separately for boys and girls as well as for the total sample, for low and high grades, and for the four combinations of sex and grade. Empathy was not found to contribute significantly to predicted or explained variance in Bullying Others when Positive Attitude to Bullying had been controlled for (entered first in the analyses). Accordingly, these results are consistent with the hypothesis that the "effects" of (dispositional) empathy are mediated by a (negative) attitude to bullying (cf. Baron & Kenny, 1986).

With regard to Empathic Distress, it was not considered meaningful to explore a possible mediating role for attitude to bullying, because the direct relationship (correlation) between this scale and Bullying Others was basically zero for both boys and girls. It is also worth emphasizing that the relationship between Empathic Distress and the aggressive behavior scale in this study did not differ for the two sexes, in contrast to what Davis (1996) found in his study of college students.

INTEGRATING THE FINDINGS

Sex-of-Subject Effect

In agreement with a number of previous studies of empathy using self-reports (see reviews by Eisenberg & Fabes, in press; Eisenberg & Lennon, 1983), we found a marked sex-of-subject effect favoring girls. Overall, without differentiating according to the sex of the stimulus object, the scores for both the Total Scale of Empathic Responsiveness and Empathic Distress were higher for girls than for boys, and the sex difference actually increased with age. Expressed in correlational terms, the point-biserial correlation between sex of subject and total empathy, for example, was .45 (for the total sample), with subject sex "accounting for" 20% of the variance of the dependent variable. It might be argued that 20% of the variance "explained" only reflects a relatively modest association. However, as previously demonstrated, the differences in the relative proportions of boys and girls at the extreme ends of the empathy distribution were striking, especially for the higher grades (Grades 8 and 9 combined). The results imply relative constancy across grades of the proportions of boys and girls at the low-empathy end of the distribution, with a massive predominance of low-empathic boys, whereas the portion of highly empathic boys actually decreased with increasing age. These marked differences in the relative proportions of boys and girls at the extreme ends of the empathy dimension make it clear that the conventional index "amount of variance explained" may underestimate the strength of an association (cf. e.g., Abelson, 1985; Rosenthal & Rubin, 1982).

In the more comprehensive analyses including sex of the stimulus as a factor, we also found, in addition to the already noted sex-of-subject effects, a strong sex-of-stimulus effect. Girls and boys responded with much more empathy toward a girl than toward a boy in distress. It is worth noting that these results represented opposite tendencies for boys and girls with regard to the sex of subjects with whom they empathized most: Girls were most empathic with stimuli of their own sex, whereas boys showed most empathy toward the opposite sex.

Although these sex-of-respondent to sex-of-stimulus interactions are important and we will discuss them further (in the context of age effects), the basic conclusion that girls responded more empathically than boys to another youth in distress is still generally valid for our data. How can this marked sex-of-respondent effect be explained? We will not go into detail at this point but limit ourselves to a brief consideration of a common explanation of such differences.

It has been hypothesized that sex differences in empathy, as measured by questionnaires, may to some extent reflect demand characteristics or social desirability biases (e.g., Eisenberg & Lennon, 1983; Lennon & Eisenberg, 1987). According to this argument, men and women may differ in how empathic they would like to appear to others (and, perhaps, to themselves), and such a mechanism may then underlie the reported overall sex difference in empathic concern in our study. However, results from studies examining this possibility are mixed. Some researchers report basically no association between empathy measures and social desirability scores (Bryant, 1982; Mehrabian & Epstein, 1972), whereas others report positive relations (Eisenberg & McNally, 1993). It is also noteworthy that some studies have shown that correction of test scores for social desirability reduces the validity of the test (McCrae et al., 1989; Nicholson & Hogan, 1990), thereby suggesting that social desirability scores actually reflect true variance rather than a confounding influence.

Although it is our basic conviction that, by and large, the main differences reported in this study actually reflect real differences in empathic responsiveness, it cannot be ruled out that demand characteristics or social desirability biases play some role in explaining the overall sex differences obtained. At the same time, we note that there is relatively little direct empirical support for such interpretations in the literature. In addition, a demand characteristic explanation would no doubt be of little help in explaining the more complex but distinct trend patterns identified in the present study.

Age Trends in Empathic Concern Involving Sex of Stimulus for Girls and Boys

As demonstrated in Figure 7.1 and related analyses, differentiation of the items with regard to sex of stimulus object was of critical importance for the discovery of the age trends in empathic concern that were present for boys and girls in our study. Girls showed the most straightforward development, with an increase in empathic concern toward girl and boy stimuli. The boys evinced a roughly similar developmental pattern with regard to girls as stimuli but showed a deviating, decreasing trend in empathic responsiveness toward stimuli of their own sex.

If differentiation according to sex of stimulus object had not been made in the questionnaire, it is likely that our findings would have shown a general developmental increase in empathic concern in girls and a basically flat or stable curve for boys (judging from the nonsignificant trend for boys for the Total Scale of Empathic Responsiveness or for a combined Girl-as-Stimulus and Boy-as-Stimulus variable). The latter curve (for boys) would then have represented a kind of average of two diverging developmental curves and actually concealed the opposite trends in empathic concern identified for boy or girl stimuli, respectively. Failure to consider the sex of stimulus in research on empathy is probably the main explanation for the inconsistent and inconclusive results that have been reported for developmental trends in empathic responsiveness from age 11 and upward. As noted in the introduction, researchers who did not differentiate the items in terms of sex of stimulus have found decreasing, stable, and increasing levels in school children and adolescents, with varying patterns for boys and girls. In this context, it is interesting to note that the markedly different developmental findings reported by Bryant (1982), when analyses were differentiated according to sex of stimulus object, have been largely neglected by the field.

What, then, is the overall relationship of self-reported empathic responsiveness to age? The answer will obviously depend on the sex of respondent, the sex of stimulus object, the particular aspect or facet of empathy studied, and the age range concerned. With regard to empathic concern, the different trends in our own data for ages 13–16 have already been briefly discussed. However, if we make certain assumptions about the comparability of our results with those of Bryant (1982), our conclusions can be broadened. These assumptions concern a rough equivalence of the dimensions measured (Bryant's two sets of sex-of-stimulus-differentiated items and our two subscales) and of the levels of empathic concern identified for the various combinations of sex of subject and sex of stimulus in the overlapping subject groups (the seventh graders with a probable modal age of 13 years in the Bryant study and our youngest subject group with the same modal age). The relative order of the means for the four groups for the seventh graders in Bryant's study (and the younger groups) is exactly the same as the one identified for the corresponding age groups in Figure 7.1 (Grade 6).

Given that these equivalence assumptions are roughly justified, we can conclude that, in girls, empathic concern for other youths in distress increases steadily with age, from age 10 up to age 16 at least. This is true with regard to girl and boy stimuli, although the levels of empathic concern are generally higher toward girls as stimuli (same-sex stimuli). In boys, however, the developmental results are more critically dependent on the sex of the stimulus object: With girls in distress as stimuli (cross-sex stimuli), we find an increasing developmental trend that is largely parallel to the one for girls overall. With boys as stimuli (same-sex stimuli), however, there is a steadily decreasing trend in empathic concern with age, from age 10 up to at least age 16 . (We do not include Bryant's findings for the youngest group age 7 in our generalizations because we see these results as more uncertain, due to the small number of participants on which they were based: 27 girls and 29 boys.)

Our findings for the boys run counter to the hypothesis that participants tend to respond more empathically to others who are similar to themselves, for instance in terms of sex and race (Hoffman, 1982; Krebs, 1970). However, results consistent with such an idea are found for the fourth graders in Bryant's study (Bryant, 1982), where both boys and girls showed most empathic concern for stimulus objects of their own sex. Accordingly, it appears that, for boys, there occurs a reversal in average degree of empathic concern for own-sex as contrasted with cross-sex stimulus objects some time between ages 10–13. From age 13 (or possibly somewhat earlier) and older, boys tend to express more empathic concern for girls than for boys in distress, as already noted. For girls, on the other hand, there are no indications of such reversals and, on average, they empathize most with other girls across the whole of the considered age span.

It should be emphasized that these generalizations apply to the particular facet of empathic responsiveness that we have defined as empathic concern and measured with questionnaire items. It is not clear to what extent they would apply if empathy were measured with other techniques as described in the introductory part of the chapter. Actually, relatively little is known about the developmental course of empathic responsiveness measured with other than self-report methods.

With regard to the other facet of empathy differentiated in the present study, Empathic Distress, the age trend for girls was of the same generally increasing form as for Empathic Concern, whereas the curve for boys was slightly decreasing. The latter result is fairly similar to what was found for boys with regard to Empathic Concern for other boys, although the decline in responsiveness with age seems to be less marked for Empathic Distress. In any case, these findings make us agree with Lennon and Eisenberg (1987), who emphasize that it is important to specify what particular facet of empathy is concerned when determination of age trends (and other comparisons) are at issue.

Some Explanations

How can the developmental changes we and others have found in empathy be explained? We will focus here on the facet of Empathic Concern and pay particular attention to the increase with age in empathic responsiveness identified overall for girls and for boys with regard to girls as stimulus objects. In addition, it is important to understand the deviating developmental trend for boys in regard to boys as stimuli.

As mentioned, cognitive and affective developments are likely to influence the nature and extent of an individual's empathic responsiveness.

Although such dimensions have not been investigated in the present research, it is reasonable to assume that maturational changes in these areas may account for part of the generally increasing developmental trends identified above. It is important to emphasize in this context that an increasing trend was found also for boys, in regard to girls as stimuli. The deviant decreasing trend in empathy toward other boys therefore cannot be adequately explained with reference to a general deficit or delay in cognitive or affective maturation in boys.

In a similar vein, one might explain the pattern of findings with reference to a general reluctance or inability in adolescent boys to communicate or even experience more tender feelings such as empathic concern. Also, this general male emotional inexpressiveness hypothesis is not viable, however, because the findings show convincingly that the boys were able and willing to communicate such affective states and reactions (although at lower level of intensity than girls) if the stimulus object was a girl.

These inadequate or insufficient attempts at explanation direct our attention to theoretical mechanisms that involve some kind of sex role expectations (however derived). Such role expectations concern behavior toward individuals of the same and opposite sex. Also, it is natural to assume that the influence of such expectations will become gradually stronger for older age groups, as the participants approach adulthood.

From such a general perspective, the boys' decrease in empathic concern for other boys may reflect an increasing identification with a masculine role and a desire to live up to expectations and ideals associated with masculinity. To feel concern for another boy in distress (who is not defined as a best friend) probably does not fit well with macho ideals held by many adolescent boys (Archer, 1992). The associated attitudes may also contain an element of contempt for weakness (cf. Olweus, 1978), and it is reasonable to assume that at least some proportion of boys in our study may have felt somewhat threatened by thoughts about being in distress (sad, hurt, or socially isolated). In response to such reactions, they may have tried to dissociate themselves defensively from such scenarios by adopting a condescending, nonempathic attitude.

In formulations derived from evolutionary psychology, or modern Darwinism (Archer, 1996; Buss, 1994), behaviors and attitudes of this kind are viewed as originating from intermale competition, and they should consequently concern and be directed to other men in particular. As stated by Archer (1996), "It is necessary for men to avoid signs of vulnerability in a masculine competitive environment that emphasizes the importance of toughness and reputation. To show feelings of vulnerability is to open oneself to exploitation." (p. 914). A more circumscribed mechanism of male emotional inexpressiveness in relation to other males, evolved over long periods of time, may thus be a major factor in the explanation of the decreasing levels of empathic concern in boys.

In contrast, the boys' increasing empathic concern for girls in distress can in part be seen as a reflection of the growing interest in and attraction to individuals of the opposite sex. To feel sorry for and to be somewhat protective of a girl in distress may not only be seen as acceptable, but in fact as part of a masculine role by adolescent boys. As mentioned, such tendencies are expected to become gradually stronger with increasing age. Also, our findings of boys' increasing empathic concern for girls seem to fit well with predictions from a modern (and old) Darwinian perspective.

For women, the situation is quite different. A feminine role and associated expectations not only allow empathic reactions, but are actually likely to contribute to the fostering of an empathic orientation in women. This orientation may involve tendencies to care for and nurture others and young children in particular, to provide emotional support to others, and generally to be tender-minded and emotionally sensitive and expressive (Archer, 1996; Eagly, 1987; Feingold, 1994; Grossman & Wood, 1993). From this perspective, it is natural that the girls in our study (as in other studies) responded with more empathic concern than the boys, and that their empathic responsiveness gradually increased as they approached adulthood. Again, these results agree well with predictions from an evolutionary paradigm.

In attempting to explain our overall pattern of findings for age trends and sex differences, we have stressed an evolutionary psychological perspective, which is based on principles of sexual selection. A main assumption in this theoretical approach is that sex differences reflect the different fitness requirements, or reproductive strategies, of men and women, and the interaction between them (Archer, 1996). Dispositions based on evolutionary processes are thus viewed as being the origin of present-day sex differences in social behavior. This does not, however, in any way rule out cultural influences such as gendered socialization in the generation of these differences. Such influences are understood in terms of coevolutionary processes that accentuate (or modify) evolved dispositions. Generally, gendered socialization is viewed as reflecting the future adaptive requirements of men and women in society and as making a distinct contribution to present-day sex differences in social behavior (Archer, 1996).

EMPATHIC RESPONSIVENESS AND BULLYING OTHERS

Another key aim of our study was to examine the relationship between empathic responsiveness and bullying behavior. Generally, we found for both boys and girls and across all grade levels the expected negative relationship between the scale reflecting aggressive behavior and the various measures of empathic concern. However, the empathy–aggression relationship was somewhat weaker than it is often assumed to be in the public debate, with negative correlations in the .10–.20 range. On the other hand, our findings fit well with results from previous related studies, as summarized in the above-mentioned meta-analysis (Miller & Eisenberg, 1988), negative, but weak, assoications were the dominating pattern.

The results from our regression analyses were consistent with the hypothesis that the participants' attitudes to bullying may mediate (all of) the effect of (dispositional) empathic concern on bullying behavior. Participants who score high on empathic concern are likely to have a more negative attitude to bullying, which in turn will reduce their involvement in bullying behavior. It should of course be emphasized that these analyses do not prove a causal empathy–attitude–aggression relationship; they show, however, that the associations among the implicated variables are compatible with such an interpretation. In addition, in this context a possible inhibitory effect of empathic concern on bullying is likely to be relatively weak.

The scale of Empathic Distress, however, had comparably much weaker correlations with the scales reflecting aggressive behavior and attitudes. These results support the idea that the scale of Empathic Distress in part measures something different than the scales of Empathic Concern (see above and Olweus & Endresen, 1998) and generally attest to the usefulness of separating the total empathy scale into subscales of concern and distress. The total pattern of correlations also suggests that it is the tendency to respond with empathic concern, rather than with empathic distress, that may have an inhibitory effect on aggressive behavior.

SUMMARY AND CONCLUSION

A major goal of the study described in this chapter was to examine age trends and sex differences in empathic responsiveness, particularly empathic concern for others in distress. The empirical analyses showed that differentiation of the items with regard to sex of stimulus object was of critical importance for the discovery of the age trends that were present for boys and girls. Girls showed the most straightforward development, with an increase in empathic concern toward girl and boy stimuli with age. The boys evinced a similar developmental pattern with regard to girls as stimuli but showed a clearly deviating, decreasing trend in empathic concern for other boys in distress. Failure to consider sex of stimulus object is probably the main explanation for the inconsistent results previously reported for developmental trends in empathic responsiveness from age 11. In addition, and in agreement with previous research, we found very marked sex differences, with a strong predominance of low-empathic boys and a similarly marked predominance of high-empathic girls. To explain the complex but consistent trend patterns identified in the present study, we mainly stressed an evolutionary psychological perspective. This is of course not to deny that the results may also be compatible with, at least in part, other theoretical orientations such as social role theory (e.g., Eagly, 1987).

The second major issue dealt with in this study was the relationship between empathic responsiveness, bullying behavior, and attitudes to bullying. In agreement with the meta-analysis by Miller and Eisenberg (1988) we found a negative, relatively weak, empathy–aggression relationship. The results from the correlation analyses also supported the suggestion that it is the tendency to respond with empathic concern when exposed to another person in distress that may have an inhibitory effect on aggressive behavior. More detailed analyses within a path-analytic framework showed that the results were consistent with a mediator interpretation: A possible inhibitory effect of empathic concern on bullying behavior was mediated by the participants' attitude to bullying. Taken together, the diverging results for Empathic Distress and Empathic Concern in the correlation analyses and the demonstrated effect of the sex of stimulus object underscore the usefulness of separating the empathy measure into subscales to attain a more differentiated picture of the relationships of empathic responsiveness to other variables.

REFERENCES

Abelson, R. (1985). A variance explanation paradox: When a little is a lot. *Psychological Bulletin, 97*, 129–133.

Adams, G. R., Schvaneveldt, J. D., & Jenson, G. O. (1979). Sex, age and perceived competency as correlates of empathic ability in adolescence. *Adolescence, 14*, 811–818.

Archer, J. (1992). Childhood gender roles: Social context and organization. In H. McGurk (Ed.), *Childhood social development: Contemporary perspectives* (pp. 31–61). Hove, England: Erlbaum.

Archer, J. (1996). Sex differences in social behavior. Are the social role and evolutionary explanations compatible? *American Psychologist, 51*, 1–9.

Barnett, M. A. (1987). Empathy and related responses in children. In N. Eisenberg & J. Strayer (Eds.), *Empathy and its development* (pp. 147–162). New York: Cambridge University Press.

Baron, R. M., & Kenny, D. A. (1986). The moderator-mediator variable distinction in social psychological research: Conceptual, strategic, and statistical considerations. *Journal of Personality and Social Psychology, 51*, 1173–1182.

Bryant, B. K. (1982). An index of Empathy for children and adolescents. *Child Development, 53*, 413–425.

Buss, D. (1994). *The evolution of desire: Strategies for human mating.* New York: Basic Books.

Cohen, J. (1977). *Statistical power analysis for the behavioral sciences* (rev. ed.). New York: Academic Press.

Davis, M. H. (1983). The effects of dispositional empathy on emotional reactions and helping: A multidimensional approach. *Journal of Personality, 51,* 167–184.

Davis, M. H. (1996). *Empathy: A social psychological approach.* Dubuque, IA: Williams C. Brown.

Eagly, A. H. (1987). *Sex differences in social behavior: A social role interpretation.* Hillsdale, NJ: Erlbaum.

Eisenberg, N., Carlo, G., Murphy, B., & Van Court, P. (1995). Prosocial development in late adolescence: A longitudinal study. *Child Development, 66,* 1179–1197.

Eisenberg, N., & Fabes, R. A. (in press). Prosocial development. In W. Damon (Ed.), *Handbook of child psychology* (5th ed.).

Eisenberg, N., & Lennon, R. (1983). Sex differences in empathy and related capacities. *Psychological Bulletin, 94,* 100–131.

Eisenberg, N., & McNally, S. (1993). Socialization and mother's and adolescents' empathy-related characteristics. *Journal of Research on Adolescence, 3,* 171–191.

Eysenck, S. B. G., Easting, G., & Pearson, P. R. (1984). Age norms for impulsiveness, ventureness, and empathy in children. *Personality and Individual Differences, 5,* 315–321.

Feingold, A. (1994). Gender differences in personality: A meta-analysis. *Psychological Bulletin, 116,* 429–456.

Feshbach, N. D. (1982). Sex differences in empathy and social behavior in children. In N. Eisenberg (Ed.), *The development of prosocial behavior* (pp. 315–338). New York: Academic Press.

Feshbach, S., & Feshbach, N. D. (1986). Aggression and altruism: A personality perspective. In C. Zahn-Waxler, F. M. Cummings, & R. Iannotti (Eds.), *Altruism and aggression: Biological and social origins* (pp. 189–217). New York: Cambridge University Press.

Feshbach, N. D., & Roe, K. (1968). Empathy in six- and seven-year olds. *Child Development, 39,* 133–145.

Grossman, M., & Wood, W. (1993). Sex differences in intensity of emotional experience: A social role interpretation. *Journal of Personality and Social Psychology, 65,* 1010–1022.

Hoffmann, M. L. (1982). Development of prosocial motivation: Empathy and guilt. In N. Eisenberg (Ed.), *Development of prosocial behavior* (pp. 281–313). New York: Academic Press.

Krebs, D. (1970). Altruism—An examination of the concept and a review of the literature. *Psychological Bulletin, 73,* 258–302.

Lennon, R., & Eisenberg, N. (1987). Gender and age differences in empathy and sympathy. In N. Eisenberg & J. Strayer (Eds.), *Empathy and its development* (pp. 195–217). New York: Cambridge University Press.

McCrae, R. R., Costa, P. T., Grant Dahlstrom, W., Barefoot, J. C., Siegler, I. C., & Williams, R. B. (1989). A caution on the use of the MMPI K-correction in research on psychosomatic medicine. *Psychosomatic Medicine, 51,* 58–65.

Mehrabian, A., & Epstein, N. (1972). A measure of emotional empathy. *Journal of Personality, 40*, 525–543.

Miller, P. A., & Eisenberg, N. (1988). The relationship of empathy to aggressive and externalizing/antisocial behavior. *Psychological Bulletin, 103*, 324–344.

Nicholson, R. A., & Hogan, R. (1990). The construct validity of social desirability. *American Psychologist, 45*, 290–292.

Olweus, D. (1978). *Aggression in the schools: Bullies and whipping boys.* Washington, DC: Hemisphere.

Olweus, D. (1989). *The Olweus Bully/Victim Questionnaire* [Mimeo]. HEMIL-senteret, Universitetet i Bergen, Norway.

Olweus, D. (1991). Bully/victim problems among schoolchildren: Basic facts and effects of a school based intervention program. In D. Pepler & K. Rubin (Eds.), *The development and treatment of childhood aggression* (pp. 411–448). Hillsdale, NJ: Erlbaum.

Olweus, D. (1993). *Bullying at school: What we know and what we can do.* Oxford, England: Blackwell.

Olweus, D. (1994). Annotation: Bullying at school: Basic facts and effects of a school based intervention program. *Journal of Child Psychology and Psychiatry, 35*, 1171–1190.

Olweus, D. (1996). *The Revised Olweus Bully/Victim Questionnaire* [Mimeo]. HEMIL-senteret, Universitetet i Bergen, Norway.

Olweus, D., & Endresen, I. M. (1998). The importance of sex-of-stimulus object: Age trends and sex differences in empathic responsiveness. *Social Development, 7*, 370–388.

Rosenthal, R., & Rubin, D. B. (1982). A simple general purpose display of magnitude of experimental effect. *Journal of Educational Psychology, 74*, 166–169.

Saklofske, D. H., & Eysenck, S. B. G. (1983). Impulsiveness and venturesomeness in Canadian children. *Psychological Reports, 52*, 147–152.

Strayer, J. (1993). Children's concordant emotions and cognitions in response to observed emotions. *Child Development, 64*, 188–201.

8

REVELLER OR STRIVER? HOW CHILDHOOD SELF-CONTROL PREDICTS ADULT BEHAVIOR

LEA PULKKINEN

For a long time I have been interested in investigating developmental paths that arise from constructive and destructive behavior in childhood. By *destructive behavior* I mean a noncollaborative or dominating behavior that initiates, escalates, or intensifies a conflict. The most common form of destructive behavior is aggression. *Constructive behavior*, on the other hand, means a collaborative or conciliatory behavior that de-escalates or inhibits potential future aggressive exchanges.

In psychological literature concerned with the study of personality the term *personality trait* is used to refer to the characteristic behavior of an individual. In adulthood, individual differences may be rather stable and fixed and unrelated to currently existing environmental factors. In childhood the process of formation of behavioral outcomes as the interaction between individual and environmental factors is more visible. In a developmental chain, individual differences observed in children's destructive and constructive behavior are both outcomes of the interaction between individual and environmental factors and stimuli to or resources for further interaction. To a certain extent, an individual's new possibilities for development are opened up or limited by his or her own behavior.

The problems that I discuss in this chapter concern the development of destructive and constructive paths beginning in childhood. My interest was to question whether children's destructive or constructive behavior is predictive of respective adult outcomes. I review several studies based on the same longitudinal data and compare their results with the findings of other researchers.

JYVÄSKYLÄ LONGITUDINAL STUDY OF PERSONALITY AND SOCIAL DEVELOPMENT

The Point of Departure

The Jyväskylä Longitudinal Study of Personality and Social Development began in 1968 as a study of interindividual differences in 8-year-old children's social behavior. The problems and hypotheses of the study have to be understood within the framework of psychological research and theory formation in the 1960s. Three trends were particularly salient at that time: (a) the dominance of trait orientation in the study of personality due to factor-analytic studies by, for instance, Cattell (1957) and Eysenck (1960); (b) the emergence of social learning theory as a result of the work of Bandura (Bandura & Walters, 1963); and (c) the increased recognition of the interface of emotion and cognition (Lazarus, 1966; Schachter & Singer, 1962).

My own studies on children's aggression had made me skeptical about the interpretation of aggression as a personality trait. Rather, I understood aggression as a behavior which, despite its biological basis, varied in strength in children's behavioral repertoire depending on learning history. Besides quantitative differences, I found that aggression was not a unified construct. There were qualitative differences in aggression between individuals (see Tremblay, 2000). For instance, there were differences in reactive and proactive aggression. The type and intensity of aggression seemed to depend on the context of behavior and social learning. Furthermore, any type of aggressive behavior was characteristic of only a small proportion of children.

There was a need to learn more about individual differences in social behavior, especially those suggesting positive social development. By the end of the 1960s, few studies had been conducted on prosocial behavior. Among the few exceptions were the study by Block and Martin (1955) on constructive behavior manifested by children under conditions of frustration and the studies by N. Feshbach and Roe (1968) and N. Feshbach and

S. Feshbach (1969) on empathy as an alternative to aggression. In the 1960s, psychological research was oriented to psychopathology, anxiety, and aggression rather than to aspects of healthy functioning and prosocial behavior, which gradually emerged as a focus of study in the 1970s and 1980s.

Nonaggression was generally referred to in psychological literature as "inhibition of aggression." From the psychodynamic point of view, inhibition of aggression was negatively evaluated because it might result in personality pathology. My criticism of this interpretation of nonaggressive behavior is based on the idea that human beings are able to regulate their emotions cognitively and consequently end up with nonaggressive, constructive behavior. In the 1960s, emotions were understood as states; the study of emotional regulation is a more recent phenomenon.

I studied the question about how children could avoid aggressive responses (i.e., what kind of alternative modes of social behavior existed in children's groups) with 8-year-old children. A theoretical framework was an impulse control model that I devised (Pitkänen, 1969; Pitkänen-Pulkkinen, 1979) and later modified (Pulkkinen, 1982, 1986). More recently it was relabeled as a model of emotional and behavioral regulation (Pulkkinen, 1995).

The two-dimensional model defines four behavioral types, differentiated by high or low self-control of emotions, and social activity versus passivity (Figure 8.1). Low self-control of emotions may be indicated either by the display of negative emotions in an externalizing way such as in aggressive behavior or by being overwhelmed by a negative emotion such as anxiety. In the latter, actions that could change the situation are inhibited. Correspondingly, high self-control of emotions may be indicated by constructive behavior in which an individual controls the display of negative emotions and acts to change the situation or by compliant behavior in which the person controls the expression of negative emotions and avoids an active involvement in the situation. Here, *emotion* refers to a mostly negative emotional state subject to control and *emotion regulation* to the redirection, control, and modification of this state, which enables an individual to function adaptively as suggested by Cicchetti, Ganiban, and Barnett (1991; see Shields & Chicchetti, 1997; Walden & Smith, 1997).

The quality of self-control of emotions is determined by several factors. As explained elsewhere (Pulkkinen, 1995), high self-control of emotions is facilitated by (a) high regulation of reactivity as a temperamental characteristic (Derryberry & Rothbart, 1984, 1997); (b) parental socialization that supports the development of the processes involved in emotion regulation; (c) transitory state, such as positive mood; (d) perceptions that increase comprehension of the situation and anticipations of successful coping; and (e) maturity. In contrast, in low self-control of emotions, an individual's attention in a situation focuses on cues that intensify a negative

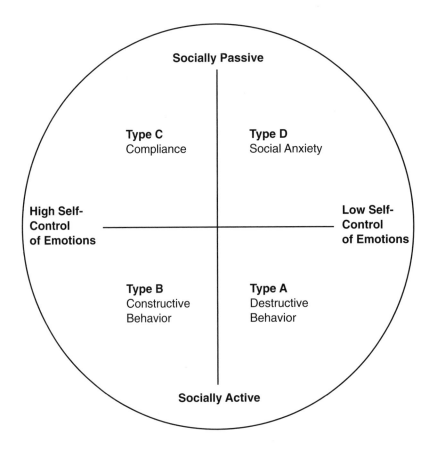

Figure 8.1 Constructive and destructive behavior within the framework of emotional and behavioral regulation. From "Behavioral Precursors to Accidents and Resulting Physical Impairment," by L. Pulkkinen, 1995, Child Development, 66, p. 1661. Copyright 1995. Adapted with permission.

emotion, for instance, anger or fear. The intensification is facilitated by low temperamental regulation of reactivity, poor parental socialization, negative moods, limited perceptions and anticipations of an emotional confrontation, and immaturity.

In this chapter, I focus on constructive and destructive behaviors (Type A and Type B). The model defines constructive and destructive behavior as overtly active reactions in an interactive situation and differentiates them on the basis of self-control of emotions. In my research, all four behavioral patterns (constructive, destructive, compliant, and anxious behavior) were obtained in children's behavior, and they were predictive of different styles of social behavior in late adolescence (Pulkkinen, 1982). Destructive behavior (i.e., aggression at age 8), was predictive of the style of life called *Reveller*. It was characterized by gathering with friends, drinking, smoking, and heterosexual interaction. This kind of pleasure-seeking behavior correlated with conflicts with the parents, weak tolerance, and feeling of aggression. Low self-control in childhood is related to poor strategies of emotional regulation in adulthood (Kokkonen & Pulkkinen, 1999). In contrast, constructive behavior in childhood was predictive of the style of life called *Striver* in which high self-control of emotions was related to optimistic expectations about the future, good success in studies, and responsible attitudes toward oneself and society.

The parents' socioeconomic status was not associated with the children's destructive behavior and only slightly associated with their constructive behavior (Pulkkinen, 1982). Child-centered, authoritative parenting promoted the development of the children's self-control and constructive behavior. In contrast, adult-centered parenting (i.e., authoritarian or indifferent behavior toward the child) correlated with aggressive behavior and other indicators of weak self-control at a later age, such as early experiments with tobacco and alcohol and norm-breaking behavior (Pulkkinen, 1982). The effects of harsh and abusive parenting on juvenile problem behavior have also been found (Fergusson & Lynskey, 1997). Below, I describe the method and provide more detail on the studies' findings.

Participants and Major Data Waves

Of a sample consisting of 196 boys and 173 girls, most participants (93.5%) were born in 1959. The average age of the participants was 8 years, 8 months. They were drawn from second-grade pupils as a sample of 12 school classes. One half of the classes were located in the center, and the other half in the suburbs of the medium-size town of Jyväskylä, which has about 70,000 inhabitants and is a busy university and industrial center of the province of Central Finland.

When the participants were age 14 a follow-up study of social behavior was conducted with 189 boys and 167 girls (96% and 97% of the original sample, respectively). Data were collected in 1974. In six years the participants had spread out from 12 school classes to 78. In 1974, approval to do an interview with the child and either of the parents was obtained from 154 parents of selected participants, representing all the basic behavioral patterns. In 1989–1990, the participants ($n = 135$) were interviewed again.

At age 27, all participants of the original sample were traced for a follow-up study in 1986. A mailed Life Situation Questionnaire was completed by 166 men and 155 women (85% and 90%, respectively), and 150 men and 142 women (77% and 82%, respectively) were interviewed. At age 36, all participants were traced again for a follow-up study in 1995. Three male participants had died. A mailed Life Situation Questionnaire was completed by 160 men and 151 women (82% and 87%, respectively), and 146 men and 137 women (76% and 79%, respectively) were interviewed.

No systematic reason for attrition in the mailed questionnaire at ages 27 and 36 could be found on the basis of data collected at age 8. The participants at age 36 represented the whole age cohort born in 1959 when compared with census data on education, marital status, and unemployment. The unemployment rate was 18% in 1995 both in the sample and in the age cohort born in 1959 because of a severe economic recession in Finland.

Measurements

Behavioral characteristics were studied at age 8 using peer nomination and teacher rating (Pitkänen, 1969; Pulkkinen, 1998). In peer nomination, each participant was asked to name same-sex subjects in his or her class who displayed specific behaviors. For example, the participant was asked to identify anyone "who may hurt another child when angry, e.g., by hitting, kicking, or throwing something." Of the 33 variables, 12 concerned aggressive behavior. They were chosen to represent different types of observable aggression in the framework of a model characterizing aggressive acts (Pulkkinen, 1987). Other variables represented nonaggressive behavioral patterns (anxious, constructive, compliant) as described in the model used as the framework of the study and characteristics of social behavior, for example, leadership and disobedience. Constructiveness was operationalized by three questions: "Who tries to act reasonably even in annoying situations?" "Who thinks that if one negotiates, everything will be better?" and "Who sides with smaller and weaker peers?" The participants were asked to name at least three same-sex children who displayed the kind of behavior that the item described. A participant's score (expressed in percentages) for each variable was formed by the "votes" he or she received in the class (votes given in relation to the number of voters). In teacher rating, these items were worded as statements, and teachers rated all pupils on a four-point scale (3 = *characteristic in question is very prominent*, 0 = *never observed the characteristic in question*).

At age 14, the number of rating variables was reduced to nine descriptions of behavior (for destructiveness, "Who attacks without reason, teases others, says naughty things?" and for constructiveness, "Who tries to solve annoying situations reasonably, negotiates, conciliates, strives for justice?"). In addition to the item for proactive aggression mentioned above, ratings were made on an item for reactive (defense-limited) aggression ("Who defends himself if teased, but does not attack without reason?"). Peer nominations were made in all school classes (78) that contained at least one participant from the original sample. Because of the move from elementary school to lower secondary school and the change of teachers and class structures, peers had changed. Consequently, nominations at the ages of 8 and 14 were largely independent.

Teacher ratings for students at age 14 were collected on the same pupils, using the same items as the peer nominations. In addition, teachers rated the pupils' behavior in some additional items, such as popularity among classmates. Data about school success were obtained from school archives.

Also at age 14, part of the sample (154 participants) and one of the parents were also interviewed. The semistructured interview lasted from 1 to 2 hours and covered many life domains, including environmental conditions and upbringing. The scale for parenting consisted of 10 items that loaded on the factor for child-centered versus adult-centered parenting (Männikkö & Pulkkinen, in press; Pulkkinen, 1982). Parental support included the following items: the parents know his or her leisure-time company, know where the child spends his or her leisure time, encourage school attendance, are sympathetic with regard to failure at school, consider the child's opinion, and implement reasonable restrictions and sanctions.

At ages 27 and 36, the Life Situation Questionnaire consisted of more than 200 questions about marital status, children, housing, length of education, work history, drinking habits, financial status, subsistence aid, satisfaction with different aspects of life, and so forth. *Career* was defined as stable or unstable based on the length of the periods of unemployment. *Problem drinking* was defined on the basis of an alcoholism screening test and arrests for public drunkenness (Pulkkinen & Pitkänen, 1994).

The interview at ages 27 and 36 was semistructured, with the difference that, at age 36, the interview included several structured parts and inventories, such as the Karolinska Scales of Personality (af Klinteberg, Schalling, & Magnusson, 1990), the Conflict Tactics Scales (Strauss, 1992), and the Aggression Questionnaire (Buss & Perry, 1992). At age 33, a Big Five Personality Inventory, an authorized adaptation of the NEO Personality Inventory (Costa & McCrae, 1985), was presented with the participants.

Criminal registers were examined at ages 20, 26, 31, and 36. At ages 20 and 26 two registers were examined: (a) the government register, which includes information about offenses for which the sentence has been imprisonment, and (b) the local, more informal register held by the police. The latter included information about petty offences (e.g.,, arrests for public drunkenness). At ages 31 and 36, only government registers were examined.

DESTRUCTIVE BEHAVIOR

Stability of Aggression from Childhood to Adulthood

A question that is typically investigated in longitudinal studies is the stability of behavior over years (i.e., whether a person's ranking on a particular variable remains the same or changes with time). There is a considerable stability in aggression (Loeber & Hay, 1997; Olweus, 1979), and differences between the genders are smaller than is generally assumed. Cairns and Cairns (1994) stated, in connection with teacher ratings on school-age children, that the median eight-year stability correlation of aggression was 0.44, whereas the median one-year stability correlation was 0.51. The stability correlations of teacher ratings on aggression were very similar for boys and girls, a finding also obtained from peer-ratings by Lefkowitz, Eron, Walder, and Huesmann (1977). When the length of the time interval became longer in the latter study (extending from ages 8 to 30), peer-rated aggression predicted scores in hostility inventories more highly in the case of men than for women (Huesmann, Eron, Lefkowitz, & Walder, 1984).

In agreement with the above-mentioned results, peer-nominated aggression was rather stable over the school years for both boys and girls (.35–.37, $p < .001$) in the Jyväskylä Longitudinal Study too, but teacher-rated aggression did not show stability for girls (Pulkkinen & Pitkänen, 1993). For girls, teacher ratings were biased by school adjustment. They predicted female drinking problems at age 27 better than did peer nominations.

Peer nominations and teacher ratings on aggression in early school-age children predicted self-ratings on aggression in adulthood only slightly, but if ratings were made in adolescence, stability correlations were higher (Table 8.1). Correlations reached statistical significance for men between ages 8 and 36 but were insignificant for women. However, peer nominations on male and female aggression at age 14 correlated significantly with self-reports on aggression at age 27 (.22 for men and .20 for women, $p < .01$ and .05, respectively; Pulkkinen & Pitkänen, 1993), as well as at age 36. For women, peer-nominated aggression in adolescence also predicted women's marital disagreement at age 36 as defined on the basis of the Conflict Tactics Scales invented by Strauss (1992). Higher scores indicate physical and verbal aggression as conflict-solving tactics.

TABLE 8.1

Intercorrelations of Aggression Variables from Ages 8 to 36 (Correlations for Females Above the Diagonal, for Males Below the Diagonal)

Variable	1	2	3	4
1. Aggression, age 8[a]		37***	06	10
2. Aggression, age 14[a]	35***		15*	20*
3. Aggression, age 36[b]	15*	21**		53***
4. Marital disagreement, age 36	14	−05	39***	

[a]Aggression at ages 8 and 14 was measured by peer nomination.

[b]Aggression at age 36 was measured by the Aggression Questionnaire (Buss & Perry, 1992).

*$p < .05$. **$p < .01$. ***$p < .001$.

Proactive and Reactive Aggression

Peer nominations on aggression in adolescence were based on the question covering aggressive initiatives (proactive aggression). For instance, in teacher ratings, proactive aggression predicted the perception of an aggressive personality more than reactive aggression (Pitkänen, 1969). Proactive and defense-limited reactive aggression in adolescence also predicted different outcomes at age 27 (Pulkkinen, 1996b). A comparison of (a) reactively aggressive, (b) proactively aggressive, and (c) nonaggressive adolescents revealed that proactively aggressive boys at age 27 were more extroverted, used more alcohol, were arrested more often, and had experienced more nonnormative life events (change of residence, workplace, partner, etc.) than did the other men. In contrast, proactively aggressive girls at age 27 were more neurotic, had less education, smoked more cigarettes, and used more alcohol than did the other women.

Reactively aggressive adolescents and the nonaggressive adolescents had higher self-control in childhood, adolescence, and adulthood than proactively aggressive adolescents. Defense-limited aggression correlated with constructive behavior and better adult adjustment than proactive aggression. Reactively aggressive girls had longer education and more stable careers than did other women. The nonaggressive adolescents were more compliant, passive, or anxious and less aggressive as adults than were the other groups.

Heterotypic Continuity from Aggression to Adult Outcomes

In addition to homotypic continuity over time in behavior that is subsumed under the same conceptual construct (such as aggression), there may be heterotypic continuity among behaviors that look different but that share theoretically interpretable common qualities. I have tested the hypothesis concerning heterotypic continuity from early aggression to adult problem drinking and criminality. For problem drinking, the results have supported the assumptions. Ratings, especially teacher ratings, on aggression at ages 8 and 14 predicted male problem drinking at ages 27 and 36 (the average correlation for teacher ratings was .21; $p < .01$; Pulkkinen & Pitkänen, 1993). Correlations were somewhat lower for women, but mostly significant. Self-reports on aggression at ages 27 and 36 correlated with problem drinking at these ages for men but not for women.

Aggressive behavior in adolescence predicted the likelihood that a person would live in a cohabitation rather than in a marriage at age 36 (Kovanen, 1998). Similarly, it predicted an unstable career, even long-term unemployment (Kokko, Pulkkinen, & Puustinen, 2000), but less if the aggressive child had also displayed constructive behavior (Kokko & Pulkkinen, 2000). The accumulation of problems in social functioning, such as problem drinking, criminality, poor financial status, poor intimate relations, few friends, and unstable career, was rooted in destructive behavior in childhood and in home adversities (Rönkä, 1999; Rönkä & Pulkkinen, 1995).

Several studies have demonstrated continuity from child aggression to adolescent and adult criminal behavior in men (Farrington, 1991; Hämäläinen & Pulkkinen, 1996; Loeber, 1988; Loeber & Hay, 1997; Pulkkinen, 1983; Stattin & Magnusson, 1989, 1996). In the Jyväskylä Longitudinal Study, the number of arrests by age 27 (including petty offences from the local police register but excluding alcohol-related offences such as public drunkenness) correlated with peer-nominated and teacher-rated aggression at age 8 from .33 to .35 ($p < .001$; Pulkkinen & Pitkänen, 1993). The correlations were insignificant for women; the number of arrests was small among women. I have also demonstrated that early aggressiveness in men predicts more serious criminality (convictions, several types of offenses, and recidivism) better than less serious criminality (arrests, one type of offense, and occasional criminality; Hämäläinen & Pulkkinen, 1995; Pulkkinen & Hämäläinen, 1995).

After age 27, the number of arrests decreased remarkably. Between the ages 15 and 26, 30 out of 196 men in the original sample were convicted, but from ages 27 to 36 only 4 men who had no previous criminal record were convicted. A declining trend after age 26 was also seen among men who had a criminal record. In the interview conducted at age 36, men claimed that they had decreased their offending because of maturation, another person's (often a wife's) influence, environmental changes, and the negative consequences of offending. A few men said, however, that they had increased their norm-breaking behavior. They attributed this to restrictions set by the social services authorities or to the low morality of society in general.

In the interpretation of correlations between early aggressiveness and later criminality, it should be noted that the correlations observed may be caused only by the individuals with the most salient problems. When the most aggressive individuals (above the 75th percentile) were excluded from correlative analyses, correlations between aggressiveness and criminality turned out to be insignificant (Pulkkinen & Hämäläinen, 1995). Significant predictive correlations may be explained by continuity in the behavior of the few most prominently aggressive and criminal individuals.

PATTERNED CHARACTERISTICS AND DESTRUCTIVE BEHAVIOR

Magnusson and Bergman (1990; Bergman & Magnusson, 1997) have strongly advocated the use of a holistic person-oriented approach to the study of behavioral continuity, in which the patterning of characteristics is considered. They have demonstrated that problem behavior is patterned in preadolescence, and that different patterns are predictive of adult behavior in different ways. Multiproblem patterns, including aggressiveness, restlessness, lack of concentration, and low school motivation, predicted multiple adjustment problems, especially criminality and alcohol abuse.

In accordance with the Swedish findings of Magnusson and Bergman (1990; Bergman & Magnusson, 1997), the results of the Jyväskylä Longitudinal Study have shown that criminal offences were best predicted if the accumulation of behavior problems over the school years was considered (Pulkkinen, 1992a, 1992b). Similar findings were also obtained in a comparative study between Finland and Canada (Pulkkinen & Tremblay, 1992). Childhood aggressiveness did not predict arrests without the presence of other problems (Hämäläinen & Pulkkinen, 1996). The risk for offenses of a variety of types was highest among boys who exhibited many types of escalating behavioral problems (aggressiveness at age 8, conduct problems and school failure at age 14). A fewer number of behavioral problems resulted in qualitatively different offenses: Childhood aggressiveness followed by norm-breaking in early adolescence predicted violent offenses, but early aggressiveness followed by poor school success (but not by conduct problems) in early adolescence predicted property offenses.

Researchers' results are consistent with other researchers findings that there were early-onset offenders (a life-course type), adolescent offenders (a limited-duration type), and adult offenders (a late-onset type; Loeber & Stouthamer-Loeber, 1998; Moffitt, 1993; Patterson, Capaldi, & Bank, 1991). Each category constituted about one third of all offenders. Childhood aggressiveness was most strongly related to early-onset offending and least strongly to adolescent offending. Adolescent offending could not be predicted on the basis of behavior problems that emerged before early adolescence (Hämäläinen & Pulkkinen, 1995, 1996). The results suggest that there are different mechanisms in the development of antisocial behavior. Family adversities and early aggressiveness constitute one of them, and another mechanism can possibly be explained on the basis of youth development and youth culture.

CONSTRUCTIVE BEHAVIOR

Continuity

Continuity in constructive behavior is studied much less often than is continuity in destructive behavior. In the Jyväskylä Longitudinal Study of Personality and Social Development, constructiveness showed significant stability from ages 8 to 14 and particularly in boys: The correlation coefficient was .23 for boys and .19 for girls in teacher ratings ($p < .001$ and .01, respectively) and .29 for boys and .11 for girls in peer nominations ($p < .001$ and NS, respectively; Pitkänen-Pulkkinen, 1981).

Constructive behavior helps the pupil adapt to school work and the peer group. Constructiveness at age 8 predicted school success and popularity at age 14 as well as length of education and stable work career by age 27 (Table 8.2; Pulkkinen, 1998). For women, early constructiveness also predicted marital satisfaction. In contrast, adult problem drinking, criminality, and financial problems were negatively related to constructiveness in childhood and adolescence.

Among women, constructive behavior at age 8 was related to a good intimate relationship at age 36 ($r = .24$, $p < .05$) and to a higher age at the birth of the first child ($.22$, $p < .05$); aggression at age 8 was associated with early motherhood ($-.18$, $p < .05$). Risk factors such as low self-control of emotions, poor school success, and home adversities increased the likelihood of early motherhood, but early motherhood had only an indirect effect through low work involvement on the accumulation of social functioning problems (Rönkä & Pulkkinen, 1998).

Career Orientation

Constructive behavior, social activity, strong self-control of emotions, and school success at ages 8 and 14 are significant determinants of career orientation in women at age 36 as shown by Pulkkinen, Ohranen, and Tolvanen (1999) using structural equation modeling. Among men, more passive behavior, compliance at age 8, also predicted career orientation. Career orientation was defined according to Ruggiero and Weston (1988) on the basis of socioeconomic status, length of education, current work status, and stability of working career.

Low career orientation, on the other hand, was predicted by low self-control of emotions: anxiety, passivity, and poor school success among women, but aggressive behavior and poor school success among men. It demonstrates a gender difference between internalizing and externalizing behaviors as predictors of problem behavior; both are indicators of low self-control of emotions as shown by the model in Figure 8.1. In general, behavioral characteristics were stronger predictors of career orientation in women than in men. This gender difference was particularly clear when the stability of career line was to be predicted (Pulkkinen et al., 1999).

CONSTRUCTIVE AND DESTRUCTIVE BEHAVIOR AND PERSONALITY TRAITS

Constructive behavior at age 8 correlated with the Socialization scale of the Karolinska Scales of Personality at age 36 for men ($.24$, $p < .05$, for

TABLE 8.2
Correlations of Constructive Behavior With Variables for Academic and Social Success

Variable	Age 8				Age 14			
	Teacher Rating		Peer Nomination		Teacher Rating		Peer Nomination	
	Females	Males	Females	Males	Females	Males	Females	Males
School success, age 14	33***	38***	33***	41***	60***	41***	30***	49***
Popularity, age 14	24**	22**	14	19**	35***	37***	29***	19*
Parental socioeconomic status	13	-01	20*	16*	07	08	-04	-07
Parental support, age 14	21*	05	21*	09	45***	25**	26**	22*
Length of education, age 27	24**	39***	29***	22**	12	29***	08	14
Stable work career, age 27	14	31***	18*	25***	25**	15	16	17*
Problem drinking, age 27	-17*	-11	-22**	-13	-17*	-19*	-18*	-16*
Criminality, age 27	-16*	-17*	-13	-09	-11	-23***	-09	-12
Marital satisfaction, age 36	26**	06	22*	04	07	-06	-07	-03
Recipient of subsistence aid, age 36	-16*	-17*	-23**	-14	-06	-18*	-10	-14

Note.

*p < .05. **p < .01. ***p < .001.

men; $p < .08$ for women), whereas aggression at age 8 was negatively associated with Socialization ($-.30$, $p < .01$ for men; $-.14$, NS, for women). Aggressive behavior at age 14 was related to the Impulsivity scale of the Karolinska Scales of Personality at age 36 ($r = .24$ for women and .23 for men, $p < .01$) and to low scores in the Conscientiousness scale of the Big Five Personality Inventory at age 33 in women (.24, $p < .05$; .12 for men). Aggressive behavior at age 8 correlated with low Agreeableness at age 33 in men (.25, $p < .05$; .14 for women) (Kovanen, 1998).

CONCLUSION

The results of the Jyväskylä Longitudinal Study have shown that there is continuity in both destructive and constructive behavior over a period of many years. Children who exhibit Type A (aggressive) or Type B (constructive) behavior (cf. Figure 8.1) are likely to follow different life paths to adulthood. Constructiveness appeared to facilitate school adjustment and career development that are characteristic of positive social functioning, whereas aggressive behavior tended to pattern with other problem behaviors.

Constructiveness in childhood implies a low risk for criminal offences, whereas low prosociality has a significant independent relationship to arrests (Hämäläinen & Pulkkinen, 1996). Low prosociality is related to low peer-group status, unpopularity, and peer rejection, which have been found to be linked to subsequent antisocial behavior (Coie & Dodge, 1998; Farrington, 1994; Loeber & Hay, 1997).

Different developmental paths for constructive and destructive behavior were also found in the study of adult personality styles and their background (Pulkkinen, 1996a, 1998). Adjusted adults, especially men, who displayed a positive adaptation to life had been more constructive in childhood than conflicted adults who had been more destructive in childhood.

The development of constructive and destructive behavior before the school years is a crucial issue. Because these behavior types seem to be crystallized by age 8, they are rather powerful predictors of adult developmental outcomes. There may be inherent temperamental differences that, in interaction with parenting behavior and other environmental variables, pave the way to individual differences in social behavior. Recent studies suggest, for instance, that secure attachment to parents in childhood may be an important protective factor for development.

In the framework of the Big Five personality traits, constructive and destructive behaviors are most likely to be exhibited by individuals characterized by high or, respectively, low Agreeableness. As suggested by Graziano and Eisenberg (1997), both highly agreeable and disagreeable behaviors may have a temperamental basis which may lead to different socialization experiences. Emotional individuals become more distressed when exposed to emotional stimuli than nonemotional individuals (Buss & Plomin, 1984). Besides affectional self-regulatory processes, there may be motivational differences in striving for intimacy and solidarity within the groups to which individuals belong (Wiggins, 1991).

Many children are exposed to risk factors such as destructive models and marital conflicts to such an extent that without strong protection and support from the parents they are vulnerable to maladjusted behavior and low school motivation, and later, to limited options for career development (Fergusson & Lynskey, 1997; Stattin & Magnusson, 1996). Discontinuous histories of behavior problems are more likely to exist if children come from backgrounds in which levels of risk are intermediate compared with those children who show persistent conduct problems or no problems (Fergusson, Lynskey, & Horwood, 1996).

The results showed that constructive behavior indicating good problem-solving abilities is correlated with school success and supportive or child-centered parenting. Positive characteristics and life conditions tended to accumulate. Similarly, the present study showed that destructive development correlated with adult-centered parenting involving authoritarian and/or neglecting parenting. Children who are temperamentally vulnerable to low self-regulation and exposed to family adversities are at a higher risk for the accumulation of social-functioning problems than children who are temperamentally more able to modulate their reactivity (Rönkä & Pulkkinen, 1995). The child's characteristics develop in interaction with his or her environment.

REFERENCES

af Klinteberg, B., Schalling, D., & Magnusson, D. (1990). Childhood behavior and adult personality in male and female subjects. *European Journal of Personality*, 4, 57–71.

Bandura, A., & Walters, R. H. (1963). *Social learning and personality development*. New York: Holt, Rinehart & Winston.

Bergman, L. R., & Magnusson, D. (1997). A person-oriented approach in research on developmental psychopathology. *Development and Psychopathology*, 9, 291–319.

Block, J. H., & Martin, B. C. (1955). Predicting the behavior of children under frustration. *Journal of Abnormal and Social Psychology*, 51, 281–285.

Buss, A. H., & Perry, M. (1992). The Aggression Questionnaire. *Journal of Personality and Social Psychology*, 63, 452–459.

Buss, A., & Plomin, R. (1984). *Temperament: Early developing personality traits*. Hillsdale, NJ: Erlbaum.

Cairns, R. B., & Cairns, B. D. (1994). *Lifelines and risks: Pathways of youth in our time*. Cambridge, England: Cambridge University Press.

Cattell, R. B. (1957). *Personality and motivation: Structure and measurement.* London: Harrap.

Cicchetti, D., Ganiban, J., & Barnett, D. (1991). Contributions from the study of high-risk populations to understanding the development of emotion regulation. In J. Garber & K. A. Dodge (Eds.), *The development of emotion regulation and dysregulation* (pp. 15–48). New York: Cambridge University Press.

Coie, J. D., & Dodge, K. A. (1998). Aggression and antisocial behavior. In N. Eisenberg (Ed.), *Social, emotional, and personality development: Handbook of child psychology* (Vol. 3, pp. 779–862). New York: Wiley.

Costa, P. T., & McCrae, R. R. (1985). *The NEO Personality Inventory manual.* Florida: Psychological Assessment Resources.

Derryberry, D., & Rothbart, M. K. (1984). Emotion, attention, and temperament. In C. E. Izard, J. Kagan, & R. B. Zajonc (Eds.), *Emotions, cognition, and behavior* (pp. 132–166). New York: Cambridge University Press.

Derryberry, D., & Rothbart, M. K. (1997). Reactive and effortful processes in the organization of temperament. *Development and Psychopathology, 9,* 633–652.

Eysenck, H. J. (1960). *The structure of human personality.* London: Methuen.

Farrington, D. P. (1991). Childhood aggression and adult violence: Early precursors and later life outcomes. In K. H. Rubin & D. Pepler (Eds.), *The development and treatment of childhood aggression* (pp. 169–188). Hillsdale, NJ: Erlbaum.

Farrington, D. P. (1994). Childhood, adolescent, and adult features of violent males. In L. R. Huesmann (Ed.), *Aggressive behavior: Current perspectives* (pp. 215–240). New York: Plenum Press.

Fergusson, D. M., & Lynskey, M. T. (1997). Physical punishment/maltreatment during childhood and adjustment in young adulthood. *Child Abuse & Neglect, 21,* 617–630.

Fergusson, D. M., Lynskey, M. T., & Horwood, L. J. (1996). Factors associated with continuity and changes in disruptive behavior patterns between childhood and adolescence. *Journal of Abnormal Child Psychology, 24,* 533–553.

Feshbach, N., & Roe, K. (1968). Empathy in six and seven year olds. *Child Development, 39,* 133–145.

Feshbach, N. D., & Feshbach, S. (1969). The relationship between empathy and aggression in two age groups. *Developmental Psychology, 1,* 102–107.

Graziano, W. G., & Eisenberg, N. H. (1997). Agreeableness: A dimension of personality. In R. Hogan, J. Johnson, & S. Briggs (Eds.), *Handbook of personality psychology* (pp. 795–824). San Diego: Academic Press.

Hämäläinen, M., & Pulkkinen, L. (1995). Aggressive and non-prosocial behaviour as precursors of criminality. *Studies on Crime and Crime Prevention, 4,* 6–21.

Hämäläinen, M., & Pulkkinen, L. (1996). Problem behavior as a precursor of male criminality. *Development and Psychopathology, 8,* 443–455.

Huesmann, L. R., Eron, L. D., Lefkowitz, M. M., & Walder, L. O. (1984). Stability of aggression over time and generations. *Developmental Psychology, 20,* 1120–1134.

Kokko, K., & Pulkinnen, L. (2000). Agression in childhood and long-term unemployment in adulthood: A cycle of maladaptation and some protective factors. *Developmental Psychology, 36,* 463–472.

Kokko, K., Pulkkinen, L., & Puustinen, M. (2000). Selection into long-term unemployment and its psychological consequences. *International Journal of Behavioral Development., 24,* 310–320.

Kokkonen, M., & Pulkkinen, L. (1999). Emotion regulation strategies in relation to personality characteristics indicating low and high self-control of emotions. *Personality and Individual Differences, 27, 913–932.*

Kovanen, S. (1998). *Mukautuva toimintastrategia–sen pysyvyys ja yhteydet elämänkulkuun.* [Compliant behavior: Continuity and associations with an individual's life-course]. Master's thesis, University of Jyväskylä, Finland.

Lazarus, R. S. (1966). *Psychological stress and the coping process.* New York: McGraw-Hill.

Lefkowitz, M. M., Eron, L. D., Walder, L. O., & Huesmann, L. R. (1977). *Growing up to be violent: A longitudinal study of the development of aggression.* New York: Pergamon.

Loeber, R. (1988). Natural histories of conduct problems, delinquency, and associated substance use: Evidence for developmental progressions. In B. B. Lahey & A. E. Kazdin (Eds.), *Advances in clinical child psychology* (Vol. 11, pp. 73–124). New York: Plenum Press.

Loeber, R., & Hay, D. (1997). Key issues in the development of aggression and violence from childhood to early adulthood. *Annual Review of Psychology, 48,* 371–410.

Loeber, R., & Stouthamer-Loeber, M. (1998). Development of juvenile aggression and violence: Some common misconceptions and controversies. *American Psychologist, 53,* 242–259.

Magnusson, D., & Bergman, L. R. (1990). A pattern approach to the study of pathways from childhood to adulthood. In L. N. Robins & M. Rutter (Eds.), *Straight and devious pathways from childhood to adulthood* (pp. 101–115). Cambridge, England: Cambridge University Press.

Männikkö, K., & Pulkkinen, L. (in press). Parenting and personality styles. A long-term longitudinal approach. In J. R. M. Gerris (Ed.), *Dynamics of parenting.* Leuven, Belgium: Garant-Vitgevers.

Moffitt, T. E. (1993). Adolescence-limited and life-course-persistent antisocial behavior: A developmental taxonomy. *Psychological Review, 100,* 674–701.

Olweus, D. (1979). Stability and aggressive reaction patterns in males: A review. *Psychological Bulletin, 86,* 852–875.

Patterson, G. R., Capaldi, D., & Bank, L. (1991). An early starter model for predicting delinquency. In D. J. Pepler & K. H. Rubin (Eds.), *The development and treatment of childhood aggression* (pp. 139–168). Hillsdale, NJ: Erlbaum.

Pitkänen, L. (1969). *A descriptive model of aggression and nonaggression with applications to children's behaviour. (Jyväskylä Studies in Education, Psychology and Social Research, 19.)* Jyväskylä, Finland: Jyväskylä University Printing House.

Pitkänen-Pulkkinen, L. (1979). Self-control as a prerequisite for constructive behavior. In S. Feshbach & A. Fraczek (Eds.), *Aggression and behavior change: Biological and social processes* (pp. 250–270). New York: Praeger.

Pitkänen-Pulkkinen, L. (1981). Long-term studies on the characteristics of aggressive and non-aggressive juveniles. In P. F. Brain & D. Benton (Eds.), *Multidisciplinary approaches to aggression research* (pp. 225–243). Amsterdam: Elsevier/North Holland Biomedical Press.

Pulkkinen, L. (1982). Self-control and continuity from childhood to adolescence. In B. P. Baltes & O. G. Brim, Jr. (Eds.), *Life-span development and behavior* (Vol. 4, pp. 63–105). Orlando, FL: Academic Press.

Pulkkinen, L. (1983). Finland. The search for alternatives to aggression. In A. P. Goldstein & M. Segall (Eds.), *Aggression in global perspective* (pp. 104–144). New York: Pergamon Press.

Pulkkinen, L. (1986). The role of impulse control in the development of antisocial and prosocial behavior. In D. Olweus, J. Block, & M. Radke-Yarrow (Eds.), *Development of antisocial and prosocial behavior: Theories, research, and issues* (pp. 149–175). Orlando, FL: Academic Press.

Pulkkinen, L. (1987). Offensive and defensive aggression in humans: A longitudinal perspective. *Aggressive Behavior, 13,* 197–212.

Pulkkinen, L. (1992a). Life-styles in personality development. *European Journal of Personality, 6,* 139–155.

Pulkkinen, L. (1992b). The path to adulthood for aggressively inclined girls. In: K. Björkqvist & P. Niemelä (Eds.), *Of mice and women: Aspects of female aggression* (pp. 113–121). Orlando, FL: Academic Press.

Pulkkinen, L. (1995). Behavioral precursors to accidents and resulting physical impairment. *Child Development, 66,* 1660–1679.

Pulkkinen, L. (1996a). Female and male personality styles: A typological and developmental analysis. *Journal of Personality and Social Psychology, 70,* 1288–1306.

Pulkkinen, L. (1996b). Proactive and reactive aggression in early adolescence as precursors to anti- and prosocial behavior in young adults. *Aggressive Behavior, 22,* 241–257.

Pulkkinen, L. (1998). Levels of longitudinal data differing in complexity and the study of continuity in personality characteristics. In R. B. Cairns, L. B. Bergman, & J. Kagan (Eds.), *Methods and models for studying the individual* (pp. 161–184). Beverly Hills, CA: Sage.

Pulkkinen, L., & Hämäläinen, M. (1995). Low self-control as a precursor to crime and accidents in a Finnish longitudinal study. *Criminal Behaviour and Mental Health, 5,* 424–438.

Pulkkinen, L., Ohranen, M., & Tolvanen, A. (in press). Personality antecedents of career orientation and stability among women compared to men. *Journal of Vocational Behavior.*

Pulkkinen, L., & Pitkänen, T. (1993). Continuities in aggressive behavior from childhood to adulthood. *Aggressive Behavior, 19,* 249–263.

Pulkkinen, L., & Pitkänen, T. (1994). A prospective study of the precursors to problem drinking in young adulthood. *Journal of Studies on Alcohol, 55,* 578–587.

Pulkkinen, L., & Tremblay, R. E. (1992). Patterns of boys' social adjustment in two cultures and at different ages: A longitudinal perspective. *International Journal of Behavioural Development, 15,* 527–553.

Rönkä, A. (1999). *The accumulation of problems of social functioning.* (Jyväskylä Studies in Education, Psychology and Social Research, 148.) Jyväskylä, Finland: Jyväskylä University Printing House.

Rönkä, A., & Pulkkinen, L. (1995). Accumulation of problems in social functioning in young adulthood: A developmental approach. *Journal of Personality and Social Psychology, 69,* 381–391.

Rönkä, A., & Pulkkinen, L. (1998). Work involvement and timing of motherhood in the accumulation of problems in social functioning in young women. *Journal of Research on Adolescence, 8,* 221–239.

Ruggiero, J. A., & Weston, L. C. (1988). Work involvement among college-educated women: A methodological extension. *Sex Roles, 19,* 491–507.

Schachter, S., & Singer, J. E. (1962). Cognitive, social, and physiological determinants of emotional state. *Psychological Review, 69,* 379–399.

Shields, A., & Cicchetti, D. (1997). Emotion regulation among school-age children: The development and validation of a new criterion Q-Sort Scale. *Developmental Psychology, 33,* 906–916.

Stattin, H., & Magnusson, D. (1989). The role of early aggressive behavior in the frequency, seriousness, and types of later crime. *Journal of Consulting and Clinical Psychology, 57,* 710–718.

Stattin, H., & Magnusson, D. (1996). Antisocial development: A holistic approach. *Development and Psychopathology, 8,* 617–645.

Strauss, M. A. (1992). *Manual for the Conflict Tactics Scales (CTS).* Durham: University of New Hampshire.

Tremblay, R. E. (2000). The development of aggressive behaviour during childhood: What have we learned in the past century? *International Journal of Behavioral Development, 24,* 129–141.

Walden, T. A., & Smith, M. C. (1997). Emotion regulation. *Motivation and Emotion, 21,* 7–25.

Wiggins, J. S. (1991). Agency and communion as conceptual coordinates for the understanding and measurement of interpersonal behavior. In D. Cicchetti & W. Grove (Eds.), *Thinking critically in psychology: Essays in honor of Paul E. Meehl* (pp. 89–113). New York: Cambridge University Press.

9

PROSOCIAL BEHAVIOR AND AGGRESSION IN CHILDHOOD AND PRE-ADOLESCENCE

GIAN VITTORIO CAPRARA, CLAUDIO BARBARANELLI,
AND CONCETTA PASTORELLI

Our central concern is to understand what prevents and controls aggressive feelings and what instigates and regulates their expression. In our work, we have emphasized individual differences in self-regulatory systems that mediate an individual's relationship with the environment and his or her social adaptation. In particular, individual differences in prosocial behavior and aggression have been studied as indicators and precursors to social adjustment in childhood and early adolescence (Caprara, & Pastorelli, 1993; Caprara, Perugini, & Barbaranelli, 1994).

In this chapter we review studies conducted over the past 10 years on prosocial behavior and aggression in children and pre-adolescents. First, we review our work on the assessment of individual differences in aggression and prosocial behavior. Second, we examine the stability of aggression and prosocial behavior and their predictive power for later social adjustment. Finally, we discuss the practical implications of our findings.

ASSESSMENT OF INDIVIDUAL DIFFERENCES

The theoretical arguments supporting the importance of individual differences in aggressive and prosocial behavior have been discussed in previous papers and corroborated by a great deal of empirical research (Caprara, 1986, 1987, 1996; Caprara et al., 1985; Caprara et al., 1987; Caprara & Pastorelli, 1989; Caprara, Renzi, Alcini, D'Imperio, & Travaglia, 1983).

Our original interest in aggression was motivated by practical concerns about the processes that regulate personality development and adaptation. Consistent with the frustration–aggression paradigm (Dollard, Doob, Miller, Mowrer, & Sears, 1939), we began studying aggressive behavior in adults. Our goal was to understand the basic mechanisms and processes that instigate or inhibit its expression.

The study of individual differences became an important strategy for understanding why some individuals are more inclined than others to counterattack after an experimental frustration manipulation and why others are more inclined to harbor and even increase a desire for vengeance toward the one causing the frustration.[1] Here the role of personality dimensions such as irritability, emotional susceptibility, and dissipation–rumination were crucial. They helped us clarify various processes underlying two forms of aggression: (a) affectively charged, impulsive, reactive, and involuntary aggression and (b) cognitively regulated, instrumental, proactive, intentional, voluntary, goal-directed, and cold-blooded interpersonal hostility.[2] The results of experimental research have confirmed the validity of the distinction that we made and suggest its extension into the developmental sphere, where it might be used to investigate the formation of these original dimensions.

We first explored the possibility of developing indicators for children similar to the ones we developed for adults. We then initiated a longitudinal study with the aim of identifying the precursors and correlates of children's and adolescents' social adjustment.

The use of self-report for children has been discouraged because of the low degree of agreement between ratings made by the self and those made by others, such as teachers, mothers, and peers. We nevertheless believed it was important to assess whether children can be reliable and valid informants. We were also interested in investigating whether children's ability to

---

[1]In our studies frustration was operationalized as a failure in a memory task or as a written insulting profile given to the experimental subject by a confederate of the experimenter. Aggression was operationalized as the levels of delivered shocks given to a confederate of the experimenter in a fake ESP experiment.

[2]*Dissipation–rumination* was defined as the inclination toward a prolonged rumination, increasing or at least maintaining the desire to retaliate in some hostile manner following an instigation.

report on their own behavior can be ascribed to problems of accuracy or to meaningful differences between self and others' perspectives.

In line with this reasoning, we conducted a number of cross-sectional studies before the longitudinal study to ascertain the psychometric characteristics of various measures designed to assess aggression and prosocial behavior. The children were Italian and ranged in age from 7 to 13 years.

We used a multimethod/multi-informant research strategy, developing self-report, teacher ratings, and peer nomination for both aggression and prosocial behavior (see Caprara & Laeng, 1988; Caprara & Pastorelli, 1993). Self-reports and teacher ratings share the same items, the only difference is that in the latter case the items are formulated in the third person. The peer nomination measures were developed on the basis of those items that proved to have higher loadings in the factorial structure of aggression and prosocial children's self-report scales. Exhibit 9.1 presents the definition of the constructs, an item sample, and the number of items in each scale for the different informants.

EXHIBIT 9.1
Definitions and descriptions of aggression and prosocial behavior scales

Aggression Scale
1. I insult other kids (S).
   He/she insults other kids (T).
   Who are the three classmates that often insult other kids (P)?
2. I kick and hit (or punch) (S).
   He/she kicks and hits (or punches) (T).
   Who are the three classmates that often kick and hit (or punch) (P)?
3. I bite others to harm them (S).
   He/she bites others to harm them (T).
   Who are the three classmates that often bite others to harm them (P)?

Prosocial Behavior Scale
1. I try to make sad people happier (S).
   He/she tries to make sad people happier (T).
   Who are the three classmates that often try to make sad people happier (P)?
2. I try to help others (S).
   He/she tries to help others (T).
   Who are the three classmates that often try to help others (P)?
3. I share things I like with my friends (S).
   He/she shares things he/she likes with friends (T).
   Who are the three classmates that often share things they like with their friends (P)?

Note. S = self; T = teacher; P = peer. For aggression, the self-report and teacher rating scale are composed of 20 items, with 5 control items (answer format: 3 = *often,* 2 = *sometimes,* 1 = *never*). Various items offer a description of child's behavior aimed at hurting others physically and verbally. For prosocial behavior, the self-report and teacher rating scale are composed of 15 items, with 5 control items (answer format: 3 = *often,* 2 = *sometimes,* 1 = *never*). Various items offer a description of positive behaviors children show in response to peers in distress: helping, sharing, and comforting behaviors.

Self-report and peer nomination were administered in the school setting. For the self-report, students had to complete the two scales related to aggression and prosocial behavior. For peer nomination, students were presented a booklet containing all questions. For example, they were asked to read the question (e.g. "Who are the three classmates who fight a lot?"), to read all the names of their classmates, and then to put a circle around the names they wished to indicate as the answers to the question. Teachers were asked to complete the prosocial behavior and aggression scales for each child in their class.

PSYCHOMETRIC CHARACTERISTICS OF THE SCALE

Aggression and prosocial behavior scales met the psychometric criteria for both informants in different age groups. As shown in Table 9.1, the percentage of variance accounted for by the first component for self-report and teacher ratings confirm the monofactorial structure of aggression and prosocial behavior scale in elementary and junior high school students. Also, the reliability coefficients further confirm the internal consistency of the two scales for both informants and age groups.

GENDER DIFFERENCES

Table 9.2 shows the means and standard deviations for the children themselves, the teachers, and the children's peers. For self-reports the results show significant gender differences in all age groups for both aggression and prosocial behavior. The boys rated themselves as more aggressive

TABLE 9.1

Percentage of variance accounted for by the first component and alpha coefficient for self-reports and teacher ratings

	Aggression		Prosocial Behavior	
	Self	Teacher	Self	Teacher
% of variance of first component				
Elementary (ages 7–10)	38.3	52.8	33.6	49.9
Junior high (ages 11–13)	37.3	61.6	38.0	65.8
Alpha value				
Elementary (ages 7–10)	0.88	0.93	0.78	0.88
Junior high (ages 11–13)	0.87	0.86	0.81	0.89

TABLE 9.2

Means and standard deviations of aggression and prosocial behavior in self-report, teacher rating, and peer nomination for different age groups, by girls and boys

| | Self-Report | | | | | Teacher Rating | | | | | Peer Nomination | | | | |
| | Boys | | Girls | | | Boys | | Girls | | | Boys | | Girls | | |
Scale/age	M	SD	M	SD	p	M	SD	M	SD	p	M	SD	M	SD	p
Aggression															
7 years	1.73	.40	1.44	.33	***	1.71	.56	1.36	.35	***	0.23	.25	0.03	.08	***
8 years	1.70	.42	1.35	.27	***	1.62	.49	1.26	.37	***	0.22	.23	0.03	.08	***
9 years	2.04	.43	1.59	.35	***	1.76	.50	1.27	.36	***	0.24	.24	0.04	.08	***
10 years	1.92	.37	1.60	.37	***	1.75	.64	1.22	.29	***	0.22	.24	0.03	.07	***
11 years	1.67	.38	1.43	.33	***	1.33	.41	1.10	.22	***	0.20	.22	0.06	.11	***
12 years	1.64	.39	1.43	.29	***	1.48	.46	1.13	.25	***	0.20	.22	0.04	.08	***
13 years	1.75	.37	1.50	.39	***	1.38	.43	1.10	.21	***	0.21	.22	0.05	.09	***
Prosocial	38	.36	**	2.45	.38	2.53	.39	NS	0.14	.19	0.13	.15	NS		NS
8 years	2.20	.40	2.35	.32	**	2.29	.38	2.48	.38	NS	0.13	.14	0.15	.18	NS
9 years	2.23	.40	2.48	.29	***	2.57	.34	2.81	.24	***	0.13	.12	0.16	.15	NS
10 years	2.40	.36	2.50	.27	**	2.38	.39	2.54	.35	**	0.13	.14	0.14	.17	NS
11 years	2.28	.38	2.45	.32	***	2.12	.51	2.33	.52	NS	0.11	.08	0.16	.11	***
12 years	2.25	.35	2.48	.32	***	2.15	.51	2.21	.52	NS	0.11	.09	0.17	.13	***
13 years	2.23	.38	2.50	.35	***	2.13	.45	2.31	.50	***	0.10	.09	0.17	.15	***

*p < .01; **p < .001; ***p < .0001. NS = nonsignificant.

than did the girls. The girls rated themselves as more prosocial than did the boys. Similar to the self-report findings, the teachers and peers rated the boys as more aggressive than the girls. However, in the case of prosocial behavior, the teachers and peers showed different results. For the peers at younger ages, the girls and boys did not differ in their mean prosocial ratings; however, gender differences consistently appeared from age 11 and older. The teachers rated the girls as more prosocial than the boys at ages 9, 10, 11, and 13.

In summary, our findings are consistent with the findings of other studies, in which boys are rated as more aggressive than girls (Eagly & Steffen, 1986). Gender differences were not, however, found in all informants for prosocial behavior, at least in the younger age ranges.

ASSOCIATIONS BETWEEN AGGRESSION AND PROSOCIAL BEHAVIOR

Following the literature (Eron & Huessman, 1984; Rushton, 1987), we expected to find a negative correlation between aggression and prosocial behavior, although it was also expected that some variations might be found among different age groups and informants (Miller & Eisenberg, 1988). As shown in Table 9.3, significant negative correlations between aggression

TABLE 9.3

Correlation between aggression and prosocial behavior, in different groups of age and informants, by boys and girls

Age	Gender	Self-Report		Teacher Rating		Peer Nomination	
		R	N	R	N	R	N
7 years	Boys	−.14	150	−.20*	150	−.12	150
	Girls	−.19	120	−.05	120	−.02	120
8 years	Boys	−.11	117	−.10	117	−.14	117
	Girls	−.24*	104	−.01	104	−.15	104
9 years	Boys	−.39***	126	−.15	126	−.21	126
	Girls	−.25*	108	.09	108	.13	108
10 years	Boys	−.03	117	−.17	110	−.18	117
	Girls	−.06	104	.15	94	.01	104
11 years	Boys	−.19*	163	−.07	147	−.37***	163
	Girls	−.07	146	−.17	132	−.16	146
12 years	Boys	−.30***	172	−.23**	163	−.24**	172
	Girls	−.12	142	−.04	140	−.17	142
13 years	Boys	−.31***	180	−.35***	160	−.28***	180
	Girls	−.30***	165	−.32***	153	−.18*	165

*$p < .01$. **$p < .001$. ***$p < .0001$.

and prosocial behavior are confirmed for 13-year-old boys and girls for all informants. Boys ages 11 and 12 showed significant and negative correlations for most of informants. Girls did not show the same pattern in early adolescence. Among the younger children, the self-report data show a significant negative correlation for 8-year-old girls and 9-year-old boys and girls, and in the case of teacher ratings, for 7-year-old girls.

Consistent with other studies (Cairns & Cairns, 1994), our results indicate that aggression and prosocial behavior are not so highly negatively correlated as to be considered at opposite ends of a single dimension (Eron & Huessman, 1984). They are usually negatively correlated (low to moderate), but for some informants in some age groups, they are not significantly correlated at all.

AGREEMENT AMONG INFORMANTS

Regarding aggression in the younger groups (ages 7–10), as shown in Table 9.4, the peer–teacher pairs show a higher number of positive and significant correlations than did the self–teacher and self–peer pairs. In the older group (ages 11–13), however, self-reports of aggression correlate positively and significantly with teachers' and peers' ratings for both boys and girls, although to a lower degree.

TABLE 9.4

Correlations across informants on the aggression scale, by girls and boys

Age	Gender	Self-Report–Teacher Rating		Self-Report–Peer Nomination		Peer Nomination–Teacher Rating	
		R	N	R	N	R	N
7 years	Boys	.16	150	.10	150	.55***	150
	Girls	.11	120	.01	120	.38***	120
8 years	Boys	.21	116	.11	117	.45***	117
	Girls	.22	104	.29*	105	.49***	105
9 years	Boys	.31***	126	.31***	126	.48***	126
	Girls	.05	108	.12	108	.45***	108
10 years	Boys	.20	101	.29**	102	.44***	102
	Girls	.31*	97	.15	97	.17	98
11 years	Boys	.22*	148	.27***	164	.47***	148
	Girls	.31***	134	.28**	146	.66***	134
12 years	Boys	.34***	163	.31***	172	.55***	162
	Girls	.24*	141	.22*	141	.45***	140
13 years	Boys	.31***	163	.40***	180	.50***	163
	Girls	.33***	154	.34***	165	.23*	154

* $p < .01$; ** $p < .001$; $p < .0001$.

TABLE 9.5

Correlations across informants on prosocial behavior scale, by boys and girls

Age	Gender	Self-Report–Teacher Rating		Self-Report–Peer Nomination		Peer Nomination–Teacher Rating	
		R	N	R	N	R	N
7 years	Boys	.19	150	.20*	150	.27**	150
	Girls	.14	120	.15	120	.29**	119
8 years	Boys	.44***	118	.16	118	.16	118
	Girls	.23*	106	.13	108	.33***	107
9 years	Boys	.11	126	.08	126	.19	126
	Girls	.09	108	.06	108	.14	108
10 years	Boys	.39***	110	.32***	120	.31***	110
	Girls	.38***	94	.30*	107	.21	94
11 years	Boys	.12	161	.22*	163	.25**	161
	Girls	.22*	142	.21*	146	.31***	142
12 years	Boys	.26*	173	.25**	172	.22*	172
	Girls	.14	140	.20*	141	.26*	139
13 years	Boys	.24*	163	.24**	180	.29***	163
	Girls	.21*	153	.26**	165	.33***	153

$*p < .01;$ $**p < .001;$ $p < .0001.$

Our results show higher correlations between teacher and peer evaluations than between self and either teacher or peer ratings and more convergence between self and others' evaluations in older age groups than in younger age groups. It appears, however, that the higher agreement between teachers and peers occurs only in the case of aggression. Prosocial behavior does not show a prevalent pattern of association between teachers and peers (Table 9.5). Therefore, it appears that the question of whether others are better informants than children are themselves remains open.

PREDICTING SOCIAL ADJUSTMENT

Finally, we examined associations between the aggression and prosocial behavior scales and a set of indices related to social adjustment: peer rejection, peer preference, externalizing scales, and total problem behavior scales of the Teacher Report Form of the Child Behavior Checklist (CBC; Achenbach & Edelbrock, 1983, 1986).

In particular, aggression was significantly and positively correlated with peer rejection and with both externalizing scales and the total problem behavior score from the CBC (parent and teacher form; Achenbach & Edelbrock, 1983, 1986), both in boys and in girls. Prosocial behavior was significantly and positively correlated with peer measures of popularity and with both children's school performance and adaptive characteristics, as measured by the CBC teacher form (Achenbach & Edelbrock, 1986).

In summary, the results obtained on our cross-sectional samples indicate that children's self-report meets the usual psychometric requirements of construct validity and attests that children are no less reliable informants than adults and no less reliable when serving as self informants (i.e., when they report about their own personality) than when serving as peer informants (i.e., when they report about peers' personality).

STABILITY

Previous studies suggest that both aggressive and prosocial behavior are relatively stable individual differences. Studies have consistently documented the stability of aggression, suggesting an underlying trait or predisposition toward physically or verbally harming other people (Olweus, 1979; Zumkley, 1992). Evidence of stability of prosocial behavior is weaker, although studies have shown some stability over periods of four years (adolescence) and longer (early adulthood; Eisenberg, Carlo, Murphy, & Van Court, 1995).

Despite evidence of some stability in both aggressive and prosocial behavior, some researchers deny the utility of traits and stress the "power" of situations in governing behavior. The presence of stable patterns of behavior cannot, however, be denied, and these suggest some form of continuity in structures or processes that guide behavior in particular contexts. Competing arguments can be made, however, about the nature of these hypothetical structures or processes.

We believe that individual tendencies to behave aggressively or prosocially are not based in genetic or other factors in place at birth, but rather they evolve from cognitive–affective–behavioral organizers that develop out of individuals' interactions with their environment (Caprara, 1996). We do not deny possible genetic contributions that may predispose the development of aggressive or prosocial tendencies more in some people than in others (Rushton, 1987). But our focus is on the reciprocal determination among biological, psychological, and social factors that develop into stable organizations. These stable structures predispose the processing of affect, cognitions, and behavior in a relatively coherent aggressive or prosocial manner across time and place. We reason that even if behavior is substantially influenced by genetic endowment, there is no real aggression or prosocial behavior without intention and attribution of meaning. Consequently, stability in both kinds of behavior depends substantially on reciprocal expectations among actors, targets, and bystanders.

People learn primarily from experience how to aggress and how to care, but experience itself is filtered through individual cognitions. The same behaviors may lead to different perceptions, attributions, and expectations, which in turn influence their stability. When behaviors related to certain kinds of situations become organized into stable patterns it makes sense to speak of stable dispositions, but the stabilization of a disposition is not entirely an individual matter.

Consensus with others and reputation, in particular, may explain to some degree an individual's tendency to interpret events, to feel, and to behave in a relatively consistent way across time and place. Most of the studies on the stability of aggression and prosocial behavior rely on others' ratings and few use self-reports, but practically none has investigated the flow of reciprocal influences between the former and the latter. Furthermore, coefficient stabilities resulting from correlations within and between informants over time may capture only a part of the phenomenon. Others' ratings and self-reports show a remarkable stability for aggression and prosocial behavior. It is not clear, however, to what degree the stability is based on internal factors such as well-established dispositional tendencies, or on external factors, such as social attributions by significant others—in essence, whether stability is in the behavior of the actor or in the eyes of observers. Disentangling the amount of stability that is due to internal factors from the amount due to external factors and to their reciprocal interactions is an empirical issue.

We embarked on a study to examine these interrelationships. We tested different structural equation models (Bentler, 1989) to assess the nature of relationships among self-reports, teacher ratings, and peer nominations for aggression and prosocial behavior on two sets of data from children in the third, fourth, and fifth grades and from the seventh and eighth grades. A number of competing models were tested separately for boys and girls to clarify the paths of influence between different informants. These models were based on similar models previously discussed in Caprara (1996); in this case, however, analyses were performed for aggression and prosocial behavior, separately for boys and girls.

The clearest result is the high stability of both aggression and prosocial behavior across all informants. When considering paths of influence among different informants, we found that teachers exert the main influence on peer nominations (especially in the case of aggression), whereas the influence on children's self-evaluations is lower. It is likely that teachers' influence is mostly exerted through labeling and differential treatment They label the behaviors, make them salient, contrast them against others' behaviors, provide models for how to deal and cope with aggression and prosocial behavior, and generally establish the grounds for reciprocal expectations. According to the models tested here, one can speculate that consensus among various informants is "led" by teachers, so that complying with others' evaluations and expectations may become a prerequisite for children in establishing continuous relations with peers.

When moving from elementary to junior high school the picture changes. Now the influential role of teachers' ratings over self-report is replaced, at least in part, by peer evaluation. Indeed, among the models tested, the most plausible were; the models positing teacher evaluations as the starting point were less plausible.

While aggression and prosocial behavior were more stable for older than younger children, slight reciprocal influence between peers and young adolescents' self-evaluations declined with the passing of time. Both the model in which the paths of influence move from self to peers and to teachers and the one in which the paths move from peers to self and to teachers are plausible, particularly in the case of prosocial behavior.

We are inclined to believe that young adolescents' judgments both reflect and influence the judgments of others by conveying their own "personality theory." At ages 8 and 9, self-reports tended to be influenced by teachers and peers, whereas at ages 12 and 13, self-reports were no more influenced by others than they influenced others' reports. By the end of junior high school there is a remarkable stability in ratings, reports, and nominations, drastically limiting the influence peers and teachers can exert on self-reports. It nevertheless remains possible that reported stability is enhanced by "dispositional heuristics," which promote perceptions of the self and others in terms of stable dispositions and which tend to maintain high stability in self-evaluations.

Again, high stability coefficients within informants do not suggest high agreement between self and others, as seen by the correlations among various informants and, in particular, between self-reports and others evaluations. Thus, it is reasonable to question whether self and others' evaluations, although reflecting different points of view, refer to the same phenomena and, ultimately, which of them is more valuable for current and future assessment of adolescent social adjustment.

Here the issues of the accuracy of various informants and the prediction of aggression and prosocial behavior at different ages come to the fore. Regarding accuracy (i.e., the capacity to capture and to convey the veridical nature of a phenomenon), we have no reason to believe that adolescents are poorer informants than adults or better informants when they report on others than when they report on themselves. Rather, we believe that different informants' ratings may reflect different aspects of the same phenomena and are differentially predictive with regard to other behavior. Boys and girls at age 14 may have better access than any others to their own feelings, intentions, and behaviors, whether aggressive or prosocial. However, access to one's own experience is not necessarily accompanied by equal access to the impact that one's behavior has on others. Others may be better informants than actors of the consequences of their behavior. In principle one may presume that the person is more accurate when the criteria correspond to internal states accompanying a behavior or a disposition to behave in a certain way, for instance the intention to hurt or to care in the case of aggression and prosocial behavior. Presumably others are better informants than the individual when criteria correspond to the social impact of a behavior or an individual tendency, for instance the harmful outcome of aggression or the comforting effect of caring. In practice researchers may benefit from the assessment of different point of views of actors and observers. In this regard our findings allow us to move further ahead with regard to accuracy by assessing the predictive power of different informants.

THE PREDICTIVE POWER OF DIFFERENT INFORMANTS

The findings so far suggest that teachers may exert a major influence on children's self-reports and peer nominations in elementary school, but their influence declines as children get older. Peer influence on self-report appears to replace that of teachers in junior high school. By the end of junior high school, both self and others' evaluations are remarkably stable, although consensus among self, peers, and teachers is moderate.

We asked next whose ratings–teachers, peers, or their own–predict best children's later adjustment? Our longitudinal research has provided evidence on the predictive validity of aggression and prosocial behavior, rated by various informants, respectively, in second and third, and sixth and seventh grades. Outcomes to be predicted included academic achievement, sociometric status, and the total problem behavior index of the Achenbach & Edelbrock (1986) YSR at the end of eighth grade.

In a preliminary analysis, two sets of multiple regression analyses were performed with school achievement, popularity, rejection, and total problem behavior in seventh and eighth grades as the dependent variables and aggression and prosocial behavior (self-report, teacher ratings, and peer nominations) in second and third grades as predictor variables. Overall, peer nominations in prosocial behavior for both boys and girls were the most important predictors of academic achievement, rejection, and problem behavior (Caprara, Barbaranelli, & Pastorelli, 1996).

Subsequently, we tested two structural equation models, respectively, for boys and girls, in which aggression and prosocial behavior (measured by self-report, teacher ratings, and peer nomination) were defined as latent variables and posited as predictors of academic achievement, rejection, and problem behavior. In one model, predictors were measured in second or third grades and in the other in sixth or seventh grades; in both models dependent variables were measured in seventh or eighth grades. Either at the distal or proximal time interval, prosocial behavior was the best predictor of all three dependent variables. Aggression was important in predicting rejection and problem behavior but unexpectedly more distally than proximally. Self-report was a poor indicator of prosocial ratings (especially for boys), and peer ratings were a very good indicator of aggression for boys but were a very poor one for girls.

In summary, peers were the most important informants for both prosocial behavior and aggression at both the distal and proximal time interval. However, the importance of self-ratings increased significantly as children increased in age. Prosocial behavior was much more important than aggression in predicting later adjustment, and peers were much more informative with regard to all three dependent variables included in the analysis.

The robust contribution of early prosocial behavior to children's developmental trajectories in academic and social domain were further confirmed in a recent study. Both prosocial and aggressive behaviors during third grade were tested as predictors of academic achievement and peer relations five years later. Prosocialness had a strong positive impact on later academic achievement and social preferences, but early aggression had no significant effect in either outcomes (Caprara, Barbaranelli, Pastorelli, Bandura & Zimbardo, 2000).

CONCLUSION

These studies suggest new interpretations of the stability of behavior. They emphasize the role that others may play in sustaining the construction and stabilization of individual dispositions through early labeling, shared consensus, reputation, and differential treatment. It is critical to ascertain how children learn to think about themselves as aggressive or prosocial individuals, how their self-reports are influenced by adult and peer evaluations, how they come to influence others' impressions of them, and how this process of building consensus among observers and actors promotes stability in behavior.

The findings we discuss in this chapter suggest that, in elementary school, children's judgments about themselves and others may be influenced by teachers' views. In junior high school, peer influence replaces teachers' influence and appears to be somewhat reciprocal. Consensus among observers contributes to the stabilization of an individual's disposition toward certain behaviors. We have no reason to doubt that observers' reports reflect what they actually perceive. We recognize, however, that the same events may be construed differently by actors and observers and that expectations and reputations influence both what is seen and how what is seen is interpreted. For example, teachers may be more likely to notice and call attention to an aggressive act of a child they perceive to be aggressive than the same behavior by another child. Or a behavior such as bumping into another child might be perceived as purposeful and reprimanded for a child who has a reputation of being a bully and as accidental and ignored for another. Thus, ratings and self-reports, particularly when they take place repeatedly, reflect not only behavioral tendencies but also expectations and reputation, which may begin to influence the actor's behavior and thus contribute to stability in behavior over time.

It therefore becomes difficult to establish whether consensus among observers over time reflects stability of a behavioral tendency or whether the latter is an effect of the former. Imagine, for example, children who are rated by teachers and peers as aggressive or prosocial in the early grades of school. Consensual attributions and expectations adhere with surprising tenacity, often regardless of what the child does. This "socially attributed stability," along with an "ipsative stability," may account for the perception of identity, continuity, and coherence that others derive from observing the target child's behavior. Labeling, differential treatment, reputation, and ultimately compliance all conspire to preserve the stability of others' consensus. In particular, lack of prosocial behavior (for girls and boys) and also aggression (only for boys) lead to rejection, and prosocial behavior leads to acceptance.

Given the role of others in shaping behavior and the value of others' communicative feedback in defining the self (Taylor, Neter, & Wayment, 1995), it is not surprising that ratings and self-report converge over the years as a result of increased consensus about personality. However, we must clarify whether the higher agreement is due to the effect of reputation on self-definition, to the effect of the latter on the former, or to both.

In some situations individuals may have no choice other than to conform to others' expectations. An ambivalent member of a gang, for example, may feel that he has to behave aggressively or violate the law to avoid censure, which could be in the form of physical harm. In other situations, such as when members of the group are more flexible in their expectations and open to having their perceptions changed, individuals may be able to convey their own view and to effectively master the impression that others form of them.

Our findings support the role of preventing aggression in fostering later adjustment, but they demonstrate also the importance of prosocial behavior. The findings suggest that the capacity to interact prosocially with peers influences not only children's acceptance, but also their academic achievements and the perception that adults have of them as more or less problematic. Early prosocial behavior may also mediate the influence of aggression on social adjustment. Clearly, prosocial behaviors such as sharing, caring, and cooperating play an important role in fostering social adjustment in school settings.

There have been a lot of discussions about social intelligence and affective education from different perspectives and not always referring to the same phenomena (Cantor & Kihlstrom, 1986; Feshbach & Feshbach, 1987). However, there is no doubt that the capacity to share the basic rules of social interaction and the ability to express affect are crucial for setting in motion important experiences for fostering social adjustment. On the other hand, it is more than likely that social disabilities will increase over the years, through others' feedback, leading to rejection and failure (Caprara & Zimbardo, 1996).

It is not surprising that aggression has received more attention than any other phenomenon in predicting social maladjustment, given the immediate visibility of its undesirable consequences. We suspect, however, that the importance of abilities associated with prosocial behavior have been underestimated, especially as they affect social acceptance and success. Being supportive of others can be a source of interpersonal influence and of positive affect, which in turn enhances children's sense of efficacy as well as their achievements. Prosocial behavior can also be a powerful antidote to aggression when earlier emotional vulnerability and negative interpersonal experiences, through rejection and stigmatization, lead to hostility, disengagement, and social withdrawal.

We believe that our findings have several implications for effective interventions aimed at preventing children's maladjustment and promoting their well-being. We are convinced that children should be listened to and that educators should be trained to listen, to comprehend, and to support the expression of children's competencies. Adults and educators in particular should provide occasions, models, and rewards for expressing and developing social abilities. Emphasis should be placed not only on prevention and correction of antisocial behavior, but also on promotion of socially valuable behaviors such as altruism, cooperation, and interpersonal skills (Deutsch, 1993). Prosocial abilities such as the capacity to help, to cooperate, to negotiate, to express emotions, and to recognize others' feelings should be encouraged and taught.

Because behavioral stability is in part the outcome of relationships and reciprocal expectations that stabilize over time, educators and peers should also be targeted in interventions designed to prevent the crystallization of labels that promote stigmatization and rejection.

REFERENCES

Achenbach, M. T., & Eldebrock, C. (1983). *Manual for the Child Behavior Checklist and Revised Child Behavior Profile*. Burlington: University of Vermont, Department of Psychiatry.

Achenbach, M. T., & Eldebrock, C. (1986). *Manual for the Teacher's Reports and Teacher Version of the Child Behavior Profile*. Burlington, VT:

Bentler P. M. (1989). *Theory and implementation of EQS: A structural equations program*. Los Angeles, CA: BMDP Statistical Software.

Cairns, R. B., & Cairns, B. D. (1995). *Lifeliness and risks: Pathways of youth in our time*. Cambridge, England: Cambridge University Press.

Cantor, N., & Kihlstrom, S. F. (1986). *Personality and social intelligence*. Englewood Cliffs, NJ: Prentice Hall.

Caprara, G. V. (1986). Indicators of aggression: The Dissipation–Rumination Scale. *Personality and Individual Differences, 7*, 23–31.

Caprara, G. V. (1987). The disposition–situation debate and research on aggression. *European Journal of Personality, 1*, 1–16.

Caprara, G. V. (1996). Structures and processes in personality psychology. *European Psychologist, 1*, 13–25.

Caprara, G. V., Barbaranelli, C., Pastorelli, C., & Perugini, M. (1994). Individual differences in the study of human aggression. *Aggressive Behavior, 20*, 291–303.

Caprara, G. V., Barbaranelli, C., & Pastorelli, C. (1997). I predittori dell'adattamento sociale, In S.M.G. Adamo e P. Valerio (Eds.), *Fattori di rischio psicosociale in adolescenza* (pp. 29–45). Napoli: La Citta' del Sole.

Caprara, G.V., Barbaranelli, C. Pastorelli, C. Bandura, A. & Zimbardo P. (2000). Prosocial foundation of children's academic achievement. *Psychological Science, 11*, 302–306.

Caprara, G. V., Cinanni, V., D'Imperio, G., Passerini, S., Renzi, P., & Travaglia, G. (1985). Indicators of impulsive aggression: Present status on research on irritability and emotional susceptibility. *Personality and Individual Differences, 6*, 665–674.

Caprara, G. V., Gargaro, T., Pastorelli, C., Prezza, M., Renzi, P., & Zelli, A. (1987). Individual differences and measures of aggression in laboratory studies. *Personality and Individual Differences, 8*, 885–893.

Caprara, G. V., & Laeng, M. (1988). *Indicatori e precursori della condotta auressiva*. Rome: Bulzoni.

Caprara, G. V., & Pastorelli, C. (1989). Toward a reorientation of research on aggression. *European Journal of Personality, 3*, 121–138.

Caprara, G. V., & Pastorelli, C. (1993). Early emotional instability, prosocial behavior and aggression: Some methodological aspects. *European Journal of Personality, 7*, 19–36.

Caprara, G. V., Perugini, M., & Barbaranelli, C. (1994). Studies of individual differences in aggression. In M. Potegal & J. F. Knutson (Eds.), *The dynamics of aggression* (pp. 123–153). Hillsdale, NJ: Erlbaum.

Caprara, G. V., Renzi, P., Alcini, P., D'Imperio, G., & Travaglia, G. (1983). Instigation to aggress and escalation of aggression examined form a personological perspective: The role of irritability and emotional susceptibility. *Aggressive Behavior, 9*, 354–358.

Caprara, G. V., & Zimbardo, P. G. (1996). Aggregation and amplification of marginal deviations in the social construction of personality and maladjustment. *European Journal of Personality, 10*, 79–110.

Deutsch, M. (1993). Educating for a peaceful word. *American Psychologist, 48*, 510–517.

Dollard, J., Doob, L. W., Miller, N. E., Mowrer, O. H., & Sears, R. R. (1939). *Frustration and aggression*. New Haven, CT: Yale University Press.

Eagly, A. H., & Steffen, V. J. (1986). Gender and aggressive behavior. A meta-analytic review of the social psychological literature. *Psychological Bulletin*, 100, 309–330.

Eisenberg, N., Carlo, G., Murphy, B., & Van Court, P. (1995). Prosocial development in late adolescence: A longitudinal study. *Child Development.*, 66, 1179–1197.

Eron, L.D., and Huesmann, L.R. (1984). The relation of prosocial behavior to the development of aggression and psychopathology. *Aggressive Behavior*, 10, 201–211.

Feshbach, N. D., & Feshbach, S. (1987). Affective processes and academic achievement. *Child Development*, 58, 1335–1347.

Miller, P. A., & Eisenberg, N. (1988). The relation of empathy to aggressive and externalizing/antisocial behavior. *Psychological Bulletin*, 103, 324–344.

Olweus, D. (1979). The stability of aggressive reaction patterns in human males: A review. *Psychological Bulletin*, 85, 852–875.

Rushton, J. P. (1987). Altruism and aggression. The heritability of individual differences. *Journal of Personality and Social Psychology*, 50, 1192–1198.

Taylor, S., Neter, E., & Wayment, A. (1995). Self-evaluation processes. *Personality and Social Psychology Bulletin*, 21, 1278–1287

Zumkley, H. (1992). The stability of individual differences in aggression. In A. Fraczek & H. Zurnkley (Eds.), *Socialization and aggression* (pp. 103–113). Berlin: Springer-Verlag.

10

DESIGNING A METHOD TO ASSESS EMPATHY IN ITALIAN CHILDREN

PAOLO ALBIERO AND ALIDA LO COCO

Measurement and evaluation are among the most difficult tasks of researchers studying empathy. In this chapter we open with a review of the conceptual issues regarding empathy and their implications for measuring empathic responses. We then present a measure of empathy for school-age children, based on the work of Feshbach and Roe (1968). These researchers developed a series of story-narratives that form the Affective Situation Test for Empathy (FASTE), which is considered a prototype in this field of inquiry. After describing how the FASTE was adapted for Italian children, we describe some empirical findings that explore the reliability of the instrument and the relationships between empathy and other indicators of social behavior such as aggressiveness, prosocial behavior, and emotional instability.

THEORETICAL AND METHODOLOGICAL ISSUES IN EMPATHY

Why is empathy difficult to evaluate? Assessing any psychological phenomena requires that some inner quality such as intelligence or emotion

This research was supported by a grant from National University Council to Alida Lo Coco.

205

is transformed and recorded into observable and quantifiable behaviors. To overcome this difficulty, scholars have tried to define psychological constructs and operationalize them according to those definitions.

Empathy serves as an excellent example of the issue of measuring underlying psychological constructs (Lo Coco, 1992). According to its etymological definition, the word *empathy* refers to one's ability to feel emotions that another person is experiencing. As many authors have noted, such a subtle, internal concept is particularly difficult to measure through direct observations and must be assessed indirectly, by inference from overt behaviors (Feshbach, 1978; Plutchik, 1987).

The lack of a comprehensive theory of empathy has further hampered measurement development. Methodological and definitional concerns are strictly interdependent and closely connected (Hoffman, 1982), and the ability to share the feelings of others has been variously conceptualized, depending on the author's theoretical lens. Given the various definitions of empathy (Eisenberg & Strayer, 1987), we do not have a single way of measuring vicarious empathic responding. Instead, different methods are linked to specific perspectives and emphasize some aspects of the construct.

The existence of various methods of assessing empathy has caused considerable misunderstanding. Empathy researchers may use a similar term but actually study different psychological phenomena. This makes it difficult to compare empirical findings, replicate research outcomes, and reach reliable conclusions about empathy: What is it? How is it measured? Why does it occur? What are its antecedents, correlates, and consequences?

The most widely used definition of *empathy* refers to the vicarious ability to share affect. Within this general definition, the most critical issue concerns whether empathy is primarily affective or cognitive or both. From a cognitive view, *empathizing* refers to the ability to recognize and understand the thoughts, intentions, and feelings of another individual. This capacity is closely linked to cognitive development, and it progresses through a number of stages, hierarchically ordered, ranging from the infant's pre-empathic diffuse sensitivity to the adolescent's empathic awareness. By the last stage, egocentrism has declined, and empathy involves the adoption of others' points of view, while self and others are truly differentiated (Borke, 1971; Deutsch & Madle, 1975; Shantz, 1975). Empathy is thus conceived as a general ability of social reasoning or cognition, connected to similar constructs such as role-taking, perspective-taking, and social perception.

The social understanding of empathy has led to the construction of instruments that assess the ability to predict behavior or accurately label the emotional state of others. Some examples include the pioneering measure developed by Dymond (1949), designed to evaluate a person's ability to judge another individual's reactions, and Borke's (1971) Interpersonal Perception Test. The latter is way of measuring children's ability to label correctly the emotion felt by another child and then to take the point of view of the other in judging emotional events. Measures that have focused on cognitive skills, such as social perception or role-taking, have been criticized for not assessing the complex skills involved in the affective sharing component of empathy (Chandler & Greenspan, 1972; Cronbach, 1955).

In the so-called affective approach, empathy denotes a vicarious experience of an emotion that is congruent with the emotion of another individual (Batson & Coke, 1981; Sawin, 1979; Staub, 1978). Central to this definition is the attention to emotional arousal and its directionality rather than accuracy in labeling what another person is feeling. Nevertheless, the requirement of emotional correspondence between the observer and the observed need not ignore the role of cognitive factors. On the contrary, the approach that is currently prominent focuses on an integrated model that takes into account both affective experience and cognitive mediators of empathy.

In N. Feshbach's theoretical paradigm (1973, 1975, 1978), *empathy* is defined as a match between the affective responses of the perceiver and a stimulus person. Empathic arousal is thought to be a function of the participant's ability to discriminate affective cues in others, assume the perspective and role of another person, and experience and share emotions. In Hoffman's developmental model (1978, 1982), *empathy* is conceived of as an affective response to distress in others and is already reflected in infant behavior. Although empathy is a primary affective reaction, Hoffman assumed that cognitive and affective processes jointly operate when a child's cognitive system develops. Thus, although empathy is defined as an affective reaction, it is likely to be mediated by different kinds of cognitive appraisal, which may be ordered in terms of increasing complexity reflecting a shift from involuntary to voluntary mediators (Strayer, 1987).

Within the affective perspective, several measures have been developed to assess the degree of empathic response to individuals in circumstances that give rise to different emotions. Generally, the instruments fall into three categories: physiological and somatic indices, paper-and-pencil questionnaires, and picture-story or verbal report indices (for a detailed review, see Strayer, 1987).

Picture-story indices are the most well-known measures of empathy and are based on participants' responses to emotionally loaded situations such as vignettes, audiotapes, or slides depicting a main character involved in an affective event. The FASTE (Feshbach & Roe, 1968) has been the most widely used verbal report measure. Developed by the authors for preschool and early elementary school-age children, it was aimed at evaluating the affective dimension of empathy while taking into account its cognitive prerequisites. The FASTE exists in three versions: written stories, audiovisual tapes, and slides. In the slide format, children are individually exposed to a series of slide sequences depicting a boy or girl in different affective situations, two each for fear, anger, sadness, and happiness. Each sequence consists of three slides, accompanied by an appropriate narration. Immediately after each slide sequence, the child is asked to state how he or she feels. An exact match with the stimulus person's emotion is scored as an empathic response, and the child's social comprehension is assessed by asking him or her how the main character in the story feels.

The FASTE index has been used in numerous empirical studies (Bazar, 1977; Eisenberg-Berg & Lennon, 1980; Fay, 1971; Iannotti, 1975). In earlier research, N. Feshbach (1973, 1975) found that empathy in children increases with age. Concerning gender differences, data were not unequivocal; although some findings suggested that girls are more empathic than boys (Eisenberg & Lennon, 1987), Feshbach and Feshbach (1969) found an inverse relationship between empathy and aggression. The predicted positive association with prosocial behavior was less consistent (Feshbach, 1978). Verbal reports remain the most often used method that taps the subjective quality of empathy. The validity of verbal reports as a measure of empathy has been criticized (Hoffman, 1982). Some criticisms stress the vocabulary needed for verbal reports to label and communicate different emotional reactions in diverse contexts. Moreover, the veridicality of verbal reports depends on participants' capacity to introspect and say what they really feel when witnessing affective events. But the most important criticism concerns the scoring of empathic responses in terms of affect match between the emotion felt by the target and that perceived by the observer. The exact correspondence between the two feelings seems to be a restrictive criterion because it does not take into account that similar emotional responses can be empathetic (Feshbach & Roe, 1968).

DESIGNING A MEASURE TO ASSESS EMPATHIC RESPONSIVENESS

Differences in methods and instruments for assessing empathy highlight the enormous difficulties researchers face when evaluating the empathic process. Each measure stresses one of the multiple components of vicariously sharing affect. In the absence of an agreed-on definition of empathy, it is not surprising that associations among empathic measures are not consistent and that different measures produce different results. Consider the case of the relationship between empathy and role-taking. Although role-taking has been thought of as an important prerequisite of empathic response and sometimes even incorporated into the definition (Borke, 1971), in several studies it has been found not to be correlated with empathy (Kagan & Knudson, 1982). Measurement of empathy is undoubtedly a challenging enterprise.

When we began to study empathy in Italy, the word *empathy* was familiar to only a few researchers, mostly psychologists and sociologists. Empathy did not have the same relevance that it had in English-speaking countries. In Italy there was minimal racial discord, limited gratuitous violence, and limited interpersonal and intergenerational conflict. This does not mean that Italians were without social problems, but people thought that serious social discord applied only to minority deviant social groups. In general, the Italians did not think of empathy as a strategy to build human relations.

Keeping in mind these cultural differences, we have conducted several studies on children's empathy and its relationship to aggressiveness and prosocial behavior (Lo Coco, Manna, & Miceli, 1991). To test the children's ability to feel empathically, we used the paper-and-pencil measure developed by Feshbach and her colleagues and based on her theoretical model (Feshbach, Caprara, Lo Coco, Pastorelli, & Manna, 1991). The results for our sample were not as reliable as those obtained in the United States. It seemed to us that the children did not fully understand what they were being asked and that social desirability was affecting their responses. At the same time, it seemed that the children's difficulties did not stem from inadequate mastery of socio–cognitive skills but from their lack of familiarity with the construct. We think that empathy is culturally constructed or at least takes different forms as a function of child-rearing and educational practices.

Using Feshbach and Roe's (1968) original essay as a point of departure, we designed a series of story narratives. They allowed us to interview the children extensively and examine how they construct the idea that another person can experience emotionally charged events. The story narratives also reveal the level and quality of the children's responses when they witness similar events.

The study that follows is an elaboration of the FASTE index, for children from 5 to 10 years old. It also depicts findings on the relationships between empathy and aggressiveness, prosocial behavior, and emotional stability.

STUDY 1

The design of the vignettes for the new measure was preceded by a lengthy preparation to ensure the measure's relevance to Italian children. We first created a semistructural questionnaire asking the children to describe what situations in daily life can give rise to happiness, fear, anger, sadness, jealousy, and shame. The first four emotions were originally used in the FASTE; the last two were new. We were interested in studying these emotions because they seem to be more culture dependent and linked to the social context.

The questionnaire was administered to 500 children, varying in grade level, gender, and socioeconomic background. The emotional antecedents were integrated and incorporated into very short stories, three for each emotion, in which the main character was involved in an event arousing a direct, intense emotional response. These stories were then submitted to two small samples: 30 adults, to assess whether the stories were correctly linked to the particular emotion, and 30 children, to ascertain whether the narration of the stories enabled them to make the correct inferences about the emotions experienced by the main character. After these checks, the written stories were presented to another sample of 50 boys and 50 girls. In a collective session, each child read the story and at the end indicated which emotion (of the six given) the main character was feeling. The scenarios in which the central emotion was recognized by the most children were chosen. Each scenario was depicted by three illustrations and accompanied by a written text (Albiero & Lo Coco, 1995). Descriptions of the six emotions and their accompanying stories are provided in Table 10.1.

The children were shown the three illustrations for each emotion while the interviewer read the appropriate narration, avoiding the use of affective terms. At the end of each narration the child was interviewed, and his or her responses were recorded. In constructing the interview, two main lines of inquiry were pursued. The first explored social comprehension, the extent to which children are able to decode correctly the events in the story, discriminating and recognizing psychological states and the facial and bodily affective cues of others. These cognitive elements involved in the empathetic process were evaluated by asking (a) "How does the main character feel?" (b) "How much does the protagonist feel? A little, quite a lot, a

TABLE 10.1
Description of the stories used in questionnaire

Emotion Scenario	Description
Anger	Two children on a balcony pour a pail of water on the child who is walking past, and they start laughing and making faces at the child.
Happiness	The child goes to the circus with his or her parents to see a performance.
Sadness	The child goes to the hospital with his or her parents to visit a relative who is very ill and must have an operation. However, the relative is so seriously ill that he dies despite the operation.
Fear	The child is coming home from school through a park when a fierce dog starts running after the child.
Jealousy	The child is watching television with his or her mother. When his or her father comes back home and watches TV, too, the mother only cares about the father.
Shame	For a medical examination, the child must strip from head to foot in front of his or her mother, the doctor, and the nurse.

lot?" and (c) "Why does the protagonist feel this way?" The second line of inquiry concerned affective responsiveness to witnessing an emotional event in which another person is involved. Focusing on the affective match between the story character and the participant, questions included "How do you feel?" (R4); "How much do you feel? (R4) A little, quite a lot, a lot?" (R5); "Why do you feel this way (R4)?" (R6).

At the end of each scenario, the children were presented a card showing the emotional categories. From these, they chose the concordant emotion for the stimulus person. Besides the six emotions, a category called "nothing" was introduced ("I feel nothing"). If a child reported more than one emotion, he or she was asked to choose the strongest. If the child reported an emotion not included in the categories, he or she was asked to choose the one most similar to their feelings.

The scoring criteria used in this study were very strict. For the social comprehension question, participants scored 1 for each correct label of the character's emotion and 0 for an incorrect label. For the empathy question, participants scored 1 for the match between the stimulus person's and participant's emotion. Hoffmann (1977, 1982) noted that requiring an exact match would simplify scoring, because the presence or absence of an exact match can be readily ascertained. However, he has argued that insisting on an exact match as a criterion would lead to discarding many empathetic responses, especially by young children, where accuracy may be undermined by competence. Despite the potential shortcomings of such strict criteria to assess empathy, in this initial phase of our work we chose to consider only those that matched exactly.

The results of the exploratory study concern the first data collected from 50 children, 25 boys and 25 girls, ranging in age from 8 to 10 years. All children were enrolled in an elementary school in the city of Palermo. The percentage of correct responses to social comprehension and empathy questions for each emotion are reported in Table 10.2.

TABLE 10.2

Percentage of correct responses to social comprehension and empathy questions for each emotion

	Total		Boys		Girls	
	Social Comprehension	Empathy	Social Comprehension	Empathy	Social Comprehension	Empathy
Sadness	98	94	96	92	100	96
Happiness	89	86	92	80	86	92
Fear	100	95	100	92	100	98
Anger	94	87	94	54	94	58
Shame	91	36	92	34	90	38
Jealousy	61	48	54	40	68	56

As expected, the children were able to decode the emotion felt by the stimulus person (social comprehension question) but often did not report sharing the emotion of another person when "witness" to an emotionally charged hypothetical event. Moreover, there were consistent differences among emotions. For social comprehension, almost all participants recognized all of the emotions, with fear being the best recognized and jealousy the least. There were few differences in the results for the boys and girls, although the girls scored higher in both social comprehension and empathy for jealousy.

The girls' higher scores on jealousy are consistent with previous findings of girls reporting more empathy (Eisenberg & Lennon, 1983 ; Feshbach & Feshbach, 1969; Feshbach & Roe, 1968; Strayer, 1987). These gender differences have been interpreted to result from socialization practices that tend to promote and permit more emotions in girls than boys (Eisenberg & Lennon, 1983). The role of gender socialization seems to be more relevant in the self-attribution report than when noting the emotions and feelings of others (Strayer, 1989). In Strayer's study there were no gender differences in the report of emotions attributed to the vignettes' protagonists, but there were gender differences in self-reported emotions. In our study, we obtained similar findings. There were no relevant differences in attributing emotions to the main character of the story. On the contrary, for happiness and shame, the boys were more accurate in recognition than were the girls, but the girls showed more overall accuracy in self-reported emotions than did the boys.

In this study we were determined, where possible, to remedy limitations raised by Hoffman (1982). This includes an index to measure the intensity of the affective match, and adding new questions to discover participants' cognitive reasons for their shared affect. Other problems, such as social desirability, are not possible to eliminate with this type of measure. Another limitation reported by Hoffman is that stories can evoke more than one emotion. This means that a response that is different from what is predetermined to be correct does not receive full credit. Each scenario was constructed following rigorous procedures, and although a mixture of different emotions is possible, we think that the scenarios focus mostly on one emotion.

The vignettes could also be criticized for not being particularly stimulating or involving for children, compared with other possible ways of presenting stimulus situations. They may not be sufficiently "emotionally charged" to provoke an affective match in children. The use of other forms of communication, such as videotapes rather than slides, could increase participant involvement and enhance empathic responses.

However, there are problems related to these forms of presentation that cannot be ignored. For instance, it is undoubtedly more difficult to control variables when making a videotape. Also, differences in photography, acting, framing, or editing can influence participant responses. Vignettes, on the other hand, allow greater control of the whole story context and its elements, such as the number of words used for each scenario. For this reason, we chose vignettes.

STUDY 2: THE DEVELOPMENT OF EMPATHY

The main purpose of the second study was to explore developmental differences in empathy, focusing on vicarious affective response and the cognitive explanations for the emotions experienced. Another aim was to analyze the relationship between empathy and aggressiveness, prosocial behavior and emotional instability. The study was designed to address these questions: To what extent does children's responsiveness in witnessing others' feelings change as a function of age? Are changes different for boys and girls? Do children's justifications of their shared emotions become more complex with age? Are the reasons given related to gender? Finally, to what extent is empathy a mediator and facilitator of prosocial behavior and a regulator of aggressive behavior? Three sets of hypotheses were examined.

The first set concerns children's emotional responses, operationalized as affect match. Many studies have found that the development of an understanding of others' feelings and needs and an awareness of other people as distinct from the self develops with age (Damon, 1977). In turn, the ability to organize one's own social experience should enhance children's capacity to share the emotional states of other individuals. We therefore expected affect matches to increase with age.

Past findings from experimental research regarding gender differences in empathy development are inconsistent. Where differences are present, they could be ascribed to the type of measures used (Bazar, 1977; Eisenberg & Lennon, 1987). Consequently, no hypotheses have been made regarding gender, and the study intends to compare findings with data from other cultures, because empathy can be considered a culture-dependent construct.

We also expected to find differences among emotions. Children appear to empathize more easily with euphoric than disphoric emotions, perhaps because it is more gratifying to share positive than negative emotions. Anger is considered an "at-risk" emotion because it may involve important changes in the self-control system (Feshbach & Roe, 1968; Mood, Johnson, & Shantz, 1978; Strayer, 1980). We hypothesized that the children may be more responsive to some emotions, especially sadness and happiness, which are more socially acceptable. No hypotheses were made for jealousy and shame, because these emotions had not been used previously in other studies on empathy responses.

The second set of hypotheses regards the cognitive attributions that children make to explain their empathic responses. According to the results reported in many previous studies, as children age they become more aware of other's emotional states (Damon, 1977). They are more able to identify the most salient emotional factors regarding events or persons (Gnepp, 1983; Thompson, 1987), more accurate in understanding others' affective situations (Hughes, Tingle, & Sawin, 1981), and more capable of verbalizing their affective and social experiences (Thompson, 1987). Following Strayer (1993), we hypothesized that the type of cognitive explanation would vary with age. The younger children were expected to make simpler attributions, based on external events and the stimulus person within the event. The older children were expected to make more complex attributions, based on their ability to apply similar personal experiences to those witnessed in others, and on the ability to take someone else's point of view. At this point we also hypothesized that emotions such as happiness, sadness, and fear should elicit more complex cognitive attributions, whereas anger and jealousy would induce explanations based on external events, without reference to the internal state of another person.

Finally, we determined to explore the relationship between empathy, aggressiveness, prosocial behavior, and emotional instability. Research carried out in the past two decades has examined the role that empathy plays in the emergence of social behaviors and the organization of interpersonal relationships (Eisenberg & Fabes, 1991). Theoretically, empathy is thought to enhance prosocial behavior and to modulate or regulate aggressive behavior. The assumption underlining this hypothesis resides in the particular nature of the constructs involved. The ability to understand and share the emotional state of another may lead the participant to display several positive social behaviors toward others in distress, such as helping and comforting. At the same time, the painful consequences of an aggressive act, experienced vicariously, may inhibit the participant's aggressive tendencies.

Although these premises have been largely accepted, empirical findings from experimental research on these topics have not been consistent. Eisenberg and Fabes (1990, 1991) proposed two reasons for the inconsistency. The first concerns the complex and multidimensional nature of the construct implied in the relation. Aggression, prosocial behavior, and empathy have many facets and involve other similar constructs.

The second explanation concerns the type of instrument or procedure used to measure or test the hypotheses. Consider the case of the relationship between empathy and prosocial behavior. When using verbal reports to assess empathy and naturalistic observations to test prosocial behavior, results have been less consistent (Eisenberg-Berg & Lennon, 1980; Fay, 1971). In contrast to this, when using questionnaires or self-reports to measure both empathy and prosocial behavior, results appear to be consistent and significant (Strayer & Robertson, 1989). In the case of the relationship between empathy and aggressive behavior, several studies have demonstrated a significant inverse relationship between the two constructs when empathy is assessed in school-age children by means of self-report and aggressive behavior is evaluated using reports from teachers and parents (Bazar, 1977). This trend, however, depends on the participant's age and the type of emotion considered to be shared (Feshbach, 1982). However, on the basis of previous research conducted in our laboratory (Lo Coco, Manna, & Miceli, 1991), we hypothesized a positive relation between verbal reports on empathy and prosocial behavior when the latter is assessed by teachers and peers. We predicted a negative relationship between verbal reports on empathy and aggressive behavior when evaluated by peers.

Applying New Methods

The participants were 200 children (100 boys, 100 girls) divided into two age groups: 6–7 years and 9–10 years. The children were administered the Italian revision of the FASTE, as previously described in Study 1. To overcome some problems discovered in the exploratory study, we introduced some modifications. The first regards the scoring criteria for affect match. We decided to adopt a less stringent criterion than in Study 1 and evaluated the affect match on a four-point scale (0 = *the child felt no emotion*, 1 = *the child's emotion was similar to his or her report of the character's emotion*, 2 = *the child's emotion was the same as the character's but different in intensity*, 3 = *both the child's emotion and the intensity are the same as the character's*).

The second modification concerns the interview used to assess the presence of an empathic response. Besides the two typical questions aimed at measuring social comprehension and empathic responsiveness, a new line of inquiry was introduced by asking the children, "If you witnessed a situation like this, what would you feel?" (R1); "How much do you feel? (R1) A little, quite lot, a lot?" (R2); "Why do you feel this way (R1)?" (R3).

Because the vignettes depict a main character in an emotionally charged context, the presence or absence of empathic responsiveness may be due more to the power of the stimulus situation than to the psychological disposition of the participant. In other words, the formulation of the questions could elicit empathic arousal in terms of "state," related to the particular condition in which the stimulus person is involved. The question "How do you feel?" is the most direct, whereas the question "If you witnessed a situation like this, what would you feel?" establishes a distance between observer and observed. Consequently, it could elicit an empathic response linked less to the specificity of the stimulus and more to individual dispositions. Another goal was to examine the patterns of affect match, cognitive attributions, and empathy scores at this more general (dispositional) level of response. We would expect the children to have higher affect match scores on the standard measure of empathy and higher cognitive attributions on the witnessing measure.

The five questions were presented in random order. We scored the children's explanations for why they felt the way they did according to Strayer's (1987) proposed procedure. Strayer suggested two cognitive levels reflecting the absence of affect match and five levels reflecting its presence. These seven levels are ordered according to participants' ability to find synchrony with the internal state of another person: L0 = an inaccurate identification of the character's emotion, L1 = an accurate identification of the character's emotion, but without affect match, L2 = no or irrelevant attributions for affect match, L3 = attributions based on events only, L4 = attributions mentioning the stimulus person in a specific event, L5 = attributions associating the stimulus person's experience to one's own, L6 = attributions mentioning the stimulus person's internal state or viewpoint, and L7 = explicit emotional role-taking.

Age and Gender Effects

To assess age and gender effects on affect match scores, we performed an analysis of variance, with age and gender as independent variables and the six scenarios depicting the emotions and the two levels of recording (empathy and witnessing) as repeated measures (see Table 10.3). The results show a significant main effect for age, Wilk's Lambda (2.195) = 0.88, $p < .0000$, and for emotions, Wilk's Lambda (10.187) = 0.41, $p < .0001$. Gender and interactions were not significant. The analysis of variance shows that the older children (M = 1.68) reported greater affect matches than did the younger children (M = 1.27) in empathy recording, $F(1.196) = 24.77$, $p < 0.000$. For witnessing, the age differences were not significant.

Emotion effects were significant for both empathy, $F(5.980) = 39.73$, $p < 0.000$, and witnessing recording, $F(5.980) = 32.70$, $p < 0.000$. Newman-Keuls post-hoc procedure shows that sadness and happiness elicited the greatest affective concordance in both situations, whereas anger, jealousy, and shame elicited less affective concordance.

TABLE 10.3

Means and standard deviations of affect match for emotions in empathy and witnessing

Emotions	Empathy	Witnessing		
	M	SD	M	SD
Happiness	1.85	1.08	1.70	1.15
Jealousy	1.22	1.05	1.13	0.9
Fear	1.29	0.9	1.38	0.9
Anger	1.24	1.07	1.30	1.01
Sadness	2.10	0.93	1.98	0.9
Shame	1.16	1.02	1.06	0.9

TABLE 10.4
Percentage of cognitive attributions type for 6- to 7-year-olds and 9- to 10-year-olds

	Age	
Cognitive Attribution	6–7 Years	9–10 Years
L3 Events in the story	6	0
L4 Stimulus person in the story	33	10
L5 Association between stimulus person's experience and one's own	41	21
L6 Stimulus person's internal states	18	45
L7 Explicit role taking	2	24

Table 10.4 shows the frequencies for the cognitive attribution in 6- to 7-year-olds and 9- to 10-year-olds. For this kind of analysis, frequency is calculated by considering the median of attributions provided by each child at two levels of recording. Only the levels strictly pertaining to the cognitive aspects were taken into account.

The children ages 6–7 most often referred to the person in the event and the association between the stimulus person's experience and their own. The children ages 9–10 were more likely to refer to the internal state of the other person (45%) and, to a lesser degree, to explicit role-taking (24%). The attributions based on the external story-event decreased. The trend was similar for all emotions except for shame and fear. With the exception of those two emotions, the older children had significantly higher responses than did the younger children.

Anger Scenario

In the empathy recording, the younger children focused on L1 (35%), and the older children distributed their cognitive explanations on L3, L4, and L5, (21, 21, and 23%, respectively). Distribution in the witnessing recording was not significant. Gender was not significant in both levels of recording.

Happiness Scenario

In the empathy recording, the younger children focused on L4 (17%) and L6 (16%), and the older children distributed their cognitive explanations on L5 (20%), L6 (27%) and, partially, on L7 (13%). In the witnessing recording, the younger children based their cognitive attributions on level 6 (21%). The older children made the same type of attributions but with higher percentages (44%). Gender was not significant at either level of recording. Gender differences were found only for sadness, with girls giving more L5 responses and boys giving more L3 responses.

Sadness Scenario

In the empathy recording, the younger children focused on level 3 (35%), and the older children distributed their cognitive explanations on level 5 (38%) and level 6 (20%). The same trend was found in the witnessing recording in which the younger children based their cognitive attributions on level 3 (28%), and the older children based their cognitive attributions on level 5 (36%) and level 6 (21%). Gender distribution was significant, with girls focusing on level 5 (36%) and boys on level 3 (34%).

Jealousy Scenario

In the empathy recording, the younger children focused on level 4 (21%), and the older children distributed their cognitive explanations on level 5 (27%) and level 7 (12%). Distribution in the witnessing recording was not significant. Gender was not significant at either level of recording. Distributions regarding age and gender in the shame and fear scenarios were not significant at either level of recording.

The findings regarding the first two sets of questions support our hypotheses on affect matches. As expected, the older children reported greater affect matches than the younger children. With age, understanding of social contexts and different emotional cues becomes more sophisticated (Gnepp, 1983). And previous research indicates that acquisition of this kind of socio–cognitive and emotional competence allows children to respond more accurately to others' affective states (Thompson, 1987).

The difference between the older and younger children concerns only the experience of empathy, not witnessing recording. This pattern of result supports our hypothesis that the question "How do you feel?" taps the affective aspect of empathy directly, and the question "If you witnessed a situation like this, what would you feel?" does not. The latter question, establishing a distance between the observer and the observed, seems to be mediated by a cognitive appraisal (the child thinks about how he or she would typically respond). As in many other previous studies, gender differences did not affect empathic responses (Strayer, 1989).

Affect match scores varied among the six emotions, as found in previous studies (Feshbach, 1982; Strayer, 1987, 1989, 1993). In particular, sadness and happiness elicited the most concordance. Scores for anger, as expected, were low, but unexpectedly, jealousy and shame were the least shared emotions. Perhaps displays of these private and intimate emotions are less salient and consequently less likely to be shared.

Findings regarding cognitive levels support the idea that the reasoning given by the children to explain their emotional experiences are organized according to a system of cognitive attributions. These are derived from models of interpersonal understanding in which the range of emotional concepts increases with age and the interpretation of an emotional experience becomes more personal and psychological (Strayer, 1989). Attributions for sadness and happiness focused on the internal experience of others, whereas attributions for anger were based on external events. Our expectations that witnessing recording would elicit more sophisticated and complex cognitive elaboration was not supported and needs further research as well as thorough theoretical examination.

RELATIONSHIPS AMONG EMPATHY, AGGRESSIVE AND PROSOCIAL BEHAVIOR, AND EMOTIONAL STABILITY

To test this set of hypotheses, a series of correlations were calculated between affect match scores and scores from the self-report, teacher ratings, and peer nominations on aggression, emotional instability, and prosocial behavior (Caprara, Alcini, Mazzotti, & Pastorelli, 1988). The only significant correlation using self-report measures involved empathy and prosocial behavior and then only for the girls. The same was found for teacher ratings.

The boys reported a significant correlation between empathy and unstable emotions. The lack of a positive association between empathy and prosocial behavior may be explained by differences in the boys' and girls' upbringing and educational practices. Girls may be encouraged to be more sensitive and caring toward emotions and distress in others, which in turn produces the display of social, positive behavior. Perhaps boys are not encouraged as much to behave prosocially regardless of their empathetic feelings. Perhaps emotionally unstable boys are more vulnerable and thus more responsive to others in need.

When the informants were peers, a negative association was found between affect match scores and aggressiveness in the boys, whereas a positive association was found between affect match and prosocial behavior in the girls. Female classmates with high scores in empathetic responsiveness were perceived as prosocial by their peers, whereas the boys who had lower affect match scores were deemed aggressive.

These results suggest that empathy has different implications for boys and girls. The findings also show that different informants evaluate constructs differently. For example, aggression was associated with boys' empathy only when it was related by peers. Perhaps peers' judgments were more reliable than the children's self-ratings of aggression because children are not reliable judges of themselves on negative dimensions.

CONCLUSION

Our general aim in these two studies was to explore empathy in Italian children and its relation to other positive social behavior. For this purpose, we created an instrument inspired by the procedure of Feshbach and Roe. Results of the exploratory study suggest that the instrument does reliably assess empathy. Nevertheless, we recommend some modifications for the questions on cognitive attributions that ask children to explain their empathetic responses. For instance, it might be useful to ask children where they obtained the idea of sharing the emotional states of others and what reasons or external cues they take into account when reacting the way they do. One could thus verify further the role of social desirability in children's responses, or their need to comply with the interviewer.

In the future, researchers should also use measures of empathy other than verbal report to gain more information on what comprises this complex and multifaceted phenomenon. Sharing the emotional state of others can signify an important step in the path toward solidarity and understanding others' points of view. Learning to care for others is an important resource for organizing human and social relationships. Unfortunately, recent political and social events in Italy have shown how violence, racism, and aggression have become part of the country's reality. The word *empathy* has now become familiar and is believed to be important for social understanding and a more peaceful society. Empathy could represent a means of surviving and better facing the future.

REFERENCES

Albiero, P., & Lo Coco, A. (1995). The Feshbach and Roe Affective Situation Test for Empathy revised and adapted for Italian children. In G. Sprini & F. Ceresia (Eds.), *Issues in cognition, development and work psychology* (pp. 121–133). Italy: Universita di Palermo.

Batson, C. D., & Coke, J. S. (1981). Empathy: A source of altruistic motivation for helping? In J. P. Rushton & R. M. Sorrentino (Eds.), *Altruism and helping behavior: Social, personality and developmental perspectives* (pp. 167–211). Hillsdale, NJ: Erlbaum.

Bazar, J. W. (1977). An exploration of the relationship of affect awareness, empathy and interpersonal strategies to nursery school children's competence in peer interactions (Doctoral dissertation, University of California, Berkeley, 1976). *Dissertation Abstracts International, 37,* 5691A.

Borke, H. (1971). Interpersonal perception of young children: Egocentrism or empathy? *Developmental Psychology, 5*, 263–296.

Caprara, G. V., Alcini, P., Mazzotti, E., & Pastorelli, C. (1988). Sviluppo e caratteristiche di tre scale per la misura dell'aggressivita fisica e verbale, del comportamento prosociale, dell'instabilita emotiva. In G. V. Caprara & M. Laeng (Eds.), *Indicatori e precursori della condotta aggressiva* (pp. 121–144) Rome: Bulzoni.

Chandler, M. J., & Greenspan, S. (1972). Ersatz egocentrism: A reply to H. Borke. *Developmental Psychology, 7*, 104–106.

Cronbach, L. J. (1955). Processes affecting scores on "understanding others" and "assumed similarity." *Psychological Bulletin, 52*, 177–193.

Damon, W. (1977). *The social world of the child.* San Francisco: Jossey-Bass.

Deutsch, F. M., & Madle, R. A. (1975). Empathy: Historic and current conceptualizations, measurement, and a cognitive theoretical perspective. *Human Development, 18*, 267–287.

Dymond, R. F. (1949). A scale for the measurement of empathic ability. *Journal of Consulting Psychology, 13*, 127–133.

Eisenberg, N., & Fabes, R. A. (1990). Empathy: Conceptualization, assessment and relation to prosocial behavior. *Motivation and Emotion, 14*, 131–149.

Eisenberg, N., & Fabes, R. A. (1991). Prosocial behavior and empathy: A multi-method developmental perspective. In M. S. Clark (Ed.), *Prosocial behavior* (pp. 34–61). Newbury Park, CA: Sage Publications.

Eisenberg, N., & Lennon, R. (1983). Sex differences in empathy and related capacities. *Psychological Bulletin, 94*, 100–131.

Eisenberg, N., & Lennon, R. (1987). Gender and age differences in empathy and sympathy. In N. Eisenberg & J. Strayer (Eds.), *Empathy and its development* (pp. 195–217). New York: Cambridge University Press.

Eisenberg, N., & Strayer, J. (1987). Critical issues in the study of empathy. In N. Eisenberg & J. Strayer (Eds.), *Empathy and its development* (pp. 3–13). New York: Cambridge University Press.

Eisenberg-Berg, N., & Lennon, R. (1980). Altruism and the assessment of empathy in the preschool years. *Child Development, 51*, 552–557.

Fay, B. (1971). The relationship of cognitive moral judgment, generosity and empathic behavior in six- and eight-year-old children (Doctoral dissertation, University of California, Los Angeles, 1970). *Dissertation Abstracts International, 31*, 3951A.

Feshbach, N. D. (1973). Empathy: An interpersonal process. In W. Hartup (Chair), *Social understanding in children and adults: Perspectives on social cognition.* Symposium presented at meeting of the American Psychological Association, Montreal.

Feshbach, N. D. (1975). Empathy in children: Some theoretical and empirical considerations. *Counseling Psychologist, 5*(2), 25–30.

Feshbach, N. D. (1978). Studies of empathic behavior in children. In B. A. Maher (Ed.), *Progress in experimental personality research* (pp. 1–47). New York: Academic Press.

Feshbach, N. D. (1982). Sex differences in empathy and social behavior in children. In N. Eisenberg (Ed.), *The development of prosocial behavior* (pp. 315–338). New York: Academic Press.

Feshbach, N. D., Caprara, G. V., Lo Coco, A., Pastorelli, C., Manna, G., & Menzes, J. (1991). *Empathy and its correlates: Cross cultural data from Italy.* Paper presented at the Eleventh Biennial Meeting of the International Society for the Study of Behavioural Development, Minneapolis, MN.

Feshbach, N. D., & Feshbach, S. (1969). The relationship between empathy and aggression in two age groups. *Developmental Psychology, 1,* 102–107.

Feshbach, N. D., & Roe, K. (1968). Empathy in six- and seven-year-olds. *Child Development, 39,* 133–145.

Gnepp, J. (1983). Children's social sensitivity: Inferring emotions from conflicting cues. *Developmental Psychology, 19,* 805–814.

Hoffman, M. L. (1977). Sex differences in empathy and related behaviors. *Psychological Bulletin, 84,* 712, 722.

Hoffman, M. L. (1978). Psychological and biological perspectives on altruism. *International Journal of Behavioral Development, 1,* 323–339.

Hoffman, M. L. (1982). The measurement of empathy. In C. E. Izard (Ed.), *Measuring emotions in infants and children* (pp. 279–296). Cambridge, England: Cambridge University Press.

Hughes, R., Tingle, B. A., & Sawin, D. B. (1981). Development of empathic understanding in children. *Child Development, 52,* 122–128.

Iannotti, R. J. (1975). The nature and measurement of empathy in children. *The Counseling Psychologist, 5,* 21–25.

Kagan, S., & Knudson, K. H. M. (1982). Relationships of empathy and affective role-taking in young children. *Journal of Genetic Psychology, 141,* 149–150.

Lo Coco, A. (1992). E possibile misurare la qualita? (Is it possible to measure quality?). In M. Ceruti (Ed.), *Evoluzione e conoscenza* (pp. 231–243). Bergamo, Italy: Lubrina.

Lo Coco, A., Manna, G., & Miceli, S. (1991). Empatia, aggressivita, prosocialita in eta evolutiva (Empathy, aggressiveness, prosocial behavior in developmental age). In *Contributi del Dipartimento di Psicologia* (pp. 130–144). Italy: Universita di Palermo.

Mood, D. W., Johnson, J. E., & Shantz, C. V. (1978). Social comprehension and affect matching in young children. *Merrill-Palmer Quarterly, 24,* 63–66.

Plutchik, R. (1987). Evolutionary bases of empathy. In N. Eisenberg & J. Strayer (Eds.), *Empathy and its development* (pp. 38–46). New York: Cambridge University Press.

Sawin, D. (1979). *Assessing empathy in children: A search for an elusive concept.* Paper presented at the biennial meeting of the Society for Research in Child Development, San Francisco.

Shantz, C. U. (1975). The development of social cognition. In E. M. Hetherington (Ed.), *Review of child development research* (Vol. 5, pp.). Chicago: University of Chicago Press.

Solomon, J. (1985). *The relationship between affective empathy and prosocial behavior in elementary school children.* Paper presented at the Biennial Meeting of the Society for Research on Child Development, Toronto.

Staub, E. (1978). Positive social behavior and morality: Social and personal influences (Vol. 1). New York: Academic Press.

Strayer, J. (1980). A naturalistic study of empathic behaviors and their relation to affective states and perspective-taking skills in preschool children. *Child Development, 51,* 815–822.

Strayer, J. (1987). Affective and cognitive perspectives on empathy. In N. Eisenberg & J. Strayer (Eds.), *Empathy and its development* (pp. 218–244). New York: Cambridge University Press.

Strayer, J. (1989). What children know and feel in response to witnessing. In C. Saarni & P. L. Harris (Eds.), *Children's understanding of emotion* (pp. 259–289). Cambridge, England: Cambridge University Press.

Strayer, J. (1993). Children's concordant emotions and cognitions in response to observed emotions. *Child Development, 64,* 188–201.

Strayer, J., & Robertson, W. (1989). Children's empathy and role-taking: Child parental factors, and relations to prosocial behavior. *Journal of Applied Developmental Psychology, 10,* 227–239.

Thompson, R. A. (1987). Empathy and emotional understanding: The early development of empathy. In N. Eisenberg & J. Strayer (Eds.), *Empathy and its development* (pp. 119–145). New York: Cambridge University Press.

III

PREVENTION
AND INTERVENTION

The prevention of negative outcomes in children has become an important issue. There have been several recent books published on the topic (e.g., Burt, Resnick, & Novick, 1998; Cowen et al., 1996; Illback, Cobb, & Joseph, 1997; Richel & Becker-Lausen, 1997). In this part, authors look at prevention at the level of early intervention programs and at school. Intervention at the adult level is also considered in the clinical context in two chapters that specifically deal with the topic of the expression of anger.

EDWARD ZIGLER AND SALLY J. STYFCO, AND L. ROWELL HUESMANN AND MEREDITH A. REYNOLDS

We first consider basic prevention efforts with two overview chapters by Edward Zigler and Sally J. Styfco and L. Rowell Huesmann and Meredith A. Reynolds. These chapters take somewhat different looks at prevention. Zigler and Styfco consider the factors that do or do not work in various prevention efforts, review several, and make recommendations. Huesmann and Reynolds present a cognitive script-based theory of the development and expression of aggression (see also Eron. chapter 2) and then review several prevention programs that have a cognitive emphasis. They also make recommendations as to the kinds of things that need to be done for more effective programs. In essence, these programs all stress the positive: improving children's life and education and teaching them positive coping skills as a way to control aggressive behavior. Zigler and Styfco also include a discussion of Head Start and how helping children do better in school may help reduce aggressive behavior, although this has not been sufficiently researched. Both chapters conclude that intervention efforts look promising but as of yet are not as powerful as is needed.

MYRNA B. SHURE

Myrna B. Shure follows with a report on a specific program that consists of a cognitive, perspective-taking, coping model of prevention. It involves training children and their parents. It includes training both in coping skills, such as how to handle conflict situations (along the lines of what Pulkkinen suggests is needed to control antisocial/aggressive behavior) and in empathic perspective-taking skills (along the lines of what Hoffman and Mussen and Eisenberg suggest is important in promoting prosocial behavior). Furthermore, it is based on the idea that the best manner of teaching is through mobilizing the students' (and parents' and teachers') own abilities to think things through, in keeping with suggestions by Bohart (chapter 16) on what is the optimal way to promote positive change in psychotherapy.

DEBORAH STIPEK

Deborah Stipek gives a detailed examination of schools and how they can promote either prosocial or destructive developmental pathways. She focuses on practices that demoralize and discourage children, such as retention and assignment to lower-level reading groups. She shows how school failure predicts dysfunctional behavior in adulthood and suggests that much of this is created by the demoralization of children through such school practices, as well as through their subsequent failure to gain needed academic skills. She suggests alternative practices by teachers to promote prosocial rather than antisocial behavior. Stipek's chapter dovetails with Zigler and Styfco's and Huesmann and Reynolds's work that suggests that the promotion of academic achievement can have a powerful preventive, or buffering, factor.

JONATHAN BLOOM-FESHBACH AND SALLY BLOOM-FESHBACH, AND ARTHUR BOHART

Finally, two chapters consider the topic of the expression of emotion, particularly anger, and its relationship to either prosocial or destructive behavior. The question is, can there be a "constructive expression of a destructive emotion?" Many argue, and supporting research exists, for the thesis that encouraging the expression of anger encourages or heightens the probability of destructive behavior (Bushman, Baumeister, & Stack, 1999), a position advocated by Eron (chapter 2) and Huesmann and Reynolds (chapter 12). Both Bohart and Bloom-Feshbach and Bloom-Feshbach conclude, however, that expression of emotion, particularly anger, can be constructive under the proper circumstances. Bohart also briefly focuses on how the expression of this same emotion can be destructive under other circumstances. In other words, expression of the same emotion can lead either to constructive change or destructive behavior. The Bohart and Bloom-Feshbach and Bloom-Feshbach chapters are in accord with the conclusions of others on emotional expression (Greenberg & Safran, 1987; Kennedy-Moore & Watson, 1999).

However, emotional expression is by no means the only way to help adults handle anger, and it is not helpful for all individuals (Kennedy-Moore & Watson, 1999). Other approaches that use interpersonal skills training, cognitive restructuring, and emotion management techniques also are effective (e.g., Feindler, 1991; Novaco, 1975). Once again, as Bohart emphasizes, what is needed is a more differentiated look. And this remains a topic in need of further research, especially because efforts to rehabilitate adult offenders who have problems with anger and antisocial behavior have so far not been highly effective (Huesmann and Reynolds, chapter 12).

REFERENCES

Burt, M. R., Resnick, G., & Novick, E. R. (1998). *Building supportive communities for at-risk adolescents: It takes more than services.* Washington, DC: American Psychological Association.

Bushman, B. J., Baumeister, R. F., & Stack, A. D. (1999). Catharsis, aggression, and persuasive influence: Self-fulfilling or self-defeating prophecies? *Journal of Personality and Social Psychology, 76,* 367–376.

Cowen, E. L., Hightower, A. D., Pedro-Carroll, W. C., Work, W. C., Wyman, P. A., & Haffey, W. G. (1996). *School-based prevention for children at risk: The Primary Mental Health Project.* Washington, DC: American Psychological Association.

Feindler, E. L. (1991). Cognitive strategies in anger control interventions for children and adolescents. In P. C. Kendall (Ed.), *Child and adolescent therapy: Cognitive-behavioral procedures* (pp. 66–97). New York: Guilford.

Greenberg, L. S., & Safran, J. D. (1987). *Emotion in psychological practices.* Washington, DC: American Psychological Association.

Kennedy-Moore, E., & Watson, J. C. (1999). *Expressing emotion.* New York: Guilford.

Novaco, R. W. (1975). *Anger control: The development and evaluation of an experimental treatment.* Lexington, MA: D. C. Heath.

Richel, A. V., & Becker-Lausen, E. (1997). *Keeping children from harm's way: How national policy affects psychological development.* Washington, DC: American Psychological Association.

11

CAN EARLY CHILDHOOD INTERVENTION PREVENT DELINQUENCY? A REAL POSSIBILITY

EDWARD ZIGLER AND SALLY J. STYFCO

Destructive behaviors harm both the individual and the community. One destructive behavior, juvenile delinquency, causes profound harm to communities. Research that can inform policy in this area should be a top priority. But policy cannot wait while scientists work toward a clearer understanding of the psychodynamics of aggression and criminologists sort out the results of various antidelinquency programs. The besieged public is demanding immediate action.

The concerns of the public are justified. Although crime rates have decreased in recent reporting cycles, crime rates among young people have not declined. Furthermore, the nature of juvenile crime has become more serious, with the violent crime index for those younger than 18 increasing almost 50% between 1988 and 1992 (Snyder & Sickmund, 1995) and another 7% in 1994 alone (Federal Bureau of Investigation [FBI], 1995). One does not have to read the *FBI Uniform Crime Reports* to grasp the meaning of these trends. In many cities, juvenile gangs have taken over entire neighborhoods. Teachers, students, and ministers are attacked in the supposedly safe havens of the school and church. On some streets, guns and drugs are as easy for children to obtain as candy bars and bubble gum. Gunfire is now the second leading cause of death among young people; for black men ages 15 to 19, gun violence is the most common cause of death (Bronfenbrenner, McClelland, Wethington, Moen, & Ceci, 1996).

The dangers presented by lawless youth have changed the fabric of life across America. Doors that were once unlocked are now double-bolted. Cars that were left at the curb with the windows down are now garaged and outfitted with electronic alarm systems. Community activities have waned as more people become afraid to venture out at night or to pass through certain neighborhoods at any time. Polling before the 1992 presidential election revealed that crime and violence had become the public's predominant fear. The public demanded that policymakers do something about them. Proposed solutions centered on the obvious: build more jails, impose harsher sentences, try violent juvenile offenders as adults, hold parents responsible, and hire more police officers to restore law and order. Citizens promised to bring these demands to the voting booth and support candidates with strong anticrime platforms.

This undeclared war on crime is in some ways reminiscent of the 1960s War on Poverty. Then, as now, intentions were good and hopes were high, but the weapons were not sufficient to the task. A review of antidelinquency strategies by Richard Mendel (1995) reveals that many touted practices are not only insufficient, but some may actually worsen the problem. For example, violent crime rates have not decreased despite longer sentences and enormous spending to expand prison capacity. Violent crime appears to be higher in states that invoke the death penalty. Trying juvenile offenders in adult criminal courts does not result in harsher penalties in many states; in some, criminals convicted in adult courts serve even shorter sentences than those convicted in juvenile courts. Incarcerating juveniles in adult facilities can heighten their likelihood for re-arrest and reduce their prospects for future employment. Mendel offered some compelling reasons why these supposed deterrents have not worked and will not work: The vast majority of criminal perpetrators are never caught and hence will never see the inside of expensive new jails or feel the sting of stronger penalties; many violent crimes are committed in the heat of the moment and often under the influence of alcohol or drugs—conditions that pre-empt thought about consequences; criminal careers are relatively short, tapering off after age 20 and plummeting after age 30, so there will always be a new supply of juveniles to replace those who have mended their ways.

Despite the expense and relative ineffectiveness of incarceration, no one in the juvenile justice system would say that hard-core delinquents should not be punished and removed from society. But the evidence is clear that punishment alone does not have a meaningful impact on youth crime. Efforts to reduce delinquency are in need of a fresh approach. In this chapter, we argue for a primary prevention approach, one that keeps children from turning to violence and crime in the first place. Primary prevention entails giving children more productive aspirations than crime and the skills and self-confidence to attain them. It requires that parents know how to nurture as well as discipline their children and have enough of their own needs met to be able to concentrate on parenting. Finally, prevention requires that communities offer children good educational opportunities and enough social support that they do not need to join a gang to feel competent and important. In essence, prevention entails changing child rearing in a society that breeds young criminals. This will be a lot harder to do than building another jail or hiring more police officers, but such actions attack only the symptoms of crime. Prevention attacks the cause.

The medical sciences have taught that preventive practices are invariably more effective than attempts to treat or cure ailments in the acute phase. If one thinks of delinquency as a behavioral ailment of sorts, the acute phase has proven to be intractable. David Farrington, the renowned British criminologist, has shown just how intractable the problem is. In expansive literature reviews (e.g., 1987, 1995; Nagin & Farrington, 1992), he has documented that antisocial behavior has amazing stability over time. Conduct problems in children as young as preschool and kindergarten age have been found to persist to the teen age and, in some studies, to the adult years. Early behavior problems are associated quite strongly with later delinquency and criminality (e.g., Loeber, 1991). These facts have convinced Farrington (1994) and others (e.g., Mendel, 1995; Watson, 1995) to recommend prevention as the only tenable solution.

The search for preventive techniques in the behavioral sciences has often been more a matter of trial and error than one of systematic methodology. Fortunately, the search has finally advanced enough to approach the status of a science, the principles of which were articulated by John Coie and his colleagues (1993). Prevention science involves identifying and reducing the incidence of risk factors for a disorder or behavior and enhancing the influence of protective factors. In this chapter we present a brief review of the risks that propel a child toward delinquency and discuss some interventions that appear to strengthen protective shields.

ROADS TO DELINQUENCY

What places a child at risk of antisocial behavior, and what protects the child from a life of crime? The answers are far from simple. There is now a substantial body of literature showing that delinquency has very broad and complex determinants. In the most general sense, these determinants lie within the child, within the child's family, and within the community where the family resides. Although researchers' views are not unanimous, several factors of each type are commonly implicated.

The most frequently mentioned child correlates of delinquency include gender, low intelligence, poor school achievement, aggressiveness, and poor intersocial skills. Family correlates involve large family size, low socioeconomic status, low educational attainment among parents, poor parenting skills, and criminality in other household members. Community factors include poor schools, poor housing, lack of employment opportunities, and a lack of positive role models. These three types of causative agents obviously occur in combination to some extent. A poor child with a low IQ who attends a substandard school is likely to do poorly academically, uneducated parents with many children may not be able to find decent housing in an area with good schools, and so forth. The more risk factors that affect a child, the more likely that she or probably he is to engage in delinquent behavior.

If the causes of delinquency are multifaceted, so too must be the solutions. That is why narrow anticrime efforts are doomed to fail. Hiring more police officers will affect the community risk factors but will do nothing to enhance parenting skills. Dropping violent television programming will not increase the supply of well-paying jobs, and increasing the number of well-paying jobs will not help parents who do not have the skills to perform them. Attempts to raise the child's IQ will not do much good if the result is not a better student but a smarter criminal.

The cumulative nature of delinquency's risk factors is one reason why, with a few exceptions, programs to stop antisocial behavior have met with little success (e.g., Feldman, 1993). Most of these programs target one or a very few of the reasons for delinquency. Many come too late, engaging the child after he or she has already been in trouble with the law. Prevention programs have had more promising results than those aimed at children already labeled as delinquent (Wilson, 1987). Yet these, too, are usually not broad enough in scope to protect the child on all sides.

More effective efforts can be inspired by the work of Hirokazu Yoshikawa (1994, 1995), who has written two cogent reviews of the risk factors in chronic delinquency. He has developed a model that encompasses the multiple risk factors and describes two pathways by which intervention might mediate their effects. Programs aimed at reducing a child's risk factors might work to enhance cognitive and social development and school achievement. Programs that focus on family risks might attempt, for example, to improve parenting skills and socioeconomic status. Yoshikawa convincingly argued that interventions that take both pathways will be the most effective in preventing chronic delinquency and later adult criminality. Comprehensive, early childhood programs that provide preschool education as well as family support meet these requirements.

EARLY INTERVENTION EFFORTS

Several programs for young children and their families appear to have reduced delinquent outcomes. Some of these projects have been subjected to years of follow-up studies, which most delinquency prevention programs have not. But most early childhood interventions were designed with goals other than delinquency in mind, so few researchers have collected data in this area. Although the findings strongly suggest positive effects on factors correlated with delinquency, there are not always convincing statistics to verify this claim (Zigler, Taussig, & Black, 1992).

One effort was the Family Development Research program at Syracuse University (Lally, Mangione, & Honig, 1988), which began with young, poor, single mothers who were in their last trimester of pregnancy. Most had not graduated from high school, and many had histories of arrests or court appearances. Paraprofessionals worked with the families once a week to encourage good mother–child relationships and to help them access needed support services. The children received four years of quality child care at the Syracuse Children's Center, beginning when they were 6 months old. Through the combination of attention to parent and child, the researchers hoped to change the environment of the home and to enable parents to support their child's development.

The attempt appears to have been successful. Although the children did not do much better in school than did the control children in the Syracuse intervention study, they were less likely to be seen at the county probation department. By the ages of 13 to 16, only 6% of the center children had been processed as probation cases, compared with 22% of the control participants. Court and penal costs for each child in the program group averaged $186. These costs were about 10 times higher for each child in the control sample.

The Yale Child Welfare Research Program offered a program more for parents than for children (Provence & Naylor, 1983). The premise was that if parents could be relieved of some of life's stresses, they would have more energy to devote to child rearing. The participants were young mothers raising children in high-risk environments. Services began prenatally and lasted until the children were 2 years old. These included parenting education and practical supports such as help in accessing housing and food programs. Professionals also guided the mothers in making decisions about future education, career, and family goals. The children received pediatric services, and most attended child care, which was an optional service made available to their parents. At the 10-year follow-up (Seitz, Rosenbaum, & Apfel, 1985), the intervention mothers had obtained more education than did the control participants, and almost all of the program families were self-supporting. An unexpected result was that the intervention mothers had fewer children and spaced their births further apart in years. (Note that education, income level, and family size were among the family correlates of delinquency listed above.) Although the researchers did not assess delinquent behavior, teacher ratings showed that the boys in the control group were more likely to skip school and to show aggressive, acting-out, pre-delinquent behavior. The program boys required fewer remedial and supportive services—including court hearings—at an average savings of more than $1,100 each academic year.

Like the Yale program, the Houston Parent–Child Development Center offered a parent-focused intervention (Johnson, 1989). Paraprofessionals conducted home visits and weekend workshops with Mexican-American families to teach them child management techniques and how to create a healthy home environment. The parents were involved for two years, and the children attended one year of nursery school. When they were in elementary school, the program children showed less aggression and fighting and were more considerate than did the control children. The differences in aggression disappeared 7 to 15 years after the program, but the home environment remained more supportive for the center children. A supportive home can be an important mediator in the prevention of delinquency.

Several other programs appear to have affected one or more of the risk factors associated with delinquency. The Nurse Home Visitation Program at the University of Rochester (Olds, 1988) provided prenatal and well-baby care to poor teenage mothers. During the two-year intervention, home visitors also worked to strengthen the family's formal and informal support systems within the community. The most striking result was a reduction in child abuse and neglect. Some researchers have linked severe abuse in childhood to delinquency and later criminality (e.g., Lewis, Mallouh, & Webb, 1989). The Rochester program may have reduced this risk factor by improving the caregiving methods of these young mothers. The Gutelius Child Health Supervision Study (Gutelius, Kirsch, MacDonald, Brooks, & McErlean, 1977) also provided support services to poor, single teenage mothers. By the time the program children were 5 or 6 years old, they showed fewer behavior problems than did the control children. As mentioned above, early misconduct is a strong precursor of chronic delinquency. Again, intensive parent education, coupled with other family supports, seems to have lowered the risks in these children's environments.

The early intervention program that most readers will associate with reduced delinquency and criminality is the High/Scope Perry Preschool. Why is it that everyone is familiar with a program that was delivered to only 58 children and graduated its last class more than 25 years ago? The fame is deserved because the project has made several valuable contributions to the knowledge base. No early intervention effort has been evaluated for a longer period. The preschool graduates were 27 years old at the last follow-up. The scope of the evaluation was extremely broad, with data collected on measures as diverse as owning a second car and how often the graduates' children use the library. The High/Scope investigators were the first to address delinquent outcomes directly, studying both self-reports and court records to ascertain arrest histories and the severity of offenses. One member of the research team, W. Steven Barnett, has conducted complex cost–benefit analyses and reported on the long-term value of the preschool investment. Finally, the results are very positive and provide strong evidence linking early intervention with reduced delinquency.

The program itself was a high-quality preschool which most of the children attended for two years. The well-trained teachers also conducted weekly home visits to teach the children's mothers to reinforce the curriculum at home. As a group, the program graduates did better in school and beyond than did the control group. They were retained in grade less often, received fewer special education services, were more likely to graduate from high school, and had higher employment rates and lower welfare use (Berrueta-Clement, Schweinhart, Barnett, Epstein, & Weikart, 1984; Schweinhart, Barnes, & Weikart, 1993). They were also less likely to be chronic troublemakers. Although more than 60% of the program men had been arrested between one and four times, only 12% of them were arrested more often. Nearly half of the men in the control group had five or more arrests.

These positive program effects saved a great deal of taxpayer money. Barnett (1993) calculated that every dollar spent on the preschool saved $7.16 in fewer special school services, less welfare use, higher employment, and reduced crime. In fact, more than 90% of the savings was in lower crime costs. Most of these benefits were projected savings to people who did not become crime victims because the crimes were not committed.

The High/Scope group's interpretation of these long-term effects is that the preschool program resulted in better school readiness, which in turn resulted in more positive expectations by kindergarten teachers. This led to a stronger commitment to school, followed by better academic performance in later grades. This snowball effect thus builds to bring more successful schooling (an argument also made by Entwisle, 1995, and Woodhead, 1988, for preschool attendance in general). Academic success is certainly a protective factor against delinquency.

Victoria Seitz (1990; Zigler & Seitz, 1993) offered an alternative explanation that emphasizes the role of the extensive home visitation component of the Perry program. She hypothesized that as a result of their involvement, parents became better socializers of their children during all those years between the time the intervention ended and the follow-up data were collected. Early in their children's lives, parents also gained experience in building proactive relationships with teachers. Thus, parents' involvement in the preschool program may have helped them create a supportive home environment and effective home–school linkages. Both of these factors may indeed enter into more successful schooling and a reduction in delinquent behavior.

Born soon after the Perry Preschool, Head Start is now the nation's largest and most enduring early intervention program. Although it has been subjected to hundreds of evaluations over the years, there is one study that looked at the criminal histories of adults who once attended Head Start (Oden, Schweinhart, & Weikart, in press). The program has been operating since 1965 and has served more than 15 million children and their families, so there is a huge subject pool that has never been tapped. We return to the lack of longitudinal research on Head Start later in the chapter. First, we describe the program and discuss the research findings that do exist.

Head Start, a centerpiece of the War on Poverty, was the only program that targeted young children. Its general goal is to prepare children for school and enhance their social competence. The planners take a whole-child approach to school readiness that focuses on much more than academic skills. Each Head Start program offers a variety of services, including health screening and referral, nutrition education and hot meals, mental health services, preschool education, social services for the child and family, and parental involvement. Each program is tailored to local needs and resources, so it is truly community-based. (The development of these features in Head Start is described by Zigler and Valentine, 1997.)

Despite these many components, most evaluations of Head Start have focused on preschool education and its effects on intelligence and school achievement. Hundreds of studies have now shown that Head Start does a good job in preparing children for school (McKey et al., 1985). When they leave the program the children have higher IQ and achievement test scores. Although these advantages eventually fade, this finding is not specific to Head Start; graduates of nearly all early intervention programs experience the same fade-out (Barnett, 1995; Consortium for Longitudinal Studies, 1983). Head Start children may also be held back in school or receive special education less often, but these findings are more sparse and less robust than those on school readiness (Barnett, 1995; Haskins, 1989).

Head Start's other components have received comparatively little empirical attention. For example, Head Start is the largest provider of health services to poor children in America. Children with disabilities make up 13% of enrollment each year. Despite the millions of physicals, immunizations, and referrals for health problems that have been given by Head Start, relatively few studies have focused on the program's impact on children's health. Those that have provide convincing data that the majority of Head Start participants receive preventive and remedial health services at much higher rates than the poor preschool population (Currie &

Thomas, 1995; Zigler, Piotrkowski, & Collins, 1994). One study showed that Head Start students had medical care comparable to middle-class preschoolers, and they were more likely to have seen a dentist (Hale, Seitz, & Zigler, 1990). This is one of the very few studies of the effects of early intervention that shows poor children surpassing wealthier children in any domain.

There is also some indication that Head Start has positive effects on parents. About one-third of Head Start personnel are parents of current or former students, showing that the program does help them secure employment. On another level, parents have reported improved relationships with their children (National Head Start Association, 1990) and greater life satisfaction and psychological well-being as a result of their involvement in Head Start (Parker, Piotrkowski, & Peay, 1987). There is a small amount of evidence that the program also has a positive impact on the communities in which it operates. Years ago, Kirschner Associates (1970) found nearly 1,500 institutional changes to improve the health care and educational systems of 48 communities that housed Head Start centers. More recently, the U.S. General Accounting Office (1992) found Head Start's community-based approach a successful way to improve families' access to services as well as to strengthen service delivery systems. Clearly, Head Start has the potential to enhance many systems that influence a child's development, and it is a shame that we do not have more data to help us understand these effects.

Why, then, do we include Head Start in a discussion of early intervention programs for which there is at least some documented evidence that they lower the risk factors associated with delinquency? Because Head Start clearly fits the mold of these programs, incorporating pathways to lessen both the child risks and the family risks that Yoshikawa described. Head Start also branches into the community so it may help alleviate some of the risks there as well. Although we are empiricists, we think that we can overlook the absence of substantial data and say with confidence that children who begin school healthier, who have the academic and social skills they need, who have parents who are involved in their education, and who have attention paid to some of their family's needs have gained some protection against the risks associated with later delinquency. The non–Head Start studies suggest that this is true, and one evaluation did show that by young adulthood, women who had attended Head Start had fewer arrests than those who did not (Oden et al., in press). Thus it is not a leap of faith to include Head Start among programs that hold promise to prevent delinquency. In fact, the logic of this argument led Watson (1995) to propose that funds from the Office of Juvenile Justice and Delinquency Prevention (OJJDP) be distributed to Head Start; although Watson believed that some of the funds should be used to support relevant research, she saw no point in waiting for longitudinal results to prove that Head Start is the best use of OJJDP resources.

It would not be difficult for investigators to examine Head Start's efficacy in delinquency prevention. Although most researchers do not have the time, patience, or funds to do an age 27 follow-up like the High/Scope evaluation, they could assess some of the early precursors of delinquent behavior right after preschool and again a few years later. Aggression, antisocial behavior, low achievement levels, and other factors that tend to be stable over time could be included. Although this would not provide the rich data that long-term study could, it would certainly provide a sense of whether a positive impact was made.

Clearly, there is a need for a commitment to research as it has provided such surprising insights into the power of early intervention. In the 1960s when this type of program began, the goal was to make children smarter or at least help them do better in school. If these were the only outcomes looked at, the lack of robust, long-term effects would probably have doomed the whole concept of early intervention. But researchers like the High/Scope team pressed on, and it is a good thing that they did. Who would have dreamed that a quality preschool experience would have any bearing on criminal behavior many years later? Who could have foreseen that a family support program like the Yale project would affect how many children a young mother eventually has? Yoshikawa (1994) noted that because substance abuse shares many of the risk factors of delinquency, early intervention might also affect the incidence of drug use. Tonry (1995) carried this idea further, arguing that the correlates of criminality are so intertwined that a reduction in one will affect others and lessen the overall tendency toward antisocial behavior. Obviously, broad-based, primary prevention might prevent a lot more than initially planned.

ENHANCING PREVENTIVE INTERVENTIONS

Thus far we have focused on the need for more research on the behavioral effects of early childhood intervention to inform antidelinquency efforts, but there are some already proven lessons that can be applied now. Years of experience in the intervention field offer the lesson that programs must last long enough to affect change. Second, programs must be of good quality to obtain desired results. Finally, there is a need for two-generation programs that empower parents to take a proactive role in optimizing their children's futures and society's future.

Beginning with the need for longer programs, many delinquency prevention efforts suffer from the same "quick-fix" mentality that once characterized early childhood interventions. The typical school-based delinquency prevention program is offered in a unit of six weeks or so within life skills courses. Students attend these courses for an hour each week—the equivalent of one school day—which is hardly enough time to learn prosocial behavior.

The brief training they receive in conflict resolution or peer counseling is ineffective in the long run not because it is the wrong type of training but because it is so short.

Many are not aware that Head Start began as a six-week program in the summer of 1965. Those were optimistic times. Some people actually believed that this brief preschool experience would make poor children smarter, guarantee their success in school, and ensure that they become self-supporting adults. It is now well-known that there is no inoculation for poverty, and one will not be found for delinquency either. It is important to intervene early, before problem behaviors appear. Farrington (1994) was so convinced of the importance of early prevention that he recommended that programs begin in the prenatal period. He believed that services such as prenatal care, substance abuse counseling, and training in child development can help mothers eliminate some of the risks that influence their children's tendency to exhibit troublesome behavior.

The Clinton administration followed the advice of the Carnegie Task Force on Meeting the Needs of Young Children (1994) and other experts and convened the Advisory Committee on Services for Families with Infants and Toddlers (1994). The committee's recommendations resulted in Early Head Start, a comprehensive program for disadvantaged families and children ages 0 to 3. The initial phase began late in 1995, when 68 grants were awarded. The program has components for health, nutrition, mental health, education, and family support not unlike those in the preschool Head Start, but there is necessarily a greater emphasis on parent involvement and services. Quality is guided by new program performance standards—the first ever issued to include Head Start programs serving children before the age of preschool. A research and evaluation component is written into the design.

Whether this program will affect delinquent outcomes as the participants grow older remains to be seen. It should certainly help create a promising beginning. But no child's development will stop when intervention does. Infants go on to become preschoolers, third-graders, and adolescents. During the teenage years, the importance of the peer group, the urge for independence, and the unavailability of age-appropriate supervision during afterschool hours are emerging factors that simply cannot be dealt with at earlier stages of development. Children need support and guidance on different levels as they progress from the early years to the preteen and teenage periods. Early childhood interventions should dovetail with school-age interventions that change with the child's developmental needs.

One program of this type is the Head Start Transition program (see Kennedy, 1993), which continues comprehensive services and parent involvement activities for preschool graduates from kindergarten to third grade. Evaluation is not yet complete, but evidence from similar interventions (reviewed by Zigler & Styfco, 1993), particularly the Chicago Child Parent

Centers (e.g., Reynolds, 1993, 1994), supports the premise of the Transition program that longer lasting programs can have more enduring benefits. Among them are more successful schooling and possibly better child rearing and family functioning—all protective factors against delinquency. The protection will surely be tested during the teenage years when delinquency rates soar, so different environmental nutrients should be offered. For instance, a number of school- and community-based programs (e.g., midnight basketball) have proven successful in keeping adolescents constructively occupied (Mendel, 1995).

Turning to the need for quality intervention, all of the preschool programs described earlier that had an impact on delinquency were of high quality. They were well-planned and well-executed by trained staff. If there is an exception, it is the poor quality of some Head Start centers. The majority of Head Start programs deliver good services (Brush, Gaidurgis, & Best, 1993), but even these had difficulty maintaining quality during the rapid expansion of the early 1990s (Office of the Inspector General, 1993). To remedy the problems, the Clinton administration appointed the Advisory Committee on Head Start Quality and Expansion (1993), a bipartisan group of policymakers, scientists, practitioners, and laypersons. The committee developed many ideas for improving those Head Start centers that need it and for improving the program as a whole. Unlike previous reports that were ignored or forgotten by policymakers, this one has been taken seriously and is already being acted on.

Some of the committee's recommendations concern strengthening Head Start's mental health component. We mention this within the area of quality for two reasons. One is that early childhood programs have been proliferating in recent years, but they are not all of good quality (Adams & Sandfort, 1994; Layzer, Goodson, & Moss, 1993). Some of the public-school-based programs in particular leave much to be desired, in that they are more like a downward extension of the older grades and are not age-appropriate. Although some have a quality education component, this is often the only component that they have. Head Start, on the other hand, attempts to enhance the many systems that influence child development by providing comprehensive services. Among these are mental health services, singled out here because they are particularly relevant to a discussion of violence and crime. Emotional disorders are another of the risk factors associated with delinquency, so early treatment and, better yet, prevention should offer some protection. Yet even when emotional or behavioral, or both, problems are identified in preschoolers, appropriate interventions are rarely available. In reviewing this problem, Webster-Stratton concluded that preschoolers with conduct problems and their families have largely been neglected by the mental health community (1997, p. 446).

The committee's recommendation to improve mental health services in Head Start has already brought some needed attention to the matter. The

American Orthopsychiatric Association (1994) formed a task force on Head Start and mental health that focused on the need for additional staff, training, and technical assistance in this area. The task force also encouraged collaboration with the larger family support and mental health community, which bodes well for improving services and expanding into the neighborhoods that house Head Start centers. This will benefit even those residents who have no connection to the preschool. The thrust of this attention to mental health in Head Start is not just toward treatment but also toward the development of effective prevention strategies for children and their families.

The final lesson that the early childhood field can offer to delinquency prevention efforts is the importance of two-generation programming. Although this approach is now accepted as a required element of effective intervention, this was not so in 1965, when Head Start's planners made the then-radical recommendation to involve parents in the program. Up until that time, educators, psychologists, and others involved in children's services had what can only be called a condescending attitude toward parents, particularly poor parents. The prevailing view was that the home was responsible for children's failures. Professionals thus had to take the child away from these bad influences for a few hours each day or week and deliver their magic through a program in another setting. What was wrong with this practice, of course, is that children spend a great deal more time with their families than with their service providers. And parents are the ones who raise children, not teachers or social workers or psychologists who design early intervention programs.

The seeds of change away from child-focused services were planted during the deliberations of Head Start's planning committee. One member was Urie Bronfenbrenner, who was just beginning to formulate his ecological approach to human development (1979). He reasoned that children are influenced by families and that the well-being of families is influenced by the community in which they reside. An intervention must therefore touch all of these areas to be effective. This philosophy fit very well with Head Start's mission as a War on Poverty program. The authorizing legislation for the antipoverty efforts being mounted during this war called for "maximum feasible participation" of poor people in the programs designed to serve them. And so it came to be that Head Start not only provided services for parents but also invited them into the planning, administration, and daily operations of their local centers.

The value of two-generation programming today is recognized throughout the professional disciplines, from pediatric services to child care settings to public schools. Until recently, the practice was justified by theorizing that parents are the primary educators and socializers of their children and in the best position to further the goals of the intervention or school program. There is now some sound empirical data to substantiate this formulation. Rothbaum and Weisz (1994) searched the literature for studies of the association between parental caregiving practices and children's externalizing behavior. Externalizing includes aggression, hostility, and noncompliance—behaviors particularly relevant to juvenile delinquency. They subjected the results of 47 studies to a meta-analysis, a complex statistical procedure that essentially pools the results of all the studies and determines whether the average result is significant. They found clear evidence linking parental caregiving, particularly maternal caregiving, with child externalizing behaviors. These findings supply the missing link in the chain of evidence that has suggested two-generation programs are more effective than child-focused programs. Those involved in designing delinquency prevention efforts now have some well-founded guidelines to inform their planning.

CONCLUSION

Quality early childhood intervention programs exemplify primary prevention. Although most of them were designed to prevent school failure, they have shown that broad, two-generation efforts that build on the strengths of families as well as children can prevent more than poor report cards. This is not to minimize the value of a good report card. Many delinquency risks are school-linked, such as grade repetition, truancy, and dropping out. By preparing children for school, early intervention programs may prevent these risks. In addition, some of these programs have demonstrated their value in preventing poor social competence, gauged by various indicators that graduates are better able to meet societal expectancies. Many programs, including Head Start, had as a central goal the improvement of children's social competencies. Not engaging in delinquent acts is one expectation with worthwhile consequences for the individual and the society. The impact of early intervention programs on delinquency reduction must of course be supported by additional research, but the evidence so far is very promising. Decades of work can be brought to fruition in one tough but paramount task: changing society's collective attitude toward children who defy social and moral laws. The war on crime has taken on warlike proportions itself lately. People are hostile. They have armed themselves. They feel rage and hatred toward young criminals. They want to lock them up and throw away the key. Some of those teenagers undoubtedly have earned this scorn, and some of them may be very hard to reach. But President Clinton delivered a poignant message in one of his State of the Union addresses. He asked Americans not to point their fingers at children who have no hope and no future. Instead, he encouraged people to reach out their hands to them. This will only be possible through a scholarly rather than emotional understanding of destructive behavior. Such a foundation will allow researchers to continue the search for more effective treatments for both the perpetrators and the victims of delinquent acts. It will allow researchers to move toward primary prevention that strengthens constructive behaviors and minimizes destructive ones.

REFERENCES

Adams, G., & Sandfort, J. (1994). First steps, promising futures. State prekindergarten initiatives in the early 1990s. Washington, DC: Children's Defense Fund.

Advisory Committee on Head Start Quality and Expansion. (1993). *Creating a 21st century Head Start*. Washington, DC: U.S. Department of Health and Human Services.

Advisory Committee on Services for Families with Infants and Toddlers. (1994). *Statement of the Advisory Committee on Services for Families with Infants and Toddlers*. Washington, DC: U.S. Department of Health and Human Services.

American Orthopsychiatric Association. (1994, April). *Strengthening mental health in Head Start: Pathways to quality improvement* (Report of the Task Force on Head Start and Mental Health). New York: Author.

Barnett, W. S. (1993). Benefit–cost analysis of preschool education: Findings from a 25-year follow-up. *American Journal of Orthopsychiatry, 63,* 500–508.

Barnett, W. S. (1995). Long-term effects of early childhood programs on cognitive and school outcomes. *Future of Children, 5*(3), 25–50.

Berrueta-Clement, J. R., Schweinhart, L., Barnett, W., Epstein, A., & Weikart, D. (1984). *Changed lives: The effects of the Perry Preschool Program on youths through age 19.* Ypsilanti, MI: High/Scope Educational Research Foundation.

Bronfenbrenner, U. (1979). *The ecology of human development.* Cambridge, MA: Harvard University Press.

Bronfenbrenner, U., McClelland, P., Wethington, E., Moen, P., & Ceci, S. J. (1996). *The state of Americans: This generation and the next.* New York: Free Press.

Brush, L., Gaidurgis, A., & Best, C. (1993). *Indices of Head Start program quality.* Washington, DC: Pelavin Associates.

Carnegie Task Force on Meeting the Needs of Young Children. (1994). *Starting points: Meeting the needs of our youngest children.* New York: Carnegie Corporation.

Coie, J. D., Watt, N., West, S., Hawkins, J., Asarnow, J., Markmam, H., Ramey, S., Shure, M., & Long, B. (1993). The science of prevention: A conceptual framework and some directions for a national research program. *American Psychologist, 48,* 1013–1022.

Consortium for Longitudinal Studies. (1983). *As the twig is bent: Lasting effects of preschool programs.* Hillsdale, NJ: Erlbaum.

Currie, J., & Thomas, D. (1995). Does Head Start make a difference? *American Economic Review, 85,* 341–364.

Entwisle, D. R. (1995). The role of schools in sustaining early childhood program benefits. *Future of Children*, 5(3), 133–144.

Farrington, D. P. (1987). Early precursors of frequent offending. In J. Q. Wilson & G. C. Loury (Eds.), *From children to citizens: Vol. 3. Families, schools, and delinquency prevention* (pp. 27–50). New York: Springer-Verlag.

Farrington, D. P. (1994, April). *Delinquency prevention in the first few years of life*. Plenary address, Fourth European Conference on Law and Psychology, Barcelona, Spain.

Farrington, D. P. (1995). The Twelfth Jack Tizard Memorial Lecture. The development of offending and antisocial behavior from childhood: Key findings from the Cambridge Study in Delinquent Development. *Journal of Child Psychology and Psychiatry, 36*, 929–964.

Federal Bureau of Investigation. (1995). *Uniform crime reports for the United States*. Washington, DC: U.S. Department of Justice.

Feldman, P. (1993). *The psychology of crime*. New York: Cambridge University Press.

Gutelius, M. F., Kirsch, A. D., MacDonald, S., Brooks, M. R., & McErlean, T. (1977). Controlled study of child health supervision: Behavioral results. *Pediatrics, 60*, 294–304.

Hale, B. A., Seitz, V., & Zigler, E. (1990). Health services and Head Start: A forgotten formula. *Journal of Applied Developmental Psychology, 11*, 447–458.

Haskins, R. (1989). Beyond metaphor. The efficacy of early childhood education. *American Psychologist, 44*, 274–282.

Johnson, D. L. (1989, April). *Follow-up of the Houston Parent-Child Development Center: Preliminary analyses*. Paper presented at the meeting of the Society for Research in Child Development, Kansas City, MO.

Kennedy, E. M. (1993). The Head Start Transition Project: Head Start goes to elementary school. In E. Zigler & S. J. Styfco (Eds.), *Head Start and beyond: A national plan for extended childhood intervention* (pp. 97–109). New Haven, CT: Yale University Press.

Kirschner Associates. (1970). A national survey of the impacts of Head Start centers on community institutions. Albuquerque, NM: Author.

Lally, R. J., Mangione, P. L., & Honig, A. S. (1988). The Syracuse University Family Development Research Program: Long-range impact of an early intervention with low-income children and their families. In D. Powell (Ed.), *Parent education as early childhood intervention: Emerging directions in theory, research and practice* (pp. 79–104). Norwood, NJ: Ablex.

Layzer, J. I., Goodson, B. D., & Moss, M. (1993). *Life in preschool: Vol. 1. An observational study of early childhood programs for disadvantaged four-year-olds. Final report* (Contract No. EALC 890980, U.S. Department of Education). Cambridge, MA: Abt Associates.

Lewis, D. O., Mallouh, C., & Webb, V. (1989). Child abuse, delinquency, and violent criminality. In D. Cicchetti & V. Carlson (Eds.), *Child maltreatment: Theory and research on the causes and consequences of child abuse and neglect* (pp. 707–721). New York: Cambridge University Press.

Loeber, R. (1991). Antisocial behavior: More enduring than changeable? *Journal of the American Academy of Child and Adolescent Psychiatry, 30*, 393–397.

McKey, R. H., Condelli, L., Ganson, H., Barrett, B., McConkey, C., & Plantz, M. (1985). *The impact of Head Start on children, family, and communities: Final report of the Head Start Evaluation, Synthesis and Utilization Project* (DHHS Pub. No. OHDS 85-31193). Washington, DC: U.S. Government Printing Office.

Mendel, R. A. (1995). *Prevention or pork: A hard-headed look at youth-oriented anti-crime programs.* Washington, DC: American Youth Policy Forum.

Nagin, D. S., & Farrington, D. P. (1992). The stability of criminal potential from childhood to adulthood. *Criminology, 30*, 235–260.

National Head Start Association. (1990). *Head Start: The nation's pride, a nation's challenge. Report of the Silver Ribbon Panel.* Alexandria, VA: Author.

Oden, S., Schweinhart, L. J., & Weikart, D. P. (in press). *The long-term benefits of Head Start study.* Ypsilanti, MI: High/Scope Press.

Office of the Inspector General. (1993). *Head Start expansion: Grantee experiences* (OEI-09-91-00760). Washington, DC: Department of Health and Human Services.

Olds, D. L. (1988). The Prenatal/Early Infancy Project. In E. L. Cowen, R. P. Lorion, & J. Ramos-McKay (Eds.), *Fourteen ounces of prevention: A handbook for practitioners* (pp. 9–22). Washington, DC: American Psychological Association.

Parker, F. L., Piotrkowski, C. S., & Peay, L. (1987). Head Start as a social support for mothers: The psychological benefits of involvement. *American Journal of Orthopsychiatry, 57*, 220–233.

Provence, S., & Naylor, A. (1983). *Working with disadvantaged parents and children: Scientific issues and practice.* New Haven, CT: Yale University Press.

Reynolds, A. J. (1993). One year of preschool intervention or two: Does it matter? *Early Childhood Research Quarterly, 10*, 1–31.

Reynolds, A. J. (1994). Effects of a preschool plus follow-on intervention for children at risk. *Developmental Psychology, 30*, 787–804.

Rothbaum, F., & Weisz, J. R. (1994). Parental caregiving and child externalizing behavior in nonclinical samples: A meta-analysis. *Psychological Bulletin, 116*, 55–74.

Schweinhart, L. J., Barnes, H. V., & Weikart, D. P. (1993). *Significant benefits: The High/Scope Perry Preschool Study through age 27* (Monographs of the High/Scope Educational Research Foundation, 10). Ypsilanti, MI: High/Scope Press.

Seitz, V. (1990). Intervention programs for impoverished children: A comparison of educational and family support models. *Annals of Child Development, 7*, 73–103.

Seitz, V., Rosenbaum, L. K., & Apfel, N. H. (1985). Effects of family support intervention: A 10-year follow-up. *Child Development, 56*, 376–391.

Snyder, H. N., & Sickmund, M. (1995). *Juvenile offenders and victims: A national report.* Washington, DC: Office of Juvenile Justice and Delinquency Prevention.

Tonry, M. (1995). Malign neglect: Race, crime, and punishment in America. New York: Oxford University Press.

U.S. General Accounting Office. (1992). *Integrating human services* (Report No. GAO/HRD-92-108). Washington, DC: Author.

Watson, J. (1995). Crime and juvenile delinquency prevention policy: Time for early childhood intervention. *Georgetown Journal on Fighting Poverty, 2,* 245–270.

Webster-Stratton, C. (1997). Early intervention for families of preschool children with conduct problems. In M. J. Guralnick (Ed.), *Effectiveness of early intervention.* Baltimore, MD: Paul H. Brookes.

Wilson, J. Q. (1987). Strategic opportunities for delinquency prevention. In J. Q. Wilson & G. C. Loury (Eds.), *From children to citizens: Vol. 3. Families, schools, and delinquency prevention* (pp. 291–312). New York: Springer-Verlag.

Woodhead, M. (1988). When psychology informs public policy. The case of early childhood intervention. *American Psychologist, 43,* 443–454.

Yoshikawa, H. (1994). Prevention as cumulative protection: Effects of early family support and education on chronic delinquency and its risks. *Psychological Bulletin, 115,* 28–54.

Yoshikawa, H. (1995). Long-term effects of early childhood programs on social outcomes and delinquency. *Future of Children, 5*(3), 51–75.

Zigler, E., Piotrkowski, C., & Collins, R. (1994). Health services in Head Start. *Annual Review of Public Health, 15,* 511–534.

Zigler, E., & Seitz, V. (1993). Invited comments. In L. J. Schweinhart, H. V. Barnes, & D. P. Weikart (Eds.), *Significant benefits: The High/Scope Perry Preschool Study through age 27* (pp. 247–249). Ypsilanti, MI: High/Scope Press.

Zigler, E., & Styfco, S. J. (1993). Strength in unity: Consolidating federal education programs for young children. In E. Zigler & S. J. Styfco (Eds.), *Head Start and beyond: A national plan for extended childhood intervention* (pp. 111–145). New Haven, CT: Yale University Press.

Zigler, E., Taussig, C., & Black, K. (1992). Early childhood intervention: A promising preventative for juvenile delinquency. *American Psychologist, 47,* 997–1006.

Zigler, E., & Valentine, J. (Eds.). (1997). *Project Head Start: A legacy of the War on Poverty* (2nd ed.). Alexandria, VA: National Head Start Association.

12

COGNITIVE PROCESSES AND THE DEVELOPMENT OF AGGRESSION

L. ROWELL HUESMANN AND MEREDITH A. REYNOLDS

Interest in programs to prevent aggression and violence has increased dramatically in recent years. This increase is seen at many levels—parents and teachers striving to modify children's aggressive behaviors, medical and mental health professionals concerned about the plight of abused children, and politicians responding to growing social concern regarding the incidence of violent crime. It is interesting to note that the growing concern with aggression does not directly reflect increased rates of overall violence and aggression in the past decade. Homicide rates, for example, changed little between 1980 and 1995 and have declined slightly since then. Rather, increasing concern with aggression parallels a decrease in the modal age of violence perpetrators. As the age of the typical violence perpetrator has decreased, and as the amount and severity of damage wrought by violent youths has increased as a result of greater access to lethal weapons, the public has become increasingly alarmed. This alarm has been exacerbated most recently by the surge in lethal violence committed by children against children in schools in small towns in Kentucky, Arkansas, and Oregon.

As concerns and fears about aggression and violence increase, demands for intervention and remediation are made more vociferously. Before discussing these strategies, it is important to highlight the distinction between prevention and treatment. Whereas *treatment* refers to attempts to alter an identified, pre-existing problem in an individual, such as modifying the behavior of a neighborhood bully, *prevention* refers to efforts aimed at precluding the development and onset of problems. Depending on the breadth of the population targeted by a program, a prevention effort is designated as "primary" or "secondary." Primary prevention programs are broad based and typically target every individual in a particular population, such as a school-based program for all second-grade students. Secondary prevention programs are focused on individuals who are at increased risk for developing problems later on, for example, children who live in particularly violent communities or who show early indications of aggressive tendencies.

A few robust findings have consistently emerged from empirical studies of aggression, which have important implications for intervention that must be taken into consideration. First, aggression emerges early in life and tends to be stable (Huesmann, Eron, Lefkowitz, & Walder, 1984; Olweus, 1979). In fact, childhood aggression is the strongest factor predicting aggression in adolescence and adulthood. Therefore, it is imperative that prevention and treatment efforts begin early, before problems develop and before aggressive behavior becomes consolidated into enduring patterns. Second, aggression has multiple causes ranging from genetic predispositions to peer group identification (Huesmann, 1994, 1998b). Causes and risk factors are embedded within all context levels—in the individual, family, peer group, school, as well as general society. The complex convergence and reciprocal interaction of factors causing any particular child to become aggressive makes it extremely difficult to determine the unique contribution any given factor makes to the development of aggression and precludes simple, "one-size-fits-all" programs that target one or two components of aggression. Finally, there is a strong learning component to aggression, which is significantly influenced by certain environmental conditions. Having numerous opportunities to observe aggression, the existence of multiple reinforcers for aggressive behavior, and being the object of others' aggression are the conditions most conducive to learning aggression.

Over the past quarter-century psychologists have responded to concerns about aggression and violence with a large number of intervention programs aimed at preventing the development of violence. Although some have achieved positive outcomes, overall the results have been disappointing (Guerra, 1994). One problem has been the tendency to focus on immediate results and rely on intuition rather than established psychological theory. As a result, although well-intentioned, many intervention efforts have had unfortunate deleterious and sometimes tragic effects. For example, some approaches to treating abusive husbands have led to increased violence and placed women at a greater risk for injury and death (Sherman, 1992). Similarly, as mentioned before, efforts to decrease and control aggression through punishment have resulted in increased levels of aggression (Huesmann & Podolski, in press). Even when interventions have been designed to avoid such obvious negative effects, suggestions of iatrogenic effects, particularly in small group interventions with antisocial youth, have been reported (Metropolitan Area Research Group, 2000; Poulin & Dishion, 1997).

In this chapter we focus on how intervention programs can benefit from an understanding of the cognitive characteristics that promote the learning and emission of aggressive behaviors and the environmental factors that interact with these characteristics. We highlight recent advances in social-cognitive, information-processing models of aggression and discuss their implications for intervention programs. However, such a focus on cognitive characteristics should not be misconstrued as de-emphasizing the importance of other factors, including biological predispositions, poor parenting, violent and stressful environments, and substance use, which typically form the backdrop against which aggressive behaviors are acquired and performed. Rather, our view is that cognitions are perhaps the most important avenue through which these other factors exert their influence on aggressive behavior.

REVIEW OF INTERVENTION APPROACHES

Before describing our social-cognitive, information-processing model and the kinds of preventive interventions that are suggested by the model, we review some of the major interventions that have been proposed to reduce aggression and violence. However, it is difficult to extract a coherent picture of successful intervention techniques from the aggression prevention and treatment literatures, as is apparent in the following review.

Intervening with Adults

Because habitual aggression tends to emerge early and rapidly, it develops into stable behavioral patterns that are extremely resistant to change. Treating aggressive individuals is much more difficult than is preventing the development of aggression. Nevertheless, the treatment of aggression has received more attention than its prevention (Kazdin, 1994). Whereas prevention and treatment programs are frequently used with children, interventions designed for adults are almost by definition treatment programs. Problems with aggression almost never develop in adulthood for individuals who were not particularly aggressive as children. When this does happen, it is generally the result of a traumatic condition afflicting the central nervous system, such as a brain tumor or head injury that occurred in adulthood.

Given the tenacity with which severe aggression resists change, particularly after it has become a chronic and stable pattern, it is not surprising that few programs exist for aggressive adults. Instead, society seems to have opted to adopt strategies that minimize the damage aggressive adults can realize, strategies that typically remove these individuals from general society through various incarceration programs. As the high incidence of violence in prison can attest, many of these programs do not suppress, let alone extinguish, the aggression and violence of these individuals. They simply allow them to aggress only against one another. Violence among (and against) prison inmates is not viewed by the public as a particularly grave problem as long as it remains confined.

Intervening with Youth

Evaluations of a number of prevention and treatment programs have reported positive results, including reducing several at-risk behaviors in children and increasing prosocial competence. Unfortunately evaluations of many other programs have shown no effects, and a sobering number have demonstrated deleterious effects. To complicate matters, when positive results do occur, the outcomes realized are not necessarily predicted or directly related to the specific factors addressed by the intervention programs. Additionally, intervention programs typically address many causes and risk factors, reflecting our understanding of aggression as multidetermined. This makes it difficult to determine what features, and combinations of features, in the intervention were mutative (Kazdin, 1994). Generally speaking, the results of interventions are consistent with the facts of aggression delineated earlier—early interventions targeting multiple causes and risk factors appear to be the most likely to produce enduring effects (Tolan & Guerra, 1994). Additionally, it is generally agreed that the discovery of efficacious intervention programs rests on the development of sophisticated theories of the development of aggression.

Of course, intervention and treatment attempts have not waited for sophisticated theories to materialize. As a result, initial attempts have been based only on global theoretical orientations and can be categorized under the general labels of behavioral modification treatments or counseling (individual and group) treatments. Arguably the most commonly used behavior modification approach to treating aggression is punishment. Kazdin (1994) reviewed many applications as well as other behavior modification programs directed at reducing aggression. According to the principles of operant conditioning, aggressive behavior should be suppressed by punishment if the punishment creates an aversive consequence or terminates or prevents a rewarding event. Unfortunately, the second part of the principle—that extinction is not produced by punishment but by the lack of reinforcement of the target behavior and the reinforcement of competing behaviors—is often forgotten. Furthermore, punishment such as spanking and confinement are often applied alone by parents to children and by society to delinquents.

Other behavior modification techniques, such as counterconditioning and problem-solving skills training, are necessary for real behavior change to take place. Counterconditioning, or replacement training as it is sometimes called, involves removing the stimuli that are reinforcing the aggressive behavior while simultaneously reinforcing alternative, competing behaviors that preclude aggression. Also, although the laws of conditioning are relatively straightforward and immutable, the successful application of them is not. There is a bewildering array of variables, many of which are not directly under anyone's control (e.g., memories, perceptions, and motivations), whose complex interactions determine whether punishment will lead to the desired outcome of decreased aggression or will actually lead to further aggression (see Huesmann & Podolski, in press, for a detailed analysis of punishment and aggressive behavior).

The most common psychodynamic formulation of violence is that it results from anger and hostile feelings. These feelings normally arise in interpersonal relationships, but because there are social and parental mandates against their immediate and open expression, they become repressed from consciousness. There they smolder and ferment until they have reached a level of intensity that necessitates some form of discharge, and they burst out uncontrollably. From this perspective, violence could be controlled and prevented if only we would consciously acknowledge and verbally articulate our anger and frustration more freely and directly. By putting these experiences into words, psychodynamic logic goes, we gain enough mastery and control over them that their expression in an aggressive behavioral form becomes unnecessary.

Intervention programs based on this formulation have advocated acknowledging and expressing anger in many forms using a variety of methods. For example, some have advocated the use of make-believe or pretend aggression in which no one is actually injured. This can be done cognitively, using visual imagery and fantasy such as telling off your boss in your mind, or behaviorally, "fighting" with Nerf batons or other toy weaponry. The assumption is that, as long as no one is actually hurt during these activities, no harm is being done.

Is this assumption reasonable? According to the unified information-processing model of aggression, the answer is no. Both fantasizing and play-acting aggression are opportunities for rehearsing and further elaborating aggressive scripts, thereby increasing the accessibility of these scripts. Such activities may also strengthen normative beliefs that support aggressive responding.

What have empirical studies found? The empirical investigations of psychodynamically oriented approaches using catharsis and make-believe aggression have found these approaches to heighten rather than prevent actual aggression (c.f. Turner & Goldsmith, 1976; Walters & Brown, 1963; Zuzul, 1989).

The group counseling approach to preventing or treating aggression has taken two primary forms: peer group counseling and family counseling. Other approaches (e.g., behavior modification, cognitive therapy) may also treat the family or peer group. What characterizes the counseling approach is the belief that by having the family members or peer group members talk about the problem, express their feelings, and give and take advice from others in the group, the target behavior will get better. This approach is often loosely based on the psychodynamic view that venting anger will reduce aggression. However, again, there is no evidence that the process has any such effect, and there is some reason to believe that such group sessions might exacerbate the problems (Poulin & Dishion, 1997).

Overall, as this brief review illustrates, most of the behavioral, counseling, and psychodynamic interventions have not produced dramatic decreases in aggression in either adults or children. We now discuss social-cognitive, information-processing theory and the interventions that have sprung out of such theorizing.

SOCIAL-COGNITIVE MODELS FOR THE DEVELOPMENT OF AGGRESSIVE BEHAVIOR

We must begin this section with a digression concerning the meaning of some terms used in theorizing about the cognitive processes influencing aggression. In particular, there is often understandable confusion over the use of the terms *information-processing* and *social-cognitive* in this literature. Information-processing models, as introduced by Simon and associates in the 1950s (Huesmann, 1998b), are models that use the language of computer science to describe the thought processes underlying behavior, whether those thoughts are conscious or unconscious, automatic or controlled. Social-cognitive is more of a generic term for theories that attempt to explain social behavior in terms of the underlying thought processes. However, the terms are often used almost interchangeably. Perhaps, the more correct approach is to conceive of information-processing models of social behavior as a particular method of social-cognitive theorizing.

Over the past 15 years two general social-cognitive, information-processing models have emerged of how humans acquire and maintain aggressive habits. One model, developed by Huesmann and his colleagues (Huesmann, 1980, 1982, 1986, 1988, 1998b; Huesmann & Eron, 1984), initially focused particularly on scripts, beliefs, and observational learning, and the other model, developed by Dodge and his colleagues (Dodge, 1980, 1986; Crick & Dodge, 1994; Dodge & Frame, 1982), focused particularly on perceptions and attributions. However, both hypothesize a similar core of information processing, both draw heavily on the work of cognitive psychologists and information processing theory, and both draw from Bandura's (1977, 1986) earlier formulations of cognitive processing in social learning as well as Berkowitz's (1990) neoassociationist thinking.

The social-cognitive, information-processing model, as elaborated most recently by Huesmann (1998b), treats people as social problem solvers. Individuals are faced repeatedly with social situations that require some appropriate behavior (e.g., they want to join a group of peers, they are insulted by someone else, they meet a new person, they are treated badly by a clerk). They evaluate the situation, their emotions and thoughts are affected by the evaluation, they decide on something to do, they do it, and then they alter the way they think about the situation in the future on the basis of what happens.

Huesmann's (1998b) model is outlined in Figure 12.1. It incorporates the premise that social behavior is controlled to a great extent by cognitive *scripts* (Abelson, 1981) that are stored in a person's memory and are used as guides for behavior and social problem solving. A script incorporates both procedural and declarative knowledge and suggests what events are to happen in the environment, how the person should behave in response to these events, and what the likely outcome of those behaviors would be. Everyone has scripts for everyday social situations like meeting a friend (smile, say hello, etc.) or going to a restaurant (speak to the hostess, go to the table,

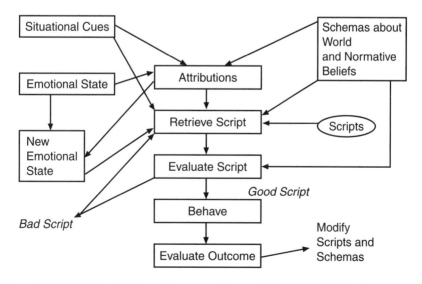

Figure 12.1. A unified social-information-processing mode for aggressive behavior.

read the menu, etc.). It is presumed that while scripts are first being established they influence the child's behavior through "controlled" mental processes (Schneider & Shriffrin, 1977), but these processes become "automatic" as the child matures. Without such automatic scripts, we would be paralyzed by the amount of thinking required to handle every small social event. Correspondingly, scripts that persist in a child's repertoire, as they are rehearsed, enacted, and generate consequences, become increasingly more resistant to modification and change.

Normative beliefs are the second kind of cognitive schema hypothesized to play a central role in regulating aggressive behavior. Normative beliefs are cognitions about the appropriateness of aggressive behavior. They are related to perceived social norms but are different in that they concern what's "right for you." For example, a husband, provoked by his wife, may think of a script involving hitting her, but will not use it because it violates a normative belief against hitting women. According to Huesmann and Guerra (1997), normative beliefs not only filter out inappropriate scripts and behaviors as in the above example, but they also prime the schemas used to evaluate other's behaviors (e.g., a belief that staring at another person is wrong primes a hostile schema for being stared at), and they guide the search for social scripts (e.g., a belief that not obeying parents is wrong limits the search for appropriate scripts to respond to a child's disobedience).

One can see within this model that there are four possible loci at which individual differences and situational variations can influence aggressive behavior. First, the objective situation is defined by the social problem and the environmental cues. However, the cues that are given the most attention and the interpretation of those cues may vary from person to person and may depend on a person's neurophysiological predispositions, current mood state, and previous learning history as reflected in activated schemas, including normative beliefs. Because emotional states may persist for some time, a person may enter a social interaction in an emotional state that is unrelated to the current situational cues. For example, a person exposed repeatedly to frustrating situations, who attributes the goal blocking to the actions of others, may enter a social interaction in an aroused state with hostile feelings toward everyone. Environmental stimuli may also directly trigger conditioned emotional reactions and may cue the retrieval from memory of cognitions that define the current emotional state. For example, the sight of an enemy or the smell of a battlefield may provoke both instantaneous physiological arousal and the recall of thoughts about the enemy that give meaning to the aroused state as anger. That emotional state may influence which cues the person attends to and how the person evaluates the cues to which he or she does attend. A highly aroused, angry person may focus on just a few highly salient cues and ignore others that convey equally important information about the social situation. Then the angry person's evaluation of these cues may be biased toward perceiving hostility when none is present.

A person who finds hostile cues the most salient or who interprets ambiguous cues as hostile will be more likely to experience anger and activate schemas and scripts related to aggression.

Second, the search for a script to guide behavior can also account for substantial differences in aggressive responding. It is presumed that the more aggressive individual has encoded in memory a more extensive, well-connected network of social scripts emphasizing aggressive problem-solving. Therefore, such a script is more likely to be retrieved during any search. However, the search for a script is also strongly affected by one's interpretation of the social cues, one's activated schemas including normative beliefs, and one's mood state and arousal. For example, anger, even in the absence of supporting cues, will make the retrieval of scripts previously associated with anger more likely; the presence of a weapon, even in the absence of anger, will make the retrieval of scripts associated with weapons more likely; and the perception that another person has hostile intentions will activate scripts related to hostility. Additionally, the schemas that have been activated, particularly the self-schema and normative beliefs, will influence the direction of the search for a script. The man who believes in "an eye for an eye" and perceives himself as "an avenger" is more likely to retrieve a script emphasizing aggressive retaliation. Finally, for the individual with a large well-learned repertoire of simple, direct aggressive scripts for solving social problems and a smaller less-well-learned repertoire of complex, indirect scripts for prosocial solutions, the arousal associated with anger will make the selection of an aggressive script even more likely. As described earlier, in high states of arousal individuals search less widely and deeply for scripts and retrieve the best connected scripts; so aggressive behavior becomes even more likely in highly arousing situations for people with predominantly aggressive scripts.

The third locus for the expression of individual differences and situational variation occurs after a script is activated. Before acting out the script, it is proposed that one evaluates the script in light of internalized activated schemas and normative beliefs to determine if the suggested behaviors are socially appropriate and likely to achieve the desired goal. Different people may evaluate the same script quite differently. The habitually aggressive person is expected to hold normative beliefs condoning more aggression and thus he or she will use more aggressive scripts. For example, if a man suddenly discovers that his wife has been unfaithful, he may experience rage and access a script for physical retribution. However, whether or not the man executes that script will depend on his normative beliefs about the appropriateness of hitting a woman. Even within the same person, different normative beliefs may be "primed" by different situations and different mood states. Going to church probably activates (in the short run) quite different normative beliefs than watching a fight in a hockey game on television. Although evaluation of the script on the basis of one's normative beliefs is the most important filtering process according to Huesmann and Guerra (1997), other evaluations also play a role. Fontaine and Dodge (1998) have proposed that a complex process of "response evaluation and decision" takes place at this point that considers response efficacy and valuation, outcome expectancy and valuation, response comparison, and response selection. They propose that children who display different kinds of aggression (e.g., proactive/instrumental versus reactive/hostile) may display different kinds of deficits in these mechanisms.

An important implication of these multiple loci for processing deficits is that the same aggressive behavior in different individuals may be produced by different deficits in social information processing (e.g., reactive aggression may stem from misinterpretation of cues or holding inappropriate normative beliefs or having a large repertoire of aggressive scripts). Likewise, differences in aggressive behavior may indicate differences in underlying information-processing deficits (e.g., instrumental aggression is probably more likely to stem from inappropriate normative beliefs than from hostile attributional bias).

Finally, as the bottom right box in Figure 12.1 shows, it is not simply society's response to a person's aggressive behavior per se that affects the person's future behavior, but the person's interpretation of society's response and how that interpretation affects the person's schemas and mood. This assumption opens several important channels for explaining how aggressive scripts may be maintained even in the face of strong negative responses from society. For example, a child who is severely beaten for behaving aggressively may attribute the beating to being disliked by the punisher rather than to anything he did. An aggressive teenage male, rather than changing his aggressive behaviors, which perhaps provide immediate gratification, may alter his normative beliefs to make the feedback he is receiving seem less negative. He might integrate some of the readily available aphorisms about aggression into his regulatory schemata. The boy who is told he is bad because he pushed others out of the way may shrug his shoulders and think "Nice guys finish last." The boy who shoves a child who bumped into him may think "An eye for an eye." Alternatively, he may mitigate society's punishments for his aggressive behavior by choosing environments in which aggression is more acceptable. Thus, the more aggressive adolescent male may spend more time interacting with other aggressive peers who accept his behaviors as a way of life. Not only do such social networks provide adolescents with environments in which aggression is not discouraged, such social networks promote the internalization of normative beliefs favoring aggression. The important point sometimes lost on social engineers is that it is not just society's response to aggression that is important, but how the aggressor interprets that response.

So far we have examined how scripts may be accessed and used to guide behavior and how certain individual and environmental factors could promote the use of aggressive scripts. Within this framework a habitually aggressive person is presumed to be someone who regularly retrieves and uses aggressive scripts for social behavior. We have noted a number of factors that might promote the retrieval and use of aggressive scripts. It may be, for example, that the cues present in the environment trigger the recall only of aggressive scripts. However, the regular retrieval and use would suggest above all that a large number of aggressive scripts have been stored in memory. Similarly, the regular execution of such scripts would suggest that normative beliefs and other schemas supporting aggression have been acquired and encoded. Thus, we must also examine how schemas and scripts are acquired.

A child's early learning experiences are surely critical to the acquisition of scripts and schemas for social behavior, just as learning plays the key role in the acquisition of procedural and declarative knowledge relevant to intellectual life. A variety of preexisting neurophysiological factors can predispose individuals toward particular schemas and scripts, and individual differences in biology interact with individual differences in environment to mold the child's social tendencies. As described above in the discussion on social learning theory, observational and inactive learning interact as the child develops to shape the child's scripts and schemas. A script is most likely to be acquired at first by observing others and then more firmly established by having its use reinforced.

What is the role of prevention within such a social-cognitive context? Obviously, aggression can be prevented either by interfering in the acquisition process through which the relevant cognitive schemas, scripts, and beliefs are acquired, or by directing prevention efforts at changing existing cognitions and replacing them with more appropriate cognitions for guiding social behavior. Later in this chapter we give some examples of each type of approach and how it might be applied.

EARLY SOCIAL-COGNITIVE PREVENTIVE INTERVENTIONS

With the advent of social-information–processing models of aggressive behavior, social-cognitive components began to be incorporated in the multifaceted intervention programs that sought to address the numerous causes and risk factors for aggression. Among the first of these was Spivak and Shure's (1989) social problem-solving intervention (see Shure, chapter 13, this volume). Spivak and Shure designed a primary prevention program to help children develop the interpersonal cognitive problem-solving skills that underlie the quality of social relationships and the capacity to cope with interpersonal problems. Although not specifically targeted toward aggressive behavior, the techniques used by this program promote skills and strategies that are conducive to prosocial interpersonal problem solving.

Through a series of structured classroom games, children are taught strategies for evaluating interpersonal problems and generating alternative solutions while taking into consideration the feelings of others and the likely consequences of alternative solutions. The goal of the program is to teach children how to think and how to generate and evaluate multiple ways for solving problems. As a result, the process of thinking, rather than the content of the thoughts, is emphasized. The act of generating multiple alternative solutions and evaluating each of these by considering their likely consequences fosters multiple scripts for behaving and decreases the likelihood that an aggressive behavioral script will be chosen. Similarly, training children how to recognize and find out what others are feeling will help overcome and prevent the hostile attribution bias. The authors have reported some empirical evidence that this intervention improves interpersonal problem-solving by strengthening prosocial behaviors while decreasing maladaptive ones, such as aggression. However the magnitude of the changes does not appear to be large, and the findings are not robust.

Guerra and Slaby (1990) conducted a social-cognitive intervention with 120 adolescents incarcerated for violent offenses. In the intervention they targeted social problem-solving skills and beliefs supporting aggression. In terms of our cognitive model, they were attempting to modify scripts for social problem-solving and normative beliefs for evaluating scripts. They found that immediate changes in beliefs and problem-solving skills were engendered by the intervention with accompanying improvements in behavior as rated by staff. However, there were no differences between the treated and untreated children in recidivism.

Hudley and Graham (1993) isolated and targeted one social cognitive process, hostile attribution bias, in their intervention program designed to reduce peer-directed aggression among African-American boys. In other words they attempted to change the way that children interpret cues at the beginning of the processing sequence in our model. Aggressive and nonaggressive boys were randomly assigned to one of three conditions: the attributional intervention, an attention training program, or a no-treatment control group. Results demonstrated that the attributional intervention reduced aggressive children's tendency to presume hostile intent in hypothetical and laboratory analog tasks involving ambiguous provocation by peers. In addition to showing reduced hostile attribution bias, the aggressive boys who participated in the attributional intervention were less likely to engage in verbally hostile behaviors toward a peer during a laboratory task than were the aggressive children in the other two conditions. Finally, only the aggressiveness of the attribution intervention participants was judged by teachers to have declined from pre- to post-intervention. These results suggest that the hostile attribution bias characteristic of aggressive children can be successfully modified through retraining and that this retraining does have an impact on aggressive behavior. Hudley and Graham's (1993) results are some of the strongest empirical results reported for social-cognitive interventions. It is hoped that replications of the effect will be reported in the near future.

Although these early social-cognitive interventions showed some success, they have not been as successful as the underlying theoretical model would lead one to expect. We believe that there are several reasons for this outcome. First, each of the existing approaches has tended to focus on only one or two aspects of the information processing involved in social problem-solving, such as hostile attributional bias, scripts for conflict resolution, and beliefs about aggression. A more comprehensive approach may be necessary. Second, as we said at the start of this chapter, aggression is multiply determined. No one factor alone causes serious aggressive behavior. Many contextual factors play important roles. It is probably unrealistic to expect that one can prevent aggression simply by changing a child's cognitive processes. Third, there is evidence that the small group approach to prevention that throws many aggressive kids together may actually breed aggression, possibly making it seem more normative. Fourth, and perhaps most important, sufficient attention may not have been paid to the developmental course of aggression and planning preventive interventions to fit into the appropriate slots in the developmental course.

DEVELOPMENT OF COGNITIONS SUPPORTING AGGRESSION

There is substantial evidence that the relation between a child's cognitions and social behavior crystallizes during the early elementary school years. Huesmann and Guerra (1997), for example, found that among first-grade children, greater levels of aggressive behavior predicted subsequent beliefs approving of aggression, but a first grader's beliefs did not predict subsequent behavior. Furthermore, although beliefs could be measured reliably among first graders, normative beliefs were unstable from one year to the next. On the other hand, fourth grader's beliefs about the acceptability of aggression were stable and did predict later aggressive behavior. Together these findings suggest that normative beliefs are first formed from self-perceptions of behavior and then, as the child grows older, crystallize and begin to influence behavior.

More recently, Huesmann, Spindler, McElwain, & Guerra (1998) reported a similar pattern for aggressive fantasies. Such fantasies can be viewed as cognitive rehearsals of aggressive behavior. As with normative beliefs, aggressive fantasizing was predicted by previous aggressive behavior in early elementary children but predicted subsequent aggressive behavior in older children.

One implication of such findings for preventive interventions is clear—the success of any preventive intervention will probably depend on the child's age. Older children need interventions designed to change existing cognitions, whereas younger children need interventions designed to help mold appropriate cognitions. A second likely implication is that interventions conducted during the early years before a child's cognitions solidify are more likely to have lasting effects.

TWO DEVELOPMENTALLY SENSITIVE SOCIAL-COGNITIVE INTERVENTIONS

At least three recent prevention research programs have been initiated that attend to developmental issues and focus on the elements that our social-cognitive model suggests should be important. In addition, the two large programs described below both accept as a fundamental principle the need for multidimensional intervention. In other words, one cannot expect social-cognitive interventions to be effective unless they are coupled with changes in the ecology supporting aggression that surrounds the child.

FAST Track

Building particularly on Dodge's social-cognitive perspective, the FAST Track—Family and Schools Together—research program (Greenberg et al., 1998) was designed to determine whether one could reduce children's disruptive behaviors (including aggression) in the home as well as at school by enhancing children's social-cognitive skills related to affect regulation and interpersonal problem-solving. To realize these broad-ranging goals, the FAST Track program is using five intervention components: (a) parent training, (b) home visiting/case management, (c) social skills training, (d) academic tutoring, and (e) teacher-based classroom intervention. Although this program is multifaceted and not simply "social-cognitive," many of its interventions derive from Dodge's social-cognitive model of aggression. For example, part of the parent-training component focuses on helping children successfully implement the strategies they are learning in school for anger control (reduce the influence of emotions on cue interpretation and script selection in our model) and effective problem-solving (script selection and outcome evaluation). In the process, these skills are enhanced within parents themselves. The social-skills–training component for the children is centered on improving social-cognitive skills, including friendship and play skills, anger and self-control strategies, and interpersonal problem-solving.

This large-scale multiyear, multisite project has been under way since the early 1990s. Final evaluation of the results will require more time as the children from the study grow into adolescence and young adulthood. The initial results are both promising and disturbing. Although there are clear indications that the intervention is changing social-cognitive information processing and reducing some aggressive behavior (e.g., on the playground), the effect sizes reported thus far are not as large as one would have hoped.

MACS Project

The Metropolitan Area Child Study (MACS; Huesmann, 1998a; Metropolitan Area Research Group, 2000) is evaluating three separate but complementary interventions based on the social-cognitive model. As with FAST Track, however, the interventions also target the ecology of the child to facilitate social-cognitive changes. Each intervention level includes all that was delivered in the less intense levels but adds a component. Level A is a general enhancement, classroom-based, social-cognitive, and peer-relationship–training program that is combined with an extensive teacher-training program focused on the enhancement of classroom and school environment. Level B adds a small group social-cognitive and peer-relationship training for high-risk children, and Level C includes a family intervention for the high-risk children and their families. As described above, the children in the Level B intervention also received the classroom intervention, and the children in the Level C intervention also received the classroom and small group intervention.

The social-cognitive elements addressed varied somewhat from condition to condition. In all conditions, attempts were initiated to change normative beliefs about aggression to make them less supportive of aggressive behavior. In the classroom and small-group components attention was also directed at reducing fantasizing about aggression (rehearsal of scripts) and at counteracting the effects of exposure to media violence on scripts and beliefs (reduce encoding of aggressive scripts and normative beliefs accepting aggression).

The MACS project particularly targeted high-risk urban children and used a between-schools evaluation design. Four schools in the Chicago metropolitan area were randomly assigned to each condition—Control, Level A, Level B, and Level C. Then each cohort of children that entered the school received the appropriate intervention for the school.

As with the FAST Track project, the MACS project was initiated in the early 1990s, and the children are still being assessed as they move into adolescence. The results are also very similar to the results from the FAST Track project. There is evidence that the intervention reduced fantasizing about aggression and reduced aggressive behavior somewhat in some schools. What is particularly interesting about the MACS results to the social-cognitive theorist is that the effects only seem to occur for children who receive the intervention when they are in the second and third grades before their cognitions about aggression solidify. Furthermore, the positive results only seem to occur in the schools that have a more facilitative ecology for the reduction of violence. In fact, there is some evidence that the small group intervention actually moves low aggressive kids toward the average level of aggression in schools with a less facilitative environment.

MORE INTENSE AND CONTROLLED SOCIAL-COGNITIVE INTERVENTIONS

Both the FAST Track and MACS projects assumed that prevention of aggression required change in the ecological context in which the children were developing, as well as individual cognitive change. Given that approach, it is all the more surprising that stronger results do not seem to be emerging. One problem may be that there is a trade-off between the multiple-school, large-sample efforts in disadvantaged neighborhoods that ecological approaches require and the kind of tight control of intervention procedures that one needs for a strong social-cognitive intervention. It is not enough to target the correct cognitions and information-processing operations for change; one must be able to use mechanisms that actually do change them.

An alternative approach to testing the principles of social-cognitive interventions is to target several specific cognitive dimensions with more powerful techniques for change than one can usually use in larger samples. One can attempt to do this, as well, in a more controllable environment where ecological change is not as necessary.

The "Communicate, Cooperate, and Believe in Yourself" (C^2 Believe) research project is being conducted among foster children and nonfoster school children in the Ann Arbor, Michigan, public schools (Huesmann et al., 2000). The goal of this research is to evaluate the effectiveness of four social-cognitive interventions designed to reduce violence. Specifically, the program seeks to reduce aggressive behavior by (a) reducing children's imitation of violence they observe or experience, (e.g., the learning of aggressive scripts); (b) reducing children's acquisition and rehearsal of attitudes and beliefs supporting violence (e.g., the learning of normative beliefs); (c) reducing children's development of biased perceptions of hostility in others (e.g., biased cue interpretation); and (d) increasing children's prosocial alternative behaviors, which can replace characteristic aggressive solutions to problems (i.e., learning prosocial scripts).

Building on an earlier intervention technique developed by Huesmann et al. (1983), we used procedures for each segment of this intervention that used well-established powerful attitude change procedures to alter children's cognitions. Specifically, the children were manipulated into publicly committing themselves to attitudes opposing aggression (e.g. "turn the other cheek," to being careful about perceiving hostility in others, and to not watching and not imitating the violent acts of others on television). To inoculate children against the imitation of violence and the acquisition of specific beliefs supporting violence from the observation of violence, the children were given the task of making a video in which they had to convince other children that imitating violent behaviors and accepting violence is bad. The second component of the intervention required children to discriminate hostile from nonhostile intent in others' behavior using videotaped vignettes. Once children solved the discrimination problems, which were designed to illustrate that even acts that appear very hostile may often be accidental, they were charged with the task of making a second videotape in which they had to convince other children to think about why others are acting as they do before automatically assuming their intent is hostile. The final component of the intervention was aimed at fostering prosocial solutions to interpersonal problems by showing a videotape in which a variety of tense social situations are resolved by nonaggressive assertive actions.

A randomized trial of this intervention on a sample of average-risk school children and another sample of high-risk foster children is currently yielding mixed results. Only preliminary results are available at present, but they suggest that, although some attitudes are changed by such an intervention approach, corresponding behaviors may not follow (Herrera, Huesmann, Parker, Eron, & Souweidane, 1997). Although the intervention has been praised extensively by the teachers and parents involved and it is in great demand, it has been hard to show to date that objective across-the-board changes in aggressive behavior followed from the intervention. However, there are strong suggestions of moderation of the intervention's effect by individual differences. For example, the results reveal that those aggressive children who rate themselves inappropriately high on social self-efficacy are more likely to respond to the intervention by reducing their aggressive behavior (Tartt, Huesmann, & Herrera, 1998). It may be that strong individual differences in responsiveness to social-cognitive interventions create large variations in children's responsiveness to such interventions—a variation that may be related to measurable individual difference.

SUMMARY

As we have illustrated in this chapter, the unified information-processing model for aggression provides a theoretical base from which systematic intervention strategies for aggression are suggested. This model highlights four important points in the cognitive processes underlying aggression—four loci that promise to be important entryways through which interventions can be made: (a) the perception and interpretation of social cues, (b) the search for scripts to guide behavior, (c) the evaluation of activated scripts, and (d) the interpretation of society's response to one's behavior. Until more systematic research is conducted, it is unclear exactly which and how many of these points need to be addressed for an intervention to be effective. Nor is it known what methods are most effective in influencing these points in the cognitive process.

Nevertheless, it seems clear from our model that one must aim interventions at fostering a nonaggressive self-schema—a schema that reflects a realistic world view, neither a "bad" nor unrealistically "good" self-schema that will be susceptible to reacting aggressively to external evaluations that challenge the unrealistic view.

Finally, in targeting interventions for these information-processing domains researchers and practitioners should establish a careful balance between providing a strong, tightly controlled intervention effort and conducting a broad ecological attack on the foundations of aggression in the child's environment. Too diffuse an effort in an attempt to broaden the ecological effect may minimize the treatment effect; too narrow a focus may yield only temporary improvements that are counteracted by ecological influences.

REFERENCES

Abelson, R. P. (1981). The psychological status of the script concept. *American Psychologist, 36,* 715–729.

Bandura, A. (1977). *Social learning theory.* Englewood Cliffs, NJ: Prentice Hall.

Bandura, A. (1986). Social foundations of thought and action: A social-cognitive theory. Englewood Cliffs, NJ: Prentice Hall.

Berkowitz, L. (1990). On the formation and regulation of anger and aggression: A cognitive–neoassociationistic analysis. *American Psychologist, 45,* 494–503.

Crick, N. R., & Dodge, K. A. (1994). A review and reformulation of social information processing mechanisms in children's adjustment. *Psychological Bulletin, 115,* 74–101.

Dodge, K. A. (1980). Social cognition and children's aggressive behavior. *Child Development, 51,* 620–635.

Dodge, K. A. (1986). A social information processing model of social competence in children. In M. Perlmutter (Ed.), *The Minnesota Symposium on Child Psychology* (Vol. 18, pp. 77–125). Hillsdale, NJ: Erlbaum.

Dodge, K .A., & Frame, C. L. (1982). Social cognitive biases and deficits in aggressive boys. *Child Development, 53,* 620–635.

Fontaine, R. G., & Dodge, K. A. (1998). On-line behavioral judgments and decision making in aggressive youth: A computational model of response evaluation and decision (RED). Manuscript submitted for publication.

Greenberg, M. T., Bierman, K., Coie, J. D., Dodge, K. A., Lochman, J. E., & McMahon, J. (1998, August). *Results of the FAST-Track prevention trial.*

Presented at the annual meeting of the American Psychological Association, San Francisco, CA.

Guerra, N. (1994). Violence prevention. *Preventive Medicine, 23,* 661–664.

Guerra, N. G., & Slaby, R. G. (1990). Cognitive mediators of aggression in adolescent offenders: II. Intervention. *Developmental Psychology, 26,* 269–277.

Herrera, C., Huesmann, L. R., Parker, J. G., Eron, L. D., & Souweidane, V. S. (1997, May). *Inoculating children against the development of aggression: The SafeMichigan Children's Initiative.* Presented at the annual meeting of the American Psychological Society, Washington, DC.

Hudley, C., & Graham, S. (1993). An attributional intervention to reduce peer-directed aggression among African-American boys. *Child Development, 64,* 124–138.

Huesmann, L. R. (1980). Toward a predictive model of romantic behavior. In K. S. Pope (Ed.), *On love and loving.* New York: Jossey-Bass.

Huesmann, L. R. (1982). Television violence and aggressive behavior. In D. Pearl, L. Bouthilet, & J. Lazar (Eds.), *Television and behavior: Ten years of scientific programs and implications for the 80's* (Vol. 2, pp. 126–137). Washington, DC: U.S. Government Printing Office.

Huesmann, L. R. (1986). Psychological processes promoting the relation between exposure to media violence and aggressive behavior by the viewer. *Journal of Social Issues, 42,* 3, 125–139.

Huesmann, L. R.(1988). An information processing model for the development of aggression. *Aggressive Behavior, 14,* 13–24.

Huesmann, L. R. (Ed.). (1994). *Aggressive behavior: Current perspectives.* New York: Plenum Press.

Huesmann, L. R. (1998a, January). A preliminary evaluation of a cognitive/ecological intervention for preventing aggression in high-risk youth. Presented at Society for Research on Adolescence, San Diego, CA.

Huesmann, L. R. (1998b). The role of social information processing and cognitive schema in the acquisition and maintenance of habitual aggressive behavior. In R. Geen & E. Donnerstein (Eds.), *Human aggression: Theories, research, and implications for social policy* (pp. 73–109). New York: Academic Press.

Huesmann, L. R., & Eron, L. D. (1984). Cognitive processes and the persistence of aggressive behavior. *Aggressive Behavior, 10,* 243–251.

Huesmann, L. R., Eron, L. D., Klein, R., Brice, P., Fisher, P. (1983). Mitigating the imitation of aggressive behaviors by children's attitudes about media violence. *Journal of Personality and Social Psychology, 44,* 899-910.

Huesmann, L. R., Eron, L. D., Lefkowitz, M. M., & Walder, L. O. (1984). The stability of aggression over time and generations. *Developmental Psychology, 20,* 1120–1134.

Huesmann, L. R., & Guerra, N. G. (1997). Normative beliefs about aggression and aggressive behavior. *Journal of Personality and Social Psychology, 72*(2), 408–419.

Huesmann, L. R., Parker, J. G., Herrera, C., Timmons, P., Eron, L. D., & Souwdain, V. (2000). Preliminary outcomes of a social-cognitive intervention to reduce risk for aggression in foster children. Unpublished manuscript. Institute for Social Research, University of Michigan, Ann Arbor, Michigan.

Huesmann, L. R., & Podolski, C. (in press). Punishment and the development of aggressive and antisocial behavior. In S. McCouville (Ed.) *Punishment*. New York: Gaggenheim Foundation.

Huesmann, R. L., Spindler, A., McElwain, N., & Guerra, N. G. (1998, August). *The roles of cognitive processes in moderating and mediating the development and prevention of childhood aggression*. Presented at the annual meeting of the American Psychological Association, San Francisco.

Kazdin, A. E. (1994). Interventions for aggressive and antisocial children. In L. D. Eron, J. H. Gentry, & P. Schlegel (Eds.), *Reason to hope: A psychological perspective on violence and youth* (pp. 341–382). Washington, D. C.: American Psychological Association.

Metropolitan Area Research Group (2000). A cognitive-ecological approach to preventing aggression in urban settings: Initial outcomes for high-risk children. Under revision for *Journal of Consulting and Clinical Psychology*.

Olweus, D. (1979). The stability of aggressive reaction patterns in males: A review. *Psychological Bulletin, 86*, 852–875.

Poulin, F., & Dishion, T. (1997 April). Iatrogenic effects among high risk adolescents aggregated within interventions: An analysis of the durability and process. Washington, DC: Society for Research in Child Development.

Schneider, W., & Shiffrin, R. M. (1977). Controlled and automatic human information processing: I. Detection, search, and attention. *Psychological Review, 84*, 1–66.

Sherman, L. W. (1992). Policing domestic violence: Experiments and directions. New York: Free Press.

Spivak, G., & Shure, M. B. (1989). Interpersonal cognitive problem solving (ICPS): A competence-building primary prevention program. *Prevention in Human Services, 6*, 151–178.

Tartt, A., Huesmann, L. R., & Herrera, C. (1998, August). *Self-esteem as a moderator of the effects of interventions to reduce aggression*. Presented at the annual meeting of the American Psychological Association, San Francisco, CA.

Tolan, P. H., & Guerra N. G. (1994). Prevention of juvenile delinquency: Current status and issues. *Journal of Applied and Preventive Psychology, 3*, 251–273.

Tolan, P. H., Guerra, N. G., Henry, D., VanAcker, R., Huesmann, L. R., & Eron, L. D. (1998, August). *Cognitive–ecological prevention: Results of the Metropolitan Area Child Study*. Presented at the annual meeting of the American Psychological Association Meeting, San Francisco, CA.

Turner, C. W., & Goldsmith, D. (1976). Effects of toy guns and airplanes on children's antisocial free play behavior. *Journal of Experimental Child Psychology, 21*, 303–315.

Walters, R. H., & Brown, M. (1963). Studies of reinforcement of aggression: III. Transfer of responses to an interpersonal situation. *Child Development, 34*, 563–571.

Zuzul, M. (1989). *The weapons effect and child aggression: A field experiment.* Unpublished doctoral dissertation, University of Zagreb, Croatia.

13

HOW TO THINK, NOT WHAT TO THINK: A PROBLEM-SOLVING APPROACH TO PREVENTION OF EARLY HIGH-RISK BEHAVIORS

MYRNA B. SHURE

In this chapter I describe how my research colleague George Spivack and I have studied children's ability to think about how to solve typical, everyday interpersonal problems; how that ability relates to an identified set of overt behaviors as early as preschool; and how intervention to train those thinking skills can reduce or prevent early high-risk behaviors from preschool through sixth grade.

EARLY HISTORY AND ICPS SKILLS

When George Spivack and I began our work in the late 1960s, we focused on children's aggression and their inability to wait and to cope with frustration because those behaviors were specifically linked to mental health dysfunction. They are now known to be particularly destructive, because research has shown them to also predict later violence, substance

The research reported in this chapter was funded by Grants MH-20372, MH-35989, MH-27741, and MH-40801, National Institute of Mental Health, Washington, DC.

abuse, and other more serious problems (Parker & Asher, 1987). We also focused on positive, prosocial behaviors such as caring, sharing, and cooperation, which are linked to good peer relations and in turn play a constructive role in preventing the serious outcomes mentioned above (Eron & Huesmann, 1984).

In this chapter I describe the way that Spivack and I studied how children resolve conflicts. When I was training to be a nursery school teacher, I noticed several ways that children tried to get a toy from another child. Some would first ask for it, but if refused, they would then hit the child, grab the toy, or tell the teacher. Some would simply give up and walk away pouting. Zachary, age 4, tried a different strategy. When he asked Richard for the wagon, which Richard predictably refused to give up, Zachary asked him why he couldn't have it. "Because I *need* it! I'm pulling the rocks," answered Richard. Now Zachary offered, "I can help you pull them. We can pull the rocks together." And Richard and Zachary went off happily pulling the wagon together.

I thought Zachary might be unusual. He was applying skills requiring highly sophisticated thinking. He was coordinating his needs with those of Richard's instead of focusing only on his own. And Zachary and Richard were both satisfied with their solution to the problem. As I began to observe more children, I noticed that although many children need negative behavior to achieve their desires, some seemed aware of, if not genuinely concerned about, the needs and feelings of others. They were not overly aggressive or overly timid and tried more and different prosocial strategies.

In 1968, Spivack was studying how adolescents could think about reaching interpersonal goals. He learned that regardless of IQ, adolescents who had the ability to plan step-by-step means to reach an interpersonal goal, to recognize potential obstacles that could interfere with reaching that goal, and to appreciate that problem-solving takes time (skills referred to as "means-ends thinking") were better adjusted than those who lacked these skills (Spivack & Levine, 1963). My first task was to test those thinking skills in fifth graders (Shure & Spivack, 1972). Youngsters who displayed impulsive or withdrawn behaviors were significantly more deficient in means-ends and other skills (e.g., consequential thinking)—two abilities in a series we later came to call Interpersonal Cognitive Problem-Solving, or ICPS skills.

Why would impulsive and socially withdrawn children be more ICPS-deficient than those not displaying those behaviors? Spivack and I hypothesized that individuals who are not adept at thinking through ways to solve a typical interpersonal problem or are unable to circumvent obstacles that may interfere with reaching that goal may make impulsive mistakes, become frustrated and possibly aggressive, or may evade the problem entirely by withdrawing. If their initial needs remain unsatisfied, and if they fail often enough, varying degrees of maladaptive behavior could result. On the other hand, someone with ICPS skills could more effectively plan a course of action, evaluate and choose from a variety of possible routes to the goal, consider a different course of action in light of its potential outcome, and consequently experience less frustration and failure.

It was Robert, a 4-year-old, who gave me further insights into how children's thinking might affect their behavior. He got what he wanted from his classmates by hitting them. When I first saw him do this to Paul, I asked him, "What happened when you hit Paul?" He answered, "He hit me back, but I don't care." Indeed he did not. He got the truck, and that was what he cared about. Robert and other children who hit, kick, scream, and grab toys from others gave me a new perspective on the significance of research on empathy, energized by Norma and Seymour Feshbach (e.g., 1969). I wondered if children who do not care or who endure their own pain when they are 3, 4, or 5 years old could possibly develop empathy for the victims they might hurt (either physically or emotionally) later on.

Did Robert not care about being hit back because he was truly unconcerned about what happened to him? Or, did he really care, but because he lacked the prosocial strategies to obtain his goal, he pursued the only course of action he knew? Did he think about how hitting a child for a toy might make that child feel? Or, was he so consumed with getting what he wanted that he did not even think about feelings at all? Is it even possible that Robert did not care whether he got hit back because he was so used to getting hit by peers (perhaps also hit in the form of spanking by his parents) that he simply became immune to those consequences of his behavior? In light of escalating substance abuse (hurting one's self) and violence (hurting others), perhaps children who say "I don't care" should make us take special pause.

Gary, age 5, who hit his brother for "bugging" him, understood when asked that his brother was "mad" when he did that. Perhaps even more important, he told me, "I feel bad when I hurt my brother." Would Gary be less likely than Robert to continue hurting others? Would Gary be still less likely if he knew what else to do?

Musings about Gary, Robert, and children like them inspired me to systematically test how (and whether) interpersonal thinking skills would distinguish preschoolers who were socially adjusted and interpersonally competent from those who were not. After considerable piloting, Spivack and I first identified two ICPS skills that produced the widest range of response in both low- and middle-income 4- and 5-year-olds within a wide IQ range (80–120+). The first skill, measured by the Preschool Interpersonal Problem-Solving (PIPS) test (Shure, 1992d; Shure & Spivack, 1974b), is *alternative-solution thinking,* the ability to think of different, relevant solutions to two types of (hypothetical) problems: (a) wanting a toy another child has and (b) damaging an object of value to a parent. The second skill, measured by the What Happens Next Game (WHNG) test (Shure, 1990;

Shure & Spivack, 1974c), is *consequential thinking*, or the ability to think of different things that might happen next if a child (a) grabs a toy from a peer and (b) takes something from an adult without first asking.

As rated by teachers on the Hahnemann Preschool Behavior Rating (HBSB) scale (Shure & Spivack, 1971), deficiencies in both ICPS skills, especially solution skills, were related to impulsivity, including impatience, over-emotionality in the face of frustration, and physical and verbal aggression (Shure, & Jaeger, 1971; Spivack, Platt, & Shure, 1976; Spivack & Shure, 1974). In addition, children who were unable to make friends, who were less concerned about (or at best unaware of) others in distress, and who were less able or willing to share and cooperate with others were also relatively ICPS-deficient compared with their more prosocial classmates (Spivack & Shure, 1974).

We found from Urberg and Docherty's (1976) measure of perspective-taking that withdrawn youngsters were more aware than impulsive ones that people could feel differently about something (e.g., a birthday party, a broken bike), and that an event may benefit one person at the expense of the other (e.g., one child receives a toy from the teacher, the other does not; Shure & Spivack, 1982b). Perhaps awareness of others' feelings is not enough to overcome social withdrawal. For example, if I know that what I did made you angry, but I don't know what to do about that anger, and if I am already afraid to relate to others, I may find it easier to simply withdraw from people and from problems I cannot solve. Is this kind of perspective-taking a necessary but not sufficient skill for well-adjusted behavior? Perhaps awareness of others' feelings is not an end in itself, but rather a prerequisite skill for good problem-solving. We believe that such insight might open up more options for solving interpersonal problems, creating a greater likelihood of success in solving those problems than would be possible for youngsters who are unaware of or unconcerned about the feelings of others.

EARLY HYPOTHESIS BUILDING

Having now discovered that there are youngsters who behave differently and think differently at very early ages, we began to wonder if how a child thinks may guide his or her behavior as much as, or perhaps more than, commands, suggestions, or even explanations given to them by adults. How could this be? Impulsive behaviors include an inability to wait when a desire has to be delayed, however temporarily. Unable to share or wait a turn, a child often grabs the toy or hits the other child as the quickest and surest way to get it now—behaviors that are often accompanied by intense distress or anger. Although less able than their adjusted age mates to think of a wide variety of potential consequences to these acts, they were able to tell us that the other child might "hit him back," "grab the toy back," or "tell the teacher." Having experienced these consequences in real life, it is possible that awareness does not stop their impulsive behaviors because they are unwilling or unable to think of what else to do. Perhaps this reasoning helps explain why Robert did not care if he got hit back when he grabbed a toy.

Once a child does have available options, that is, alternative solutions for a problem, the next question becomes whether it is the quality or quantity of those solutions that has relevance for behavior. This question has been the subject of some debate among those who have examined *interpersonal* or, as some call it, *social problem-solving* (Elias & Clabby, 1992; Rubin, 1985). For us, the number of relevant alternative solutions supersedes the quality of those solutions in distinguishing the behavior groups. Adjusted, impulsive, and inhibited youngsters could all think of forceful ways to obtain a toy (e.g., hit the other child, grab the toy, throw sand in the other's face). The difference was that well-adjusted children could also think of a greater variety of nonforceful options (e.g., trade a toy, take turns, play together) and more creative ones such as "Show her how to play with it," "You'll have more fun if you play with me," or some form of loan such as "I'll just play with it for a little while." When withdrawn children thought of nonforceful ways to obtain a toy, most were limited to "ask," "say please," or "tell the teacher" (to solve the problem for them). It is important to note that no matter how hard I probed for new ideas, these youngsters got stuck, repeated those same solutions, and were unable to think of a wider variety of ideas. Even though the content of solutions given by withdrawn youngsters was positive and nonforceful, being so limited in repertoire gave these children fewer options to fall back on in case of failure. It was this deficiency that related to maladaptive behaviors.

Regarding content, we learned something interesting about another solution to obtain a toy from a peer. Children who said "Wait 'till he's not looking and then take it" were not the impulsive ones, as one might think based on the content "take it," nor were they the withdrawn, suggested by the possibility that the content "when he's not looking" is nonconfrontational. In fact, it was more likely the adjusted youngsters who gave that solution. We came to realize that this solution shows rather sophisticated thinking. It involves a plan. It includes a nonimpulsive waiting period. However rudimentary, it includes two components of the more developmentally advanced means-ends thinking described earlier: a means and a statement of time. This "plan for future," the ability of these adjusted youngsters to think of multiple solutions, and the nonforceful but limited repertoire of the withdrawn children led us to believe that perhaps it is not what children think that relates to behavior but *how* they think; that is, the process of thinking about how what they do affects their own and others' feelings and other potential consequences of their acts—and then what else they could do to solve the problem. Would these skills provide a stronger mediator of behavior than the content of a few limited options, however prosocial in content? Perhaps an adequate repertoire of solutions could prevent a child from giving up too soon.

At a conversation hour at the meetings of the Society for Research in Child Development (Shure & Selman, 1977), a panel discussed issues in social cognition. Norma Feshbach inquired, "Should a child who shows understanding (in a test situation) be expected to behave accordingly when observed at a later time?" Carolyn Shantz noted, however, that it is not always possible to tell what a child is thinking by the action he takes. She suggested, for example, that "a child [in physical pursuit] of another may not [in his view] be displaying antisocial behavior at all; he may merely be coming to the defense of a vulnerable friend." Such a child may indeed be experiencing empathy (it hurts me to see my friend attacked) and may even be actively perspective taking (my friend is afraid of the attacker; I am not). And, as Seymour Feshbach noted, "It could be that the more a child understands the nature of a social injustice the angrier he may become." I do not mean to suggest that even if in this case the end would justify the means. But if one can understand the situation from the child's point of view, one might come to understand that the problem was not that the child he pursued was hitting but that his friend needed help. The issue for the adult now was to help the child find a different way to solve the problem he defined.

Why is ICPS competence so important? Research has confirmed that it is ICPS-related behaviors—aggression and impatience, lack of concern for the feelings of others, and inability or unwillingness to share and cooperate—that predict such later, more serious problems as violence, substance abuse, teenage pregnancy, school dropout, and some forms of psychopathology (Parker & Asher, 1987). Research has also confirmed that social withdrawal, if left untreated, can predict more internalized kinds of problems such as depression and, in extreme cases, even suicide (Rubin, 1985). Social withdrawal may, in some cases, predict aggression. A 14-year-old boy in suburban Philadelphia, who was bullied by a classmate for three years, brought a gun to school, and in front of several classmates, shot and killed the bully. As reported in the newspapers, the boy never expressed his feelings or told anyone about what was happening. This, and many similar cases reported (in which neighbors of a murderer say "He was so quiet, he just stuck to himself"), makes me think that very soon researchers will identify extremely withdrawn behavior as a predictor of violence as well. Although researchers do not yet have direct evidence that ICPS skills prevent violence, only its predictors, I ask that, if this boy had been guided to express his feelings early in life and helped to think of other ways to solve his problems, might this act have been prevented?

To test the linkage between ICPS ability and behavioral adjustment, we experimentally altered ICPS skills (through intervention) and then observed changes in children's behaviors. If we could demonstrate that ICPS skills could mediate behavior, independent of IQ, we would have the beginnings of a new approach to the prevention of behavioral dysfunction in young children.

THE INTERVENTIONS IN PRESCHOOL AND KINDERGARTEN

The first interventions were designed for teachers to use in inner-city preschools (Spivack & Shure, 1974) and kindergartens (Shure & Spivack, 1974a). Teachers taught the prerequisite and problem-solving thinking skills in hypothetical situations during the daily, 20-minute lessons for about 3 months.

The first level of the curriculum consisted of age-appropriate lesson-games that taught key word concepts needed to set the stage for later problem-solving thinking. For example, games with word pairs such as *is/is not* and *same/different* were first played in non-problem–solving situations, "Johnny *is* painting. Who is *not*?" "Who is doing the *same* thing as Peter?" "Who is doing something *different* from Peter?" These words were used in game form so that their association with fun would help children later enjoy thinking about *different* ways to solve a problem and about whether an idea *is* or *is not* a good one. The second level focused on children's own and others' feelings, opening up more possibilities for the third level, alternative-solution and consequential thinking.

With ultimate emphasis on the problem-solving *process*, not content of solutions, teachers learned to help children first think through hypothetical problems and then real ones. Early techniques included holding up a picture of a scene depicting two or more children in a conflict situation (or role-playing with puppets) and then asking, "What happened?" "What's the problem?" "Do (James) and (Shawn) see what happened the *same* way or a *different* way?"

Building on the ICPS word pairs, children were asked to think about how people, including themselves, feel about things. They first had to be able to identify and verbalize words that describe those feelings. To that end, children were asked to talk about what made them feel a particular way and how they thought another child might feel about the *same* thing.

Recognizing that different people can feel different ways about the same thing can help a child who wants something from his friend to think about what would make that friend happy and what would not. Using previously learned "ICPS words" and feeling concepts, children could think about the idea that if one way does *not* make another feel happy, it is possible to try a *different* way.

About 6 weeks into the program, children were exposed to games and dialogues designed to enhance the problem-solving skills to be learned.

Through pictures, puppets, and simple role-play, children began to solve hypothetical problems (e.g., Lakisha wanted to join others in play, but they wouldn't let her in), and were asked the following questions:

- What is happening in this picture? What is the problem?
- How does (e.g., Lakisha) feel about this?
- What can (e.g., Lakisha) do or say to (e.g., get the others to let her play)?

After focusing on identifying the problem, people's feelings, and brainstorming several possible alternative solutions to the problem (regardless of content), the words *might/maybe* and *why/because* were introduced in preparation for the next series of lessons. Children were guided to evaluate their solutions with the added questions

- What *might* happen if (e.g., She screamed "I want to play!")?
- *Why might* that happen? *Because* . . . .
- How *might* she feel if that happens?

After brainstorming several different consequences and considering the feelings of each person involved, children evaluated each offered solution in light of whether it was a good idea or not a good idea and why. They were then ready to offer a solution, its immediate consequence, a new solution, its consequence, and so on. This solution–consequence pairing was designed to help children later think "I'll do this but *not* that *because* of what *might* happen next."

It was during the early 1970s, when the curriculum was first being piloted, that I observed a teacher asking the problem-solving questions similar to those about Lakisha as she showed pictures of hypothetical children. The children answered these questions quickly and competently, and I felt very proud to have designed a program that children so young could respond to so well. I was just about to leave feeling fully satisfied, but just then one child pushed another. The teacher, who moments earlier had asked the group how to solve a problem with hypothetical children, yelled at the perpetrator, "How many times do I have to tell you we don't push children in this classroom!" While this boy was sitting off in a corner in "time-out," I thought to myself, "Something's missing here. Why doesn't this teacher use the same line of questioning in real life that she just used with the pictures?" That was how "ICPS dialoguing" was born.

Punishing, threatening, suggesting, or even explaining to children what they should and should not do are monologues. The adult is doing all the talking for the child. To help children develop their own thinking in real-life contexts, teachers were trained to ask questions similar to those about hypothetical children. For example, the teacher asks a child who has hit another "What's the problem?" "What happened when you hit him?" "How do you think he feels when you hit him?" "How did you feel when . . . (e.g., he hit you back)?" "Can you think of a different way to solve this problem so you both won't feel (mad) and he won't hit you?" Now the adult and child are participating in a two-way conversation, a dialogue. These kinds of questions engage children in the process of identifying the problem, thinking about the consequences of what they do, including their own as well as others' feelings, and what else they can do to solve the problem.

What did the training intervention program, which included both the group games and the real-life ICPS dialoguing, do for the thinking and behavior of the children? With varying amounts of ICPS training over a 2-year period from preschool through kindergarten, we examined immediate and follow-up cognitive and behavior gains (Shure & Spivack, 1979a, 1980, 1982b; Spivack & Shure, 1974).

- ICPS-trained preschool and kindergarten children could generate more and different relevant alternative solutions, both forceful and nonforceful in nature, to real-life interpersonal problems than could control children, as measured by the earlier-described PIPS test. They could also conceive of more relevant consequences of interpersonal acts such as grabbing a toy, as measured by the WHNG. The gains in consequential thinking were greater in the kindergarten-trained than in the preschool-trained groups, perhaps because thinking simultaneously of what to do (now) and what might happen (later) is more difficult for 4-year-olds than for 5-year-olds.
- ICPS gains were not explained by initial IQ or IQ gains as measured by the Peabody (Dunn, 1965), the Slosson (Slosson, 1963), or the Stanford Binet (Terman & Merrill, 1960) tests.
- One exposure to the 3-month training (in preschool or in kindergarten) was sufficient for significant ICPS gains. As measured by the earlier-described HPSB teacher-rating scale, behavioral improvements were shown in decreased impulsivity and inhibition and increased prosocial behaviors such as concern for others, cooperation, sharing, and the degree to which the child was liked by peers. If training was not done in preschool, kindergarten was not too late, although preschool youngsters whose behavior improved as a function of ICPS training may have had a social advantage when they began kindergarten.
- In addition to overall training and control group differences in ICPS and behavior gains, a significant linkage was found within the training group. Youngsters who most improved in the trained ICPS skills, especially alternative-solution skills,

were the same youngsters who also improved in behavior—supporting the theoretical position that ICPS ability significantly mediates overt behaviors. Although gains in consequential thinking were more strongly related with gains in behavior in kindergarten than in preschool, alternative-solution skills remained the most powerful mediator of behavior in both groups.

- During 1- and 2-year follow-up periods, gains were maintained. It is important to note that trained youngsters who had not previously shown behavior problems were less likely than the initially comparable control children to begin showing problems during the follow-up periods, suggesting a preventive as well as a treatment component to ICPS interventions.

In addition to the quantitative data, two children highlight how the ICPS intervention helped. With guidance from his teacher, Benji, age 4, learned how to cope with frustration when he could not get what he wanted. Tanya, age 4, learned how to get what she wanted. Benji had asked his teacher for some Playdough, which was out of reach at a time when the teacher was occupied. The ICPS-trained teacher, who taught both the formal lessons and had learned to apply ICPS dialoguing in real problem contexts, told Benji that she was helping another child with his project. She then asked, "Can you think of something *different* to do while you wait?" Benji thought for a moment, then smiled and said "I'll go paint." He zealously pulled an apron off the hook, put it on, and approached the easel. Would Benji have gone to paint had the teacher given him the same explanation of why she couldn't get him the Playdough at that moment and then suggested that he go paint?

Tanya was painfully shy and always hovered around the doll corner, wanting to join in but not knowing how. Before training, her well-meaning teacher tried to help by modeling a problem-solving strategy. She told the group that "Tanya would like to help pack the suitcase." Even if the group had complied, Tanya was not yet ready to enter the group. But 7 weeks into training, she watched for a while, then proudly announced, "If you need a fireman, I'm a fireman." One of the children noticed a pretend fire, and Tanya began playing. Now able to think of her own solution for entering the group, Tanya felt less timid (a feeling perhaps previously sensed by her peers), was now accepted by those peers, and could join without trepidation. Her pathway to social competence had begun.

EARLY RESEARCH WITH PARENTS

Our early studies examined how (and whether) ICPS skills of low-income African-American mothers (or primary caretakers) would correspond to the ICPS skills and behavior of their 4-year-old children (Shure & Spivack, 1978, 1979b).

Children were tested with the earlier-described PIPS test (measuring alternative solutions), the WHNG (measuring consequential thinking), and the HBSB (measuring teacher-rated behaviors in the classroom). Unlike our research with teachers, mothers were tested pre-post on

- *Child-rearing Style.* Mothers were asked to describe how they handle a series of typical problem situations (e.g., when a child says "no" a lot; when a child says another child hit him or her). Each statement in the mother's report was scored along a continuum from commands and demands, to suggestions without explanation (e.g., "You should ask, not grab"), to explanations and reasons (e.g., "You'll hurt him if you hit him"), including an explanation of feelings (e.g., "He'll feel angry if you hit him"), to a problem-solving style of communication like ICPS dialoguing, (e.g., "How might he feel if you hit him?" "What might happen next?" "How will you feel if that happens?" "Can you think of something different to do so that will not happen?").
- *Problem-Solving Skills.* Mothers were tested for their ability to name alternative solutions and consequences and to conceptualize means-ends plans to achieve a goal in adult-type problems (e.g., keeping a friend from being angry for being very late to a movie) and means-ends thinking about child-related problems (e.g., her two children are squabbling while she's trying to make dinner).

Regarding child-rearing style, we found, as did Hoffman and Saltzstein (1967), that parents who used induction techniques ("If you hit him, you'll lose a friend") had better-adjusted children than those who used more power-assertive techniques, such as demanding, commanding, and spanking. However, in our studies of African-American low-income 4-year-olds, these findings held only for girls.

Why not for boys? We do not know for sure, but as others have found, it appears that boys comply less often (Baumrind, 1971), thereby forcing parents to apply more pressure on them. Or it could be that the boys were mostly from father-absent homes, and Hoffman (1971) has found that older boys in father-absent homes reported that their mothers showed more affection toward their daughters than toward their sons. Whether this affection creates a cognitive bond that affects interpersonal problem-solving is not known.

As was the case with training of teachers, Spivack and I set out to learn whether inner-city parents of preschoolers could become effective

ICPS training agents and how (and if) mothers' enhanced ICPS skills and problem-solving child-rearing styles would affect the ICPS skills and behavior of their children.

The lessons designed for parents included the same concepts as those used in the above-described school curricula, modified for use with a single child at home (Shure & Spivack, 1978). Trained in small groups of 10, mothers met for 3 hours, once a week, for 10 weeks. During each session, I demonstrated the formal lesson-games they would take home to their children that week, and the mothers then practiced them. Each training session also included discussions about the week's successes and failures, practice in the use of the ICPS word pairs that applied to home settings (e.g., things that are the same and different at the dinner table), and practice in the real-life dialoguing techniques. Time was also given to help the mothers think of solutions, consequences, and means-ends planning regarding their own problems, including situations in which their children created a problem for them (such as not listening or doing what they asked). Thus parents learned ICPS skills of their own as they learned to guide their children to think through and solve actual problems that arose during a typical day.

For the child, the goals were the same as in the teacher-training studies. For mothers, the goals were (a) to increase awareness that their children's point of view may differ from their own; (b) to discover that there is more than one way to solve a problem; (c) to discover that thinking about what is happening may, in the long run, be more beneficial than immediate action to stop it; (d) to provide a model of problem-solving thinking by becoming better problem-solvers themselves; and (e) to learn how to engage their children in the process of solving problems by dialoguing with guiding questions instead of demanding, suggesting, or explaining.

For the mother–child pairs, we found that

- Mothers' gains in their ability to solve hypothetical child-related (but not adult-related problems) were positively associated with their children's gains in ICPS skills.
- Mothers who could learn to think of sequenced steps to reach a stated hypothetical goal were also most likely to apply ICPS dialoguing with their child in real life. However, controlling for mothers' skills suggested it was still the child's own ICPS skills, especially alternative-solution skills, that functioned as the most significant direct mediator of behavior observed in the classroom.

The research results over the 2-year period suggest that inner-city youngsters, boys as well as girls, who were trained by their mothers could significantly increase their ICPS skills and reduce behavior problems in school. In light of pretest findings that child-rearing style related to ICPS skills of daughters only, why did boys benefit as much as girls? We do not know for sure, but before training, the highest level of child-rearing style that mothers exhibited was induction, or explaining to their children what not to do and why. When mothers took their communication skills to the next level of ICPS dialoguing, children were less frequently told what to do or given explanations as to why they should do it. If boys were more resistant to modeling ICPS skills of their mothers before training, it is possible that they were less resistant to it when guided to think for themselves.

The impact of the ICPS approach on children's thinking and behavior may be best illustrated by two mothers who observed their sons grabbing a toy from an invited friend. What follows is the dialogue between the first (untrained) mother and her child:

> M: Why did you grab that truck from John!
> C: 'Cause it's my turn.
> M: Give it back, James!
> C: I don't want to. It's mine.
> M: Why don't you play with your cars?
> C: I want my fire truck.
> M: You should either play together or take turns. Grabbing is not nice.
> C: But I want my truck now!
> M: Children must learn to share. John will get mad and he won't be your friend.
> C: But mom, he won't give it to me!
> M: You can't go around grabbing things. Would you like it if he did that to you?
> C: No.
> M: Tell him you're sorry. (Shure & Spivack, 1978, p. 32)

Although this mother did explain consequences to her child, nothing was communicated that would teach her child how to think. Preoccupied with teaching her child to share, she did the thinking for him. When she angrily asked James why he snatched the truck from John, she might have shifted from a mere accusatory, non-information–seeking question to questions that would provide information about the problem from her child's point of view. This mother would probably have told him to give it back no matter how James answered her question. She was thinking about what was important to her, not about what was important to him. Parents often complain that their children do not listen to them; James might have thought that no one was listening to him.

What follows is the dialogue between the ICPS-trained mother and her child:

> M: Ralph, what happened? What's the matter?
> C: He's got my racing car. He won't give it back.
> M: Why do you have to have it back now?
> C: 'Cause he's had a long turn.

In eliciting her child's point of view, this mother learned something she would not have learned had she simply demanded that he share. She learned that, in fact, her son had shared his toy. The nature of the problem now appeared different.

> M: How do you think your friend feels when you grab toys?
> C: Mad, but I don't care. It's mine.
> M: What did your friend do when you grabbed the toy?
> C: He hit me. But I want my toy!
> M: How did that make you feel?
> C: Mad.
> M: You're mad and your friend is mad, and he hit you. Can you think of a different way to get your toy back so you both won't be mad and so he won't hit you?
> C: I could ask him.
> M: And what might happen then?
> C: He'll say no.
> M: He might say no. What else can you think of doing so your friend will give you back your racing car?
> C: I could let him have my match-box cars.
> M: You thought of two different ideas. (Shure & Spivack, 1978, pp. 36–37)

Ralph's mother did not try to solve the problem from her point of view. She did not tell him to share his racing car or not to grab toys. Instead, the problem shifted from Ralph's grabbing to how Ralph could get the toy back. Ralph's mother helped her child think about the nature of the problem, about how the other child feels, and equally important, how he felt when his friend hit him. She helped him think of his own solutions to the problem and to evaluate the consequences of his act. She taught her child *how* to think, not what to think.

As documented by the HPSB teacher-rating scale, children exposed to ICPS training at home improved their behavior in a different setting, school. We believe this happened because children learned how to generalize their new skills to more than one situation. The ICPS and behavior changes in children trained by their mothers were similar to those trained by their teachers. It was encouraging to learn that inner-city mothers, many of whom lacked ICPS skills themselves, could improve their own abilities and those of their children in only 3 months.

Another question asked of our research was whether the measured outcome behaviors really improved because of the child's hypothesized improvement in ICPS skills or whether it was merely a function of added special attention given to them by their mothers. A placebo attention group in preschool, wherein children played teacher-led non-ICPS games (e.g., singing songs with finger puppets), confirmed our notion that attention alone did not account for gains in the ICPS skills or in behaviors, nor for the linkage between gains in one with gains in the other (Shure, Spivack, & Gordon, 1972).

ICPS FOR OLDER CHILDREN

We then asked whether beginning ICPS training at a later age would have a significant impact on ICPS thinking and behavior. With age-appropriate lessons and the addition of means-ends thinking to the intervention, we found that as rated by independent observers (Achenbach & Edelbrock, 1983), low-income African-American youngsters improved positive prosocial behaviors in Grade 5, but that it took longer (training in Grades 5 and 6) to reduce negative behaviors. However, placebo control children showed more negative behaviors in Grade 6 than in Grade 5, suggesting again the preventive impact of ICPS programs (Shure, 1984; Shure & Healey, 1993). It is important to note that standardized achievement test scores and reading levels improved, especially in Grade 6. Although there was no direct teaching of academic skills, and improving them was not a stated goal, it may have been that releasing emotional tension helped the children concentrate better on the task-oriented demands of the classroom and subsequently to do better in school. These results are consistent with other research that demonstrates a relationship between maladaptive behaviors and school achievement (e.g., Hinshaw, 1992).

FIVE-YEAR LONGITUDINAL STUDY

In our most recent research project we returned to the younger children. The primary aim was to address the issues of the long-term impact of the training for low-income African-American youngsters and the relative effectiveness of combining the training of children by the teacher (in kindergarten) and the parent (in Grade 1).

The Training Programs

All school interventions, originally called "Interpersonal Cognitive Problem-Solving", were renamed to a more palatable "I Can Problem Solve", and significantly revised based on comments and help from teachers (Shure, 1992a, 1992b, 1992c). The intervention used for parents, originally called "Problem-Solving Techniques in Child-Rearing" (Shure & Spivack, 1978), was also revised and is now found in *Raising a Thinking Child* (Shure, 1996), and most recently, in *Raising a Thinking Child Workbook* (Shure, 2000). Essentially, the same word pairs, feeling concepts, and problem-solving skills were taught at school and at home, applying them to situations unique to the setting at hand.

During the implementation of this longitudinal project I realized that I had to differentiate more clearly the ways adults communicate with children. A number of teachers and parents said things like, "I already dialogue with children. I say things like, 'You'll make him mad if you hit him.' See, I talk about feelings." It was then that I knew I had to more clearly distinguish the content of telling the child how someone will feel from the process of asking the child to tell us.

I asked teachers and parents how many times they thought that children had heard the explanations and reasons for why they should and should not do something. I asked them whether they thought they were telling children something they already knew. I followed that with, "Do the children tune out on the 1,001st time they have heard what you are saying? Do you then get angry because a child is not listening?" Because the answer to all or most of these questions was yes, I methodically divided the way we talk with children into four levels. Instead of focusing primarily on the goal, which is how to dialogue, as we did in our previous research, these parents and teachers now had examples of all four levels right in front of them. They could now say, "I do this, but I don't do that." The levels that I gave them were

> *Level 1: Demands, Commands, Belittles, Punishes*
> Examples: How many times have I told you . . . !
> Give it back!
> Do you want a spanking! (or actually spank)
>
> *Level 2: Offers Suggestions Without Explanation*
> Examples: Why don't you ask him for it?
> Children must learn to share.
>
> *Level 3: Offers Explanations and Reasons, Including Feelings*
> Examples: If you hit you might hurt him.
> If you grab toys, you'll lose your friends.
> He (I) will feel angry if you do that.
>
> *Level 4: Problem-Solving Dialoguing*
> Examples: What's the problem? What's the matter?
> How do you think I (he or she) feel(s) when . . . ?
> How did you (would you) feel about that?
> What happened when … (might happen) if . . .?
> Can you think of a different way to solve this problem?

I explained that the goal was now to engage the child in the process of solving the problem, a process that cannot be done unless the child is listening, a process that makes the child more likely to feel empowered and proud of his or her own ability to think.

Research Findings

Over the 5-year period, we found that

- As in earlier research, immediate problem-solving and behavior gains were found for all three groups of ICPS-trained youngsters. These gains lasted through Grade 2.
- Gains of trained youngsters were lost in Grade 3, suggesting a need for a booster.
- At the end of Grade 4, 3 years after completion of the final (Grade 1) training, initial behavior gains re-emerged for youngsters trained by their teachers in both kindergarten and Grade 1.
- As measured by the child-rearing style scores, children whose parents moved toward ICPS dialoguing for real problems showed more behavioral improvement than those whose parents did not. These behavior gains were observed immediately after Grade 1 and were maintained at the end of Grade 4.
- Standardized achievement test scores also improved among ICPS-trained children in kindergarten and Grade 1, especially social studies, reading, and math, but these gains diminished after the training had ended.

Some insurmountable methodological difficulties emerged during the 5 years of this study (e.g., staff changes, many parents not continuing the training once their training was completed, and attrition), and we would have liked longer-lasting effects in the kindergarten-only trained group. It was, however, encouraging to find that after 3 years, the behavior gains of the 2-year teacher-trained and some parent-trained youngsters could be linked to exposure to ICPS (Shure, 1993).

FINAL THOUGHTS

Although our research has focused exclusively on low-income urban African-American youngsters, ICPS training of both parents and teachers has now been evaluated with very positive behavior changes in White youngsters from middle- and upper-middle-income homes (Baumgardner, 1996), including children with attention deficit hyperactivity disorder (Aberson, 1987, 1996).

I began thinking again about Gary, who said that he felt bad when he hurt his brother. If parents would talk to their children in the problem-solving way, perhaps they would grow up to be thinking, feeling human beings who would not want to hurt others. Maybe then Robert could also come to care what happens to himself—and to others.

REFERENCES

Aberson, B. (1987). I Can Problem Solve (ICPS): *A cognitive training program for kindergarten children* (Report to the Bureau of Education). Dade County, FL: Dade County Public Schools.

Aberson, B. (1996). An intervention for improving functioning and social/emotional adjustment of ADHD children. Three single case design studies. Unpublished doctoral dissertation, Miami Institute of Psychology.

Achenbach, T. M., & Edelbrock, C. S. (1983). *Manual for Child Behavior Checklist and Revised Child Behavior Profile.* Burlington: University of Vermont.

Baumgardner, S. Personal communication, May, 1996.

Baumrind, D. (1971). Current patterns of parental authority. *Developmental Psychology Monograph* (Whole No. 4).

Dunn, L. M. (1965). *Expanded manual: Peabody Picture Vocabulary Test* (PPVT). Minneapolis, MN: American Guidance Services.

Elias, M. J., & Clabby, J. F. (1992). Building social problem solving skills: Guidelines from a school-based program. San Francisco, CA: Jossey-Bass.

Eron, L. D., & Huesmann, L. R. (1984). The relation of prosocial behavior to the development of aggression and psychopathology. *Aggressive Behavior, 10,* 201–211.

Feshbach, N. D., & Feshbach, S. (1969). The relationship between empathy and aggression in two age groups. *Developmental Psychology, 1,* 102–107.

Hinshaw, S. (1992). Externalizing behavior problems and academic underachievement in childhood and adolescence: Causal relationships and underlying mechanisms. *Psychological Bulletin, 111,* 127–155.

Hoffman, M. L. (1971). Father absence and conscience development. *Developmental Psychology, 4,* 400–406.

Hoffman, M. L., & Saltzstein, H. D. (1967). Parent discipline and child's moral development. *Journal of Personality and Social Psychology, 5,* 45–57.

Parker, J. G., & Asher, S. R. (1987). Peer relations and later personal adjustment: Are low-accepted children "at risk?" *Psychological Bulletin, 102,* 357–389.

Rubin, K. H. (1985). Socially withdrawn children: An "at-risk" population? In B. H. Schneider, K. H. Rubin, & J. E. Ledingham (Eds.), *Peer relations and social skills in childhood: Issues in assessment and training* (Vol. 2, pp. 125–139). New York: Springer-Verlag.

Shure, M. B. (1984). *Interpersonal problem solving and mental health of 10- to 12-year olds* (Final Report MH 35989). Washington, DC: National Institute of Mental Health.

Shure, M. B. (1990). *The What Happens Next Game (WHNG): Manual* (2nd ed.). Philadelphia: Hahnemann University.

Shure, M. B. (1992a). I Can Problem Solve (ICPS): An interpersonal cognitive problem solving program (Preschool). Champaign, IL: Research Press.

Shure, M. B. (1992b). *I Can Problem Solve (ICPS): An interpersonal cognitive problem solving program* (Kindergarten/Primary Grades). Champaign, IL: Research Press.

Shure, M. B. (1992c). *I Can Problem Solve (ICPS): An interpersonal cognitive problem solving program* (Intermediate Elementary Grades). Champaign, IL: Research Press.

Shure, M. B. (1992d). *Preschool interpersonal problem solving (PIPS) test: Manual* (2nd ed.). Philadelphia: Hahnemann University.

Shure, M. B. (1993). *Interpersonal problem solving and prevention. Research and training final report* (MH-40181). Washington, DC: National Institute of Mental Health.

Shure, M. B. (1996). *Raising a thinking child: Help your young child to resolve everyday conflicts and get along with others.* New York: Pocketbooks.

Shure, M. B. (2000). *Raising a thinking child workbook.* Champaign, IL: Research Press.

Shure, M. B., & Healey, K. N. (1993, August). *Interpersonal problem solving and prevention in urban school children.* Paper presented at the annual meeting of the American Psychological Association, Toronto.

Shure, M. B., & Selman, R. L. (1977, April). *Issues in social cognition.* Modified conversation hour at the meetings of the Society for Research in Child Development, New Orleans.

Shure, M. B., & Spivack, G. (1971). *Hahnemann Preschool Behavior (HPSB) rating scale.* Philadelphia: Hahnemann University.

Shure, M. B., & Spivack, G. (1972). Means-ends thinking, adjustment and social class among elementary school-aged children. *Journal of Consulting and Clinical Psychology, 38,* 348–353.

Shure, M. B., & Spivack. G. (1974a). Interpersonal cognitive problem solving (ICPS): A mental health program for kindergarten and first grade children (Training Script). Philadelphia: Hahnemann University.

Shure, M. B., & Spivack, G. (1974b). *Preschool Interpersonal Problem Solving (PIPS) test: Manual.* Philadelphia: Hahnemann University.

Shure, M. B., & Spivack, G. (1974c). *The What Happens Next Game (WHNG): Manual.* Philadelphia: Hahnemann University.

Shure, M. B., & Spivack, G. (1978). *Problem solving techniques in child-rearing.* San Francisco, CA: Jossey-Bass.

Shure, M. B., & Spivack, G. (1979a). Interpersonal cognitive problem solving and primary prevention: Programming for preschool and kindergarten children. *Journal of Clinical Child Psychology, 8,* 89–94.

Shure, M. B., & Spivack, G. (1979b). Interpersonal problem solving thinking and adjustment in the mother-child dyad. In M. W. Kent & J. E. Rolf (Eds.), *The primary prevention of psychopathology: Social competence in children* (Vol. 3, pp. 201–219). Hanover, NH: University Press of New England.

Shure, M. B., & Spivack, G. (1980). Interpersonal problem solving as a mediator of behavioral adjustment in preschool and kindergarten children. *Journal of Applied Developmental Psychology, 1,* 29–44.

Shure, M. B., & Spivack, G. (1982b). Interpersonal problem solving in young children: A cognitive approach to prevention. *American Journal of Community Psychology, 10,* 341–356.

Shure, M. B., Spivack, G., & Gordon, R. (1972). Problem solving thinking: A preventive mental health program for preschool children. *Reading World, 11,* 259–273.

Shure, M. B., Spivack, G., & Jaeger, M. A. (1971). Problem solving thinking and adjustment among disadvantaged preschool children. *Child Development, 42,* 1791–1803.

Slosson, R. L. (1963). *Slosson Intelligence Test (SIT) for children and adults.* East Aurora, NY: Slosson Educational Publications.

Spivack, G., & Levine, M. (1963). *Self-regulation in acting-out and normal adolescents* (Report M-4351). Washington, DC: National Institute of Health.

Spivack, G., Platt, J. J., & Shure, M. B. (1976). *The problem solving approach to adjustment.* San Francisco, CA: Jossey-Bass.

Spivack, G., & Shure, M. B. (1974). *Social adjustment of young children.* San Francisco, CA: Jossey-Bass.

Terman, L. M., & Merrill, M. A. (1960). *Stanford-Binet Intelligence Scale.* Boston, MA: Houghton Mifflin Co.

Urberg, K. A., & Docherty, E. M. (1976). Development of role-taking skills in young children. *Developmental Psychology, 12,* 198–203.

14

PATHWAYS TO CONSTRUCTIVE LIVES: THE IMPORTANCE OF EARLY SCHOOL SUCCESS

DEBORAH J.STIPEK

Academic achievement and educational attainment are two of the most important factors affecting an individual's life opportunities and productivity. High school completion, highly associated with academic achievement, is particularly important. Dropping out of high school seriously limits subsequent opportunities and is associated with socially destructive and self-destructive behaviors, including substance abuse, unemployment, low income, welfare dependency, delinquency, and crime (Haveman & Wolfe, 1984; Hawkins & Lishner, 1987; Hawkins, Lishner, Catalano, & Howard, 1986; Hinshaw, 1992; Loeber & Stouthamer-Loeber, 1987; Rutter & Giller, 1983; Steinberg, Blinde, & Chan, 1984).

Children's achievement trajectories are influenced by experiences in their homes, at school, and in other contexts throughout their school careers. But research discussed in this chapter suggests that preschool and the early elementary grades may be especially critical. Children's academic skills at the beginning of school are highly predictive of long-term academic success and the amount of education acquired. There is also some evidence suggesting that family socioeconomic status (SES) is particularly important in early childhood, in part because it affects academic skills at school entry.

The proposed model is based on speculations about the mechanism by which early achievement levels affect educational achievement and attainment much later (see Figure 14.1). I propose that children's initial academic performance puts into motion a set of experiences in school which, in turn, affect their behavior and their later performance. Specifically, initial academic skills are presumed to affect children's conduct and motivation (especially their self-perceptions). They also affect the learning opportunities that children have, because these are influenced by their teachers' expectations (regarding their academic competencies and promise), attendant behavior toward them, and decisions such as class placement (e.g., prekindergarten or transition classroom versus regular classroom), retention, and ability group assignment.

The experiences described above, presumed to result from children's initial skills, should affect their rate of learning. Thus, children who begin with relatively good skills should learn more than children who begin with relatively poor skills. The result would be increasing disparity in skill levels among children. Coleman et al. (1996) referred to this amplification as "fan-spread." A study by Gersten, Becker, Heiry, and White (1984) provides

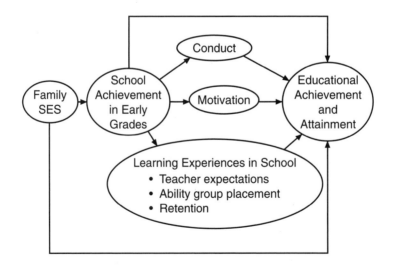

Figure 14.1. Proposed model: Effects of early achievement on later achievement and educational attainment

some supportive evidence. Children who entered school with a relatively low IQ (which is strongly associated with academic performance) made relatively more modest gains on a variety of achievement tests over the first three grades in school than did children who entered school with a high IQ.

Bloom (1976) made a similar proposal related to opportunities to learn. He claimed that prior skills limit a child's ability to learn new skills and that children with relatively high skills are able to take better advantage of the instructional program than are children with poorer skills. Bloom's proposal, however, did not acknowledge the possibility that teachers might unintentionally limit opportunities for relatively low-skilled children to learn.

In this chapter I first summarize evidence on the importance of intellectual competencies and experiences in early childhood for long-term educational outcomes. Second, I review a few studies suggesting that SES in early childhood has long-term effects on achievement, which may be mediated by its short-term effects on school performance. Third, I discuss potential effects of children's academic skills when they enter school on their behavior, motivation, and learning opportunities. The chapter is not intended as a comprehensive summary of the literature. The goal is to stimulate research that examines directly the question of why children who enter school with relatively low skills tend to continue to do relatively poorly throughout their school years and to be less likely to graduate from high school. As the second section on SES shows, the issues I address in this chapter are particularly important to children in low-income families, who typically begin school at an academic disadvantage and never catch up.

The model offered here is by no means the only explanation. On the contrary, it is compatible with others, including models that focus on contemporaneous effects of variables, such as SES, which are fairly stable and continue to affect children's achievement levels throughout their school years.

EARLY ACADEMIC SKILLS AND LATER SCHOOL ACHIEVEMENT AND ATTAINMENT

Predicting Achievement

According to Bloom (1964):

> The first period of elementary school (grades 1 to 3) is probably the most crucial for the development of general learning patterns . . . all subsequent learning in the schools is affected and in large part determined by what the child has learned . . . by the end of grade 3. (p. 110)

Many longitudinal studies have examined how well cognitive assessments given before or in the first few years of school predict later academic performance.

Findings of moderate to high correlations suggest substantial stability, although early achievement certainly does not "determine" later school achievement.

One study, for example, found that the Hess School Readiness Scale, given either in pre-kindergarten or kindergarten, correctly identified at least 70% of children who had academic difficulties 5 years later (evidenced in grade retention and teacher reports of a lag of at least 1 year on a standardized achievement test; Hess & Hahn, 1974; see also Tramontana, Hooper, & Selzer, 1988). Stevenson and Newman (1986) found correlations ranging from .60 to .68 between scores on four assessments of cognitive competencies (naming letters, paired associates, reversals, and category naming) that were given before children entered kindergarten and children's 10th-grade reading achievement. Luster and McAdoo (1996) reported a correlation of .71 between achievement test scores in 1st grade and achievement in 8th grade for the sample of children in the well-known High Scope study. Baydar, Brooks-Gunn, and Furstenberg (1993) reported that, in their analyses of African-American children in two longitudinal samples, verbal skills assessed for children ages 4–6 were highly predictive of literacy skills in early adulthood (ages 18–21). Chen, Lee, and Stevenson (1996) reported that cognitive ability assessments and achievement test scores from 1st grade were significantly correlated with achievement test scores in 11th grade (mean r of .33 and .43, respectively). And finally, Cunningham and Stanovich (1997) reported that three indices of reading achievement in 1st grade correlated very highly with reading ability and content knowledge in the 11th grade, even with measures of IQ held constant.

The correlations between academic skills in the early grades and academic skills much later become stronger over the first few grades of school. They continue to increase so that the closer the grade is to the predicted grade, the higher the correlation, but the increases tend to level off after 3rd or 4th grade. Bloom (1976, p. 40), for example, in a chart of correlations for achievement between adjacent grades, showed relatively steep increase until 4th grade; after then, correlations remained relatively level through the 11th grade. There is a relatively steep increase between Grades 2 and 4 in how well performance in the early grades predicted 11th-grade performance. He described other data that were collected by Bracht and Hopkins (1972), in which the correlation between 3rd- and 11th-grade composite achievement scores was .82 and increased only to .90 between 7th and 11th grade (Bloom, 1976). In his own data Bloom found a correlation of .60 between achievement at Grade 2 and achievement in Grade 12 and a correlation of .78 between achievement at the 6th and 12th grades. More supportive evidence comes from Newman (1984). He reported that the correlation between math achievement from 2nd to 5th grade (.55) was about the same as the correlation between 2nd and 10th grade (.58) and only a little less than the correlation between 5th and 10th grade (.70).

Taken together, these studies support the importance of children's academic performance in the early grades of elementary school. The predictive power of early performance increases a fair amount over the first few grades but then levels off, suggesting greater malleability during the early years.

Predicting High School Completion

Studies have shown likewise that academic achievement as early as 1st grade predicts high school completion, presumably in large part because low academic performance in the early grades predicts low academic performance in the later grades, which in turn is associated with dropping out. The effect of early performance on education attainment may also be mediated by motivational variables. Children who perform poorly early in their school careers may develop negative attitudes toward school and low expectations for success, for example, which in turn result in their choosing to leave school when the law allows.

In a study by Garnier, Stein, and Jacobs (1997), the correlation between academic performance in 1st grade and dropping out of high school (–.24) was almost as high as the correlation between academic performance in 6th grade and dropping out (–.30). Preschool general ability (concept recognition, associative vocabulary, and social responsiveness) also predicted high school completion in a study by Brooks-Gunn, Guo, and Furstenberg (1993). Using a 55 percentile score on the 3rd-grade Iowa Basic Skills Tests as the cutoff, Barrington and Hendricks (1989) predicted dropping out of high school with 70% accuracy. Following participants even longer, Luster and McAdoo (1996) found that 1st-grade achievement, as well as IQ assessed before school, were significantly associated with years of education at age 27. Ensminger and Slusarcick (1992) found that inner-city, primarily African-American children in their sample, who received As and Bs in arithmetic at the end of 1st grade had 1.46 times the odds of graduating as had those who received Cs or Ds.

In summary, children's relative academic skills when they enter school are highly predictive of educational achievement and attainment much later. The high correlations must not, however, be misinterpreted to mean that children who perform relatively poorly when they enter school are doomed to school failure and dropping out. The highest correlations found in research leave plenty of unexplained variance, allowing for many children to change, even dramatically, in their academic status. There is also substantial evidence from educational reforms and interventions that academic achievement can be substantially raised (see Henderson & Berla, 1994, for a review). But the evidence reviewed above suggests that children who achieve at a relatively high level in the first few grades of school are much more likely to fare well later on than children who achieve at a relatively low level in the early school grades.

The stability of academic achievement is of particular concern to low-income children, who, as I demonstrate in the next section, on average enter school with very poor skills.

SES AND SCHOOL ACHIEVEMENT AND ATTAINMENT

SES Differences in Academic Skills at School Entry

Studies have found repeatedly that children from families of low SES, even those who have had the benefits of early intervention, begin school, on average, with significantly poorer academic skills than do more economically advantaged children (Brooks-Gunn, Duncan, & Britto, 1999; Case, Griffin & Kelly, 1999; Entwisle & Alexander, 1990; Entwisle, Alexander, Cadigan, & Pallas, 1987; Willms, 1999). SES is not assumed to have direct effects on student achievement. Rather many studies have shown that SES effects are mediated by particular circumstances and experiences that are associated with SES, such as the home intellectual environment; number of siblings; family constellation; and parents' teaching behaviors, psychological health, stress, expectations and aspirations for their child, and involvement in school.

A study I completed recently with my colleague, Rosaleen Ryan, is one of the more comprehensive documentations of SES differences in young children's preparation for schooling (Stipek & Ryan, 1997). The study included 262 children who were assessed at the beginning and end of their last year of preschool or kindergarten. The sample was ethnically diverse, about half Latino and about a quarter each African American and White. Many of the low-income children had been or were enrolled in preschool programs specifically designed to enhance their preparation for elementary school.

Children were assessed with a traditional test of basic literacy and mathematics skills (an adapted version of the Woodcock–Johnson Achievement Tests (Woodcock & Johnson, 1989), supplemented with items from the Peabody Individual Achievement Tests (Dunn & Markwardt, 1970) and a test designed to assess cognitive problem-solving, reasoning, and creativity (the short form of the McCarthy Test [McCarthy, 1972]). The children also were assessed on a variety of motivation measures, which I discuss in a later section of this chapter.

The middle-class children scored substantially higher than did their disadvantaged peers on all eight cognitive measures. The F values for the SES main effect ranged from 13.99 to 91.18, with a mean of 43.16 (all p values < .001). For four of the eight cognitive tasks (word knowledge, number memory, conceptual grouping, and letters/reading achievement), the middle-class preschool children scored higher, on average, than did the disadvantaged kindergarten children, indicating that the low-income children began school more than a year behind in cognitive skills. Other studies also have found that low-SES children begin school as much as a year and a half behind their high-SES peers in terms of age equivalents (see Case et al., 1999).

Studies suggest that income may be the more important SES variable. In my study with Ryan (Stipek & Ryan, 1997), analyses were conducted to identify the family variables measured that were the most strongly associated with children's cognitive skills at school entry. Stepwise regressions were run separately for the letters/reading achievement test, the numbers/math achievement test, and the McCarthy total score. Three of the predictors were fathers' education, mothers' education, and family income. As in other studies, these variables were highly correlated to each other. The correlation coefficient between mothers' and fathers' education was .78 ($p < .0001$); it was .58 ($p < .0001$) between family income and both mothers' and fathers' education. Of these three SES variables, income was by far the strongest and most consistent predictor of cognitive competencies for the children ages 4–6. Our finding is consistent with White's (1982) meta-analysis of many studies examining associations between SES and school achievement, in which income emerged as a stronger predictor of school achievement than did the other indices of SES (see also, Duncan, Yeung, Brooks-Gunn, & Smith, 1998).

Importance of Early Childhood

There is some evidence suggesting also that SES-related variables affect children more in early childhood than later in their lives. For example, Duncan et al. (1998) assessed the relative importance of income in different stages of childhood using data from the Panel Study of Income Dynamics (PSID).[1] Analyses were conducted to examine income effects on educational attainment for children when they were in three age spans: 0–5, 6–10, and 11–15 years. The earliest age period (0–5), and the most distant from decisions about school leaving, was by far the strongest predictor of educational attainment. Early childhood income effects were particularly strong in the lower income ranges. A comparison of family income for children under age 6 revealed that for each additional $10,000 in family income, children stayed in school one full year longer (see also Axinn, Duncan, & Thornton, 1997). Income during the preschool years also was shown to have substantially greater effects on cognitive skills than income in later years in analyses of data from the National Longitudinal Survey of Youth–Child Supplement and the Infant Health and Development Program (Brooks-Gunn et al., 1999).

---

[1]A longitudinal survey of U.S. households that began in 1968 and includes a representative sample of about 5,000 families.

Also suggesting the greater importance of income in early childhood are findings that contemporaneous associations between income and school achievement appear to decrease over time to very modest levels in adolescence (Peters & Mullis, 1997); see Brooks-Gunn & Duncan, 1997. White (1982), for example, reported from analyses using the Coleman et al. (1966) data that the correlations between SES and achievement diminished across the 1st, 6th, 9th, and 12th grades (r = .21, .21, .17, .15 respectively).

Analyses of other SES-related variables also suggest greater impact during early childhood. In the analyses by Baydar et al. (1993), family variables (living arrangements, physical and emotional quality of the home environment, maternal commitment to education, and economic well-being) measured in early childhood predicted 28% of the variance in young adult literacy scores, compared with 14% and 15%, respectively, of the variance accounted for by these variables measured in middle childhood and adolescence.

The number of siblings may also be more important in early childhood than later on. Baydar et al. (1993) found in a sample of African Americans that the number of siblings a child had during early childhood (ages 0–4) predicted literacy scores at ages 19–21 (controlling for the quality of the home environment, maternal education, and economic well-being), but the number of siblings during middle childhood (ages 5–10) and adolescence (ages 11–15) did not predict later literacy skills. Krein and Beller (1988) found in their analyses of the National Longitudinal Study (NLS) data that educational attainment was lower for individuals who lived in single-parent homes during the preschool years but not for individuals who lived in single-parent homes during elementary school or high school, even with family income controlled. Education was reduced by about a year and a half for men and by a year for African-American women who spent the entire preschool period in a single-parent family. In the Sameroff, Seifer, Baldwin, & Baldwin (1993) study, a statistical model in which family stress during children's first three years directly predicted dropping out of high school provided a better fit with the data than an indirect model in which the effects of family stress were assumed to be mediated through children's behaviors and attitudes in adolescence.

Studies also have suggested the particular importance of the home intellectual environment in early childhood. Bradley, Caldwell, and Rock (1988), for example, found that some subscales of the Home Observation of Measurement of the Environment (HOME) (availability of toys and parental involvement with the child) administered when children were 2 years of age predicted academic achievement scores at age 10, controlling for HOME scores at 6 months and 10 years. Different subscales (emotional climate, active involvement in enriching activities, and participation) administered at age 10 were associated with children's academic achievement, with HOME scores from 6 months and 2 years controlled. These results suggest that different aspects of the home environment may be important at different stages of children's lives.

Similarly, Chen et al. (1996) found that the home intellectual environment in 1st grade (e.g., parents teaching a child words, phrases, and sentences; parents reading newspapers or taking courses) was associated with children's mathematics ($r = .41$, $p < .001$) and reading ($r = .15$, $p < .05$) achievement in 11th grade. The path analysis suggested that the effect of family SES at 1st grade on children's academic performance in 11th grade was mediated by these parental behaviors in early childhood.

In summary, extant research on the effects of SES-related variables on later academic achievement clearly suggests the importance of children's early years. Even long-term SES effects, however, may be explained at least in part by early academic performance.

Early Academic Skills and School Achievement as a Mediator

A few studies suggest that the effects of SES in the early years on later achievement are mediated by the effect of SES on early school achievement. For example, Hess, Holloway, Dickson, and Price (1984) found that behaviors of mothers interacting with their children on a task (e.g., affective rating, directiveness in teaching, use of authority-based appeals, criticism of child errors), which are associated with SES, predicted children's academic achievement in 6th grade. But the predictive power of these SES-related variables was reduced substantially when children's preschool academic skills were forced first into the equation.

In the Garnier et al. (1997) study, the correlation between family SES, assessed at age 6, and academic achievement and decisions in later grades, became stronger as children advanced through school ($r = .13$, $p < .05$ in first grade; $r = .18$, $p < .01$ in sixth grade; $r = .25$, $p < .001$ with decisions to drop out of high school). Results of latent variable structural equation models suggested that the effect of family SES in 1st grade on decisions to drop out or stay in school was not direct. The model that best fit the data suggested that family SES affected cognitive skills in 1st grade, which predicted school performance in 6th grade, which predicted school completion decisions in high school. Longitudinal analyses by Baydar et al. (1993) also support the notion that SES effects on school attainment are mediated by SES effects on early academic skills. They found that the significant effects of income on school completion disappeared when early childhood cognitive developmental level was controlled.

In summary, the data reviewed are consistent with the proposed model, in which family SES affects academic achievement in the early grades of elementary school, which in turn predicts academic achievement and educational attainment much later. This conclusion does not imply that contemporaneous SES-related variables do not affect school performance in the later grades. To the contrary, there is a vast literature demonstrating contemporaneous effects. The findings reviewed here do, however, indicate that family variables in early childhood have particularly profound effects and that some of their long-term effects may be explained by their effects on initial academic performance.

SES AND SCHOOL QUALITY

Children who enter school with relatively poor cognitive skills have another strike against them. Low-achieving children are disproportionately represented in low-income families, and children in low-income families are more likely to attend schools that have relatively poor resources. On average, compared with schools that serve predominantly middle- and high-income students, schools that serve low-income children have lower per-pupil expenditures (National Center for Education Statistics [NCES], 1998a). Principals in low-income schools claim to have more difficulty hiring teachers (NCES, 1998c), and the teachers they hire are less likely to be certified in the subject matter that they teach (NCES, 1998b). Teachers in schools with a relatively high concentration of poverty claim to spend more time maintaining classroom order and discipline, which means less time for instruction (NCES, 1998c), and report that they lack necessary teaching materials (NCES, 1998b).

In a recent study my colleagues and I observed directly the quality of instruction in 128 classrooms in 79 schools, as a function of the proportion of low-income and non-White children in the school. All of the schools served predominantly low-income children; the mean proportion of children eligible for subsidized lunch was 58%. Even within this restricted range, in kindergarten and 1st grade, the higher the proportion of low-income children in the school, the poorer the quality of math instruction, the more negative the classroom climate, and the less intense the focus on children's learning (Stipek & Byler, 2000).

These between-school differences presumably contribute to the stability of children's academic achievement levels in studies that include a diverse set of schools. Low school quality makes it all the more difficult for relatively low-skilled young children to improve their relative achievement status.

CONSEQUENCES OF INITIAL POOR PERFORMANCE IN SCHOOL

I next examine possible consequences of low academic performance in the early grades that might undermine future learning and thus make it difficult for children to increase their relative skill levels. In the first section I propose that low academic skills exacerbate conduct problems, which in turn limit opportunities to learn. In the second section I suggest that children who perform poorly develop negative views of their competencies and low expectations for success, which undermine effort and persistence and thus learning. In the final section I propose that initial performance affects teachers' perceptions, behaviors, and decisions in ways that can limit children's opportunities to learn.

Conduct

Behavior and attention are strongly associated with early academic competencies, even before children enter kindergarten (Arnold, 1997; Hinshaw, 1992; McGee et al., 1985; Morrison, Mantzicopoulos, & Carte, 1989; Richman, Stevenson, & Graham., 1982; Stevenson, Richman, & Graham, 1985). Like low academic skills, conduct problems, especially hyperactivity (i.e., restlessness, poor concentration), are also more prevalent among low- than among middle- or high-income children (Duncan, Brooks-Gunn, & Klebanov, 1994; Korenman, Miller, & Sjaastad, 1995; McLoed & Shanahan, 1993; Offord, Alder, & Boyle, 1986).

The evidence suggests, moreover, that poor academic performance in school promotes conduct problems, especially hyperactive behavior (Farrington, 1979; Hinshaw, 1992; Jorm, Share, Matthews, & Maclean, 1986; Maughan, Gray, & Rutter, 1985; McGee, Williams, Share, Anderson, & Silva, 1986; Schonfeld, Shaffer, O'Connor, & Portnoy, 1988). For example, Hinshaw (1992) found that externalizing behavior problems increased for children who experienced early reading failure.

Conduct problems, in turn, limit children's opportunities to learn. Time spent engaged in or being punished for misbehavior is time lost from attending to instruction and academic tasks. Children who are difficult to manage are also likely to develop negative, conflictual relationships with teachers and increasingly negative attitudes toward school, which could undermine their investment in doing well. The continued or even declining poor academic performance would, in turn, generate more conduct problems. Thus, the child is caught in an increasingly stable spiral that becomes more and more difficult to escape.

This reciprocal relationship between academic skills and conduct is illustrated in a study by Arnold (1997). First, he found that the correlation between academic skills and disruptive behavior increased with age ($r = .37$, .54, .64, and .84 for children from 36–43, 44–54, 55–64, and 65–74 months, respectively). Second, he found in path analyses of data from his study of children ages 3–6 years that externalizing behaviors predicted academic skills, and academic skills predicted externalizing behaviors. In an attempt to understand the mechanisms of the associations between conduct and academic problems, he assessed children's attention and teachers' instructional input. He found that children who had relatively low academic skills paid relatively less attention to academic tasks (measured by direct observations). The poor attention alone should undermine learning. But teachers appeared to contribute to the problem by providing fewer learning opportunities for children with conduct problems. They were less likely to question, call on, or provide information to students with conduct problems than they were with students without problems.

There are other ways in which poor performance might engender behavioral problems. For example, peers typically have less regard for and may reject low-achievers, making it harder for children who perform poorly to form the kind of positive peer relationships that help children develop appropriate social interaction skills (Ladd, Kochenderfer, & Coleman, 1997). Negative relations may also develop with teachers, and these may foster negative feelings about school and a decreased desire to be actively involved in the learning enterprise. This proposal is consistent with evidence that teachers claim to have more intimate relationships with children who perform well academically (Birch & Ladd, 1997).

In summary, extant research suggests that poor academic skills in preschool and the early elementary grades may create or at least exacerbate behavioral problems, which in turn may undermine children's further learning. Among others, this process may explain why children with poor initial skills have difficulty breaking out of their relatively low status as learners.

Motivation

A parallel argument can be made for motivation. Children's early performance in school may affect their perceptions of their academic competence and other motivational variables, which in turn affect their effort and future performance. Many motivation-related variables are assumed to influence children's behavior and learning in academic settings. Most researchers have emphasized two sets of variables: (a) beliefs (e.g., about their own competence, the likelihood of success, and the causes of academic outcomes) and (b) values (e.g., intrinsic interest in academic skills, perceptions of the importance of doing well in school and of the utility of academic skills outside of school).

There is a vast amount of evidence suggesting that performance affects motivation and some evidence demonstrating that motivation affects performance (Helmke & van Aken, 1995; see Stipek,1998, for a review). Alexander and Entwisle (1988), for example, found significant, albeit modest, effects of first and second graders' expectations on their academic performance.

Past research indicates that children's motivation-related beliefs at the beginning of school are usually very positive, but the self-perceptions of children who perform poorly in school decline over the first few elementary grades (see Stipek, 1984; Stipek & Mac Iver, 1989, for reviews). My study with Ryan (Stipek & Ryan, 1997) is typical of studies finding an optimistic bias of children at school entry. Children from economically disadvantaged and middle-income families were very high on the motivation variables that we assessed. For both the perceptions of competencies and the attitude-toward-school measures, average scores were about 4.5 on a 1–5-point scale. Average expectancy scores were well above the midpoint of the scales. Anxiety ratings were close to 1, on average, and children's ratings of how much they worried averaged about 2 on the 5-point scale. Analyses of 13 motivation variables resulted in only one significant SES difference. Entwisle and Hayduk (1982) also reported particularly unrealistic expectations for academic performance among early elementary-age low-income children, although middle-income children also overestimated their performance (see also Stipek et al., 1998; Stipek & Greene, in press). Taken together, these results suggest that most young children, whatever their family economic circumstances, enter school with considerable enthusiasm, self-confidence, and willingness to take on learning challenges.

Average scores on motivation measures begin to decline for children who perform poorly soon after they enter school (Stipek, 1984; Stipek & Mac Iver, 1989; Stipek & Greene, in press, for reviews). Some studies find significant associations between academic achievement and perceived competence as early as kindergarten and 1st grade. For example, in a study of nearly 300 low-income children that I am currently conducting, kindergarten and 1st-grade children's ratings of both their literacy and their math competence were significantly associated with teachers' ratings of their literacy and math skills. Some studies have found these associations insignificant because there was almost no variance in children's self-perceptions (they were almost all very high; e.g., Nicholls & Miller, 1984). However, motivation scores become increasingly associated with academic performance over the elementary grades and are clearly associated by the 2nd or 3rd grades (Eshel & Klein, 1981; Nicholls & Miller, 1984; Wigfield et al., 1997; see Stipek & Mac Iver, 1989, for a review).

There is also evidence that motivation becomes more stable, and perhaps less malleable, as children progress through school. One study, for example, found that academic achievement was a stronger predictor of self-perceptions of ability several years later for children in elementary school (2nd–5th grades) than for children in later grades (5th–10th grades; Newman, 1984). Wigfield et al. (1997) assessed competence beliefs, values (usefulness and importance), and interest in math and reading in three cohorts of children for three years. Consistency from year to year increased substantially as children progressed through the early grades. For example, adjoining year correlations for perceived competence in reading increased each year from Grades 1–2 to Grades 5–6 as follows: .26, .36, .50, .60, .61.

These findings suggest that children's achievement motivation becomes increasingly stable until the 4th or 5th grade and then may level off.

In summary, although most children enter school high in motivation regardless of their motivations scores, self-perceptions of competence and accompanying expectations for success decline for those children who perform poorly in high school. The decline in motivation lags a little behind actual performance. Clearly, there is a direct effect of early academic achievement on motivation variables, which affect effort. Declines in effort caused by decreases in motivation, in turn, undermine children's academic achievement—again making it increasingly difficult for children who enter school with low skills to improve their relative academic status.

Learning Opportunities and Teacher Expectations

Early achievement levels may affect children's learning opportunities, which in turn affect their rate of learning. Children who have difficulty learning to read, for example, may be less inclined to seek opportunities to read, attenuating their growth in reading skills. Cunningham and Stanovich (1997) provide supportive evidence. They found that 1st-grade reading achievement predicted children's exposure to print, which in turn was highly correlated with their academic achievement in the 11th grade.

Early achievement also may affect later achievement as a consequence of its effects on teachers' expectations for academic performance and attendant decisions that affect children's learning opportunities. Thus, teachers may ask less of or give easier work to children who enter school with relatively low academic skills because they expect them to have difficulty with more difficult work. Or they may place children with low entry skills in the lowest reading group or in a developmental kindergarten or transitional class, or they may retain them in the regular class. Some of these consequences of low entry skills may be pedagogically appropriate. Some also may unnecessarily restrict learning opportunities and progress in developing skills.

Rosenthal and Jacobson (1966) demonstrated that students' learning outcomes could be influenced even by giving contrived information about students' intellectual potential. What is often missed in this classic study is that the false information affected academic performance only for children in the 1st and 2nd grades. The findings were not significant for older children, suggesting that children in the first few grades may be particularly vulnerable to low teacher expectations.

Further evidence for the importance of teacher expectations is provided by studies of naturally occurring differences in teacher expectations, which found that expectations at the beginning of the year predicted performance at the end of the year over and above what would be expected if predictions were based on initial performance (Jussim & Eccles, 1992). Low-SES children are particularly vulnerable to the effects of low expectations. One study found that preschool teachers were much more likely to underestimate a low-SES than a high-SES child's IQ, and teachers' perceptions of children's intellectual ability at age 4 predicted children's school achievement 14 years later (Alvidrez & Weinstein, 1999).

Explanations for the effects of teacher expectations on children's learning have also been studied. There now is substantial evidence that some teachers treat children for whom they have high academic expectations in ways that are more likely to enhance learning than is their treatment of low-expectancy children (see Stipek, 1998). Rosenthal (1974) categorized differential treatment into four categories: (a) the social–emotional climate that they provide (e.g., smiling, being friendly), (b) instructional input (e.g., the amount of information given to learn or number of problems to complete), (c) intellectual output (e.g., the number of times a teacher calls on a student, the time a teacher waits for a student to respond), and (d) affective feedback (amount of criticism or praise). Even well-meaning behavior (e.g., expressing pity toward or offering to help a child having difficulty) can undermine children's self-confidence ("she must think I'm not able to do this") and thus eventually undermine their learning (Graham, 1984; Graham & Barker, 1990)

Entwisle and Hayduk (1982) reported fairly stable teacher expectations from 1st through 3rd grade. Because academic performance is by far the best predictor of teachers' expectations, stability in expectations is most likely primarily a consequence of stability in children's performance. But it may also be a consequence of biased practices and selective attention. Many teachers' expectations do not change despite changes in children's skill levels because they create situations in which only confirming evidence is possible or because their expectations bias what they see and their interpretations of student behavior. Thus, for example, a teacher might not notice that Simon is reading books that are below his skill level because she does not give him a more difficult book to try. She might not adjust her expectations for Yolanda who completed a math assignment with fewer errors than usual because she attributes her success to help from a classmate rather then improvement in her math competencies. As a consequence, Simon is not given more challenging reading assignments (and thus more opportunities to improve his reading skills), and Yolanda is not praised for her effort and improvement in ways that might build her academic self-confidence.

Initial teacher expectations also may affect decisions teachers make about a child's academic program that could have long-term effects on their learning opportunities, such as ability group placement and class placement or retention.

Ability Group Placement

Ability group placement is based primarily on teachers' judgments of children's academic skills, which may be biased or erroneous. There is, moreover, evidence that the placement itself affects achievement gains (e.g., Pallas, Entwisle, Alexander, & Stluka, 1994). Weinstein (1976), for example, found that the reading group to which students were assigned contributed 25% to the prediction of midyear achievement over and above students' initial readiness scores. Children in low-skilled groups gained substantially less in reading skills than did children in high-skilled groups.

The differences in achievement gains have been explained partly by qualitative differences in teaching. Reading lessons for high-skilled compared with low-skilled groups have been observed to be structured more loosely, to involve more meaningful questions and opportunities to connect reading to personal experiences, and to be more fun. Decoding skills, rather than meaning, and repetitive ("drill and kill") tasks are often stressed more with the low-skilled group (Borko & Eisenhart, 1986; Collins, 1982; Grant & Rothenberg, 1986; Haskins, Walden, & Ramey, 1983; Hiebert, 1983; McDermott, 1987). Studies also have found that students in high-skilled reading groups were given more opportunity for self-directed learning (Grant & Rothenberg, 1986; Haskins et al., 1983) and to engage in personal conversations with the teacher (Grant & Rothenberg, 1986).

In addition, research suggests that teachers' and parents' perceptions of children's competencies and their expectations for future success are influenced by children's ability group placement regardless of their actual skill level (Pallas et al., 1994). In turn, these expectations are known to affect children's own judgments of their skills (Jacobs & Eccles, 1992).

Initial reading group assignment may have long-term implications for the rate at which children improve their skills. Children initially assigned to a low-skilled group because their skills are relatively low when they enter school will likely have difficulty catching up with higher-skilled classmates.

Class Placement and Retention

Teachers and school administrators also make decisions about class placements. Children who enter school with very low skills (both academic and social) are sometimes placed in "developmental kindergartens" with the expectation that they will advance to the regular kindergarten the following year. Children who fare poorly in kindergarten are occasionally placed in "transition" classrooms, providing an extra year before they enter 1st grade, or they are retained in a regular kindergarten. Retention is common in the first few years of elementary school. Extant research suggests that these alternative placement and retention decisions typically do not benefit children, and they may be harmful to their long-term achievement and attainment.

Grade retention has consistently been shown to predict dropping out of high school, even when achievement is held constant (House, 1989; Nason, 1991). One set of investigators estimated that when a student repeats a grade, the probability of later dropping out increases by 20–40% (Neill & Medina, 1989). Stroup and Robins (1972) found in their sample of African-American men that the numbers of quarters individuals repeated in elementary school predicted the number of years of high school completed better than any other variable measured. In the Brooks-Gunn, Duncan, Klebanov, and Sealande (1993) study, the number of grade retentions during elementary school was the strongest predictor among all the many school and family variables studied (e.g., father presence, years on welfare, parental aspirations) of both high school completion and postsecondary schooling. Grade retention predicted dropping out more strongly even than general ability assessed in early childhood.

Ironically, this cost of retention in the early grades is not offset by the learning gains that retention is designed to produce. Similarly, few benefits have been derived from other options, such as developmental kindergartens and transitional classrooms. Most studies have found no differences between children who were retained or placed in developmental or transitional classrooms and matched control children, or advantages for the children who were promoted (Dennebaum & Kulberg, 1994; Ferguson, 1991; Porwancher & de Lisi, 1993; Sandoval & Fitzgerald, 1985; Shepard, 1989). And a few studies have found more negative attitudes toward school among the retained children (Shepard & Smith, 1987, 1989).

In summary, children who perform poorly in the early school grades are more likely to be retained and, as a consequence, to develop negative attitudes toward school and drop out before high school graduation. Current policy trends at the national, state, and district level, which impose accountability standards for schools and even mandate retention for children who do not achieve at pre-specified levels, suggest that retention will be used more in the future (Meisels, 1992). Again, children who enter school with poor academic skills are put at a disadvantage.

CONCLUSION

Academic skills in early childhood clearly have long-term implications for children's educational achievement and attainment. The early years are particularly important, in part, because children's academic skills in the first few years of school set into motion a set of experiences and decisions about their educational program that affects the opportunities they have to develop their intellectual competencies.

Are children who enter school with relatively poor skills doomed to low achievement and dropping out? Certainly not. Statistically, early cognitive skills account for no more than half of the variance in later cognitive skills. Moreover, there is considerable evidence that family interventions and school reform efforts can improve substantially children's academic skills, raising the floor if not rearranging the queue. Although the research reviewed in this chapter does not bear directly on the value of preschool education programs, it certainly suggests the importance of improving intellectual skills of children who are likely to enter school at an academic disadvantage.

The important message in this analysis is that the rate of learning for children who begin school with low skills is unnecessarily limited by practices and policies that could be changed. There are many strategies that teachers can use to make sure that instruction and tasks are not frustrating for children who have low skills, thus reducing the number who will develop conduct problems. And there are ways to minimize the lost instructional time for children who have conduct problems. There are also many strategies available for minimizing negative effects of relatively low skills on children's motivation (see Stipek, 1998). Teachers can read individually with children on a regular basis, using materials of varying difficulties to identify the appropriate level of challenge. Frequent and individualized assessment will ensure that teachers' perceptions are corrected quickly when children's skills change. Many alternatives to ability grouping have been suggested and implemented successfully in classrooms across the country (Slavin, 1987). Policies that result in increased retention as a solution to low academic skills, especially when implemented without equal attention to the quality of instruction children receive, is misguided according to findings from a fairly substantial body of research. Summer school programs and tutoring are a better alternative because they should have fewer negative effects on children's self-perceptions and motivation, and they do not result in children being older than their classmates as they advance through school.

Regardless of their family's income, children who enter school with low academic skills face obstacles in reaching their intellectual potential. Low-income children, however, are the most vulnerable. On average, their skills are far behind their middle-class peers, and they are more likely to attend schools that have relatively fewer resources and fewer well-trained and experienced teachers. They are, therefore, most needy and the most likely to benefit from efforts to minimize the negative long-term consequences of relatively poor skills at school entry.

REFERENCES

Alexander, K., & Entwisle, D. (1988). Achievement in the first two years of school: Patterns and processes. *Monographs of the Society for Research in Child Development, 53*(2).

Alvidrez, J., & Weinstein, R. (1999). Early teacher perceptions and later student academic achievement. *Journal of Educational Psychology, 91*, 731–746.

Arnold, D. (1997). Co-occurrence of externalizing behavior problems and emergent academic difficulties in young high-risk boys: A preliminary evaluation of patterns and mechanisms. *Journal of Applied Developmental Psychology, 18*, 317–330.

Axinn, W., Duncan, G., & Thornton, A. (1997). The effects of parental income, wealth and attitudes on children's completed schooling and self-esteem. In G. Duncan & J. Brooks-Gunn (Eds.), *Consequences of growing up poor* (pp. 518–540). New York: Russell Sage Foundation.

Barrington, B., & Hendricks, B. (1989). Differentiating characteristics of high school graduates, dropouts, and nongraduates. *Journal of Educational Research, 82*, 309–319.

Baydar, N., Brooks-Gunn, J., & Furstenberg, F. (1993). Early warning signs of functional illiteracy: Predictors in childhood and adolescence. *Child Development, 64*, 815–829.

Birch, S., & Ladd, G. (1997). The teacher–child relationship and children's early school adjustment. *Journal of School Psychology, 35*, 61–79.

Bloom, B. (1964). *Stability and change in human characteristics*. New York: Wiley.

Bloom, B. (1976). *Human characteristics and school learning*. New York: McGraw-Hill.

Borko, H., & Eisenhart, M. (1986). Students' conceptions of reading and their experiences in school. *Elementary School Journal, 86*, 589–611.

Bracht & Hopkins (1972), reported in Bloom (1976).

Bradley, R., Caldwell, B., & Rock, S. (1988). Home environment and school performance: A ten-year follow-up and examination of three models of environmental action. *Child Development, 59*, 852–867.

Brooks-Gunn, J., & Duncan, G. (1997). The effects of poverty on children. *Future of Children, 7*, 55–71.

Brooks-Gunn, J., Duncan, G., & Britto, P. (1999). Are socioeconomic gradients for children similar to those for adults? In D. Keating & C. Hertzman (Eds.), *Developmental health and the wealth of nations* (pp. 94–124). New York: Guilford Press.

Brooks-Gunn, J., Duncan, G., Klebanov, P., & Sealand, N. (1993). Do neighborhoods influence child and adolescent behavior? *American Journal of Sociology, 99*, 355–395.

Brooks-Gunn, J., Guo, G., & Furstenberg, F. (1993). Who drops out of and who continues beyond high school? A 20-year follow-up of black urban youth. *Journal of Research on Adolescence, 3*, 271–294.

Case, R., Griffin, S., & Kelly, W. (1999). Socioeconomic gradients in mathematical ability and their responsiveness to intervention during early childhood. In D. Keating & C. Hertzman (Eds.), *Developmental health and the wealth of nations* (pp. 125–149). New York: Guilford Press.

Chen, C., Lee, S., & Stevenson, H. (1996). Long-term prediction of academic achievement of American, Chinese, and Japanese adolescents. *Journal of Educational Psychology, 18,* 750–759.

Coleman, J., Campbell, E., Ilobson, C., McPartland, J., Mood, N., Weinfeld, F., & York, R. (1966). *Equality of educational opportunity.* Washington, DC: U.S. Government Printing Office.

Collins, J. (1982). Discourse style, classroom interaction and differential treatment. *Journal of Reading Behavior, 14,* 429–437.

Cunningham, A., & Stanovich, K. (1997). Early reading acquisition and its relation to reading experience and ability 10 years later. *Developmental Psychology, 33,* 934–945.

Dennebaum, J., & Kulberg, J. (1994). Kindergarten retention and transition classrooms: Their relationship to achievement. *Psychology in the Schools, 21,* 463–470.

Duncan, G., Brooks-Gunn, J., & Klebanov, P. (1994). Economic deprivation and early childhood development. *Child Development, 65,* 296–318.

Duncan, G., Yeung, W., Brooks-Gunn, J., & Smith, J. (1998). How much does childhood poverty affect the life chances of children? *American Sociological Review, 63,* 406–423.

Dunn, L., & Markwardt, F. (1970). *Peabody Individual Achievement Test, Vol 1.* Circle Pines, MN: American Guidance Service, Inc.

Ensminger, M., & Slusarcick, A. (1992). Paths to high school graduation or dropout: A longitudinal study of a first-grade cohort. *Sociology of Education, 65,* 95–113.

Entwisle, D., & Alexander, K. (1990). Beginning school math competence: Minority and majority comparisons. *Child Development, 61,* 454–471.

Entwisle, D., Alexander, K., Cadigan, D., & Pallas, A. (1987). Kindergarten experience: Cognitive effects or socialization? *American Educational Research Journal, 24,* 337–364.

Entwisle, D., & Hayduk, L. (1982). *Early schooling: Cognitive and affective outcomes.* Baltimore: Johns Hopkins University Press.

Eshel, Y., & Klein, Z. (1981). Development of academic self-concept of lower-class and middle-class primary school children. *Journal of Educational Psychology, 73,* 287–293.

Farrington, D. (1979). Environmental stress, delinquent behavior, and convictions. In J. Sarason & C. Spielberger (Eds.), *Stress and anxiety* (Vol. 6, pp. 93–107). Washington, DC: Hemisphere.

Ferguson, P. (1991). Longitudinal outcome differences among promoted and transitional at-risk kindergarten students. *Psychology in the Schools, 28,* 139–146.

Garnier, H., Stein, J., & Jacobs, J. (1997). The process of dropping out of high school: A 19-year perspective. *American Educational Research Journal, 34,* 395–419.

Gersten, R., Becker, W., Heiry, T., & White, W. (1984). Entry IQ and yearly academic growth of children in direct instruction programs: A longitudinal study of low SES children. *Educational Evaluation and Policy Analysis, 6,* 109–121.

Graham, S. (1984). Communicating sympathy and anger to Black and White children: The cognitive (attributional) consequences of affective cues. *Journal of Personality and Social Psychology, 47,* 14–28.

Graham, S., & Barker, G. (1990). The downside of help: An attributional–developmental analysis of helping behavior as a low ability cue. *Journal of Educational Psychology, 82,* 7–14.

Grant, L., & Rothenberg, J. (1986). The social enhancement of ability differences: Teacher student interactions in first- and second-grade reading groups. *The Elementary School Journal, 87,* 29–49.

Haskins, R., Walden, T., & Ramey, C. (1983). Teacher and student behavior in high- and low-ability groups. *Journal of Educational Psychology, 75,* 865–876.

Haveman, R., & Wolfe, B. (1984). Schooling and economic well-being: The role of nonmarket effects. *Journal of Human Resources, 19,* 377–407.

Hawkins, J., & Lishner, D. (1998). Schooling and delinquency. In E. H. Johnson (Ed.), *Handbook of crime and delinquency prevention* (pp. 179–221). New York: Guilford Press.

Hawkins, J., Lishner, D., Catalano, R., & Howard, M. (1986). Childhood predictors of adolescent substance abuse: Toward an empirically grounded theory. In S. Griswold-Ezekoye, K. Kumpfer, & W. Bukoski (Eds.), *Childhood and chemical abuse: Prevention and intervention* (Vol. 18, pp. 11–48). New York: Haworth Press.

Helmke, A., & van Aken, M. (1995). The causal ordering of academic achievement and self-concept of ability during elementary school: A longitudinal study. *Journal of Educational Psychology, 87,* 624–637.

Henderson, A., & Berla, N. (Eds.). (1994). *A new generation of evidence: The family is critical to student achievement.* Washington, DC: National Committee for Citizens in Education.

Hess, R., & Hahn, R. (1974). Prediction of school failure and the Hess School Readiness Scale. *Psychology in the Schools, 11,* 134–136.

Hess, R., Holloway, S., Dickson, W., & Price, G. (1984). Maternal variables as predictors of children's school readiness and later achievement in vocabulary and mathematics in sixth grade. *Child Development, 55,* 1902–1912.

Hiebert, E. (1983). An examination of ability grouping in reading instruction. *Reading Research Quarterly, 18,* 231–255.

Hinshaw, S. (1992). Externalizing behavior problems and academic underachievement in childhood and adolescence: Causal relationships and underlying mechanisms. *Psychological Bulletin, 111,* 127–155.

House, E. (1989). Policy implications of retention research. In L. Shepard & M. Smith (Eds.), *Flunking grades: Research and policies on retention* (pp. 202–213). Philadelphia: Falmer Press.

Jacobs, J., & Eccles, J. (1992). The impact of mothers' gender-role stereotypic beliefs on mothers' and children's ability perceptions. *Journal of Personality and Social Psychology, 63,* 932–944.

Jorm, A., Share, D., Matthews, R., & Maclean, R. (1986). Behavior problems in specific reading retarded and general reading backward children: A longitudinal study. *Journal of Child Psychology and Psychiatry, 27*, 343.

Jussim, L., & Eccles, J. (1992). Teacher expectations II: Construction and reflection of student achievement. *Journal of Personality and Social Psychology, 63*, 947–961.

Korenman, S., Miller, J., & Sjaastad, J. (1995). Long-term poverty and child development in the United States: Results from the National Longitudinal Survey of Youth. *Children and Youth Services Review, 17*, 127–151.

Krein, S., & Beller, A. (1988). Educational attainment of children from single-parent families: Differences by exposure, gender, and race. *Demography, 25*, 221–234.

Ladd, G., Kochenderfer, B., & Coleman C. (1997). Friendship quality as a predictor of young children's early school adjustment. *Child Development, 68*, 1181–1197.

Loeber, R., & Stouthamer-Loeber, M. >(1987). Prediction. In H. Quay (Ed.), *Handbook of juvenile delinquency* (pp. 325–392). New York: Wiley.

Luster, T., & McAdoo, H. (1966). Family and child influences on educational attainment: A secondary analysis of the High/Scope Perry Preschool Data. *Developmental Psychology, 32*, 26–39.

Maughan, B., Gray, G., & Rutter, M. (1985). Reading retardation and antisocial behavior: A follow-up into employment. *Journal of Child Psychology and Psychiatry, 26*, 741–758.

McMarthy, D. P. (1972). *Manual for the McCarthy Scales of Children's Abilities*. New York: Psychological Corporation.

McDermott, R. (1987). The explanation of minority school failure, again. *Anthropology and Education Quarterly, 18*, 361–364.

McGee, R., Williams, S., Bradshaw, J., Chapel, J., Robins, A., & Silva, P. (1985). The Rutter Scale for completion by teachers: Factor structure and relationships with cognitive abilities and family adversity for a sample of New Zealand children. *Journal of Child Psychology and Psychiatry, 26*, 727–739.

McGee, R., Williams, S., Share, D., Anderson, J., & Silva, P. (1986). The relationship between specific reading retardation, general reading backwardness, and behavioural problems in a large sample of Dunedin boys: A longitudinal study from five to eleven years. *Journal of Child Psychology and Psychiatry, 27*, 597–610.

McLoed, J., & Shanahan, M. (1993). Poverty, parenting and children's mental health. *American Sociological Review, 58*, 351–366.

Meisels, S. (1992). Doing harm by doing good: Iatrogenic effects of early childhood enrollment and promotion policies. *Early Childhood Research Quarterly, 7*, 155–174.

Morrison, D., Mantzicopoulos, P., & Carte, E. (1989). Preacademic screening for learning and behavior problems. *Journal of the American Academy of Child and Adolescent Psychiatry, 28*, 101–106.

Nason, R. (1991). Retaining children: Is it the right decision? *Childhood Education, 67,* 300–304.

National Center for Education Statistics. (1998a). *The condition of education 1998* (NCES 98-013). Washington, DC: U.S. Department of Education, Office of Educational Research and Improvement.

National Center for Education Statistics. (1998b). *Statistical analysis report: America's teachers: profile of a profession, 1993–94* (NCES 97-460). Washington, DC: U.S. Department of Education.

National Center for Education Statistics. (1998c). *Statistical analysis report: Urban schools: The challenge of location and poverty* (NCES 96-184). Washington, DC: U.S. Department of Education.

Neill, D., & Medina, N. (1989). Standardized testing: Harmful to educational health. *Phi Beta Kappan, 70*(9), 688–698.

Newman, R. (1984). Children's achievement and self-evaluations in mathematics: A longitudinal study. *Journal of Educational Psychology, 76,* 857–873.

Nicholls, J., & Miller, A. (1984). Development and its discontents: The differentiation of the concept of ability. In J. Nicholls (Ed.), *Advances in motivation and achievement: The development of achievement motivation* (Vol. 3, pp. 185–218). Greenwich, CT: JAI Press.

Offord, D., Adler, R., & Boyle, M. (1986). Prevalence and sociodemographic correlates of conduct disorder. *American Journal of Social Psychiatry, 6,* 272–278.

Pallas, A., Entwisle, D., Alexander, K., & Stluka, M. (1994). Ability-group effects: Instructional, social, or institutional? *Sociology of Education, 67,* 27–46.

Peters, E., & Mullis, N. (1997). The role of the family and source of income in adolescent achievement. In G. Duncan & J. Brooks-Gunn (Eds.). *Consequences of growing up poor.* New York: Russell Sage Foundation.

Porwancher, D., & de Lisi, R. (1993). Developmental placement of kindergarten children based on the Gesell School Readiness Test. *Early Childhood Research Quarterly, 8,* 149–166.

Richman, N., Stevenson, J., & Graham, P. (1982). *Preschool to school: A behavioural study.* San Diego, CA: Academic Press.

Rosenthal, R. (1974). On the social psychology of the self-fulfilling prophecy: Further evidence for Pygmalion effects and their mediating mechanisms. New York: MSS Modular. Rosenthal, R., & Jacobson, L. (1966). Teacher expectancies: Determinants of pupils' IQ gains. *Psychological Reports, 19,* 115–118.

Rutter, M., & Giller, H. (1983). *Juvenile delinquency: Trends and perspectives.* New York: Guilford Press

Sameroff, A., Seifer, R., Baldwin, A., & Baldwin, C. (1993). Stability of intelligence from preschool to adolescence: The influence of social and family risk factors. *Child Development, 64,* 80–97.

Sandoval, J., & Fitzgerald, P. (1985). A high school follow-up of children who were nonpromoted or attended a junior first grade. *Psychology in the Schools, 22,* 164–170.

Schonfeld, I., Shaffer, D., O'Connor, P., & Portnoy, S. (1988). Conduct disorder and cognitive functioning: Testing three causal hypotheses. *Child Development, 59*, 993–1007.

Shepard, L. (1989). A review of research on kindergarten retention. In L. Shepard & M. Smith (Eds.), *Flunking grades: Research and policies on retention* (pp. 64–78). London: Falmer.

Shepard, L., & Smith, M. (1987). Effects of kindergarten retention at the end of first grade. *Psychology in the Schools, 24*, 346–357.

Shepard, L., & Smith, M. (1989). Academic and emotional effects of kindergarten retention in one school district. In L. Shepard & M. Smith (Eds.), *Flunking grades: Research and policies on retention* (pp. 79–107). London: Falmer.

Slavin, R. (1987). Ability grouping and student achievement in elementary schools: A best-evidence synthesis. *Review of Educational Research, 57*, 293–336.

Steinberg, L., Blinde, P., & Chan, K. (1984). Dropping out among language minority youth. *Review of Educational Research, 54*, 113–132.

Stevenson, H., & Newman, R. (1986). Long-term prediction of achievement and attitudes in mathematics and reading. *Child Development, 57*, 646–659.

Stevenson, J., Richman, N., & Graham, P. (1985). Behavior problems and language abilities at three years and behavioral deviance at eight years. *Journal of Child Psychology and Psychiatry, 26*, 215–230.

Stipek, D. (1984). Young children's performance expectations: Logical analysis or wishful thinking? In J. Nicholls (Ed.), *Advances in motivation and achievement: The development of achievement motivation* (Vol. 3, pp. 33–56). Greenwich, CT: JAI Press.

Stipek, D. (1998). *Motivation to learn: From theory to practice* (3rd ed.). Needham Heights, MA: Allyn & Bacon.

Stipek, D., & Byler, P. (2000, April). *Quality of classroom instruction as a function of student population, teachers, and school climate.* Paper presented at the annual meeting of the American Educational Research Association, New Orleans.

Stipek, D., Feiler, R., Byler, P., Ryan, R., Milburn, S., & Salmon, J. (1998). Good beginnings: What difference does the program make in preparing young children for school? *Journal of Applied Developmental Psychology, 19*, 41–66.

Stipek, D., & Greene, J. (in press). Achievement motivation in early childhood: Cause for concern or celebration? In S. Goldbeck (Ed.), *Psychological perspectives on early childhood education: Reframing dilemmas in research and practice* (in press). Mahwah, NJ: Erbaum.

Stipek, D., & Mac Iver, D. (1989). Developmental change in children's assessment of intellectual competence. *Child Development, 60*, 521–538.

Stipek, D., & Ryan, R. (1997). Economically disadvantaged preschoolers: Ready to learn but further to go. *Developmental Psychology, 33*, 711–723.

Stroup, A., & Robins, L. (1972). Elementary school predictors of high school dropout among black males. *Sociology of Education, 45*, 212–222.

Tramontana, M., Hooper, S., & Selzer, S. (1988). Research on the preschool prediction of later academic achievement: A review. *Developmental Review, 8,* 89–146.

Weinstein, R. (1976). Reading group membership in first grade: Teacher behaviors and pupil experience over time. *Journal of Educational Psychology, 68,* 103–116.

White, K. (1982). The relation between socioeconomic status and academic achievement. *Psychological Bulletin, 91,* 461–481.

Wigfield, A., Eccles, J., Yoon, K., Harold, R., Arbreton, A., Freedman-Doan, C., & Blumenfeld, P. (1997). Change in children's competence beliefs and subjective task values across the elementary school years: A 3-year study. *Journal of Educational Psychology, 89,* 451–469.

Willms, J. (1999). Quality and inequality in children's literacy: The effects of families, schools, and communities. In D. Keating & C. Hertzman (Eds.), *Developmental health and the wealth of nations* (pp. 72–93). New York: Guilford Press.

Woodcock, R., & Johnson, M. (1989). *Woodcock-Johnson Psycho-Educational Battery,* revised. Allen, Texas: DLM.

15

CATHARSIS AS A CONSTRUCTIVE EXPRESSION OF DESTRUCTIVE AFFECT: DEVELOPMENTAL AND CLINICAL PERSPECTIVES

JONATHAN BLOOM-FESHBACH AND SALLY BLOOM-FESHBACH

A theme in this book is empathy's (the affective and cognitive capacity to appreciate the emotional position of the "other") ability to be pivotal in diminishing aggression toward the "other." In this chapter, we wish to turn this relationship around. Emphasizing a clinical perspective, we consider the ways in which the appropriate expression of aggressive feelings leads to well-being and to a greater capacity for constructive and empathic interpersonal relationships.

Discussion of the benefits of expressing negative affect immediately raises the thorny set of dilemmas that surround the topic of catharsis, a complicated, but significant, theoretical and clinical domain relevant to our position. As a result, we briefly address the arguments regarding the catharsis hypothesis: To what extent is it adaptive or desirable to promote the expression of negative feelings? We conclude that the natural value of catharsis is clarified by considering a developmental perspective. We focus on the issue of how certain features of emotional expression—including necessary degrees of aggressive affect expression—are basic ingredients in the attachment process. The failure to traverse these avenues of self-expression, in turn, shapes both interpersonal relations and internal psychological capacities and biases in ways that may diminish the potential for mutuality in human relationships. Finally, to better clarify our theoretical views, especially in the face of conflicting research and clinical findings, we offer a psychotherapy case example to illustrate how the clinician might conceptualize and technically address the benefits and the pitfalls of heightened affective expression.

CATHARSIS: SHORT-TERM RELIEF OR VEHICLE FOR ENDURING CHANGE?

The concept of catharsis has a lengthy history, reflecting the ways in which scholars and healers through the ages have attempted to conceptualize the process of achieving release and relief from the burden of negative emotion. The ancient Greeks believed that the psyche was "therapeutically" cleansed through exposure to religious rites, philosophy, music, and artistic and dramatic productions. The Greek term *katharsis* originally meant purification, and by Aristotle's time, negative emotions, including fear, were thought to produce a catharsis of such passions. Aristotle's favorable view of the theater's cathartic function contrasted with the views held by his teacher; Plato condemned dramatic productions for arousing passions that could undermine the well-being of the State. This early debate among the Greek philosopher psychologists of the day framed the controversy that continues to concern modern theorists (Jackson, 1994): Do experiences of emotional expression—catharsis—arouse or diminish pre-existing levels of troubling emotion?

The use of catharsis in mental health treatment is generally seen as originating in the work of Breuer and Freud (1895/1955), whose work marks the beginning of psychoanalysis and of modern psychotherapy. The famous case of Anna O. revealed that hysterical symptoms could be relieved when the patient, under hypnosis, re-experienced traumatic events. Breuer encouraged Anna to associate freely to the origins of her symptoms, to speak about the events that came to her mind, and to express the feelings accompanying these memories—a process that appeared to relieve her symptoms. Nichols and Efran (1985) have emphasized that Breuer happened on this method serendipitously and that the process operated with rather little input from him. They noted that the spontaneous, relieving, and seemingly natural quality of catharsis in Breuer's reports is consistent with the nature of many other "discoveries" of cathartic therapeutic processes.

The ongoing struggle to determine the degree to which abreactive experiences are a necessary treatment component can be observed in the evolution of psychotherapy approaches throughout the 20th century. Although the original psychoanalytic breakthrough in the psychological understanding of symptoms and their modification rapidly reframed the therapeutic task into a more cognitive and less dramatic experience, over time, many came to feel that something vital had been filtered out. Indeed, the reduced role of emotional expression in psychoanalysis probably helped instigate some of the alternative therapeutic movements of the past 30 years. The Gestalt therapy of Fritz Perls, the bioenergetics of Lowen, the Primal scream approach of Janov, the psychodrama technique introduced by Moreno, and other such therapies share an assumption that heightened emotional expression is a crucial component of psychotherapeutic change. In fact, many behavioral therapies that might be considered superficial or narrow by an insight-oriented therapist (such as assertiveness training or role playing) tend to emphasize real-life activities that naturally include more vivid emotional experience. Similarly, the competing contemporary psychoanalytic approaches that have been proposed as alternatives to the classical analytic model, including the object relations, self-psychology, relational, and intersubjective approaches, all tend to emphasize a more affective therapeutic climate and a more interactional therapeutic relationship.

RESEARCH ON CATHARSIS AS A CLINICAL TOOL

The research literature about the clinical efficacy of catharsis shows mixed results, but in general the work is not impressive in either scope or methodology. Although there are some studies that challenge the notion of the effects of emotional release as being desirable or effective (e.g., Lewis & Bucher, 1992; Warren & Kurlychek, 1981), there are a number of studies that have yielded findings more favorable to catharsis (e.g., Eisel, 1988; Madonna & Chandler, 1986; Mohr, Shoham-Salomon, Engle, & Beutler, 1991; Nichols, 1974; Nichols & Bierenbaum, 1978). Further, Bohart (1980) offered a research investigation that reformulates the way in which catharsis operates, supporting the process but emphasizing the cognitive coping shifts that occur in the context of emotional expression (see Bohart, chapter 16, for further elaboration of this model and related findings).

It should be noted that our focus on catharsis does not include studies of the exposure to emotionally charged stimuli, such as dramatic productions, film, sporting events, and the like that Feshbach (1984) has termed the "dramatic" cathartic domain. These experiences constitute complicated sources of emotional stimulation that may be arousing and not cathartic and hence do not bear on the issue of therapeutically focused affective experience. Further, we do not address the extensive experimental literature that has examined the creation and sequelae of emotional reactions, including the stimulation and expression of aggression, in the laboratory setting. Several authors have explained why these data do not bear on the abreactive phenomena relevant to the broader psychological–clinical context (e.g., Feshbach, 1984; Nichols, 1974; Nichols & Efran, 1985). Such research may actually be studying other psychological dynamics such as the motivation for retaliation rather than the regulation of traumatic affect.

QUALIFIED ENDORSEMENT OF CATHARSIS

Given the conflicting clinical and research evidence, what are we to make, then, of this catharsis debate? There are many accounts of emotional expression as a central component of symptom relief, and the persistent rediscovery of cathartic approaches by a variety of clinicians is compelling. Historical studies of catharsis and abreaction techniques (Jackson, 1994; Nichols & Efran, 1985; van der Hart & Brown, 1992) are replete with independent discoveries of the curative power of heightened emotional expression across cultures and historical eras. At the same time, the insufficiency of emotional expression as a treatment approach has been addressed by a wide spectrum of researchers and clinicians. And even among sympathetic observers, the importance of cognitive shifts as a crucial factor accompanying emotional expression is widely accepted (Bohart, 1980; Feshbach, 1984; Horowitz, 1986; Nichols & Efran, 1985).

Thus, despite the recurrent critiques of the benefits of such abreaction, there remains a powerful, broadly held clinical and commonsense adherence to the efficacy of cathartic procedures. We suggest, as have others, that the answer to this dilemma lies in better specification of the psychological problem, the mode and intensity of emotional expression, its cognitive context, and mediating psychological conditions that must be articulated to determine whether and under what circumstances catharsis harms or heals.

A reasoned approach in this polemical terrain suggests that we underline, at the outset, that an unmodulated degree of emotional expression is clearly problematic and that there are many individuals—especially those with unstable psychological capacities—for whom the encouragement of emotional expression may indeed be an unhealthy and potentially disintegrating experience. In fact, in all individuals, it is the combination of appropriate psychological control capacities in concert with affective releasing expressions that provides a basis for the therapeutic function of cathartic processes.

Our position, then, based on clinical reports, empirical studies, and our own clinical observations, is that in the clinical context, where there is a secure relationship and an opportunity for intense emotional expression, catharsis is a potentially powerful ingredient that can facilitate marked and enduring psychological change. However, it can only do so if there are other conditions at hand that facilitate integration of the emotional expression itself. As with the lancing of an infection, sometimes such cleansing is curative, sometimes an antibiotic will also be necessary, and sometimes the lancing will necessitate a deep cut that requires stitching. Furthermore, indiscriminate lancing will likely promote further pain and infection.

ATTACHMENT AND SEPARATION, REPRESENTATION AND AGGRESSIVE AFFECT

In this section we outline our view of why catharsis operates as a naturally occurring developmental and clinical phenomenon. We discuss how the establishment of secure attachment bonds requires positive conditions for the expression and reception of negative emotions including aggressive affects. Within this framework, we hope to theoretically clarify why individuals feel the motivation for emotional release and under what conditions this may be a crucial clinical tool.

The recognition of the fundamental importance of attachment relationships in early life has far-reaching implications for the constructive expression of destructive affect. The elevation of core affective and interpersonal needs as a primary motivational system, through the work of Harlow, Bowlby, Ainsworth, Spitz, Sroufe, Mahler, Stern, and others (reviewed in Bloom-Feshbach & Bloom-Feshbach, 1987), establishes the attachment system as a biologically based, evolution-linked dimension of human functioning. The increasing period of infantile dependence that occurs through the ascension of the evolutionary ladder points to the fundamental importance of the set of psychological mechanisms that promote and maintain this intense, temporally lengthy, parent–child bond.

Within the body of research on attachment are many studies underscoring the adaptive merits of secure parent–child attachment, including correlates with better psychological functioning at later ages (e.g., Sroufe, 1983). Today, there is widespread agreement about the importance of the early nurturing environment in child development (e.g., Goldberg, Muir, 1995), a position that psychoanalysts pioneered much earlier through qualitative observations.

REPRESENTATIONAL PATTERNS AND ATTACHMENT BONDS

Early parent–child transactions become the building blocks of psychological functioning through representational templates that shape the experiencing of self and others. These representational patterns, developed through the quality and nature of formative attachment experiences, continue to mold attachment relationships throughout life. This working model concept that Bowlby (1969, 1973) adopted in his attachment studies offers a conceptual bridge to the representational models in psychoanalytic conceptions of the psyche. Elsewhere (Bloom-Feshbach & Bloom-Feshbach, 1987) we have detailed the convergence among research and clinical findings and theories about attachment and separation processes. Studies of maternal deprivation, attachment research in developmental psychology, and more speculative clinical and developmental observations of psychoanalytic scholars and practitioners, all support the far-ranging implications of how the quality of early parent–child bonds give rise to core representational templates that significantly shape interpersonal and affective behavior.

PSYCHOLOGICAL AUTONOMY AND AGGRESSION

There is general agreement that a developmental shift occurs around the child's third year that permits increased autonomy and less vulnerability to separation experiences. We examine the inner psychology of this enhanced security of the attachment bond, considering, in particular, the role of anger.

In our view, theoretical positions that solely emphasize the biological basis of aggression, and the related drive orientation within psychoanalytic theory, miss the mark. Although undoubtedly there is a physiological substrate underlying aggressive impulses, just as there are physiological bases to other affective and cognitive processes, we think that aggressive affect is so substantially shaped by socialization, attachment, and other psychological experiences, that the dominant consideration ought to be the psychological influences that shape these emotional response patterns. Beyond biology, it is useful to focus on the many highly frustrating aspects of life experience that intrinsically give rise to angry emotions. We share, for example, Mitchell's (1993) view that aggression is a biologically mediated response that takes form and meaning from the interpersonal context in which it is felt.

Infancy and early childhood inevitably evoke helplessness, dependent longings, and distress that give rise to frustration and rage. Even a secure nurturing context entails many normal, expectable experiences of intense frustration, distress, and painful separation, from lonely moments of going to sleep, to periods of diverted parental attention, to times of actual physical absence of attachment figures. As observations of parent–child interaction reveal, children's expressions of protest or anger are part of a communication pattern that signals to adults that the children are frustrated and seek an alternative nurturing response. There are innumerable micro-interactions in which a child's anger serves a communication function in restoring security and a sense of well-being within the attachment system. From this perspective, childhood anger that is evoked by frustrations within attachment relationships can be conceptualized as an expression of the self that seeks understanding and response. Over the course of later development, even when this instrumental function of aggressive display is not clear or conscious, there may well be an unconscious, foundational meaning to angry feelings; that is, an early and significant function of anger is the motivation to restore closeness.

When separation protest is responded to by the restoration of a satisfying connection within the attachment relationship, angry feelings diminish and well-being ensues (thereby reinforcing the instrumental and attachment functions of the expression of anger). In more extreme circumstances of separation, when the child's capacity to be rebuffed on protest is exhausted, depression and eventually apathy result (Bowlby, 1973). When this occurs, the adaptive function of the expression of anger, as a stage in the process of restoring ruptures in the attachment bond, can be damaged or muted. But before the need to express anger is extinguished at the more extreme degree of traumatic experience, the child will persistently and even desperately seek to find a workable channel for the expression of aggressive feelings. It is as if when hostile affect expressions fail to be communicated and understood, they create an unfinished emotional sequence that blocks the individual from reuniting with the attachment figure.

CATHARSIS AND SEPARATION

We now examine a clinical intervention approach with a blind infant who experienced a circumscribed but traumatic separation. We offer this case illustration because the young age of the child and the psychology of the disability put the separation and affective process in clear focus. Writing 25 years ago, Selma Fraiberg (1971) described a case of 14-month-old Jackie, who had been blind from birth. Jackie was developing normally, for a blind child of his age, both motorically and verbally, when his mother was called out of town suddenly on a family matter for 3 days. In her absence, the boy was cared for by various friends and relatives. When the mother returned, Jackie began to regress in nearly all areas of development and displayed alarming symptoms. His screaming fits would last for hours. When the mother sought clinical help after 2 weeks of ceaseless fits, the clinicians found these "screams or shouts of a repetitive, chanting character" to be "nearly indescribable" (p. 361). During the attacks, the child's face was strangely "immobile and expressionless." When the mother held Jackie, he would "crawl desperately all over her body as if trying to get as much as possible of his own body surface in touch with his mother's body. This frenzied crawling was as nerve-wracking to the mother as the shouting" (p. 361). During this time period, Jackie had lost interest in toys, games, and activities; his sleep was severely disrupted, and after a few mouthfuls of food he would vomit.

Although the mother realized that the crisis was precipitated by the sudden separation, she was at her wit's end as to how to reassure her son. Fraiberg and her colleagues presumed that a sighted child could have clung to his mother and visually kept her in sight but that Jackie's blindness continually re-exposed him to the possibility of another separation. Furthermore, they realized that he had a great need to express rage; although it was difficult to detect this component in the fits, the lack of a target for the rage added to the unsatisfying resolution of the child's emotional situation.

The clinicians suggested as an intervention that each time Jackie began his shouting fits, the mother should provide him with pots and pans or banging toys and encourage the child "to pound and bang with his hands and fists" (p. 364). In just a few days the mother reported that the banging games were working, in her words, "like magic." Happily, this banging activity was dramatically successful and led to a diminution in the screaming fits and a return to the adaptive level at which the child had functioned prior to the separation. Several weeks later, the mother reported that Jackie was his old self again, and she was amazed at the impact of the banging intervention.

HYPOTHESES ABOUT CATHARTIC EFFICACY

That the intervention was effective in Jackie's case is compelling and suggests many possible causative hypotheses. It should be noted that the child had been ineffectively releasing affect previously—the screaming and fits—and not found relief. There may have been something about the physical channel of expression that was either developmentally more in synch with or possibly relevant to being blind. It might have allowed the child to feel some self-efficacy and control, or it might have paralleled some previously meaningful experience in the child's life. Whether it was some of these or other factors, the hitting of pots and pans somehow struck the right mode and intensity level for the youngster and was acceptable to the mother. Hence, her receptivity to this expression brought the child's release into a communication within the attachment relationship that was workable. The broadcast channel was well-calibrated, and the reception was properly tuned-in.

We are struck by how this case demonstrates the curative impact of a well-designed avenue for the expression of aggressive affect. Inferences from this and other cases must be carefully drawn, and we are not suggesting that this technique be universally applied, or that traumatized older children and adults should be supplied bo-bo dolls or boxing gloves. But it is noteworthy that before clinical intervention, Jackie's mother clearly realized the cause of her child's distress. He was attempting to express himself by shouting, but the problematic intensity and unsatisfying mode of aggressive expression and the mother's discomfort in receiving the nature of the aggressive out-pouring precluded any interactional pattern that could be successful in restoring the bond between them. Fraiberg, presaging modern relational trends in psychoanalytic theory, emphasized the role of the parenting figure in receiving and modulating the child's separation-induced anger as critical in the resolution of disturbances in the attachment relationship. If the experience of satisfying closeness in a relationship is largely defined by mutual communication, the transmission and reception of anger that is evoked by interrupted closeness may be essential in the restoration of rup-tures in closeness.

EXPRESSION AND RECEPTION OF ANGER

It is important to note the feedback cycle that characterizes attach-ment relations (Beebe & Lachmann, 1992). When children are nurtured and feel satisfied, they act in a gratifying manner that readily evokes more attention and loving reactions. When children are overly frustrated and express distress, these affective displays may be more difficult for a parent to receive, thus prompting parental rejection and withdrawal. Further distance may evoke more separation distress, and thus a negative cycle can be engaged between parent and child, as increasing desperation by the child leads to mounting parental frustration.

We view the case of Jackie as an exaggerated illustration of what hap-pens when less dramatic yet nonetheless heightened experiences of frustra-tion occur within the attachment relationship—experiences that may be rather common. In this situation, both parent and child appeared motivated to reunite after the separation but were unable to achieve a satisfactory reunion and healing of the separation wound. This failure to resolve the attachment rupture reflected the child's need for aggressive affect expres-sion to occur in a manner that was tolerable within the relationship and in a mode and intensity level that felt relieving. This case supports the view that the development and maintenance of a secure attachment bond is therefore not only dependent on parental efforts to gratify needs for nurtu-rance, but also on the caregiver's ability to tolerate and to help construc-tively channel the inevitable fury that results from disruptions in secure relations.

It is interesting to note that a parenting style thought to be develop-mentally facilitative of competence in children is, in research (e.g., Baumrind,

1967, 1971) and clinical studies (Bloom-Feshbach, Bloom-Feshbach, & Gaughran, 1980), one that is high both in nurturance and the establishment of firm limits. A high degree of nurturance directly satisfies the child's attachment motivation, whereas an authoritative disciplinary approach provides a steady, nonpunitive boundary and foil that permits the containment of aggressive expressions.

SEPARATION, CATHARSIS, AND ADAPTATION

Object Constancy

It might be useful here to review the way in which psychoanalytic object relations theorists conceptualize the representational schemata that underlie a secure attachment bond (Blatt & Blass, 1992; Bloom-Feshbach & Bloom-Feshbach, 1987; Mahler, Pine, & Bergman, 1975). The psychoanalytic concept of object constancy (which is unrelated to Piaget's object permanence) refers to a psychological representational capacity to maintain an integrated internal image of caregiving figures. Integration here refers to a capacity to maintain a stable affective memory for the gratifying as well as the frustrating dimensions of the attachment relationship. In regard to the self, it refers to the ability to tolerate both positive and negative elements in maintaining healthy self-esteem. The theory suggests that this psychological template permits the child to remain more secure in the face of parental separation and also to feel less aggressive toward the parent during periods of loss. The notion is that separation difficulty is in part fueled by unbalanced and hence heightened aggressive impulses that cause the child to fear destruction of the loved figure.

We clarify the object constancy concept by the example of a 3-year-old who is starting nursery school. Here we have a noncrisis life transition that entails a separation experience that occurs in the midst of consolidating the psychological capacity to better tolerate separation. The secure child who is left at school may miss the parent and even express a degree of distress and protest but will nonetheless have more secure expectations of the parent's return. The insecure child has less solid expectations about reunion, and these less secure expectations generate more powerful sadness and anger during the separation experience. It is clearly more distressing to fear that one has been permanently rather than temporarily abandoned. Furthermore, the insecure expectation of parental abandonment is fueled by more intense angry feelings that are generated by repeated experiences of unmet dependency needs. Thus, a negative cycle occurs where the lack in sense of security gives rise to a more traumatic perception of the separation experience, which leads to heightened separation protest and then to heightened aggressive feelings. These feelings, in turn, lead to a more troubling view of the separation event, and so forth. It is because of the mounting intensity of this snowballing affective cycle that more intense emotional expression may be a crucial component of release from this pattern.

Separation and Nursery School Adjustment

A short-term longitudinal study of nursery school adjustment during the third year of life conducted by Sally Bloom-Feshbach (1987) provides a number of findings that bear on the constructive expression of destructive affect. The children's separation reactions at school were assessed during each of the first 6 weeks of the semester. Overall preschool adjustment was then assessed toward the end of the school year, measuring both prosocial as well as uncooperative and aggressive behavioral patterns. The children who eventually adjusted well did show some degree of sadness and anger during the early weeks of school. In contrast to this pattern of normal separation protest, the children who eventually displayed more problematic school adjustment fell into two separation protest patterns. One category of children who did not eventually adjust well exhibited separation distress that lasted even through the fourth week of school; these children expressed more intense and longer periods of upset and anger. The other problematic category included children who expressed virtually no separation reaction at school during the early weeks of preschool; this "indirect" affective group also had more problems in their eventual adjustment. Thus, children who failed to express the affect (including anger) evoked by the separation experience, as well as youngsters who expressed a very high degree of intense emotion in response to the stress on their attachment system, failed to achieve the personal and social competence associated with positive adaptation to preschool. Although we cannot say that the moderate degree of separation protest is a causative factor shaping adaptation, we can say that it is clearly associated with better adaptation. This finding adds some strength to our theoretical model in which the constellation of factors promoting secure attachment relations includes the individual's modulated negative affect expression regarding separation. Like many other psychological phenomena, such as anxiety in advance of surgery or test performance, the degree of emotional expression that appears to be adaptive is in the moderate mid-range.

SECURE ATTACHMENTS AND LATER RELATIONSHIPS

In the psychoanalytic developmental model, early difficulties in the achievement of object constancy (or failures in the provision of what the Kohutians call "self-object needs") shape later interpersonal functioning. The notion is that the failure to derive an adequate sense of security from attachment relationships renders the individual overly vigilant in fulfilling unmet dependency needs and impairs the psychological capacity to function in a mutual, empathic mode within intimate relationships. The individual may become overtly self-centered and needy, or self-protective and distant in avoiding intimacy, or adopt a combination of these dependent and defensively dependent styles. Usually, the conceptualization of unmet attachment needs in early childhood that instigates this continued pattern of insecure interpersonal functioning emphasizes a lack of or inconsistency in parental nurturance and does not sufficiently highlight the developmental need for sufficient expression of frustrated attachment strivings. It is often the frustrated need to be free to feel, and appropriately express, aggressive affect expression that emerges in later psychotherapeutic treatment. The therapeutic reshaping of the representational patterns that govern and mediate affective regulation and interpersonal relations may require the reactivation of unexpressed, unfinished, or maladaptive emotional sequences. But this reactivation is only a pre-stage in the eventual restructuring of more constructive, adaptive core psychological schemas and constructs.

We presented the Fraiberg case as an example to graphically illustrate our view that the affective intensity that must be achieved in the re-working of core representational levels far exceeds what may be typically thought of as sufficient in clinical intervention. Hence, corrective clinical movements and techniques arise that emphasize raw affective experience. On the other hand, the history of cathartic techniques in the treatment of trauma stands as a reminder of the notable lack of permanent change that results when affective experience is not placed in a cognitive, integrative context.

INTERPERSONAL ILLUSTRATIONS OF CONSTRUCTIVE EXPRESSION OF ANGER

If the analysis presented here is sound developmentally and in the later course of human relations aggressive affect expression can be constructive and facilitate more satisfying close interpersonal interactions—we should be able to point to a variety of real-life contexts that demonstrate this perspective. We turn to several of these illustrations which, although not buttressed by research confirmation, have been noted through observation and clinical reports.

Sibling Relationships

In sibling relationships, parents are faced with the challenge of absorbing a new family member with significant needs for attention and nurturance while maintaining sufficient resources to meet the needs of the older child, enabling that child to adapt well to the new configuration of family relationships. If we think of emotional resources as analogous to financial supplies, the older child, whose salary has just been cut in half with the arrival of a new sibling, will naturally feel angry and resentful—even if there is excitement stimulated by the potential for new family bonds. When parents are able to maintain sufficient nurturance for the first child while also constructively identifying, helping articulate, and modulating the expression of the rage that accompanies this inevitably frustrating family transition, the older sibling will be freer to develop a loving, mutual sibling bond. Parents who are able to tolerate the expression of anger can permit some of the fury to be directed at them rather than at a brother or sister. Furthermore—and this point is relevant more generally—parents who are empathic in receiving their children's anger present a model that encourages children to receive the full range of affective communications of others in intimate relationships, even if the content communicated is frustrating and predominantly addresses the emotional agenda of the other. This capacity to be receptive to the emotional needs of the other—especially when these needs or perspectives do not coincide with those of the self—is central to empathic relations.

Intimate Adult Relationships

Nowhere is the need for open but modulated conflict more central than in the maintenance of enduring intimate adult relationships. A central emotional challenge of a long-term, marital-type relationship is managing the negative affects that naturally arise. Inevitably there will be unmet needs, times when partners step on each other's toes, or divergent perspectives and values that require negotiation. Furthermore, the depth and intensity of a marital bond reactivates attachment schemas, the sensitivities and biases that derive from formative attachment relationships. These powerful representational patterns amplify and render more problematic frustrations and deprivations that life brings. Thus, some individuals may be quite capable of effective adaptation in social and professional relationships but have difficulty coping well in intimate relationships that activate deeper, attachment-linked psychological patterns.

The breakdown of some marital relationships is clearly traceable to an overabundance of aggressive affective communication (that is, too much fighting) and a failure to understand the principles by which such negative emotion can be effectively integrated in a growth-promoting way. Such conflict-ridden relationships in which there is too much hostile affect expressed stand in contrast to the troubled relationships that suffer from insufficient expression of anger and inadequate identification of conflictual issues. In part because of a well-meaning recognition of the problems that attend too much conflict in relationships, some couples err in the direction of attempting to overlook frustration, ignore negative emotions, and too readily forgive their partners. Although a certain degree of these conflict-reducing approaches facilitates marital stability and satisfaction, a problematic lack of expression of angry feelings in the relationship will lead to distance and alienation. When people harbor negative feelings that are not adequately communicated to those they love, they do not feel known or close. As long as negative feelings are not clearly expressed (and indeed often are not even clearly articulated internally), the empathy of the significant other cannot be felt, and the bond remains disrupted. When anger is voiced constructively in a marriage, both parties have opportunities to express themselves and to be understood. This strengthens the bond and precludes the marital breakdowns that occur when the unexpressed reservoir of built-up discontent can no longer be contained, or when it has led to a quiet but unbridgeable alienation.

Educational and Vocational Settings

There are many other applications of this principle whereby the constructive expression of destructive affect promotes a positive interpersonal climate. In educational and vocational settings, opportunities for airing student (Schmuck & Schmuck, 1971) or employee discontent (Hackman & Lawler, 1971) lead to a more productive and emotionally satisfying atmosphere. Groups that permit members to express frustration in a direct manner are better able to function than groups that demand wholesale suppression of negative emotion (Leavitt, 1966). From a broad perspective, our democratic form of government is based on social mechanisms that permit the expression of political anger in ways that lead to problem-solving, diffusion of tension, or at least better understanding of the conflicts between groups. Some have seen these struggles with aggression as reflections of biological impulses bubbling over, rather than as reactions to the concrete and symbolic frustrations that are a part of the psychology of human experience.

BEYOND ATTACHMENT

Although we place an emphasis on attachment and separation processes, we have not meant to imply that only these core issues can generate powerful aggressive emotional reactions. We certainly realize that life is replete with a spectrum of potentially frustrating experiences, from physical deprivation, to frustrations with the adequacy of the self, to social and political constraint. Rather, our focus on the attachment developmental perspective is emphasized to underscore the communicational need attendant to aggression—the natural impulse to express angry feelings as a positive, relationship-building phenomenon.

CLINICAL APPLICATION

The theoretical perspectives we have discussed have important implications for clinical technique. Although the scope of this chapter does not permit a detailed account of ways to incorporate a greater emphasis on the expression of aggressive affect in developmental consultation or in adult psychotherapy, we briefly note a case example that illustrates the flavor of this approach. It should be noted that this example is one of several cases that we have treated in which (a) the individuals involved were deemed psychologically appropriate for such intervention, (b) the diagnostic assessments indicated that the problems at hand could be treated with cathartic elements, and (c) a variety of steps were taken to clarify limitations regarding affective expression. These steps emphasized the distinction between reality and fantasy, between what is felt and what can be expressed, in recognition that many troubling affects and fantasies are often unconscious. There is often a need to link affective expression with accurate cognitive interpretation, so emphasis must be placed on the difference between what can be appropriately expressed in a psychotherapeutic context and what can be communicated in family, intimate, or other social relationships.

Dan, a bright, engaging man of about 30, entered treatment to resolve an inability to make a commitment to a romantic relationship. He had moved from another geographic location for professional reasons and was maintaining the relationship long distance. Outside the realm of intimate relationships, he was quite well functioning—a highly successful achiever with excellent social skills, long-term friendships, and positively toned feelings about life. After sifting through Dan's realistic and irrational complaints about his girlfriend and enduring various go-rounds as to the legitimate long-term viability of the relationship, a therapeutic consensus developed as to the unconscious, illogical nature of his reluctance to commit.

The resolution of this particular issue, both practical and psychological, hinged on one dramatic session in which Dan's deepest core struggle regarding closeness came into focus. In this session, he reported a dream concerning his mother, and an associational link was made between mother and girlfriend. After experiencing an associational block regarding his friend, the therapist asked Dan what feeling or impulse might be so troubling to him that he did not want to permit its expression; that is, Dan was asked, "what upsets you so much, that you can't bear to think about it?"

The paradoxical request to reveal what the patient did not want to bring to mind brought about a powerful sequence of vivid images of murdering his girlfriend. Encouraged to report these as graphically and specifically as possible, Dan began to imagine himself choking her. With eyes closed, and hands raised in a choking position, shaking in the air, he descended into a trembling, sobbing, rageful state that lasted several intense moments. He vacillated between an outpouring of murderous, hate-filled rage and a grieving, bereaved state of having destroyed someone he loved deeply. One cannot discount the value of the self-discovery processes preceding this session, including various oedipal dreams of bombing a factory linked to his father's business. Nor can one diminish the importance of the post-breakthrough sessions, in clarifying Dan's schizoid dilemma, his competitive struggles, and his conflicts in self-image. But the intense, focused uncovering of deeply felt fury that emerged in a highly visual, sensory, and specific representational form was a notable turning point in Dan's treatment.

In Dan's case, the therapeutic function of catharsis did not lie simply in the expression of negative feelings. Providing Dan with pillows to beat or exercises in gesticulation and shouting would not have been therapeutic. The critical elements were the intensely felt expressions of anger and sadness in relation to a particular attachment figure and the exploration and connection of these feelings to their previously unrecognized source. Furthermore, the breakthrough session was predicated on considerable preparatory work clarifying the nature of the unconscious; the special role of the therapy context; and other interventions that regulate, de-mystify, and render meaningful the expression of highly charged and usually taboo affects and wishes.

SUMMARY

Throughout this chapter, we have taken a relational view of aggressive reactions, examining the role of anger in the regulation of the attachment bond, emphasizing the inevitable separation-evoked aggressive reactions that punctuate development. The depth, significance, and prolonged meaning of attachment relationships throughout childhood, adolescence, and the entire life course highlight the continued ubiquitous communicative function of affective reactions that are intrinsic to attachment processes. When one conceptualizes the expression of aggression as part of an effort to restore the psychological equilibrium derived from security in the attachment realm, the natural healing phenomenon of emotional catharsis becomes understandable. But because of controversy regarding both research and clinical views of the benefits versus the negative effects of cathartic processes, additional theoretical and conceptual analyses and further research efforts will be needed to better determine what is the "baby" versus the "bathwater" in this domain.

Again, because of the highly charged polemical context surrounding these issues, we have taken pains to carefully qualify our views about the constructive expression of destructive affect. From the perspective of clinical application, we have suggested that aggressive affect may be more intense and more difficult to access at sufficient intensity than is typically recognized. Because of the difficulty in gaining therapeutic access to pivotal, deeply troubling, and often disavowed aggressive feelings, we have expanded the clinician's familiar exploration to include selective therapeutic inquiry into what does not come readily to mind, thereby facilitating the constructive expression of destructive affect.

When individuals are able to work through the problematic emotional reactions that promote the maintenance of less developed, internalized representational templates of intimate relations, they are able to evolve more naturally mutual, close, empathically oriented response patterns that govern inner psychology and interpersonal behavior. If human closeness deepens when the full range of emotional reactions is transmitted and received within a relationship, then a proper dose of aggressive affect expression allows relationships to become more stable and rich, and more mutual.

REFERENCES

Baumrind, D. (1967). Child care practices anteceding three patterns of preschool behavior. *Genetic Psychology Monographs, 75,* 43–88.

Baumrind, D. (1971). Current patterns of parental authority. *Developmental Psychology Monographs, 4*(1), Part 2.

Beebe, B., & Lachmann, F. M. (1992). The contribution of mother-infant mutual influence to the origins of self- and object representations. In N. J. Skolnick & S. C. Warshaw (Eds.), *Relational perspectives in psychoanalysis.* Hillsdale, NJ: Analytic Press.

Blatt, S. J., & Blass, R. B. (1992). Relatedness and self-definition: Two primary dimensions in personality development, psychopathology, and psychotherapy. In J. W. Barron, M. N. Eagle, & D. L. Wolitzky (Eds.), *Interface of psychoanalysis and psychology.* Washington, DC: American Psychological Association.

Bloom-Feshbach, J., & Bloom-Feshbach, S. (1987). Psychological separateness and experiences of loss. In J. Bloom-Feshbach & S. Bloom-Feshbach (Eds.), *The psychology of separation and loss: Perspectives on development, life transitions, and clinical practice.* San Francisco, CA: Jossey-Bass.

Bloom-Feshbach, S. (1987). From family to classroom: Variations in adjustment to nursery school. In J. Bloom-Feshbach & S. Bloom-Feshbach (Eds.), *The psychology of separation and loss: Perspectives on development, life transitions, and clinical practice* (pp. 207–231). San Francisco, CA: Jossey-Bass.

Bloom-Feshbach, S., Bloom-Feshbach, J., & Gaughran, J. (1980). The child's tie to both parents: Separation patterns and nursery school adjustment. *American Journal of Orthopsychiatry, 50,* 505–521.

Bohart, A. C. (1980). Toward a cognitive theory of catharsis. *Psychotherapy Theory, Research and Practice, 17*(2), 192–201.

Bowlby, J. (1969). *Attachment and loss. Vol. 1: Attachment.* New York: Basic Books.

Bowlby, J. (1973). Attachment and loss. Vol. 2: Separation: Anxiety and anger. New York: Basic Books.

Breuer, J., & Freud, S. (1955). Studies on hysteria. In J Strachey (Ed.), *The complete works of Sigmund Freud, standard edition* (Vol. 2). London: Hogarth. (Originally published 1895)

Eisel, H. E. (1988). Age regression in the treatment of anger in a prison setting. *Journal of Offender Counseling, Services and Rehabilitation, 13*(1), 175–181.

Feshbach, S. (1984). The catharsis hypothesis, aggressive drive and the reduction of aggression. In *Aggressive behavior*.

Fraiberg, S. (1971). Separation crisis in two blind children. *Psychoanalytic Study of the Child, 26*, 355–371.

Goldberg, S., Muir, R., & Kerr, J. (1995). *Attachment theory: Social, developmental, and clinical perspectives.* Hillsdale, NJ: Analytic Press.

Hackman, J. R., & Lawler, E. E. (1971). Employee reactions to job characteristics. *Journal of Applied Psychology Monographs, 55*, 259–286.

Horowitz, M. J. (1986). *Stress response syndromes* (2nd ed.). Northvale, NJ: Jason Aronson.

Jackson, S. W. (1994). Catharsis and abreaction in the history of psychological healing. *Psychiatric Clinics of North America, 17*(3), 471–491.

Leavitt, H. J. (1966). Some effects of certain communication patterns on group performance. In A. Smith (Ed.), *Communication and culture* (pp.). New York: Holt, Rinehart & Winston.

Lewis, W. A., & Bucher, A. M. (1992). Anger, catharsis, the reformulated frustration–aggression hypothesis, and health consequences. *Psychotherapy, 29*(3), 385–392.

Madonna, J. M., & Chandler, R. (1986). Aggressive play and bereavement in group therapy with latency-aged boys. *Journal of Child and Adolescent Psychotherapy, 3*(2), 109–114.

Mahler, M. S., Pine, F., & Bergman, A. (1975). *The psychological birth of the human infant.* New York: Basic Books.

Mitchell, S. A. (1993). *Hope and dread in psychoanalysis.* New York: Basic Books.

Mohr, D. C., Shoham-Salomon, S. V., Engle, D., & Beutler, L. E. (1991). The expression of anger in psychotherapy for depression: Its role and measurement. *Psychotherapy Research, 1*(2), 124–134.

Nichols, M. P. (1974). Outcome of brief cathartic 34 psychotherapy. *Journal Consulting and Clinical Psychology, 42*(3), 403–410.

Nichols, M. P., & Bierenbaum, H. (1978). Success of cathartic therapy as a function of patient variables. *Journal of Clinical Psychology, 34*(3), 726–728.

Nichols, M. P., & Efran, J. S. (1985). Catharsis in psychotherapy: A new perspective. *Psychotherapy, 22*(1), 46–58.

Schmuck, R., & Schmuck, P. A. (1971). *Group processes in the classroom*. Iowa: Brown.

Sroufe, L. A. (1983). Infant-caregiver attachment and patterns of adaptation in preschool: The roots of maladaptation and competence. In M. Perlmutter (Ed.), *Minnesota Symposium in Child Psychology* (Vol. 16). Hillsdale, NJ: Erlbaum.

van der Hart, O., & Brown, P. (1992). Abreaction re-evaluated. *Dissociation Progress in the Dissociative Disorders, 5*(3), 127–140.

Warren, R., & Kurlychek, R. T. (1981). Treatment of maladaptive anger and aggression: Catharsis vs. behavior therapy. *Corrective and Social Psychiatry and Journal of Behavior Technology, Methods and Therapy, 27*(3), 135–139.

16

HOW CAN EXPRESSION IN PSYCHOTHERAPY BE CONSTRUCTIVE?

ARTHUR C. BOHART

Bob has been let go from his job. The company recently decided to lay off 100 workers. Although Bob knew this was coming, his work had been well-regarded, and he did not expect to be one of those let go. When his supervisor called him in to tell him, the supervisor acted distant and cold and offered no explanation other than that some people had to be let go. Bob is frightened and angry. He feels unfairly treated because he can't see why he was one of the ones let go while others were kept. His work, he thinks, was better than their work. This is a traumatic experience, and Bob is having trouble sleeping at night. He feels humiliated and devalued. He ruminates over how unfairly he has been treated. He is having trouble putting the experience out of his mind and seeking a new job, even though he keeps telling himself that he should be able to forget and move on.

Bob talks to a therapist. The therapist empathically listens while Bob expresses his feelings and thoughts about this problem. Initially Bob's expression is highly emotional. He is angry and pounds his fist on the chair as he talks about how unfairly he has been treated. He describes revenge fantasies (filing a grievance, letting the air out of the supervisor's tires, marching in and telling his supervisor off in front of everyone). Throughout, the therapist listens intently, and responds with occasional empathic reflections such as "It's so hard to understand, and you would like to do something about it, but there doesn't seem to be anything really to do," or "it really hurts that he chose you to let go when others seem no more competent than you," or "It is such a shock—you had your feet knocked right out from under you."

After expressing his anger for a while, Bob suddenly takes a deep breath, looks down to the floor, and says, "I'm really scared. I feel really vulnerable. I'm 52, and I'm out of work. My wife—she doesn't work. What will we do for income? I guess I'll have to go on unemployment until I get a job. But that is so humiliating. There's an unemployment office I pass on my way to work. I see all those people milling around outside waiting for it to open. I can't imagine being one of those. But I don't have any choice. I could ask my brother for a loan. But it is too humiliating, too."

Bob sits quietly with the feeling of humiliation for a moment. Then he says, "You know—when my boss fired me, he seemed cold. But I think it was something else. He looked humiliated! Almost like he hated doing this—as if he was ashamed that he had to do this. I was blaming him. But I wonder if he was feeling bad and guilty. If he was, I shouldn't get angry with him—I should go in and talk to him like a friend. I bet he would like to help. If I get him all defensive then he won't be able to help me. But if I get him on my side I bet he'll be motivated to help me get a new job. At least I should go sound him out . . . Gad. Maybe it would be better to borrow the money from my brother. I think I might be able to get a new job fairly soon. I'd rather do that than go on unemployment. Besides, it'll motivate me to work harder to get a job." Bob is now looking up, his face clearer, the tight constricted look of anger gone.

After another minute or two Bob says, "Well, oddly enough, I feel better. I'm not sure exactly why. I still don't have a job . . .. In fact, I feel really scared. But I also feel like I got my anger off my chest and at least I can go on. Maybe we could talk a little about strategies for finding a job. I feel like I can focus on that now."

Although fictionalized, the case of Bob is based on how several real psychotherapy cases of mine have progressed. Psychotherapy exists because individuals behave in ways that are destructive to themselves or to society. The forms of self-destructive behavior include clinical conditions that interfere with adaptive behavior, such as obsessions and compulsions, agoraphobia, anorexia, substance abuse, depression, anxiety, and self-criticism. Other destructive behaviors include antisocial acting out, violence, abuse, insensitivity, manipulativeness, and abandonment of responsibilities. The goal of psychotherapy is to help individuals behave more constructively toward themselves and others.

Psychotherapeutic interventions range from highly active and structured ones designed to alter the client's thoughts, behaviors, and emotions, such as those used by cognitive–behaviorists, to the radically "noninterventionist" approach of client-centered therapy. In client-centered therapy the therapist provides empathic support, listens, and responds primarily by checking his or her understanding of what the client is expressing and trying to accomplish. The goal is to provide an "empathic workspace" for clients to work out problems (Bohart & Tallman, 1999; Bozarth, 1998).

The scenario of Bob is an example of the client-centered approach and is presented to raise a fundamental question: Can individuals spontaneously move from dysfunctional and self-destructive ways of functioning to constructive ways of functioning through the activity of expressing feelings and thoughts to an empathic listener, without more active interventions by the therapist designed to alter the client's perceptions and beliefs? One argument is that instances of expression such as Bob's can help because they allow for emotional *catharsis*—the expression and draining off of destructive affects such as anger, sadness, or fear. Another argument is that the notion of catharsis is itself harmful and that promoting sheer expression will merely reinforce dysfunctional ways of thinking, feeling, and behaving. The latter argument suggests that Bob's expressions of anger at best would bring only temporary relief but would not really change his dysfunctional ways of thinking and feeling. At worst, his expressions of anger may reinforce dysfunctional, angry ways of interpreting situations. In this chapter my goal is to demonstrate that both of these positions are inadequate to understand what happens when a person expresses emotions and thoughts in psychotherapy, why expression in psychotherapy can be beneficial, and why expression is beneficial when clients are in a "therapeutic state of mind."

CATHARSIS

Catharsis has been a topic of enduring conflict (Bloom-Feshbach & Bloom-Feshbach, chapter 15; Bohart, 1980; Bushman, Baumeister, & Stack, 1999; Eron, chapter 2; Feshbach, 1971, 1984; Greenberg & Safran, 1987; Huesmann & Reynolds, chapter 12; Kennedy-Moore & Watson, 1999; Nichols & Efran, 1985; Tavris, 1982). Part of this conflict is due to a lack of clarity in what different people mean by the term.

Conflicting Views

The term *catharsis* is used in different ways. First, catharsis often refers to a theoretical explanation of how emotions work and how people can gain constructive emotional relief (the hydraulic model). Second, catharsis is used to refer to an empirical phenomenon, namely that expressing thoughts and feelings when one is troubled can make individuals feel better. Nested under this distinction are two other distinctions: direct versus vicarious catharsis and emotional expression alone versus expression as a complex whole-person interpersonal act.

Theoretical Explanation

The hydraulic model, as held by the public and some professional psychologists, assumes that affects are like energies that build up inside if not expressed. Expression leads to a "draining off" of these affects. This relieves internal tension and promotes constructive behavior. Holding in such affects is detrimental to both emotional and physical health.

There have been two versions of the hydraulic model, based on a distinction between affect and drive. Affects are temporary responses to situations. They energize the person for immediate action (Feshbach, 1971; Greenberg & Safran, 1987). Drives are motivational mechanisms that produce energy and impel the person to pursue certain kinds of behavior. The affective version of the catharsis notion holds that if an emotion is aroused and not expressed, it can interfere with effective psychological adjustment, damage physical health, and create interpersonal problems. The drive version assumes that people have an aggressive drive that impels them to act aggressively. One version of the drive theory is Freud's. For Freud, aggressive drive is innate. He believed that an aggressive instinct (derived from the death instinct) periodically generates aggressive energy that must be discharged. This version assumes that people have a need to act aggressively and will so act unless safe outlets are found, such as through viewing aggression in the media.

Another version of the drive theory is Feshbach's (1971). For Feshbach, aggressive drive is a learned desire to retaliate when provoked (i.e., a desire to hurt). The drive is stimulated by provocation, which is distinct from the natural, built-in emotional response of anger, whose primary adaptive function is "expressive, serving as a warning signal to other organisms" (p. 285). Expression of anger is really more like what others have called *reactive aggression* and is a defensive, self-protective response to provocation. Learning how to appropriately express anger can be beneficial because it mobilizes one to take care of oneself (Greenberg & Safran, 1987). Aggressive drive is more like *proactive aggression* and is a motivated desire to inflict pain on others. Encouraging the expression of aggressive drive could easily lead to reinforcement of the desire to hurt, thereby increasing the probability of future aggression. Therefore, some kinds of expression can be beneficial and others not.

Because of such complications and for purposes of understanding psychotherapy I focus on catharsis as the expression of emotion in this chapter.

Empirical Phenomenon

Empirically people often report feeling better after having expressed an emotion such as anger or sadness. The existence of this phenomenon is easily demonstrated by asking a random group of people whether they have ever had this experience. At least some will so report (some will also report that it did not help). More formally, a survey found that many people believe that letting out anger is beneficial (Steinmetz, 1977).

The distinction between catharsis as a theoretical explanation (the hydraulic model) and catharsis as an empirical phenomenon is crucial. Most of the debates confuse these two. The hydraulic theoretical model would lead us to assume that expression is always good. Yet, as opponents of catharsis gleefully point out, there is no dearth of evidence showing that expression frequently is not helpful and can even be harmful (e.g., Bushman et al., 1999). On the other hand, viewing catharsis as an empirical phenomenon suggests more differentiated questions and perspectives. First, when and where is expression helpful? Expression might be beneficial in the special relationship of psychotherapy but not necessarily in everyday life relationships (Greenberg & Safran, 1987). Second, it may benefit some people but not others (Kennedy-Moore & Watson, 1999). If we do not assume that expression is helpful because it drains off emotions, then we ask what factors distinguish situations in which expression is helpful versus nonhelpful? I look at some of these factors in this chapter, in the discussion of how an empathic workspace encourages beneficial expression.

Direct Versus Vicarious

Another important distinction is between catharsis involving the direct expression of emotion or drive and the vicarious experience of expression through either the viewing of media material (television, movies, drama, novels) or through internal fantasy activity. Much of the dispute on catharsis rests on debate over whether it is beneficial or harmful to observe aggressive material or to aggressively fantasize (Eron, chapter 2; Fowles, 1999; Freedman, 1984; Huesmann & Eron, 1986; Huesmann & Reynolds, chapter 12; Tedeschi & Felson, 1994).

However, direct and vicarious catharsis can only be seen as reflecting the same phenomenon if one adheres to the hydraulic model, which assumes that all of these activities drain off affect or drive. Taking another theoretical position, direct expression and watching, reading, or listening to media material and fantasizing are quite different, and there is no reason to assume that these kinds of experiences operate in the same ways. Furthermore, even these activities may require additional distinctions: Is viewing a drama the same as reading a novel or a poem? Is all fantasy the same? In this chapter I focus on direct expression in psychotherapy and not on watching media depictions.

Emotional Expression Alone versus Expression as a Complex Whole-Person Act

Theorists who hold to the hydraulic model focus on the expression of emotion. There is reason to believe that the activation and experiencing of emotion is an important component of change in psychotherapy (Greenberg & Safran, 1987; Kennedy-Moore & Watson, 1999; Safran & Greenberg, 1991). Cognitive–behaviorists believe that emotions associated with dysfunctional thoughts and behaviors must be present and "hot" in the therapy situation to be altered (e.g., Barlow, 1988; Foa & Rothbaum, 1997; Safran & Greenberg, 1982).

However, when people talk about the acts of expression that make them feel better, they are not talking about expressive acts that are purely emotion, even if all they are doing is crying. They are almost always also verbalizing thoughts and perceptions, and if they are not verbalizing them, they are thinking to themselves as they express. The expressive acts that can be therapeutic are holistic acts: They include thoughts and feelings. Unless we could decorticate people as they express it is hard to imagine that there could ever be an act of pure emotional expression. Bob, in the example presented at the opening of this chapter, is holistically thinking, verbalizing, and engaging in motoric behavior as he expresses emotion.

Therefore in this chapter, when I refer to *expression* I mean a holistic act that includes thoughts and feelings and in therapy is done in an interpersonal context. When individuals engage in the activity of expressing their problems to a therapist, they are engaging in a complex set of interpersonal and cognitive–affective activities. Expression in therapy usually involves at least two other things: (a) self-disclosing to another person (an interpersonal act) and (b) thinking out loud. To be even more specific, when I express anger to a therapist I am probably (a) experiencing the anger as well as expressing it, (b) engaging in complex verbal behavior, (c) thinking as I express and trying to make sense out of my experience, (d) observing and noticing my own reactions, (e) observing the therapist's reaction to my expression, (f) trying to make myself clear to the therapist, (g) trying to explain myself to another human being, (h) searching my memory and relating this experience to my values and beliefs, and so on. This complex web of emotions and cognitions applies even if the focus of the therapeutic activity is on emotional expression. It applies even when the activity involves physical acts of expression, such as hitting pillows with rubber bats.

In addition, the "cathartic" experience of relief associated with expression is not tied exclusively to emotion. For example, people often feel a sense of relief when they finally tell the truth about something that they have been holding back. Furthermore, relief can be experienced as a consequence of expressing a thought associated with positive emotions. Consider a woman who is "bursting" to tell her supervisor about her new idea. Expressing the idea may lead to the same feeling of relief and satisfaction that expressing an emotion may lead to. The cathartic experience of relief comes from the sharing of information (although emotion is also involved). The woman does not feel a sense of relief because she has shared an emotion with her supervisor but because she has shared her idea.

Therefore, I focus on the therapeutic benefits of expression holistically conceived and argue that, although emotion is an important part of it, we cannot really understand why expression can be helpful if we only focus on its emotional component.

The Crux of the Debate: Is Expression Helpful or Harmful?

The debate over catharsis has been primarily between two different theoretical models: the hydraulic model and cognitive–behavioral views. The hydraulic model posits that expression is beneficial because emotions are quantities, like fluids or energies, that build up inside and create havoc if not expressed. They may drive the person to behave in dysfunctional ways. Expression is beneficial because it drains off emotion, thereby freeing up productive thinking, reducing internal distress, and allowing the person to choose more constructive behavior.

In contrast cognitive–behavioral views have held that expression of emotion can be harmful. Behavioral views (Eron, chapter 2) originally viewed expression as a behavior that gets strengthened through rehearsal. Contrary to being beneficial, anger expression would increase anger and destructive behavior. More recent cognitive–behavioral views (e.g., Eron, chapter 2; Huesmann & Reynolds, chapter 12) see behaviors such as expressing anger or fantasizing about anger as the rehearsal and thus strengthening of cognitive scripts and schemas. Thus, talking about anger to an empathic therapist who does not intervene or challenge one's perspective will merely strengthen the dysfunctional ways in which one is seeing the situation, along with attendant emotional reactions.

Ironically, despite this negative view of expression, one cognitive–behavioral treatment heavily emphasizes expression. Foa and Rothbaum's (1997) treatment for posttraumatic stress disorder rests on having the traumatized person express and describe his or her traumatic experience, including the relevant feelings, over and over to a tape recorder. The theoretical rationale does not rest on the value of emotional expression per se. Instead, the theoretical mechanism is exposure: exposing oneself to the traumatic experience and the attendant emotions habituates one and extinguishes the negative emotional responses. Nonetheless, the empirical process is similar to that advocated by those who believe that emotional expression is beneficial.

The Evidence

A thorough review of the research relevant to catharsis is beyond the bounds of this chapter. Instead, I note that there is evidence on both sides of the conflict. There are studies showing that expression can be dysfunctional and harmful (e.g., Bushman et al., 1999) and studies showing that expression can be beneficial. A comprehensive review is given in Kennedy-Moore and Watson (1999; but see also Bohart, 1980; Nichols & Efran, 1985).

In general, several reviewers have concluded that the hydraulic model is probably wrong but that expression can be helpful if (a) it leads to some kind of cognitive restructuring, and (b) it has some interpersonal benefits (Bohart, 1980; Kennedy-Moore & Watson, 1999; Greenberg & Safran, 1987; for a specific theoretical view of how expression might have an important interpersonal role, see Bloom-Feshbach and Bloom-Feshbach, chapter 15). In other words, expression is not helpful because of its hydraulic benefits but instead because of more complex problem-solving and interpersonal aspects. Next, I present a theoretical model that synthesizes theory and research to explain how expression in psychotherapy can be beneficial.

CONSTRUCTIVE EXPRESSION IN PSYCHOTHERAPY: AN ALTERNATIVE MODEL

Most models of psychotherapy are "therapist-centric" (Bickman & Salzer, 1996); they present psychotherapy as something therapists do to clients. Techniques and procedures are viewed along the lines of the drug metaphor (Stiles & Shapiro, 1989), as medical-like treatments that operate on dysfunctional processes in clients. In contrast, Karen Tallman and I (Bohart & Tallman, 1999; Tallman & Bohart, 1999) have argued that research evidence suggests that the primary healing force in psychotherapy comes from the client. Therapy ultimately works by mobilizing clients' strengths and their proactive self-healing processes. The therapeutic relationship, as well as therapeutic procedures and methods, are prosthetic devices that aid clients in their self-healing efforts.

Tallman and I (Bohart & Tallman, 1999) have presented a model of progressively active facilitation of client self-healing by the therapist. Different clients need different things at different times. The most basic prosthetic offered by the therapist is the provision of a safe, structured "workspace" in which clients can do their work. Many clients need nothing more than an empathic listener to solve personal problems: a place to think, talk out loud, spread ideas and problems out, look at them, reflect, and feel and experience. Others require more active therapist interventions, such as externally provided insight (e.g., psychodynamic interpretation), cognitive restructuring (cognitive therapy), or exposure and skills training (behavior therapy). In this chapter I focus on the provision of an empathic workspace because it provides a case of relatively pure client expression. I say "relatively pure" because the therapist is not an inert ingredient. The therapist's empathic reflections provide support and help clients clarify. However, their primary function is to support productive client expressive activities rather than to guide how the client sees things or behaves. Tallman and I (Bohart & Tallman, 1999) discussed some of the processes involved in clients self-healing through expression. I extend that discussion by examining how clients use such a workspace to engage in productive personal thinking and processing.

The Empathic Workspace

An *empathic workspace* is a therapeutic relationship in which the therapist listens carefully to receive and understand client expressions of both thoughts and affects and responds with empathic reflections. Empathic reflections are responses designed to help the therapist check understanding of the client's expression; they are not designed to "give feedback" in the form of providing alternative points of view, provocative questions, or advice. The underlying structure of an empathic reflection is "If I understand you correctly, you're saying/feeling/experiencing/wanting to do. . ."

Given an empathic workspace, many clients can productively think through their problems themselves. Evidence for this contention comes from controlled studies that have found that client-centered therapy can be helpful for a wide range of client problems (Elliott, 1996; Greenberg, Elliott, & Lietaer, 1994; Greenberg & Watson, 1998). Another study, by Burton, Parker, and Wollner found that breast cancer patients about to undergo surgery who received a single 45-minute preoperative interview from their surgeons dealing with a variety of concerns and issues related to the surgery had less distress about body image, anxiety, and depression and were coping with the results of surgery better at a 1-year follow-up than were control patients who did not have the interview. The surgeons were trained in empathic listening and encouraged to allow the patient to express feelings but made no active attempts to intervene therapeutically.

But how do clients grow in an empathic-listening climate[1] without the therapist actively intervening to alter clients' beliefs and behaviors? The

---

[1]Other data have shown that expression has benefits, even when not done in an empathic-listening context. Journaling has a variety of physical and mental health benefits (see Pennebaker, 1990). Expressing into a tape recorder can be beneficial (Segal & Murray, 1994; Schwitzgabel, 1961). An empirically supported treatment for posttraumatic stress disorder (Foa & Rothbaum, 1997), for instance, has as its most basic component the client's expressing her traumatic experience over and over again into a tape recorder.

hydraulic model would hold that the treatment is effective because the client has the opportunity to "vent." Cognitive–behaviorists would be skeptical that such a climate can help. To quote Burns (1980),

> when you do feel better as a result of achieving emotional release with an empathic and caring therapist, the sense of improvement is likely to be short lived if you haven't significantly transformed the way you evaluate yourself and your life . . . if the therapist does not provide objective feedback about the validity of your self-evaluation, you may conclude that [he or she] agrees with you. . . . As a result you will probably feel even more inadequate. (p. 60)

In the long run clients should be worse off because all they have done is "rehearsed" their dysfunctional thoughts and feelings and perhaps had them "reinforced" by the therapist's empathy.

Both of these perspectives overlook a third alternative, that under appropriate conditions clients are themselves capable of thinking and reprocessing their experience as they express. A highly active, synthetic, complex cognitive–affective process can occur. The two competing models—hydraulic and reinforcement/rehearsal (e.g., cognitive–behavioral)—are both models of human mindlessness. The hydraulic model assumes that emotion and drive are like "fluids" or energies that can be discharged through either direct or vicarious expression. Thinking and cognition have no role. The opposing point of view, although cognitive, still assumes, paradoxically, a "mindless" position—expression "stamps in" cognitive scripts and schemas. Thinking itself is scripted and runs off like a computer program. No possibility of active client self-generated thinking and reprocessing exists in this model either. Cognitive change in schemas is initiated from outside by the therapist. Thus, neither model portrays the person as capable of generative thinking.

I argue that expression can be helpful if it provides the opportunity for an active, thinking human being to use his or her own cognitive-processing capabilities to work through problems and to self-heal. For this to occur, the therapeutic context must foster and support a therapeutic state of mind and effective self-healing and processing activities on the part of the client.

How Does an Empathic Workspace Help?

Not all individuals seem to learn productively and process their problems when they express. The reinforcement position is partly correct in that sometimes individuals may express anger and simply become more angry (Bohart, 1980) and more mired in their dysfunctional states of mind. I suggest that one factor involved in whether clients in psychotherapy can productively use expression to think through and reprocess problems and feelings is if they are in a therapeutic state of mind. Clients can either enter therapy in a state of mind ready to work on their problems or in a state of mind that precludes therapeutic work. If they enter therapy in a dysfunctional state of mind, the therapeutic environment must be such that it promotes them moving into a more reflective, productive state of mind. The therapist's provision of an empathic workspace is one key component of such an environment.

Stress and Threat as Precipitators of Dysfunctional Thinking and Processing

When clients first enter therapy they are often in a dysfunctional state of mind. They are feeling demoralized, overstressed, and helpless. Such conditions are not optimal for them to use their capacities for productive problem-solving and creative thinking. Instead, they are more likely to be defensive and to think in various dysfunctional ways. Theorists of psychotherapy have written extensively on these dysfunctional client states of mind, including discussions of repression, resistance, defense, dysfunctional cognitive processing or irrational thinking, avoidance of feeling, intellectualization, and so on. Clients who enter therapy who are acting defensive, ruminating, overfocusing on external causes of their problems, feeling helpless, acting passively, presenting "canned" versions of their problems, not reflecting but rather simply reporting on their experience and then passively waiting for the therapist to come up with the answers, and thinking in general and abstract terms will be less likely to be able to engage productively in therapy. Unless they are able to get out of such negative mindsets and switch to a more productive mindset, expressing their feelings and thoughts in therapy will not be likely to help. Moreover, expression may simply mire them deeper and deeper in their problems, as reinforcement theorists have suggested.

When clients come to therapy they are operating under conditions that are more likely to induce, magnify, or reinforce a dysfunctional state of mind. Stress and threat create many of the dysfunctional processing characteristics that interfere with therapeutic work. According to Pennebaker (1989) research has shown that stress lowers the level of a person's thinking. The breadth of their thinking tends to narrow. They do not feel "free" to stand back and scan. Their attention stays focused only on the most immediate source of threat, and they lose context. Pennebaker (1989) also noted that under conditions of high stress individuals are less likely to engage in self-reflection. Finally, individuals are less likely to be aware of their emotions.

Stress or other forms of cognitive overload also leads to a greater likelihood of the person operating with automatic beliefs instead of thinking (Wegner & Bargh, 1998). For instance, Gilbert, Tafarodi, and Malone (1993) found in a jury trial simulation that false information about a defendant was nevertheless believed by participants and affected their sentencing decisions if participants' attentional resources were diverted by a secondary task. Under cognitive load we are more likely to attribute others' behavior to their dispositions and to ignore situational constraints (Gilbert, 1989). This means that under conditions of threat or stress we might be more likely to blame others for our problems and not empathize with their perspective. This external attribution would be more likely to lead to anger toward other persons and to attack, avoidance, or defensive behaviors instead of to approach, problem-solving, or compromise behaviors. An example is Bob, the client who has been laid off and initially focuses his anger outward on his supervisor.

Wegner and his colleagues have found that "ironic processes," in which attempts to avoid doing something produce the very thing that one is trying to avoid, occur most when control processes are overwhelmed by distractions or stress (Wegner & Bargh, 1998). For instance, under cognitive load, people who try to control the expression of sexist thoughts (Wegner, Erber, Bowman, & Shelton, 1996) end up expressing more sexist thoughts than those who are not trying to control their expression. Thus, under stress or cognitive load, attempts to control drinking, obsessive thoughts, overeating, anxiety, or depression might paradoxically backfire to strengthen these states and behaviors.

Finally, stress may also precipitate a helpless or outcome-focused state of mind. Helplessness and an outcome-oriented state of mind can be either dispositional or situational (Dweck & Leggett, 1988). Dispositionally, it appears to be a product of holding entity beliefs rather than incremental beliefs about both intelligence and personality (Dweck & Leggett, 1988). Those who are more prone to helplessness believe that intelligence and personality are fixed and unchangeable. Thus, if one succeeds it is because one is good, whereas if one fails it is because one is bad and ineffective. In that case one has no control over success or failure. Situations can also trigger feelings of helplessness. In fact, situations of stress, cognitive overload, and severe trauma are particularly likely to trigger feelings of helplessness. For instance, Janoff-Bulman (1989) has suggested that one of the major outcomes of trauma is to make individuals feel that the world is no longer safe and predictable, a shift in mindset that makes an individual feel more helpless.

In sum, feelings of stress and trauma are more likely to create feelings of helplessness and an outcome-focused state of mind and to interfere with functional thinking. Being in an outcome-focused state of mind instead of a more functional process-focused state of mind is less likely to lead to effective problem-solving. Therefore, an individual under high stress is more likely to (a) externalize his or her problems and make negative dispositional attribution to others, such as his or her supervisor; (b) not think about the context, (c) have a narrowed focus of attention on the threat, and (d) be less self-reflective. He or she may be defensive. He or she may dwell on the injury, engage in ruminative thinking, going over and over a perceived injustice. A greater tendency to make a dispositional attribution to the other party involved increases the odds of antisocial or aggressive behavior because some research has found that aggressive children are more likely to attribute negative motives to others' behavior (Dodge, 1986). The loss of empathy and the loss of attention to context is also characteristic of those who act violently (Toch, 1992). These conditions could lead to an acting out of emotion instead of to a reflective self-examination of the situation. Even if the individual does not act out he or she may not behave in ways that are productive.

In the case of Bob, he enters therapy feeling a high level of stress and also helpless. As a result he is overfocused on the initial source of threat—his job loss—and what he perceives as the cause of that threat—his supervisor. He makes dispositional attributions to his supervisor—he sees his supervisor as treating him unfairly. He feels "driven" to focus again and again on how wronged he has been. He cannot get it out of his mind. He cannot let it go and focus on more productive thinking. The result is that, at the moment Bob comes into therapy, he is consumed with the experience of threat and is not able to think through in a more intelligent and proactive sense about what to do. Bob has probably talked to friends. Most likely, they commiserate for a moment and then immediately launch into advice: "forget about it and get a new job," or "don't let him get away with it—file a grievance." Such expression to friends has not helped support productive processing activities on his part and maybe even has made him feel more mired and ruminative. He has not been successful in processing this experience on his own because (a) he has no one who will "sit with him" while he does it; (b) if anyone does sit with him they do not supply the kind of careful empathic listening that can support his own productive processing; and (c) he does not really grant himself the emotional time to do it, despite the fact that it is all he can think about. Although he cannot get it off his mind, he keeps telling himself that he should be thinking more productively and tries to banish his anger at his supervisor. Like Wegner's (1994) research on ironic processes, such attempts to banish it only seem to make it linger stronger and stronger. His attempts to self-engineer (Gendlin, 1964) and tell himself rationally what he should do backfire and actually block him from "reprocessing" the loss. He does not "stay with" the pain and the sense of loss and betrayal. As a result he does not really give himself a chance to stand back, see this all in context, and then decide what to do, until he talks to the therapist.

Effective Client Processing—Therapeutic States of Mind

In contrast, if clients enter therapy in a productive, working state of mind, or if the therapeutic environment facilitates a shift into a working state of mind, then clients may productively benefit from expression. This is a state of mind in which clients are involved and absorbed in the work of therapy, optimally open to examining their problems, reflective, open to their experience of the problem and of relevant emotions, and creatively synthesizing or discovering new ways of being and behaving. Evidence is consistent with this proposition, in that client involvement and openness to experience appear to be the two most potent variables in predicting therapeutic success (Orlinsky, Grawe, & Parks, 1994; Orlinsky & Howard, 1986).

Below I sketch out a schematic of the components of this state of mind. This schematic is drawn from a variety of sources, including research, clinical observation, and theory.

1. The Client Is Reflective.

Clients sometimes come into therapy and do not reflect. Instead, they are defensive and self-justifying. Or they provide a canned account of their problem, do not themselves actively engage in reflecting on it, and wait for the therapist to tell them what to do. Or they focus only on what is wrong and repetitively go over how they are mistreated, how they are bad, how awful life is, and so on. They do not stand back to reflect on (a) the contexts of their problems; (b) the relationships of their problems to their own personal values, goals, and meanings; and (c) their own actions. Several research scales of effective client processing have at the low or ineffective end of the scale, unreflective, externalized accounts of problems and experiences (e.g., the Experiencing Scale, Mathieu-Coughlan & Klein, 1984; the Levels of Perceptual Processing Scale, Toukmanian, 1992; and the Assimilation of Problematic Experience Scale, Stiles et al., 1990). In contrast, effective client processing includes self-reflection on personal meanings, cognitions, emotions, and experiences (Mathieu-Couglan & Klein, 1984; Stiles et al., 1990; Toukmanian, 1992; Watson & Rennie, 1994). Watson and Rennie (1994) found that effective therapeutic processing was associated with adopting a reflective stance on one's experience.

2. Functional Thinking and Processing Are Based on Adopting a Preaffirmative Position.

A *preaffirmative position* (Jenkins, 1996) is one in which one suspends not only judgment but also old frames of reference in order to take a fresh look at the problem. This is one of the often-emphasized commonalities about productive therapeutic processing (Bohart & Todd, 1988). Freud originally tried to encourage the adoption of a preaffirmative position through the use of the free-association technique. Client-centered therapists adopt a nonjudgmental "tracking" of experience through their empathic reflections, which can provide a model for clients. Cognitive therapy actively encourages clients to stand back and suspend old ideas in order to consider the data anew. The encouragement of "mindfulness," of simple observing of experience, is another example of encouragement of adopting a preaffirmative position (Martin, 1997). Adopting a preaffirmative position and suspending preconceptions is also a key part of fostering creativity (Ward, Finke, & Smith, 1995) and new insight (Sternberg & Davidson, 1995).

3. Functional Thinking and Processing Include Adopting a Broad Perspective.

Adopting a broad perspective goes along with adopting a preaffirmative position. Clients stand back and see the broader context. This is similar to Selman's (1980) theory of perspective taking. More advanced levels of perspective taking allow individuals to move beyond their egocentric perspective. I speculate that a good therapeutic environment promotes clients moving from a narrow, egocentric perspective to a broader perspective within limits of the clients' cognitive development in that area. Pennebaker's (1989) levels of thinking scale, developed from his work on measuring the helpful effects of journaling on stress, found that higher levels of thinking were associated with a broader perspective.

4. Functional Thinking and Processing Are Dialectical.

Dialectical (Jenkins, 1996; Rychlak, 1994) means that the thinking poses questions to itself—comparing and contrasting alternative points of view and possibilities. It is not merely algorithmic and deductive, following a rigid chain of logic or applying pre-existing solutions and shoulds; it attempts to stand back and consider alternative perspectives, alternative sources of information, and so on, and to compare and contrast them and synthesize and integrate them. This is a key component in synthetic, creative thinking. It is the opposite of automatic schema or script activation.

5. Functional Thinking and Processing Include Being Personally Involved in the Activity.

This dimension of involvement is included in the Experiencing Scale (Mathieu-Coughlan & Klein, 1984), which has been found to correlate with outcome in therapy. Orlinsky et al. (1994) have concluded that client involvement in therapy is the best predictor of outcome. Rice and Kerr (1986) have found that a focused vocal tone, indicative of involvement, is correlated with therapeutic outcome, whereas an external vocal tone, more indicative of someone simply describing events, is not.

6. Therapy Deals with Personal Meaning.

Dealing with personal meaning is defined as examining the relationship of events in one's life and one's problems with respect to what things mean to the self. This includes the impact on the self in terms of one's experience, emotion, plans and goals, hopes and dreams, or values. Another way of saying this is that the client has to be self-reflective. An external focus on events seems to be unproductive (Mathieu-Coughlan & Klein, 1984; Toukmanian, 1992). The turning point on the Experiencing Scale is when the person begins to talk in terms of "I" and to reflect on personal meanings and the impact on the self of whatever experience the client is processing. Pennebaker (1989) has found higher levels of thinking associated with more use of the personal pronoun "I" and has argued that higher levels of thinking are more self-reflective. Personal meanings are what is most significant to the person and are intimately connected to emotion, which may be one reason accessing emotion in therapy is so important.

7. The Level of Material Lies Somewhere Between Too Detailed and Too Abstract.

In effective therapeutic processing, the way the client explores his or her problems seems to lie somewhere between being too abstract and being too detailed. Too-abstract thinking is distanced and intellectual and does not deal with the concrete experienced details of life (Mathieu-Coughlan & Klein, 1984; Toukmanian, 1992). It also often does not deal with personal meaning. Too-detailed thinking is wrapped up in the details, does not get the whole picture, and does not provide a broad perspective. Too-detailed thinking has been found to be less therapeutic (Mathieu-Coughlan & Klein, 1984; Toukmanian, 1992) and correlated with lower levels of thinking (Pennebaker, 1989). It may well be that effective therapeutic processing focuses on the "middle levels" of categorization that have been identified by Rosch (1978).

8. A Therapeutic State of Mind Is Experiential.

The converse of distanced, abstract intellectual exploration is being experientially involved in the exploration/learning process. The idea that functional processing in therapy includes a dialogue between intellectual, cognitive thinking and concrete, bodily, experiential aspects (e.g., using imagery, accessing concrete situations and memories, thinking in the context of concrete experiential exercises such as exposure and role-play activities, focusing on direct emotion, shifting between "left- and right-brain" processing and between verbal and nonverbal processing [Bucci, 1995; Martin, 1994]), goes back to Freud (1963). This idea has been emphasized theoretically by myself (Bohart, 1993), Greenberg and his colleagues (Greenberg & Safran, 1987; Watson & Greenberg, 1996), Gendlin (1964), Epstein (1990), Bucci (1995), and Martin (1994), among others.

The idea that insights have to be at the gut level to be useful has been mentioned by Beck (1987) from a cognitive perspective and by Shapiro

(1995) in the use of Eye Movement Desensitization and Reprocessing (EMDR). EMDR, which appears to be a useful treatment for trauma (Shapiro, 1995), is speculated to increase connections between memories that are stored in concrete, imagistic nondeclarative form and declarative knowledge. Similarly, learnings that occur through direct experience, such as "I can be effectively assertive," are more powerful than self-statements not tied to experiential data (Bandura, 1997). In general the principle is that cognitions and insights need to be tied to direct experience in one form or the other to be helpful. Insights need to arise in the context of direct experience, accessing experiential referents of past experiences (memories, images, etc.); or present experiences in therapy; or experiences created through training exercises, homework assignments, and the like.

9. Functional Thinking and Processing Involves Accessing and Involving Emotion.

The importance of therapy accessing and involving emotion has been stressed by both theoreticians and researchers (e.g., Greenberg & Paivio, 1997; Safran & Greenberg, 1991). Mohr, Soham-Salomon, Engle, and Beutler (1991) found that the expression of anger in therapy could be beneficial. Other research has shown that an emotional vocal tone correlates with positive outcome in therapy (Rice & Kerr, 1986). Pennebaker (1989) has developed a levels-of-thinking scale based on his studies of coping with stress through journaling. Accessing and dealing with emotion is a component of a high level of thinking, and the number of emotion words in journals has been found to correlate significantly with an overall high level of thinking score.

The emphasis on the activation of strong feeling is not limited to humanistic and experiential therapy approaches. I have previously noted that it is a key component in cognitive–behavior therapy as well. Mahrer, Fairweather, Passey, Gingras, and Boulet (1999) found that therapists of all persuasions used methods to promote the experiencing of strong feelings. Therefore, the presence of emotion appears to be an important component of an effective therapeutic processing state (Kennedy-Moore & Watson, 1999; Greenberg & Paivio, 1997; Greenberg & Safran, 1987; Mahrer, 1996; Safran & Greenberg, 1991).

For all approaches, the presence of emotion is important because it allows for reprocessing, not because of discharge aspects. Most would probably agree with Feshbach (1971), who has said,

> Most psychotherapists agree that the reduction in anger that occurs in patients for whom anger has been a major problem is primarily a result of insight and more refined discrimination rather than the cathartic expression of the affect. Cognitive reorganization may be a far more effective means of reducing violence than promoting its sublimated or free expression." (p. 288)

For cognitive–behavior therapists the presence of emotion facilitates the restructuring of dysfunctional cognitions (Safran & Greenberg, 1982), as well as the restructuring of fear structures through exposure (Foa & Rothbaum, 1997). For humanistic therapists the activation of emotion helps access more functional aspects of the personality (Greenberg & Paivio, 1997; Mahrer, 1996), as well as promote cognitive restructuring and insight (Bohart, 1980).

10. The Client Is in a Process-Focused State of Mind.

Following up on Dweck's (e.g., Dweck & Leggett, 1988) work, Tallman (1996; Bohart & Tallman, 1999) has suggested that in any given task situation individuals can be in either a process-oriented or an outcome-oriented state of mind. In a *process-oriented state of mind*, the primary focus of the individual's attention is on the task at hand, on learning, and on problem-solving. The individual is asking himself or herself questions such as: What can I do right now to begin to find solutions to this problem? A learner who encounters obstacles asks What are alternative strategies? Can I imagine or invent new ways of handling this? A learner who encounters failure asks What can I learn from this? What is the problem-solving information value here? Focusing on learning and mastery rather than on ultimate success or failure has a number of benefits. If something goes wrong or if he or she "fails," the focus is on the information that this provides for further problem-solving. He or she examines errors curiously, generates new hypotheses and, most important, attends to the task at hand. Attention is focused on problem-solving and not on blame neither in the environment nor in himself or herself. Basically, he or she does not engage in looking for dispositional attributions of things that he or she cannot change. Instead, he or she focuses on things that he or she can change. He or she will risk mistakes to learn and focus on the immediate demands of the task rather than think too far ahead to what the outcome might be. He or she adopts learning goals; that is, the focus is on how to learn to solve a problem rather than on performance goals or on how well he or she performs. Essentially, being process-focused is what humanistic therapists have more vaguely described as "living in the here and now."

In contrast, a person in an *outcome-oriented state of mind* focuses on success or failure but less so on the tasks and processes of learning. In any given moment he or she is asking Am I succeeding or failing? Am I doing it right? Am I adequate or inadequate? What are the consequences of this for my future life? If I fail now, am I doomed? Why can't I solve this? What is wrong with me that I can't solve this? What deficits or problems in my past have caused me to be paralyzed now? The result is that if things are going badly (i.e., he or she is "failing," as many people who come to therapy believe themselves to be), a client may give up prematurely; become passive and helpless; persist in a rigid, repetitive dysfunctional manner; or divert their attention from the task to either self-criticism or self-defense.

Clients often come to therapy in an outcome-oriented state of mind (Tallman 1996; Bohart & Tallman, 1999). They are feeling frightened and helpless, and their focus is on what has gone wrong and what could go wrong in the future, more so than on what can be done here and now. Tallman believed that many of the unproductive behaviors exhibited by clients, such as defensiveness, rationalization, resistance, rigid ruminative thinking, passivity, and the like, are the results of clients feeling threatened and helpless because they are in an outcome-oriented state of mind. Tallman argued that different approaches to therapy all have ways of helping clients shift into a process-focused, working state of mind. A supportive empathic-listening atmosphere is one element that can shift clients from an outcome-focused state of mind into a more process-focused state of mind. Feeling understood helps reduce fear, and clients' attention can move from panicky contemplation of negative outcomes to what can be done in the here and now. Feeling impotent and devalued often leads to aggressive feelings (Feshbach, 1964), and feeling understood can counter this by raising one's sense of efficacy (White, 1965). In addition, empathic listening and responding by the therapist is a process of carefully following the client's meanings in the moment. It models going step by step, thereby encouraging the client to "slow down" and begin to take things step by step themselves. Finally, empathic listening models a listening, observing, nonjudgmental attitude toward personal experience, thereby helping shift clients out of an outcome-focused state of mind.

CONSTRUCTIVE EXPRESSION

Once clients achieve a constructive-processing state of mind, how can they use the opportunity for expression to an empathic listener productively to alter their problems? There are two ways. First, self-disclosure and expression can lead to productive learning about the self in an interpersonal context. Second, expression can lead to reprocessing of destructive or harmful experience.

Accruing Benefits from an Empathic Interpersonal Context

Many clients inhibit feelings because they do not feel that they have a right to feel what they feel. When one holds feelings to oneself because one is ashamed of them, one (a) feels bad about oneself and thereby engages in self-invalidation (see Tangney, chapter 6), and (b) one disempowers oneself because feelings mobilize the person to take action (Greenberg &

Paivio, 1997). For instance, if a person feels that he or she does not have a right to anger, he or she may not feel that he or she has a right to defend himself or herself against injustice.

Inhibiting feelings takes physiological work (Stiles, 1995). In addition, inhibiting feelings increases the probability of ruminative thinking (Wegner & Lane, 1995). Therefore, expressing feelings to an empathic listener who does not make one feel the need to justify feelings will bring a feeling of relief simply because one is able to let one's guard down (S. Feshbach, personal communication, October 1997). The feeling of relief comes not from the discharge of the emotion, but rather from feeling free to openly express oneself. This may help "clear a space" for more productive cognitive work toward resolving whatever problems precipitated the distressing feelings.

In addition, there are important interpersonal learnings (see also Bloom-Feshbach and Bloom-Feshbach, chapter 15). Taking a feminist self-in-relation perspective, Jordan (1997) has talked about the importance of bringing feelings into relationships. Through expression and self-disclosure to an empathic listener, individuals learn that it is easier to bear feelings together than to bear them alone, and they learn better how to do this. Furthermore, individuals learn how to bring their own voice into relationships. In fact, it could be said that they discover their own voice through expression in such a relationship.

Reprocessing Destructive Experience

When clients are expressing in therapy they are not merely venting emotions. They are also thinking, to themselves (Rennie, 1990) and out loud to the therapist. Such thinking, in the context of experiencing of relevant emotions, can lead to constructive processing. There are several ways this can occur (described in more detail in Bohart & Tallman, 1999). If clients are in a productive processing state of mind, they can think in constructive ways that allow them to (a) observe and track their experience and articulate it in words, thus facilitating productive reflection on it (Watson & Greenberg, 1996; Watson & Rennie, 1994); (b) gain insights and new perspectives on their problems (Bohart & Tallman, 1999); (c) engage in role-taking activities that allow them to gain an outside perspective on themselves (Clark, 1993) while also enhancing the chances of their gaining an empathic perspective on the behavior of others; (d) engage in productive narrative "restorying" of the problematic circumstances (Harvey, Orbuch, Chwalisz, & Garwood, 1991; Pennebaker, 1990); (e) run mental simulations of possible problem solutions; and (f) discover creative, new solutions. In addition, they may reprocess negative emotional experiences through a spontaneously occurring exposure process.

Consider the example of Bob. What is going on when Bob expresses his problem to an empathic-listening therapist? First, he is opening up and self-disclosing. This by itself can be therapeutic (Pennebaker, 1990; Stiles, 1995). He is getting to say all the things he has been inhibiting, that he did not feel he had a right to say at work. By sharing his fear, anger, and concern with another person, who responds in a way that makes him feel like he is understandable, he feels validated. He feels less crazy (Bachelor, 1988). He feels less out of control. Also, the therapist's empathic concern makes him feel that his problem is sensible and that he is still okay even if he has been laid off and is feeling vulnerable. Second, as he expresses, he is actively working with the material. To put it into words, he has to actively construct an account—he is "account making" (Harvey et al., 1991). Research by Harvey and his colleagues has found that account-making helps people get over trauma. In actively constructing an account, Bob is sorting out relationships—among emotions, beliefs, and perceptions of what happened; thoughts about what to do; and so on. He is examining the implications of what has happened for his life. He may for the first time be articulating in words some of the implications that he has only dimly sensed until now (Watson & Rennie, 1994). Furthermore, by accessing and expressing his anger, he gets in touch with his right to be angry (i.e., his right, in essence, to protect and defend himself; Greenberg & Safran, 1987). Expressing the anger, then, is an act of self-validation and self-assertion, or "self-ownership." Similarly, by expressing his fear and vulnerability, he learns that it is okay to be vulnerable, and again this becomes a form of self-validation.

For Bob, the very act of expressing forces him to begin to take an outside perspective on his problem (Clark, 1993). He begins to see things more in context. He may begin to gain some insight into and some empathy for his supervisor.

Finally, Bob is not exploring in a distanced, abstract, intellectual way. He is "re-presenting" his experience to himself as he explores, and he re-exposes himself to the trauma of losing his job. Concrete images of his encounter with his supervisor flash into his head, along with the accompanying rage, shock, and humiliation. But in therapy he can have these experiences while reflecting on them in a safe place, allowing him to now begin to "reprocess" the experience. He begins to be able to see things in context more. He may see new connections. The "problem space" becomes clearer— the relationships become clearer, his priorities begin to stand out. Gaining some distance and seeing things in context, he begins to feel more in charge of the situation, and the sense of threat diminishes. What was initially peripheral and in the background—his concern about his own future—is now in the foreground, whereas what was in the foreground—his anger and outrage and sense of injustice—now becomes background. In the foreground, now, he feels more of a concern about what he is going to do to make his life work. And this is empowering. Even though Bob still feels frightened, he feels freer to focus more proactively on what needs to be done. The next steps might be for him to run some mental simulations of searching for new jobs and, in so doing, he might even make a creative discovery of a whole new career path—perhaps something he has always wanted to do but never took seriously before.

In sum, through expression to an empathic-listening other, a number of productive processes can occur that lead to constructive change. These will not necessarily occur. Some clients may require more support and structure than that provided by just an empathic workspace to move into a productive therapeutic state of mind and begin to resolve their problems. For such clients, the procedures and approaches of psychodynamic, experiential, strategic, and cognitive–behavior therapies may better "scaffold" their problem-solving and self-healing efforts. However, even in these approaches, the opportunity for the client to talk out problems in a supportive-listening context seems to be an important healing element (Phillips, 1984).

HOW DOES EMPATHIC LISTENING FACILITATE CONSTRUCTIVE EXPRESSION?

Due to space restrictions, I can only briefly sketch how providing an empathic-listening context and then using expression to productively process a personal problem help a person move from a dysfunctional state of mind into a more therapeutic state of mind (see Bohart, in press, for a more detailed account). Empathic listening and responding is not doing nothing. Intent empathic listening is virtually all that is needed with some clients, who can then "carry the ball" on their own. It is their desire to communicate their feelings and thoughts to an empathic-listening other, which seems to be sufficient for them to engage in the productive problem-solving processes described above. With other clients, more active empathic responding may be needed to help them engage in productive expression.

Empathic responding could be thought of as actively joining with and supporting of productive client processing. I have already noted that it can help support the client's moving from an outcome-oriented into a process-oriented state of mind by (a) reducing fear; (b) increasing a sense of personal effectiveness; (c) modeling and supporting a careful step-by-step process; and (d) modeling a listening, observing, nonjudgmental attitude toward personal experience. In addition, the therapist carefully listens and checks his or her understanding with empathic reflections. By so doing he or she supports the client's clarification of personal meanings and the client's closeness to the actual experience of problems so that thinking does not become too abstract. The therapist's attempts to test out understanding allow the client to step back and gain perspective on what he or she is saying. Finally, the therapist is "there" with the client emotionally. This provides support and also helps the discussion not become too abstract.

CONCLUSION

I hope it is clear that the expression of emotion in psychotherapy is part of a complex holistic act that includes cognitive, motoric, and interpersonal elements. These are all woven together, and the debate over whether the expression of emotion is helpful or not has been simplistic in its overfocus on emotion. When individuals express emotion they are also thinking, relating, and acting. To understand whether this is useful or not, one needs to look at the whole complex of activities that the individual is engaging in.

Expression in psychotherapy is therefore neither automatically beneficial nor automatically harmful. I have suggested that the two dominant models—the cathartic and the cognitive–behavioral—are both inadequate. The cathartic model simplistically assumes that expression should mechanistically be beneficial because it drains off negative affect. The cognitive–behavioral model simplistically assumes that expression should mechanistically be harmful because it strengthens the behavior of expressing, the underlying affect, and the cognitive scripts and schemas involved. Neither model assumes the possibility that, under the right conditions, individuals can use expression to engage in a complex set of cognitive–affective processing activities and to learn, think out new solutions, and reprocess problematic experience on their own.

As Greenberg and Safran (1987) have noted, expression may be beneficial in psychotherapy but may not be beneficial everywhere. On the way to therapy the client may be cut off by another motorist. The client rolls down his window and hollers obscenities at the other motorist. Will this be constructive? Probably not. Yet expressing his anger to the therapist when he gets to the office may be. Why the difference? The therapy situation is defined as a self-change/learning/problem-solving environment. In such an environment when the client expresses, he may know that he is expected to "work on" the problematic experience in a productive fashion. Therefore, when he expresses, he may begin to reflect on the meaning of the experience, try to understand it, and try to move toward productive ways of dealing with it. Expression is a step in a problem-solving process. However, in an altercation with another motorist, the person has neither the time nor the space to reflect on the meaning of his experience and to creatively learn and problem-solve. It is not a "self-change" context. The person much more likely will automatically act on his agendas and scripts. Anger expression in such a context, then, may act exactly as the cognitive–behaviorists (see Huesmann & Reynolds, chapter 12, and Eron, chapter 2) predict—to strengthen dysfunctional ways of perceiving, construing, feeling, and behaving in the situation. In sum, there is no simple relationship between expression (even expression that is heavily emotion focused) and constructive or destructive behavior.

REFERENCES

Bachelor, A. (1988). How clients perceive therapist empathy: A content analysis of "received" empathy. *Psychotherapy, 25*, 227–240.

Bandura, A. (1997). *Self-efficacy.* New York: W. H. Freeman.

Barlow, D. H. (1988). *Anxiety and its disorders.* New York: Guilford Press.

Beck, A. T. (1987). Cognitive therapy. In J. K. Zeig (Ed.), *The evolution of psychotherapy* (pp. 149–163). New York: Brunner/Mazel.

Bickman, L., & Salzer, M. S. (1996, August). *Dose–response, disciplines, and self-help: Policy implications of Consumer Reports findings.* Paper presented as part of the symposium "Consumer Reports Mental Health Survey Results—Practice and Policy Implications" at the Annual Meeting of the American Psychological Association, Toronto, Ontario, Canada.

Bohart, A. (in press). How empathy promotes client active self-healing. *Journal of Psychotherapy Integration.*

Bohart, A. (1980). Toward a cognitive theory of catharsis. *Psychotherapy: Theory, Research, and Practice, 17*, 192–201.

Bohart, A. (1993). Experiencing: The basis of psychotherapy. *Journal of Psychotherapy Integration, 3*, 51–67.

Bohart, A., & Tallman, K. (1999). *How clients make therapy work: The process of active self-healing.* Washington, DC: American Psychological Association.

Bohart, A., & Todd, J. (1988). *Foundations of clinical and counseling psychology.* New York: Harper & Row.

Bozarth, J. D. (1998). *Person-centered therapy: A revolutionary paradigm.* Ross-on-Wye, England: PCCS Books.

Bucci, W. (1995). The power of the narrative: A multiple code account. In J. W. Pennebaker (Ed.), *Emotion, disclosure, and health* (pp. 93–124). Washington, DC: American Psychological Association.

Burns, D. D. (1980). *Feeling good.* New York: William Morrow.

Burton, M. V., Parker, R. W., & Wollner, J. M. (1991). The psychotherapeutic power of a "chat": A verbal response mode study of a placebo attention control with breast cancer patients. *Psychotherapy Research, 1*, 39–61.

Bushman, B. J., Baumeister, R. F., & Stack, A. D. (1999). Catharsis, aggression, and persuasive influence: Self-fulfilling or self-defeating prophecies? *Journal of Personality and Social Psychology, 76*, 367–376.

Clark, L. F. (1993). Stress and the cognitive–conversational benefits of social interaction. *Journal of Social and Clinical Psychology, 12*, 25–55.

Dodge, K. A. (1986). A social information processing model of social competence in children. In M. Perlmutter (Ed.), *The Minnesota Symposium on Child Psychology* (Vol. 18, pp. 77–125). Hillsdale, NJ: Erlbaum.

Dweck, C. S., & Leggett, E. L. (1988). A social–cognitive approach to motivation and personality. *Psychological Review, 95*, 644–656.

Elliott, R. (1996). Are client-centered/experiential therapies effective? A meta-analysis of outcome research. In U. Esser, H. Pbast, & G. W. Speierer (Eds.), *The power of the person-centered approach: New challenges—Perspectives—Answers* (pp. 125–138). Koln, Germany: GwG Verlag.

Epstein, S. (1990). Cognitive–experiential self-theory. In L. A. Pervin (Ed.), *Handbook of personality: Theory and research* (pp. 165–192). New York: Guilford Press.

Feshbach, S. (1964). The function of aggression and the regulation of aggressive drive. *Psychological Review, 71,* 257–272.

Feshbach, S. (1971). Dynamics and morality of violence and aggression: Some psychological considerations. *American Psychologist, 26,* 281–292.

Feshbach, S. (1984). The catharsis hypothesis, aggressive drive and the reduction of aggression. *Aggressive Behavior, 10,* 91–101.

Foa, E. B., & Rothbaum, B. O. (1997). Treating the trauma of rape: Cognitive behavioral therapy for PTSD. New York: Guilford Press.

Fowles, J. (1999). *The violence against television violence.* Thousand Oaks, CA: Sage.

Freedman, J. L. (1984). Effect of television violence on aggressiveness. *Psychological Bulletin, 96,* 227–246.

Freud, S. (1963). Observations on "wild" psychoanalysis. In P. Rieff (Ed.), *Sigmund Freud: Therapy and technique.* New York: Crowell-Collier. (Original work published 1910.)

Gendlin, E. T. (1964). A theory of personality change. In P. Worchel & D. Byrne (Eds.), *Personality change.* New York: Wiley.

Gilbert, D. T. (1989). Thinking lightly about others: Automatic components of the social inference process. In J. S. Uleman & J. A. Bargh (Eds.), *Unintended thought* (pp. 189–211). New York: Guilford Press.

Gilbert, D. T., Tafarodi, R. W., & Malone, P. S. (1993). You can't not believe everything you read. *Journal of Personality and Social Psychology, 65,* 221–233.Greenberg, L. S., Elliott, R., & Lietaer, G. (1994). Research on experiential psychotherapies. In A. E. Bergin & S. L. Garfield (Eds.), *Handbook of psychotherapy and behavior change* (4th ed., pp. 509–542). New York: Wiley.

Greenberg, L. S., & Paivio, S. (1997). *Working with emotions in psychotherapy.* New York: Guilford Press.

Greenberg, L. S., & Safran, J. D. (1987). *Emotion in psychotherapy.* New York: Guilford Press

Greenberg, L. S., & Watson, J. C. (1998). Experiential therapy of depression: Differential effects of client-centered relationship conditions and process-experiential interventions. *Psychotherapy Research, 8,* 210–224.

Harvey, J. H., Orbuch, T. L., Chwalisz, K. D., & Garwood, G. (1991). Coping with sexual assault: The roles of account–making and confiding. *Journal of Traumatic Stress, 4,* 515–531.

Huesmann, L. R., & Eron, L. D. (1986). The development of aggression in American children as a consequence of television violence viewing. In L. R. Huesmann

& L. D. Eron (Eds.), *Television and the aggressive child: A cross-national comparison* (pp. 45–80). Hillsdale, NJ: Erlbaum.

Janoff-Bulman, R. (1989). Assumptive worlds and the stress of traumatic events: Applications of the schema construct. *Social Cognition, 7,* 113–138.

Jenkins, A. H. (1996, August). *Enhancing the patient's dialectical abilities in psychotherapy.* Paper presented at the symposium "How Clients Create Change in Psychotherapy: Implications for Understanding Change" at the annual meeting of the American Psychological Association, Toronto, Ontario, Canada.

Jordan, J. V. (1997). Relational development through mutual empathy. In A. Bohart & L. S. Greenberg (Eds.), *Empathy reconsidered: New directions in psychotherapy* (pp. 343–352). Washington, DC: American Psychological Association.

Kennedy-Moore, E., & Watson, J. C. (1999). *Expressing emotion: Myths, realities, and therapeutic strategies.* New York: Guilford Press.

Mahrer, A. R. (1996). The complete guide to experiential psychotherapy. New York: Wiley.

Mahrer, A. R., Fairweather, D. R., Passey, S., Gingras, N., & Boulet, D. B. (1999). The promotion and use of strong feelings in psychotherapy. *Journal of Humanistic Psychology, 39,* 35–53.

Martin, J. (1994). The construction and understanding of therapeutic change. New York: Teachers College Press.

Martin, J. (1997). Mindfulness: A proposed common factor. *Journal of Psychotherapy Integration, 7,* 291–312.

Mathieu–Coughlan, P., & Klein, M. H. (1984). Experiential psychotherapy: Key events in client-centered interaction. In L. N. Rice & L. S. Greenberg (Eds.), *Patterns of change* (pp. 194–212). New York: Guilford Press.

Mohr, D. C., Shoham-Solomon, V., Engle, D., & Beutler, L. E. (1991). The expression of anger in psychotherapy for depression: Its role and measurement. *Psychotherapy Research, 1,* 125–135.

Nichols, M. P., & Efran, J. S. (1985). Catharsis in psychotherapy: A new perspective. *Psychotherapy, 22,* 46–58.

Orlinsky, D. E., Grawe, K., & Parks, B. K. (1994). Process and outcome in psychotherapy—noch einmal. In A. E. Bergin & S. L. Garfield (Eds.), *Handbook of psychotherapy and behavior change* (4th ed., pp. 270–376). New York: Wiley.

Orlinsky, D. E., & Howard, K. I. (1986). Process and outcome in psychotherapy. in S. L. Garfield & A. E. Bergin (Eds.), *Handbook of psychotherapy and behavior change* (3rd ed., pp. 311–384). New York: Wiley.

Pennebaker, J. W. (1989). Stream of consciousness and stress: Levels of thinking. In J. S. Uleman & J. A. Bargh (Eds.), *Unintended thought* (pp. 327–350). New York: Guilford Press.

Pennebaker, J. W. (1990). Opening up: the healing power of confiding in others. New York: Morrow.

Phillips, J. R. (1984). Influences on personal growth as viewed by former psychotherapy patients. *Dissertation Abstracts International, 44,* 441A.

Rennie, D. L. (1990). Toward a representation of the client's experience of the psychotherapy hour. In G. Lietaer, J. Rombauts, & R. Van Balen (Eds.), *Client-centered and experiential therapy in the nineties* (pp. 155–172). Leuven, Belgium: Leuven University Press.

Rice, L. N., & Kerr, G. P. (1986). Measures of client and therapist vocal quality. In L. S. Greenberg & W. M. Pinsof (Eds.), *The psychotherapeutic process: A research handbook* (pp. 73–106). New York: Guilford Press.

Rosch, E. H. (1978). Principles of categorization. In E. Rosch & B. B. Lloyd (Eds.), *Cognition and categorization.* Hillsdale, NJ: Erlbaum.

Rychlak, J. F. (1994). *Logical learning theory.* Lincoln: University of Nebraska Press.

Safran, J. D., & Greenberg, L. S. (1982). Eliciting "hot cognitions" in cognitive behavior therapy: Rationale and procedural guidelines. *Canadian Psychology, 23,* 83–87.

Safran, J. D., & Greenberg, L. S. (1991). (Eds.), *Emotion, psychotherapy, and change.* New York: Guilford Press.

Schwitzgebel, R. (1961). *Streetcorner research: An experimental approach to the juvenile delinquent.* Cambridge, MA: Harvard University Press.

Schwitzgabel, R. (1961). Streetcorner research: An experimental approach to juvenile delinquency. Cambridge, MA: Harvard University Press.

Segal, D. L., & Murray, E. J. (1994). Emotional processing in cognitive therapy and vocal expression of feeling. *Journal of Social and Clinical Psychology, 13,* 189–206.

Selman, R. L. (1980). *The growth of interpersonal understanding.* New York: Academic Press.

Shapiro, F. (1995). *Eye movement desensitization and reprocessing.* New York: Guilford Press.

Steinmetz, S. K. (1977). *The cycle of violence.* New York: Praeger.

Sternberg, R. J., & Davidson, J. E. (Eds.). (1995). *The nature of insight.* Cambridge, MA: MIT Press.

Stiles, W. B. (1995). Disclosure as a speech act: Is it psychotherapeutic to disclose? In J. W. Pennebaker (Ed.), *Emotion, disclosure, and health* (pp. 71–92). Washington, DC: American Psychological Association.

Stiles, W. B., Elliott, R., Llewelyn, S. P., Firth-Cozens, J. A., Margison, F. R., Shapiro, D. A., & Hardy, G. (1990). Assimilation of problematic experiences by clients in psychotherapy. *Psychotherapy, 27,* 411–420.

Stiles, W. B., & Shapiro, D. A. (1989). Abuse of the drug metaphor in psychotherapy process-outcome research. *Clinical Psychology Review, 9,* 521–544.

Tallman, K. *The state of mind theory: Goal orientation concepts applied to clinical psychology.* Unpublished master's thesis, California State University Dominguez Hills.

Tallman, K., & Bohart, A. (1999). The client as common factor: Clients as self-healers. In M. A. Hubble, B. L. Duncan, & S. Miller (Eds.), *The heart and soul of change: The role of common factors in psychotherapy, medicine, and human services* (pp. 91–131). Washington, DC: American Psychological Association.

Tavris, C. (1982). *Anger: The misunderstood emotion.* New York: Simon & Schuster.

Tedeschi, J. T., & Felson, R. B. (1994). *Violence, aggression, and coercive actions.* Washington, DC: American Psychological Association.

Toch, H. (1992). *Violent men* (rev. ed.). Washington, DC: American Psychological Association.

Toukmanian, S. G. (1992). Studying the client's perceptual processes and their outcomes in psychotherapy. In S. G. Toukmanian & D. L. Rennie (Eds.), *Psychotherapy process research: Paradigmatic and narrative approaches* (pp. 77–107). Newbury Park, CA: Sage.

Ward, T. B., Finke, R. A., & Smith, S. M. (1995). *Creativity and the mind.* New York: Plenum Press.

Watson, J. C., & Greenberg, L. S. (1996). Emotion and cognition in experiential therapy: A dialectical constructivist perspective. In H. Rosen & K. Kuehlwein (Eds.), *Constructing realities* (pp. 253–276). San Francisco, CA: Jossey-Bass.

Watson, J. C., & Rennie, D. L. (1994). Qualitative analysis of clients' subjective experience of significant moments during the exploration of problematic reactions. *Journal of Counseling Psychology, 41,* 500–509.

Wegner, D. M. (1994). Ironic processes of mental control. *Psychological Review, 101,* 34–52.

Wegner, D. M., & Bargh, J. A. (1998). Control and automaticity in social life. In D. T. Gilbert, S. T. Fiske, & G. Lindzey (Eds.), *The handbook of social psychology* (4th ed., Vol. I, pp. 446–496). New York: McGraw-Hill.

Wegner, D. M., Erber, R., Bowman, R., & Shelton, J. N. (1996). *On trying not to be sexist.* Unpublished manuscript cited in Wegner, D. M., & Bargh, J. A. (1998).

Wegner, D. M., & Lane, J. D. (1995). From secrecy to psychopathology. In J. W. Pennebaker (Ed.), *Emotion, disclosure, and health* (pp. 25–46). Washington, DC: American Psychological Association.

White, R. W. (1965). The experience of efficacy in schizophrenia. *Psychiatry: Journal for the Study of Interpersonal Processes, 28,* 199–211.

IV

WHAT HAVE WE LEARNED?

17

WHAT HAVE WE LEARNED?

ARTHUR C. BOHART AND DEBORAH J. STIPEK

The high school murders by alienated adolescents in Littleton, Colorado, captured more public and political attention than most events involving violence, but shootings and other violent acts are hardly unique to the small community in which those murders occurred. The Littleton tragedy was followed closely by other noteworthy shootings by White supremacists in Chicago and in northern California. Less dramatic acts of aggression against humans and property occur daily. What does this book say about preventing such aggression and about promoting interpersonally responsible and caring behavior?

One thing is clear, the promotion of prosocial and the reduction of antisocial behavior involves many different factors. Accordingly, many sites and strategies for intervention were reviewed by the authors in this volume. Chapters by L. Rowell Huesmann and Meredith A. Reynolds (chapter 12) and by Edward Zigler and Sally J. Styfco (chapter 11) point out that no single intervention program has had more than modest effects, presumably because extant programs are short and address only one or a few factors affecting developmental pathways and behavior. Evidently the promotion of constructive and the decrease of destructive behavior require a multifaceted and long-term approach.

We concur with Zigler and Styfco that primary prevention is the most effective strategy—providing children with the social environments, parenting practices, and opportunities for success in school that are known to support the development of constructive developmental pathways (although we prefer the term *primary promotion* to *primary prevention*, to focus attention on promoting positive pathways rather than preventing negative pathways). Additional efforts will be required, however, for children who do not have the advantages of such facilitative environments or who for some other reason show signs of inappropriate aggressive behavior. We differentiate between two levels of intervention for these children, intervention to prevent problems before they become serious and remediation of problems after they have developed.

When we use the term *prevention*, we therefore are referring to what community psychologists have called both primary and secondary prevention–intervention to prevent problems before they even develop, or the early identification of relatively minor problems followed by intervention, often consisting of adjustments in the child's social or academic contexts. Making changes in school practices to help students who are behind in reading before their skill deficiencies create serious learning problems is an example of prevention, as discussed by Deborah Stipek (chapter 14). *Remediation* involves attempts to fix problems after they have become serious or to reverse clearly defined negative pathways. Clinical interventions, such as psychotherapy, are an example.

We organize what we have learned from the authors of the chapters in this volume around three major topics: (a) the developmental pathways to prosocial and antisocial/aggressive behavior; (b) factors within the individual that cause or mediate behaving either prosocially or antisocially; and (c) factors in the social environment that contribute to the development and maintenance of constructive and destructive behaviors, both directly and by affecting mediators of behavior. We weave promotion, intervention, and remediation considerations throughout our discussion.

DEVELOPMENTAL PATHWAYS

Is behavior stable over developmental periods? If so, how early does it stabilize? Are the pathways of development different for boys and girls? How do we understand the meaning of destructive behavior to the actor? These and related questions are considered below.

Stability

Stability is a key issue in the development of prosocial and aggressive behavior. The degree to which such behavior is stable, when it stabilizes, and why it is stable have important implications for how and when we try to influence it.

Theoretical Considerations

Some theories of human behavior promote the notion of stability. For example, one view of personality development focuses on internal structures as the causes of behavior. The structures may be genetically based or conceptualized as underlying dispositions (personality traits) to behave in certain ways, which some believe have a genetic component (Caspi, 1998). There is some evidence to suggest the relevance of genetic factors in both prosocial and antisocial/aggressive behavior (Coie & Dodge, 1998; Eisenberg & Fabes, 1998), and although a genetic component does not necessarily manifest itself in the same way across developmental periods, it is often believed that if something is genetic it is relatively immutable.

Psychodynamic theories have stressed early childhood causes of the development of personality structures. Traditional psychodynamic theorists also favored the idea of personality traits, although traits were seen as developing out of early experiences rather than based on genetic predispositions. Cognitive representations have been stressed by recent psychodynamic theories as the enduring structures that mediate behavior throughout life. Attachment theory (Bowlby, 1988) has been one of the most influential. The early attachment between mother and child is believed to significantly influence later development. The underlying mechanism is the development of the child's "working model" of relationships. In a secure attachment, the child develops a working model of self and relationships that fosters effective social behavior and relationships later.

Robert B. Cairns and Beverly D. Cairns (chapter 1) oppose the idea that behavior is as fixed and determined as both genetic and psychoanalytic theory are often interpreted to presume. They note that current evidence suggests biological mechanisms are partners with social experiences. Although there is a clear role of inherent factors in the development of aggression, genetic effects for aggressive behavior are highly malleable over time. Their effects are dynamic and can be manipulated and modified by environmental events. Developmental timing has a significant impact on their role. In particular, learning mechanisms at different stages of development can either promote preservation of previously existing genetically influenced patterns, or modify them.

Using attachment to illustrate their point, Cairns and Cairns propose that researchers have been biased toward gathering evidence to confirm the stability of attachment categories over time. For instance, researchers have tried to show that an insecurely attached infant will have insecure adult attachments in love relationships. Although there is some evidence for this prediction, Cairns and Cairns argue that these researchers have tended to overlook or minimize research showing malleability of attachment phenomena over contexts, development, persons, and conditions. The authors conclude that social behavior is multidetermined and dynamic over time. Many different factors dynamically and continuously interweave to create change or stability in developmental pathways, and there is danger in looking primarily for continuity.

Notwithstanding Cairns and Cairns's warning, the assumption that the internal structures that constitute an individual's personality develop early and then remain relatively fixed is widely held and may be one reason why intervention programs have tended to focus on early and middle childhood and not on adolescence. The guiding belief is that if early intervention can build in the right structures, the child should be set on the right path from then on: As the twig is bent, the child will grow. If Cairns and Cairns are correct, however, there is no reason to expect early intervention to alter a developmental pathway so that it is impervious to later events.

Research suggesting that the effects of extant intervention programs diminish over time supports Cairns and Cairns's notion of continued malleability. Myrna B. Shure (chapter 13) similarly notes the need for "boosters" to her early training efforts to maintain gains, and both Huesmann and Reynolds and Zigler and Styfco promote longer intervention programs that continue into adolescence.

Empirical Evidence

Paolo Albiero and Alida Lo Coco (chapter 10), Inger M. Endresen and Dan Olweus (chapter 7), and Gian Vittorio Caprara, Claudio Barbaranelli, and Concetta P. Pastorelli (chapter 9) all present evidence suggesting developmental changes in prosocial behavior, empathy, and aggressive/antisocial behavior throughout childhood and into adolescence. There is also evidence for some stabilization of aggressive pathways as early as middle childhood (Lea Pulkkinen, chapter 8). But the correlations Pulkkinen found between aggression in childhood and in adulthood are low to moderate, suggesting some malleability as well. Moreover, predictability does not imply immutability. Pulkkinen hypothesizes that the stability observed in antisocial/aggressive behavior from childhood to adulthood may primarily be explained by a small subset of individuals with serious problems. Pulkkinen also finds, congruent with other research (e.g., Coie & Dodge, 1998), that antisocial behavior in adults begins to decline by age 26, and by age 36 many offenders have significantly decreased their offending.

These findings on developmental change suggest that early intervention may be particularly useful. But they also support Zigler and Styfco's contention that intervention programs need to continue at least into adolescence. Even if developmental pathways stabilize in early adolescence, stability is not so high as to suggest immutability.

Although research so far has not found clinical intervention with adult offenders to be particularly productive (Huesmann & Reynolds, chapter 12), the finding that most young offenders eventually cease offending offers reason for optimism and possibly clues for remediation. Pulkkinen speculates that some of the factors involved in this gradual reduction in adulthood include maturation, the influence of other people (often a spouse), environmental changes, and the negative consequences of offending. Perhaps a better understanding of why most young offenders spontaneously change could be used to develop more effective remediation programs.

Mechanisms of Stability

What are the underlying mechanisms of stability? Personality traits are often referred to as an explanation for stability in prosocial and antisocial/aggressive behavior. We consider the concept of personality traits as more a description than an explanation for continuity in behavior patterns, and the authors in this volume offer other criticisms. Pulkkinen claims that aggression is too heterogeneous a category to be considered a single personality trait. Furthermore, the type and intensity of aggressive behavior depends on context and social learning factors. And aggression takes on different forms as children develop. Pulkkinen shows, for example, that aggression and criminality in adulthood are better predicted by a pattern of norm-breaking behavior in childhood than by aggression alone.

Pulkkinen proposes an alternative explanation for apparent stability in behavioral patterns. She suggests that skills, particularly related to self-control in frustrating and conflictual situations, rather than a trait, are at issue. The picture she paints is even more complex because self-control is a multidimensional set of skills involving the ability to take multiple perspectives, choose positive modes of behavior, and experience positive emotions. Low self-control results from limited, self-centered perceptions, choosing unsanctioned and ineffective modes of behavior, and experiencing only negative emotions. Pulkkinen proposes that stability in behavior is the result of persistence in skill levels, not underlying personality traits.

In emphasizing skills, Pulkkinen's explanation of stability is congruent with the perspectives of Shure and of Huesmann and Reynolds in this volume. Continuity in norm-breaking behavior is not due to some genetically based predisposition to act antisocially, but to a serious lack of self-control and social-problem-solving skills for dealing with difficult situations. One implication for intervention, taken by Shure and discussed by Huesmann and Reynolds, is to teach better social-problem-solving skills associated with prosocial behavior.

Caprara et al. also address the issue of stability, suggesting that the stability found in behavioral ratings, whether done by others or the self, is to some degree based on external factors such as the social attributions of other people.

They claim that the reciprocal expectations among actors, targets, and bystanders influence the perception of stability in a particular individual. A consensus of people agreeing with one another and an individual's reputation may serve as both effects and causes of stability to act, feel, and respond in a consistent way over time.

Consider, for example, a child who gets labeled as aggressive. Others' consistent perceptions and reactions to the child in terms of the label may create a self-fulfilling prophecy. If such a child gets involved in a conflict he or she may more likely be seen as the provoker of the conflict or as a troublemaker and be treated more harshly, provoking resentment in the child and a greater likelihood of acting out at a later time. Or the child may be rejected, leading to resentment and aggressive feelings. Once impressions are formed, they are remarkably resistant to modification and thus continue to exert pressure for particular kinds of behavior.

The concept of personality trait, as an explanatory mechanism for constructive and destructive behavior, does not lend itself well to intervention. Skill deficits and social–interactional role expectations, in contrast, have specific implications for promotion, intervention, and remediation. Parenting practices need to foster the development of effective social skills, and intervention programs need to increase the skills of children who show some evidence of deficits, such as those described by Shure and Huesmann and Reynolds. If Cairns and Cairns are correct, however, we should not expect early skills training by itself to be sufficient. As children mature and face new and more complex conflict situations, new skills are demanded and therefore need to be trained.

To the degree that social–interactional role expectations promote consistent antisocial or aggressive behavior, adults and peers need to try to avoid labeling children with trait names like "aggressive," or "bully." It might be important, as Stipek has suggested, to encourage teachers to develop more differentiated views of their students and particularly to look for and point out counterexamples to some of their preconceptions. It might sometimes be useful for a child with a seriously bad reputation to get a fresh start in a new school.

Gender

Are boys more prone to aggression than girls, and are girls more empathic and prosocial than boys, as is commonly believed and as the study described in the chapter by Caprara et al. found? If so, interventions would apparently need to be focused more on boys.

Current evidence suggests a more complex picture. Differences between girls and boys may have more to do with how aggression and empathy are expressed than with underlying potentialities (Coie & Dodge, 1998; Eisenberg & Fabes, 1998). For example, boys may be more likely to express aggression physically, whereas girls may express it more relationally, such as through social rejection. Girls may be more likely to present themselves as empathic because it is more in keeping with the gender role they have learned.

In the current volume, Olweus and Endresen and Albiero and Lo Coco found that girls scored as more empathic than boys. The evidence suggests, however, that the difference was not necessarily in underlying capacity but possibly in how boys and girls used their empathic capacities. Albiero and Lo Coco found that boys and girls differed in the emotions with which they were empathic, suggesting gender-related attunement to different aspects of the social environment. Olweus and Endresen found that the target of empathy made a difference. Both boys and girls were more empathic with girls than with boys. As girls got older, their empathy for both boys and girls increased. Boys' empathy for girls increased, but their empathy for boys actually decreased. Olweus and Endresen propose that the gender difference is explained by gender role expectations, boys being expected to be "tough" with other boys. If their analysis is correct, the decrease does not appear to reflect a loss in underlying capacity, but rather a shift in how boys use empathy with other boys.

These observed gender differences suggest the possible benefit of different interventions for boys and girls. For example, if boys and girls are prone to empathize with different emotions, then efforts to enhance empathy may be most effective when particular emotions are targeted. Helping both boys and girls increase their ability to empathize with all emotions should increase their capacities for situationally sensitive prosocial behavior. The findings on gender difference suggest also the value of efforts to make the expression of empathy more acceptable for boys.

The possibility that gender differences observed in research represent differences in how boys and girls use their capacities for empathy, prosocial behavior, and aggression suggests also that we not be fooled by phenotypic differences in expression. Research methods that examine subtle differences in the use and expression of capacities as well as the capacities themselves are needed.

A Constructive Perspective on the Development of Destructive Behavior

Cairns and Cairns observe that social scientists often fail to appreciate the adaptive qualities of children's problem behavior. They point out that aggression has evolved as part of our "package" of behaviors because it can be adaptive when we cannot avoid an aversive interaction and when we see no other way to cope with it.

If dysfunctional expressions of anger and aggression can be motivated by adaptive tendencies, then it is possible that children who act aggressively may subjectively perceive themselves to simply be trying to take care of themselves. Caprara et al. note that from the perspective of aggressive individuals, their behavior, although seeming to reflect hostile intentions to those outside, may not be seen as aggressive from within, or at least not inappropriate. Instead, individuals may perceive themselves as justifiably protecting themselves, righting wrongs, or struggling against injustice, which is perhaps why they often become outraged and resistant when they are incriminated by adult authority figures.

Being completely negative when looking at children who behave aggressively may also lead us to overlook important strengths on which intervention efforts could capitalize. Indeed, some aggressive children may have important problem-solving skills and other capacities that they use to protect themselves from serious harm and that are overlooked in efforts to ameliorate their behavior.

A more positive, or at least open-minded perspective is congruent with the recent development of "positive psychology," championed by Seligman (1998) and others. Arthur Bohart (chapter 16), for example, proposes that clients in psychotherapy (who are typically viewed as "pathological") have a great deal more proactive problem-solving potential than is usually granted them. Indeed, some may have enough to "self-heal" simply through expressing and reflecting on thoughts and feelings with an empathic listener. Jonathan Bloom-Feshbach and Sally Bloom-Feshbach (chapter 15) similarly point out potentially constructive consequences of expressing anger.

Cairns and Cairns's suggestion that the need to attend more to the adaptive qualities of problem children has implications for intervention. First, focusing attention on positive qualities and skills of aggressive children could engender positive self-fulfilling prophecy effects, countering the effects of negative expectations described by Caprara et al. In addition, reinforcing children's prosocial behavior and helping them develop skills and other tools for coping with frustration and conflict should be more effective than concentrating only on reducing aggressive behavior. It might even be possible to build on the strategies some highly aggressive children have developed to protect themselves from serious harm, such as for de-escalating conflict or terminating a fight when it becomes truly threatening.

Second, the suggestion that aggression may have its adaptive side leads us to consider the difference between motives for aggression and its expression. Pulkkinen sees aggression as an attempt to handle frustration and conflict. What is dysfunctional is not the motive, but rather the means. This analysis fits also with Shure's emphasis on teaching prosocial means for dealing with frustrating or conflictual situations and with other intervention programs discussed in this book that teach a focus on developing skills and positive coping behaviors.

The point that aggressors may view their behavior as adaptive and justified also has clear implications for intervention. Clearly adults, whether parents, teachers, or therapists, need to understand how the child views the situation instead of simply condemning their behavior (and often their motives as well). This reaction is less likely to incite more anger, which interferes with the effectiveness of any intervention. Listening to the child's perspective also models appropriate prosocial behavior.

Trying to understand the child's perspective is also consistent with Bohart's claim that a "therapeutic state of mind"—an open mind instead of a defensive, self-protective mind—is critical to successful therapy. An empathic therapist helps people move out of defensive, resistant stances (Newfield, Kuehl, Joanning, & Quinn, 1991). Thus, Shure trains parents and teachers to listen carefully to children so they can, through the use of appropriate questions, help children develop their own capacity to consider alternative points of view and move beyond their impulsive, egocentric perspectives.

Consider, for example, the gunmen in the Littleton, Colorado, tragedy. Both Dylan Klebold and Eric Harris claimed to feel oppressed by popular classmates. It is highly likely that they believed that they were justified in striking back at injustices they had endured for many years. In fact, despite the inappropriateness of their behavior, there may have been some reality in their outrage. We have seen that bullies can be socially popular. Had these two students seen a therapist who could have gained their trust, perhaps as they expressed their outrage to an empathic-listening therapist who understood their point of view while offering alternative perspectives and ways of dealing with these feelings, the students might have been able to shift into a more proactive problem-solving set. They might have had less need to defend their point of view and may have become more open to alternatives. This could have helped them shift their attention from a narrow overfocus on the injustices they were experiencing to consideration of more socially integrative solutions that would have been life-enhancing for them, and less socially destructive as well.

INDIVIDUAL FACTORS: CAUSES AND MEDIATORS

In addition to understanding the nature and stability of constructive and destructive developmental pathways, it is important to understand factors that affect children's trajectories. We turn next to four sets of factors within individuals—emotions, cognitions, self-concept, and social-problem-solving skills—which authors in this volume propose as important mediators of aggressive and prosocial behavior. Emotional mediators include shame, guilt, empathy, and emotional expression. Cognitive mediators include scripts, fantasy, and cognitive desensitization. Self-concept includes self-esteem, perceptions of competencies, and personal identity. Social-problem-solving skills include social perception, perspective taking, and thinking of alternative prosocial solutions in conflict situations. Following this discussion, we summarize what we know, according to the books' authors, about how variables in different contexts, including home, school, and the broader society, affect children's behavior, either directly or by affecting these internal mediators.

Emotional Mediators

Pulkkinen suggests that destructive behavior is mediated by negative emotions, and constructive behavior is mediated by positive emotions. Other authors suggest making further differentiations in the role played by emotions in behavior. June Price Tangney's research (chapter 6), for example, suggests that although shame and guilt are both negative emotions, shame is associated with destructive behavior, and guilt appears to be more constructive. Also, it can be painful to experience another's distress, but such empathic pain can promote prosocial behavior. Furthermore, the expression of negative feelings can be destructive or constructive depending on how the listener receives it and whether the expression contributes to the development of a cognitive–affective problem-solving process.

Guilt and Shame

Tangney explains why guilt and shame affect behavior differently. Shame is based on feeling bad about the whole self ("*I* did that horrible thing"), whereas guilt is based on feeling bad about what one did (I *did* that horrible *thing*"). Her research finds that feeling bad about the whole self is associated with destructive behavior, whereas feeling bad about one's actions is associated with constructive behavior. In particular, proneness to shame is related to a proneness to anger and hostility and an inability to handle anger constructively. Guilt is associated with the constructive handling of anger, such as seeking corrective action, discussion, and cognitive reappraisals.

One implication of Tangney's findings is that discipline that shames children and makes them feel badly about themselves will be counterproductive. Instead, discipline that calls children's attention to the effects of their behavior on others, and thus engenders guilt, will be more productive. An example of using guilt-inducing discipline is the empathy-based induction, identified by Paul Mussen and Nancy Eisenberg (chapter 5) as the most productive parental discipline method. An additional implication of Tangney's findings for intervention is that reducing shame in individuals who may have been angered should reduce the chances of aggressive behavior. This is seen in Bohart's illustrative case of an employee who has lost his job, unfairly in his eyes. He is enraged at his employer and also feels intensely shamed. The shame keeps the individual's attention focused on the shame-inducing provocation, the employer's actions, instead of allowing the individual's attention to flow to more productive concerns, such as finding another job. Helping reduce the client's shame will not necessarily reduce his anger, but it can allow him to begin to focus his attention on more productive concerns.

Empathy

Empathy is typically defined by developmental psychologists in terms of an emotional reaction to another's experience. For instance, for Albiero and Lo Coco a person is empathizing with another if he or she experiences the same emotion the other is experiencing. Martin L. Hoffman (chapter 3) broadens this definition, claiming empathy is feeling an emotion that is more relevant to another's state than to one's own. If I am watching a friend in pain because he or she has been unjustly treated, I am feeling empathy if I feel empathic anger at the person who has mistreated my friend. Olweus and Endresen divide empathy into two components—empathic distress and empathic concern—using a self-report measure to assess both. Empathic distress is feeling distress relevant to what another is feeling, but one's focus is more on oneself than on the other; with empathic concern, the focus is on the other's welfare.

Although defined as an emotion, all the authors who discuss empathy in this volume assume that it has motivational properties—that experiencing another's pain motivates one to help rather than hurt. Consistent with this view, some studies have found that empathy and aggression are inversely related (e.g., Feshbach, & Feshbach, 1969, 1982). Miller and Eisenberg (1988) found in a meta-analysis a relationship, albeit a modest one, between empathy and aggression (-.18) In the current volume, Olweus and Endresen, Albiero and Lo Coco, and Caprara et al. all report evidence for an inverse relationship between empathy or prosocial behavior on the one hand, and aggression on the other. Albiero and Lo Coco found some evidence of a significant correlation between empathy and prosocial behavior in girls, but not in boys.

There is also evidence suggesting that empathy mediates prosocial and aggressive behavior by promoting guilt. Tangney found that those who experience guilt rather than shame are more empathic and also less likely to act aggressively. Her findings fit with Hoffman's contention that effective socializing involves mobilizing children's guilt by focusing them (empathically) on the consequences of their actions for others. Mussen and Eisenberg review the literature on parenting and conclude, in support of Hoffman, that empathy-inducing inductions and preachings are the best forms of parental teaching methods.

Both Hoffman and Mussen and Eisenberg suggest also that using empathy to socialize children helps them develop moral rules and scripts. Moral rules are generalizations from specific discipline encounters where the child has transgressed and where the parents have called the child's attention to the impact of the child's behavior on others. The child empathically understands the other's distress and may eventually develop a moral rule that one should not hurt but instead help others. These moral rules and scripts can then begin to generate prosocial behavior that conforms to the rule, even in the absence of direct empathy. Olweus and Endresen provide some evidence for this claim, finding that empathy seemed to influence bullying behavior indirectly, through its impact on negative attitudes toward bullying.

The effects of empathy can be moderated by how a person uses empathy to make decisions about how to handle a situation. Hoffman sees empathic distress as the beginning of empathy in early childhood. To achieve more mature forms of empathy the person must develop a sense of self, differentiated from others. This means that the person must be able to recognize the empathic nature of the distress he or she is feeling and to put it in its proper perspective. A lack of self-other differentiation can lead to overidentification, too much pain, and a desire to flee rather than help, or to inappropriately take on the other's burdens (e.g., Rosette, 1999).

Hoffman discusses a number of other situations, such as when justice concerns conflict with feeling empathy for the other person, in which empathy does not necessarily lead to caring behavior. Empathy can also have negative consequences when there is empathic bias, such as when individuals can empathize with members of their in-group but not with members of outgroups. Hoffman proposes that individuals need to deliberately try to expand their empathy to outgroup members.

In summary, the relationship of empathy to behavior is both mediated and moderated by other factors. Nonetheless, there seems to be clear evidence that empathy has an impact, however indirect, on both prosocial and aggressive behavior. Efforts to increase children's capacities for empathy, therefore, should have considerable value. Note, however, that although empathy, aggression, and prosocial behavior are roughly related as expected, the relationships are modest and sometimes vary as a function of gender. Taken together, the research evidence suggests that intervention efforts need also to address directly the links between empathy and prosocial behavior and control of aggression. Although there is some evidence that empathy training can promote prosocial behavior and reduce aggressive behavior (e.g., Feshbach & Feshbach, 1982), the effects might be strengthened by deliberate attempts to link the use of empathy to conflict situations. Training needs to include how to handle empathic experience productively and also "empathic decision-making," that is, how empathy would play a role in effective prosocial decision-making. Shure's program, designed to increase a child's empathic understanding of other children when trying to solve an interpersonal conflict situation, is one example of how this might be done.

The relevance of empathy to social problem-solving could also be enhanced by embedding empathy training as part of other, routine social-problem-solving activities. For instance, a recent program designed to reduce interethnic conflict in schools builds empathy training into the regular school curriculum, thus making empathy a part of how children think about many different life situations (Feshbach & Feshbach, 1998). An example is inducing children to think about how Native Americans felt when Columbus arrived, inducing children to consider the issue of one culture imposing itself on another one.

Emotional Expression: Catharsis

One of the most enduring controversies in psychology, with direct implications for destructive behavior, has been over the value of emotional expression. The issue is simple: If you are feeling a troubling and dysphoric emotion, such as sadness or anger, is it beneficial to express it? The "catharsis" idea, that emotional expression is helpful, is often explained in terms of a "hydraulic model." Emotions and drives are forms of energy that build up if they are not expressed, causing internal disruption. For Freud, energy could be released either directly through emotional expressions or indirectly through various substitute activities, such as artwork. Vicarious experience, such as through watching sexual or aggressive activity in films, is also considered by some theorists as a productive form of release.

The catharsis of anger and aggressive feelings has been of particular concern. Is it healthy to "release" anger, either directly through expression or indirectly through engaging in fantasy or viewing media material? This book's authors take different positions on the question. Huesmann and Reynolds and Leonard D. Eron (chapter 2) hold that expression of anger or aggression simply strengthens the propensity to feel angry and act aggressively. Huesmann and Reynolds explicitly object to intervention programs that rely on pretend aggression, such as those involving the use of batakas. Eron objects to the idea that fantasy aggression, such as through watching violence in the media or through playing video games, can reduce aggression.

In contrast to these negative perspectives on catharsis, Bohart and Bloom-Feshbach and Bloom-Feshbach propose a more differentiated view, claiming that under some conditions, particularly in the learning situation of psychotherapy, anger expression can be beneficial. The Bloom-Feshbachs and Bohart focus on the direct expression of anger rather than on the vicarious experience of aggression, either through fantasy or through watching aggressive media. They claim that expression of negative emotions in a supportive interpersonal situation can be beneficial, particularly if that interpersonal situation is a psychotherapeutic one. They emphasize, in particular, the value of an empathic interpersonal relationship and the development of cognitive understanding.

The Bloom-Feshbachs suggest that the benefits of catharsis can be clarified by a developmental perspective. Expression of affect in infancy, they suggest, is a key component of learning how to regulate affect by expressing it appropriately in secure relationships. It is through such expression and its reception by an empathic listening other (e.g., the mother) that the child begins to sort out how to handle anger in an interpersonal relationship. Anger is an expression of self that seeks understanding and response. What is key is that the infant's expression of rage, frustration, or other emotions are heard. It is the message they convey that is important, not the discharge of affect. The failure of hostile affect expression to be communicated and understood creates unfinished emotional sequences that block the individual from reuniting with the attachment figure.

According to the Bloom-Feshbachs' theory, individuals whose caretakers did not respond effectively to their expressions of anger as infants may have anger regulation problems as adults. For some, being able to express anger in therapy is an important precondition to restructuring basic ways of construing interpersonal relationships and managing emotions.

Bohart notes that expressing anger in the supportive context of relating to a therapist is not the same as expressing anger in everyday life. Expressing anger by gesturing obscenely or shouting at a driver on the freeway may increase rather than reduce anger by feeding one's temper. Expressing anger to an empathic therapist sets in motion a set of processes that can reduce anger. Expression that leads to emotional sharing with another and being understood can reduce shame and increase a sense of efficacy. Both of these consequences could serve to reduce inappropriate and maladaptive expressions of hostility. In addition, when the client enters therapy, he or she may be in a dysfunctional, overfocused, ruminative, and steaming angry state of mind. Expressing anger to an empathic listener in a supportive context can move the individual from frustrated, ruminative, and "venting" into a more reflective position in which one begins to examine one's angry response and to learn from it. This process can facilitate cognitive processing.

The implications of theory and research on catharsis extend beyond psychotherapy. Bohart's analysis suggests that parents and other significant adults in children's lives should neither model simple "venting" for their children nor encourage it. Rather, when a child is angry, they should encourage the child to express the anger by talking it out with an adult who tries to understand their perspective. The adult should model and encourage expression as communication rather than expression as discharge. For adults who are angry and distressed the implication is that it would be useful to find an empathic listener to share feelings with, as well as someone who encourages them to think through the source and the meaning of the emotion. Psychotherapy is only one such situation.

Cognitive Mediators

Along with feelings, how one thinks about a conflict situation is also important in whether one handles it constructively or destructively. A number of cognitive factors postulated to mediate prosocial and antisocial/aggressive behavior were discussed in this book, including scripts, fantasy, and cognitive desensitization. Each of these is discussed below.

Scripts

This volume's authors favor the concept of "script" (Nelson, 1989) as an important cognitive construct to explain antisocial/aggressive and prosocial behavior. Scripts are general frameworks for dealing with social situations. For example, research has shown that as children mature their scripts for such familiar social situations as going to a restaurant (e.g., sit down, order, wait, eat, pay) develop and become more complex with time (salad is served first in restaurants with tablecloths; Nelson, 1989).

Hoffman uses the concept of scripts to describe how individuals develop prosocial behavior. Consider a child who has transgressed against another child. If the parent promotes empathy by calling the child's attention to what the other child is feeling, and the transgressing child feels guilty, the child may extract the rule that "it isn't good to hurt others." From this a script develops that links guilt with transgressions and the moral injunction not to harm others. Rules for reparation and for helping others may also get incorporated into the script. Over time the parents' role in these scripts gradually drops out, and the scripts themselves become the internalized set of rules for prosocial behavior.

Eron and Huesmann and Reynolds use scripts to explain the development of aggressive behavior. Huesmann and Reynolds suggest that individual differences in biology predispose individuals to differentially develop scripts. This suggests that a temperamentally shy child, for instance, might be more prone to develop scripts that include avoiding conflict situations. Then, through early learning in the form of observation and reinforcement, scripts are further elaborated and developed. If children do not reject aggressive behavior as inappropriate, they may rehearse aggressive behavior in conflict situations and eventually develop an aggressive script linking conflict and aggression.

In a potentially aggressive situation, when confronted with a possible cue that could be interpreted as a provocation, individuals search for a script. The search for a script is affected by how the person interprets social cues, the activation of normative beliefs, and mood. If the person is in a bad mood or interprets the social cues as provocative, he or she is likely to access an aggression script. Anger arousal also makes selection of aggressive scripts more likely in people who have more aggression scripts available. In high arousal, individuals search less widely and deeply and retrieve the best-connected scripts. Scripts are then evaluated in relation to normative beliefs about what is appropriate behavior in a given situation. Then the person evaluates potential responses and ultimately chooses how to respond. Accordingly, the same aggressive behavior may be produced by different cognitive deficits. For example, aggressive behavior could arise because of deficits in (a) interpreting social cues, (b) accessing scripts, (c) applying normative beliefs, and (d) choosing which behaviors to engage in.

The concept of scripts in which situations, emotions, and behaviors become linked has implications for intervention, many of which have been mentioned by chapter authors. First, intervention strategies should help children learn how to read interpersonal cues accurately, so that they do not see purposeful provocation when it is not there. Second, children need to develop scripts for conflict situations that do not include aggression. Hoffman suggests the value of prosocial moral scripts that can be promoted through direct attempts to engender empathic responses. Third, children need to learn what truly is normative and sanctioned in society and how to translate normative beliefs into behavior. And finally, children need practice in evaluating and choosing effective, prosocial behavioral strategies. Huesmann and Reynolds describe several intervention programs that have addressed various aspects of this list, with promising, albeit mixed, results.

Fantasy

Eron discusses other factors that mediate aggression, such as cognitive and emotional desensitization, cognitive justification, and fantasy. Of particular importance is fantasy because of the many activities that encourage fantasy participation in violence, including comic books, music, movies, television, and video games. Eron argues against the idea that fantasizing aggression as a form of catharsis helps control overt aggressive behavior. Instead, he claims that fantasizing is a form of rehearsal, which strengthens aggressive scripts. He acknowledges, however, that fantasizing aggression could be used in psychotherapy constructively if it leads to the generation of socially appropriate problem-solving.

Eron's claims are, to be sure, consistent with commentators who have expressed concern about the role that media violence might have played in acts of violence, such as the one in Littleton, Colorado. Consistent with Eron's theory, the two adolescent gunmen in Littleton participated extensively in violent video games. They had ample opportunities to rehearse violent behavior, opportunities that presumably presented such behavior as an acceptable and appropriate strategy for achieving their goals. In addition to offering opportunities to practice aggressive acts, their continual engagement in simulated aggression may have desensitized them to its real consequences.

Eron's claims are also consistent with a substantial number of studies suggesting that fantasy violence in movies and on television promotes violent behavior (Coie & Dodge, 1998; Huesmann & Eron, 1986). The implications for policy and practice, however, are complicated. Although support for limiting violence in media can be found, concerns about infringing on first amendment rights have limited this as an option.

Clearly, any serious effort to reduce aggression in children that does not tread on first amendment rights will need to either minimize children's access to media violence or intervene somehow to reduce the effects of media violence on their behavior. In research by S. Feshbach (1972), media violence perceived as real was more likely to incite actual violence than media violence perceived as fantasy. Accordingly, helping children differentiate between fantasy and reality is an approach that may be useful. Eron mentions one such study that attempted to train children to make such a discrimination and had a positive result (Huesmann, Eron, Brice, Klein, & Fisher, 1983). There may be other strategies that merit investigation, such as trying to promote empathy by focusing children's attention on the pain and suffering of the victims of violent acts on television as well as in real life or by perhaps using situations viewed on television to discuss alternative, more prosocial strategies for dealing with conflict.

Self-Concept and Identity

Tedeschi and Felson (1994) and S. Feshbach (1971) consider the need to preserve self-esteem and to promote a positive self-concept and identity to be important motives for aggression for some children. We consider three topics related to their proposal that are discussed in the chapters in this volume: shame, perceived competence, and group identity.

Tangney notes that the emotion of shame is associated with a negative evaluation of the whole self. When one does something bad, instead of evaluating one's act, one evaluates one's self. Tangney has found in her research that shame is associated with a self-focus that appears to interfere with feeling empathy for others and to promote destructive emotions of anger and hostility. These findings suggest that shaming people is likely to enhance the probability of aggression, and reducing shame may reduce its probability. Her findings suggest the importance of the language that adults use to discipline children. A difference as subtle as "you have *been* bad" and "you have *behaved* badly" may have consequences for how children feel about themselves and thus their behavior. The implications of Tangney's research on shame dovetail with Mussen and Eisenberg's exhortation to focus children's attention on the transgression itself and its consequences.

Stipek notes that schools may contribute to a negative self-concept by engaging in practices that lead some students to develop perceptions of themselves as academically incompetent. By about age 9 or 10 children's motivational structures have begun to stabilize. Children who initially entered school self-confident but who experienced substantial academic failure may develop a negative self-concept that leads to antisocial and aggressive behavior. Indeed, some children appear to strive to develop a reputation for being a rebel or a bully, perhaps to find a domain in which they can enjoy some sense of competence.

Researchers have also suggested identification with larger groups as a factor in constructive and destructive behavior. Robert A. Hinde (chapter 4) focuses on the national level, noting that there are two different ways in which one identifies with one's country—nationalism and patriotism. Nationalism is a sense of superiority about one's country and may lead to using aggression to impose by force one's will or customs on other countries. He proposes that patriotism, in contrast, has more to do with defending one's country if it is attacked.

Hinde speculates that the dynamics of self-esteem in the case of the individual may generalize to those of the group, so that those who are nationalistic may be proactively aggressive to enhance the perceived superiority of their group, whereas those who are patriotic are more likely to act aggressively only to protect their group's identity and pride when it is under attack. He cites research from S. Feshbach (1991) suggesting that nationalists may have been insecurely attached as children, whereas patriots were securely attached. It is interesting to speculate that insecure attachments may contribute to a sense of self-esteem that needs bucking up by identification with and enhancement of a larger group identity. Note that the two gunmen in Littleton apparently identified with a group called the "trenchcoat mafia." Their well-planned attack seemed more like a "nationalistic" attack against members of other high school groups, particularly the "jocks," than an effort to protect their group.

If Hinde's distinction between nationalism and patriotism can be applied meaningfully to unofficial subgroups within nations, researchers need to understand how to foster a desire to protect and take pride in the identity of one's group rather than to aggress against other groups. The distinction Hinde makes could be useful in understanding, for example, the differences in the behavior of sports teams and gangs.

Social Problem-Solving

Several authors suggest that to promote prosocial behavior and reduce antisocial/aggressive behavior it is necessary to help children develop social-problem-solving skills. In this volume the skills emphasized are social perception, perspective taking, and thinking of alternative prosocial solutions in conflict situations.

Social Perception

Social perception has been a major area of concentration for the prevention of aggressive behavior. Eron suggests that children who approve of aggressive solutions to conflict are more likely to interpret ambiguous cues in others' behavior as hostile. Huesmann and Reynolds suggest that children learn how to interpret cues. They propose that children who interpret cues as hostile and who have well-developed aggression scripts are likely to access them when angry and consequently act aggressively. Their claims are consistent with other studies(e.g., Dodge, 1986), which have found that aggressive children are biased to interpret the actions of others as reflecting hostile intentions.

Accordingly, researchers have developed remediation programs designed to change aggressive children's social perceptions. Huesmann and Reynolds discuss in their chapter a program based on Dodge's (1986) work and another program, the C^2 program, in which children practice discriminating hostile from nonhostile intent in videotaped vignettes. The C^2 program, like others, also promotes more reflective behavior. For example, children are encouraged to think about why others are acting as they do before automatically assuming hostile intent. The program has had some success, but results are mixed.

Perspective Taking and Thinking of Alternative Solutions

We define *perspective taking* broadly as the ability to view a situation from the perspective of another as well as to view an interaction between people in terms of the broader social context. Pulkkinen suggests that people who are high in self-control are able to see a situation from multiple perspectives, not just from the perspective of the other person involved, but from that of adults and the broader society. She claims that a long-term time perspective regarding the consequences of one's actions is also important.

Hinde, Shure, Hoffman, Mussen and Eisenberg, Pulkkinen, Bohart, and other chapter authors all consider the importance of encouraging or training people to look at things from multiple perspectives. Shure describes impulsive children who were unable to adopt multiple perspectives in peer conflict situations and did not anticipate potential negative consequences to their actions. These observations became the basis for the development of a training program. Bohart suggests that when individuals come into therapy in a high state of distress their perspective-taking ability is often reduced. They think narrowly and ruminatively and are unable to stand back and see things in context. This may play a role in much of the self-destructive behavior (e.g., substance abuse, depression, anxiety) in which highly distressed individuals engage.

Being able to generate alternative prosocial solutions to conflict situations is another skill that appears to be lacking in children who use aggression to deal with conflict. The intervention approach described by Shure illustrates proactive attempts to teach both perspective-taking and problem-solving strategies. Shure coached 4- to 5-year-olds to think of others' feelings and reactions and to think of the consequences of various courses of action. Teachers and parents also were trained to respond to children in ways that would enhance the children's decision-making capabilities. Instead of saying "don't do" something, the trained teacher or parent engaged in a dialogue with the child. This training resulted in improved ability to think of solutions, decreased impulsivity, decreased inhibition, and increased prosocial behavior, which was maintained at a 1- and 2-year follow-up. An additional benefit of this training was that the mothers used the training to solve their own problems.

HOW THE SOCIAL ENVIRONMENT PROMOTES CONSTRUCTIVE OR DESTRUCTIVE BEHAVIOR

This volume's authors describe ways in which social contexts influence and shape prosocial and antisocial/aggressive behavior. We consider three contexts: home, school, and society. Social interactions and norms in these three contexts affect constructive and destructive behavior directly and indirectly through their effects on the internal mediators described in the previous section. All three are potential sites for promoting constructive developmental pathways and for intervention and remediation when destructive behaviors appear.

The Home

Authors of chapters in this book discuss practices that affect early attachment relationships and parenting discipline practices. Each is discussed below.

Attachment

As mentioned earlier, attachment theory holds that the early attachment between mother and infant is an important factor in the course of later development (Bowlby, 1988). Children of warm, empathic, responsive, and caring mothers form secure attachments; insensitive, abusive, punitive, overcontrolling, intrusive, or neglectful mothers promote insecure attachments. Therefore, Mussen and Eisenberg's claim that parenting practices work better if they are embedded in warm, nurturing, and supportive environments is supported by attachment theory.

Also emphasizing the relevance of the parent–child bond, Eron cites early research that found that children who identify with their parents accept punitive punishment and internalize the principles of behavior the punishment was designed to teach more than children who reject their parents and do not identify with them. Thus, the effect of punishment appears to depend on the parent–child relationship.

Cairns and Cairns give examples from animal research that appear to contradict attachment theory. In the studies they describe, punitive relationships seemed to create strong mother–infant bonds. The research they cite, however, involved situations in which infants could not escape because their survival depended on their mothers. Perhaps, as Cairns and Cairns suggest, children who are unable to escape a punitive or abusive parent organize their behavior around the parent. Thus, for example, children who have parents who use harsh and critical discipline practices to instill moral rules but who have no other option but to bond with them may internalize their parents' moral standards (e.g., principles against murder, robbery, cheating). They therefore may not necessarily become antisocial in their behavior. However, their principles would not be based in an empathic understanding of others, and we might expect these principles to be applied in a rigid, moralistic, and nonempathic way or to break down easily when challenged.

Although attachment theory predicts that insensitive parenting should lead to insecure attachments, and subsequently to a greater likelihood of dysfunctional behavior, Cairns and Cairns's suggestion implies that sometimes children of insensitive parents may internalize prosocial moral rules and not act dysfunctionally. This apparent contradiction may be one explanation for why the correlations between early attachment relationships and later behavior are relatively weak (Thompson, 1998). The survival-based bond that children form with abusive caretakers may explain also why children sometimes defend their abusers.

Nevertheless, both theory and research suggest the value of nurturing and sensitive caretaking. The attachment bond in this case is likely to lead to more flexible and stronger internalization of the parents' moral principles than a bond based on a need to survive.

Parental Discipline Practices

Mussen and Eisenberg review research on parenting practices that foster the development of prosocial behavior. Overall they conclude that empathy-arousing techniques are the most effective. These are techniques that help the child understand the perspective of others and to empathize and sympathize with them.

They also recommend, on the basis of research evidence, inductions—explaining a transgression and offering reasons for why the child should behave differently. Mussen and Eisenberg, following Hoffman, claim that inductions that focus the child's attention on the consequences of behavior for others are the most effective.

Preaching about caring and universal ethical standards is the third discipline strategy they recommend. They suggest that empathy-inducing preaching ("economically disadvantaged people suffer from challenging circumstances") is better than simply preaching norms ("we should help economically disadvantaged people").

Modeling and reinforcement are also promoted by Mussen and Eisenberg as productive parenting practices. Parents can model prosocial behavior, as well as empathy, perspective taking, problem-solving, and the other mediators of constructive behavior discussed above. The most effective reinforcement, they suggest, is praise that attributes children's actions to their positive behavior, their dispositional kindness, or their intrinsic motives. Social reinforcement is considered more effective than tangible rewards because social psychologists have found that tangible rewards tend to shift children's attention to the reward, rather than moral principles, as the reason for the behavior. Thus, the prosocial behavior may disappear when no reward is promised.

The research Mussen and Eisenberg review suggests clearly that punitive discipline does not produce prosocial behavior. Physical abuse is associated with both low empathy and prosocial behavior. Although Cairns and Cairns's analysis suggests that abused children may learn prosocial rules if their parents teach them, without empathy, these rules are not likely to lead to consistent and meaningful prosocial behavior. Research does not, however, suggest that occasional use of punishment by supportive, authoritative parents has negative consequences.

Parent training is an obvious strategy for promoting constructive behavior in children, and in fact, as Zigler and Styfco point out, it is common in programs, such as Head Start, that are designed for children at risk of negative developmental outcomes. Parent training is also a key component of the intervention programs discussed by Huesmann and Reynolds and by Shure.

Parent training is usually focused on only a subset of the factors that the book's authors suggest are important. Perhaps its effects could be enhanced by expanding it to address the kinds of discipline approaches described by Mussen and Eisenberg as well as the experience and expression of emotion, cognitive skills, perspective taking, social problem-solving, and self-concept and identity issues described by other authors. A comprehensive approach might be particularly useful for intervention programs designed for children who have shown signs of moving on to a destructive pathway.

School

School has been the site of many programs designed to promote constructive and reduce destructive behavior. Zigler and Styfco summarize research indicating that preschool intervention programs such as Head Start can have positive effects. Huesmann and Reynolds discuss two developmentally sensitive social–cognitive interventions: FAST Track, based on Dodge's work, and MACS. It is assumed in both programs that prevention requires ecological changes in the context in which children develop as well as individual change. Both programs included interventions with teachers, along with parent training or family intervention, and social skills training for children. FAST Track also includes academic tutoring. And both programs have shown some positive effects.

Stipek suggests that changes in some school practices might reduce aggressive and other destructive behaviors. She notes that academic success substantially affects life opportunities. High school completion, for example, is positively associated with constructive behavior, and inversely with substance abuse, unemployment, low income, welfare dependence, delinquency, and crime. Consequently, intervention that increases school success and completion is likely to promote more constructive behavior.

Stipek describes particular school practices that may undermine opportunities to succeed for children who enter school with low academic skills. She describes a process in which teachers develop negative perceptions, assign them to low reading groups that receive less effective and motivating instructional approaches, and retain them when they do relatively poorly. Retention, research has shown, is strongly associated with dropping out of school. Compounding problems related to these instructional practices, children who are at a high risk for academic failure and dropping out of school are likely to attend schools that have relatively less well-prepared teachers and a high concentration of other high-risk students.

In summary, in addition to thinking of schools as sites for interventions, researchers need to consider ways in which the educational programs and other aspects of school can be changed to foster constructive behavior. What we have learned from the Littleton tragedy suggests that the social climate of the school is as important as the academic program.

Society

Norms

At the broader level of society, cultural norms can teach, support, and legitimize aggression, or they can promote prosocial behavior. Ironically, although aggression is not sanctioned by American societal norms, violence is evident in many social artifacts, such as television, games, and comic books. Children, therefore, get contradictory messages. What is the norm? Is it what most adults preach, or is it what is modeled in the media?

Norms related to aggressive behavior are addressed in this volume by Huesmann and Reynolds and Eron. They point out that violence in the media and in other fantasy materials, such as video games, teaches aggressive scripts and cognitively and emotionally desensitizes people to violence. Huesmann and Reynolds claim that when children are primed to consider an aggressive act by some provocation, they use norms to evaluate alternative responses. If they accept what they see in the media as normative, they may conclude that aggression is an appropriate solution to a problem. One could imagine that the two adolescents in Littleton, Colorado, had learned from the video games they played that violence was an acceptable solution. When they were provoked by rejection at school, they applied these norms based on fantasy situations to their real-life problems. The video games may also have desensitized them to violence.

Also, as Eron points out, realistic violence has a greater probability of stimulating the modeling of violent behavior than does fantasy violence (see also S. Feshbach, 1972), and fantasy and realism can be confused. The video games that the two Littleton students played were apparently highly similar to the actions they took, suggesting that although at some level they may have understood that the video games did not depict real-life events, the scenes were similar enough to real life for them to mistakenly apply them to situations with real human beings.

Clearly, children need to learn that aggressive solutions to social conflict and violence are not sanctioned, normative behavior. To achieve this, access to violent models needs to be limited, or strategies are needed to counteract the lessons learned from such models. Huesmann and Reynolds discuss one example of such an intervention. In the C^2 program they describe, children are manipulated into publicly committing themselves to attitudes opposing aggression and to not watching and imitating violent acts on television. Their strategy to influence children's beliefs is to have them make a video to convince others of the evils of aggression and violence.

Institutions

Hinde's concern is about the most dramatic form of destructive behavior, war. He claims that work on aggression at the individual level does not help us understand aggression at the group level. His analysis is important; in addition to addressing aggression between nations, his points most likely apply to serious forms of destructive behavior within nations. In the United States, for example, violence between gangs or individuals from different racial groups are commonplace. Often the perpetrators lash out at groups that have no intention or desire to be embroiled in a violent conflict, such as in the case of the murders by the White supremacists, mentioned in the introduction, and the members of the Littleton trenchcoat mafia shooting the "jocks."

Hinde argues that people do not go to war because they are aggressive, but because they are coerced into it or feel that it is their duty. Hinde argues that it is not human aggression that causes war, but rather war that causes human aggression. Men who kill in war are rarely motivated by factors that lead to individual acts of aggression. His analysis may apply equally well to newly initiated gang members who, although not inclined toward violence themselves, are motivated to act according to the norms of the group they desire to join.

According to Hinde, war is a societal institution, and as such it has constituent roles for all its participants—generals, soldiers, politicians, nurses, transportation workers, broadcasters, and so on. It also is supported by a variety of cultural factors, such as language, toys, religious ideas that support violence, nationalism and patriotism, propaganda, and the military–industrial–scientific complex. Regarding the latter, arms dealers and huge budgets help support war as a societal institution. On a smaller scale, groups such as the Ku Klux Klan, whose members have committed serious acts of violence in the United States, share many of these same attributes.

How do we minimize the likelihood of war, and possibly violence within nations that share some of the qualities of war that Hinde describes? Hinde suggests that children should be educated to be patriotic, to take pride in their own nation or group, but not to be nationalistic. Rather than feeling superior to other nations or groups, they need to learn to respect the values and traditions of others. This goal is the hallmark of the currently popular educational movement for multicultural education, in which children are taught about different cultural practices and encouraged to respect and value ethnic and cultural differences.

FINAL THOUGHTS ON PROMOTION, INTERVENTION, AND REMEDIATION

Promoting prosocial behavior and instilling in children negative attitudes toward aggressive behavior are the best strategies for increasing constructive and decreasing destructive behavior in society. We agree with Zigler and Styfco, that intervening to develop effective parenting, productive aspirations and skills in individuals, and communities that offer good educational activities and social support ultimately will be more profitable than intervening to "fix" individuals who are already acting aggressively and antisocially.

Zigler and Styfco also note, and we concur, that solutions must be multifaceted. Reducing violence on television does not improve parenting skills or develop perspective taking. It is not surprising that programs targeting one or very few reasons for antisocial behavior have not been very successful.

It is likewise unlikely that intervening at any one point in children's development will be very effective. The notion that we can intervene early in children's lives and set them permanently on a positive developmental pathway is no longer tenable. As useful as interventions such as Head Start are, their effects are short lived. Similarly, Shure has found with her social problem-solving training that children need "boosters" to continue to use the skills they learn. Evidence that empathy, aggression, and prosocial behavior continue to develop into late childhood and even into adolescence before they stabilize suggests considerable malleability and the need for ongoing preventative efforts.

With regard to the substance of those efforts, there are two general points we wish to make. One general theme that runs through many of the chapters in this volume concerns interpersonal sensitivity, particularly in the form of empathy. The second theme concerns what is modeled through parental, school, and societal practices. We focus brief attention on these two themes because they have clear and powerful implications for the nature of efforts to increase constructive and decrease destructive behavior.

Interpersonal Sensitivity (or "Empathy")

Interpersonal sensitivity, broadly defined, appears to be a key to the promotion of constructive behavior and the control of destructive behavior. Learning how to be interpersonally sensitive is influential in choosing proactive behavior over aggressive behavior. Interpersonal sensitivity also appears to be an important modality through which one learns moral rules, according to Hoffman. Children acquire such rules by arousing their empathy for victims of transgression. Finally, socializing agents use interpersonal sensitivity to facilitate the development of secure attachments, and the motivation to internalize caretaker's values and moral principles.

This book emphasizes empathy (Albiero and Lo Coco, Olweus and Endresen, Hoffman, Shure, Mussen and Eisenberg), taking the perspective of others (Shure, Hoffman, Hinde, Pulkkinen), and accurate interpretation of social cues (Huesmann and Reynolds, Eron) as forms of social sensitivity that children need to learn. Furthermore, authors Hoffman and Mussen and Eisenberg promote discipline practices that mobilize children's empathy for others and engender feelings of guilt, which in turn motivate prosocial behavior. Finally, several writers suggest that socializing agents themselves must be interpersonally sensitive. Bloom-Feshbach and Bloom-Feshbach suggest that it is a mother's ability to accurately read and respond to a child's distress that helps a child integrate and learn to control potentially destructive affects such as anger. Stipek exhorts teachers to challenge their own preconceptions and expectations about their students, which she claims can blind them to ways to promote their students' academic success in school. Furthermore, she suggests responding on a more individualized basis to children who are deficient in skills, using strategies that will encourage and build self-confidence to participate in the learning process. To teach parents and teachers how to help children learn to solve social problems effectively, Shure encourages them to listen more than to tell, order, preach, or command. Bohart similarly suggests that clients in therapy can think of their own solutions if therapists sensitively listen and respond in a way that supports the client's proactive problem-solving capacities.

To avoid complicating further the debate about the meaning of empathy (Bohart & Greenberg, 1997; Eisenbert & Strayer, 1987), we refer to this set of skills and propensities to be sensitive to others' perspectives, needs, and feelings as social sensitivity. Empathy is usually defined as the affective end product of a set of social–cognitive processes–as having feelings more relevant to another's state than to one's own (Hoffman) or feeling the same feeling as another (Albiero and Lo Coco). Preceding this affective outcome, however, are many cognitive processes, including (a) accurate identification of the social environment, (b) accurate reading of the other person's nonverbal cues, (c) accurate attribution of the other's intentions, (d) imagining oneself in his or her shoes, (e) accurately interpreting the other person's thoughts and feelings, and (e) predicting the other's reactions to his or her own behavior. Skills related to all of these cognitive process, we suggest, are necessary prerequisites of prosocial, empathic behavior. We agree with N. Feshbach (1997) that true empathy is more complex than simply experiencing the emotion of another; it also requires a number of social–cognitive skills.

All of these social–cognitive skills, however, do not guarantee prosocial behavior. Indeed, accurate reading of social cues may give sociopaths a tool for manipulation, as might a well-developed capacity for perspective taking. The skills provide the means, but not the motivation, to use them. Because such "cold" perspective taking by itself would not necessarily motivate prosocial behavior, some theorists claim that feeling the same feeling as another is the key to empathy and prosocial behavior, (e.g., Strayer, 1987). But even feeling the same feeling as another does not guarantee prosocial behavior. As Olweus and Endresen note, empathic distress can motivate people to avoid people in distress, and it is possible that sadists might even enjoy vicariously feeling another's pain.

What else is needed? Two answers are implied in this book. First, Mussen and Eisenberg and Hoffman suggest that empathy needs to be connected to moral principles or rules for prosocial behavior, as well as social–cognitive skills. Second, one must in some sense care about the other person's welfare. Although empathy may increase the probability of caring, more may be required. Caring for those who are different from oneself probably requires recognition of some common dimension of humanness. As Bordo poetically points out, it is important to recognize that ". . . wherever one goes that the other's perspective is fully realized, not a bit of exotic 'difference' to be incorporated within one's own world . . . by sight-seeing" (Bordo, 1993, as cited in Gendlin, 1997, p. 36). In other words, empathy needs to include more than just "sight-seeing" in another's world, it must be combined with respecting and valuing others because they are fellow human beings. (The same principle may apply to the treatment of animals because they share a more abstract quality of having feelings.)

Parents are clearly key to the motivational dimensions of prosocial behavior. Children must not only learn social–cognitive skills, they must also learn to care about others. Certainly, learning to put themselves in others' shoes and to feel others' pain contributes to this learning. It is probably the caring and concern of socializing agents themselves, however, combined with their capacities for empathy and sensitivity to children, that ultimately provide the basis for children's learning to identify with the humanness in others. Our view is similar to Mussen and Eisenberg's claim that socializing practices are more effective when they are embedded in a warm and nurturing social context. Ultimately, we suspect that it is as important for adults to model caring and sensitivity to others as it is for them to teach children the social–cognitive skills they need to negotiate conflict situations successfully. We elaborate on this point below.

Modeling as Support of Prosocial Behavior

Modeling is stressed throughout the chapters in this book. We use the word *modeling* broadly to refer to any practice that provides, either explicitly or implicitly, a model of particular ways of behaving as well as certain attitudes.

At the family level, parents teach by modeling empathy, respect, and caring. When they use empathy-arousing inductions, they are also modeling the importance of paying attention to another's feelings. When they use Shure's methods for stimulating their children's productive problem-solving thinking, they are modeling respect for the process of taking others' feelings into account and for trying to formulate win–win solutions for everyone involved. Furthermore, they are respecting and reinforcing the child's capacity for proactive, prosocial problem-solving, and in general conveying the expectation to children that they can solve problems. When they listen to a child's anger and try to understand the child's frustration, they are modeling strategies for showing respect of another's point of view and for engaging in problem-solving dialogue. In contrast, children who are subjected to child abuse or high levels of family violence or punitive discipline are given models of aggressive, destructive problem-solving.

At school, teachers and other adults can model respect for others—including children and adults—or they can model disrespectful, aggressive, and punitive attitudes and behavior. The behavior that is modeled is likely to have more substantial effects on children's own propensities than the behavior that is preached. The same applies to what children see in the media. In brief, to promote prosocial behavior and reduce aggression, children have to be given a will as well as a way. Institutions and social practices may need to be restructured so that they model and support prosocial behavior.

Research Implications: What Don't We Know?

Finally, we concur with an observation made by Huesmann and Reynolds, who suggest that to improve intervention we need better theory. Put another way, what we need is a better understanding of the underlying mechanisms of constructive and destructive behavior, in particular of their complex interactions. Cairns and Cairns suggest that there is an ongoing, dynamic interplay between social–ecological circumstances and individual variables. Genes are not fixed in their manifestations nor are traits, scripts, or internal working models. Yet we have few theories that handle the dynamic quality or the interplay of factors within individuals and in their social–ecological environments. Continued investigation is needed to show the way. Much also needs to be done in society to find the will to devote resources to make the tragedy of Littleton, Colorado, a historic event implausible for future generations.

REFERENCES

Bohart, A., & Greenberg, L. S. (1997). Empathy: Where are we and where do we go from here? In A. Bohart & L. Greenberg (Eds.), *Empathy reconsidered: New directions in psychotherapy* (pp. 419–450). Washington, DC: American Psychological Association.

Bordo, S. (1993). *Unbearable weight.* Berkeley: University of California Press.

Bowlby, J. (1988). *A secure base: Clinical applications of attachment theory.* London: Routledge.

Caspi, A. (1998). Personality development across the life course. In N. Eisenberg (Vol. Ed.) & W. Damon (Ed.-in-Chief), *Handbook of child psychology: Vol. 3. Social, emotional, and personality development* (5th ed., pp. 311–388). New York: Wiley

Coie, J. D., & Dodge, K. A. (1998). Aggression and antisocial behavior. In N. Eisenberg (Vol. Ed.) & W. Damon (Ed.-in-Chief), *Handbook of child psychology: Vol. 3. Social, emotional, and personality development* (5th ed., pp. 779–862). New York: Wiley.

Dodge, K. A. (1986). A social information processing model of social competence in children. In M. Perlmutter (Ed.), *The Minnesota Symposium on Child Psychology* (Vol. 18, pp. 77–125). Hillsdale, NJ: Erlbaum.

Eisenberg, N., & Fabes, R. A. (1998). Prosocial development. In N. Eisenberg (Vol. Ed.) & W. Damon (Ed.-in-Chief), *Handbook of child psychology: Vol. 3. Social, emotional, and personality development* (5th ed., pp. 701–778). New York: Wiley.

Eisenberg, N., & Strayer, J. (Eds.). (1987). *Empathy and its development*. New York: Cambridge University Press.

Feshbach, N. D. (1997). Empathy: The formative years—Implications for clinical practice. In A. Bohart & L. S. Greenberg (Eds.), *Empathy reconsidered: New directions in psychotherapy* (pp. 33–62). Washington, DC: American Psychological Association.

Feshbach, N. D., & Feshbach, S. (1969). The relationship between empathy and aggression in two age groups. *Developmental Psychology, 1*, 102–107.

Feshbach, N. D., & Feshbach, S. (1982). Empathy training and the regulation of aggression: Potentialities and limitations. *Academic Psychology Bulletin, 4*, 399–413.

Feshbach, N. D., & Feshbach, S. (1998). Aggression in the schools: Toward reducing ethnic conflict and enhancing ethnic understanding. In T. K. Trickett (Ed.), *Violence against children in the family and the community* (pp. 269–286). Washington, DC: American Psychological Association.

Feshbach, S. (1971). Dynamics and morality of violence and aggression: Some psychological considerations. *American Psychologist, 26*, 281–292.

Feshbach, S. (1972). Reality and fantasy in filmed violence. In J. P. Murray, E. Rubinstein, & G. A. Comstock (Eds.), *Television and social behavior: Television and social learning* (Vol. 2, pp. 318–345). Washington, DC: U.S. Government Printing Office.

Feshbach, S. (1991). Attachment processes in adult political ideology: Patriotism and nationalism. In J. L. Gewirtz & M. Kurtines (Eds.), *Intersections with attachment* (pp. 207–226). Hillsdale, NJ: Erlbaum.

Gendlin, E. T. (1997). How philosophy cannot appeal to experience, and how it can. In D. M. Levin (Ed.), *Language beyond postmodernism: Saying and thinking in Gendlin's philosophy* (pp. 3–41). Evanston, IL: Northwestern University Press.

Huesmann, L. R., & Eron, L. D. (1986). The development of aggression in American children as a consequence of television violence viewing. In L. R. Huesmann & L. D. Eron (Eds.), *Television and the aggressive child: A cross-national comparison* (pp. 45–80). Hillsdale, NJ: Erlbaum.

Huesmann, L. R., Eron, L. D., Brice, P., Klein, R., & Fisher, P. (1983). Mitigating the imitation of aggressive behaviors by changing children's attitudes about media violence. *Journal of Personality and Social Psychology, 44*, 899–910.

Miller, P. A., & Eisenberg, N. (1988). The relation of empathy to aggression and externalizing/antisocial behavior. *Psychological Bulletin, 103*, 324–344.

Nelson, K. (Ed.). (1989). *Narratives from the crib*. Cambridge, MA: Harvard University Press.

Newfield, N. A., Kuehl, B. P., Joanning, H. P., & Quinn, W. H. (1991). We can tell you about "psychos" and "shrinks": An ethnography of the family therapy of adolescent drug abuse. In T. C. Todd & M. N. Selekman (Eds.), *Family therapy approaches with adolescent substance abusers* (pp. 277–310). Boston: Allyn & Bacon.

Rosette, P. A. (1999). *An exploratory test of three predisposing personality variables for threat perception in nursing and non-nursing students.* Unpublished doctoral dissertation, Saybrook Graduate School, San Francisco, CA.

Seligman, M. E. P. (1998). Positive social science. *APA Monitor, 29*(4), p. 2.

Strayer, J. (1987). Affective and cognitive perspectives on empathy. In N. Eisenberg & J. Strayer (Eds.), *Empathy and its development* (pp. 218–244). New York: Cambridge University Press.

Tedeschi, J. T., & Felson, R. B. (1994). *Violence, aggression, and coercive actions.* Washington, DC: American Psychological Association.

Thompson, R. A. (1998). Early sociopersonality development. In N. Eisenberg (Vol. Ed.) & W. Damon (Ed.-in-Chief), *Handbook of child psychology: Vol. 3. Social, emotional, and personality development* (5th ed., pp. 25–104). New York: Wiley

AUTHOR INDEX

Numbers in italics refer to listings in the reference sections.

Rushton, J. P., 114–115, *123*, *125*, 192, 195, *203*
Rutherford, E., 111, 114, *125*
Rutter, M., 291, 301, *312–313*
Rutter, R. A., 113, *125*
Ryan, R., 296–297, 303, *314*
Rychlak, J. F., 351, *363*

Saarni, C., *223*
Sackett, G. P., 34, *47*
Safran, J. D., 228–229, 339–342, 344, 352–354, 357, 359, *361*, *363*
Sagi, A. R., 63, *85*
Saklofske, D. H., 148, *165*
Salmon, J., 303, *314*
Saltzstein, H. D., 106, 108, *124*, 281, 288
Salzer, M. S., 344, *360*
Sameroff, A., 298, *313*
Sandfort, J., 242, *245*
Sandoval, J., 307, *313*
Sanna, L. J., 76, *85*
Sarason, J., *310*
Sawin, D. B., 73, *85*, 207, 214, *222*
Schachter, S., 168, *185*
Schaffer, H. R., 23–24, *47*
Schalling, D., 173, *181*
Schaps, E., 118–120, *126*
Scheff, T. J., 128, 136, 140, *144*
Schenin, M., *46*
Scherer, K. R., 128, 130, *142*, *145*
Schlegel, P., *268*
Schmitt, M., 79, *85*
Schmuck, P. A., 330, *335*
Schmuck, R., 330, *335*
Schneider, B. H., *288*
Schneider, W., 256, *268*
Schneirla, T. C., 25, *47*
Schonfeld, I., 301, *313*
Schulman, M., 128, *144*
Schvaneveldt, J. D., 148, *163*
Schweinhart, L. J., 237–239, *245*, *247*
Schwitzgabel, R., *363*
Scott, P. M., 105, 108, 111, 119, *126*
Sealand, N., 295, 297, 307, 309
Sears, R. R., 23–25, 33, *47*, 188, *203*
Seay, B., 33–34, *47*
Segal, D. L., *363*
Segall, M., *184*
Seifer, R., 298, *313*
Seitz, V., 235, 237, 239, *246–248*
Seligman, M. E. P., 374, *397*
Selman, R. L., 276, 289, 351, *363*
Selzer, S., 294, *314*
Shaffer, D., 301, *313*

Shanahan, M., 301, *312*
Shantz, C. U., 206, 213, *222*
Shapiro, D. A., 344, 350, *363*
Shapiro, F., 352–353, *363*
Share, D., 301, *312*
Shea, C., 105, *122*
Shell, R., 105, 107, 113, 115, *122*, *124*
Shelton, J. N., 348, *364*
Shepard, L., 307, *311*, *314*
Sherif, C. W., 38, *47*
Sherif, M., 37, *47*
Sherman, S., 81, *86*
Sherman, L. W., 251, *268*
Shields, A., 169, *185*
Shiffrin, R. M., 256, *268*
Shoham-Salomon, S. V., 319, 334, *362*
Shure, M. B., 233, *245*, 259, *268*, 271–274, 276–277, 279, 281–287, 288–290
Sickmund, M., 231, *247*
Siegler, I. C., 157, *164*
Silberstein, L., 128, *144*
Silva, P., 301, 306, *312*
Simon, H. A., 50, *59*
Singer, J. E., 168, *185*
Singer, R. D., 22, *45*
Sjaastad, J., 301, *312*
Skolnick, N. J., *333*
Slaby, R. G., 260, *267*
Slavin, R., 308, *314*
Slosson, R. L., 279, *290*
Slusarcick, A., 295, *310*
Smetana, J. G., *85*
Smith, A., *334*
Smith, C. L., 111, 114, *123*, *125*
Smith, D. W., 107, *125*
Smith, J., 297, *310*
Smith, M. C., 169, *185*, 307, *311*, *314*
Smith, S. M., 351, *364*
Smiutis, Z. M., 115, *123*
Snyder, H. N., 231, *247*
Solomon, D., 118–120, *126*
Solomon, J., *120*, *126*, *223*
Souwdain, V., 264, *268*
Souweidane, V. S., 265, *267*
Speer, A. L., 82, *122*
Speierer, G. W., *361*
Spielberger, C., *310*
Spindler, A., 254, 261, 264, *268*
Spivack, G., 259, *268*, 271–274, 277, 279, 281–285, 289–290
Sprini, G., *220*
Sroufe, L. A., 321, *335*
Stack, A. D., 228–229, 339, *360*
Stack, S. A., *58*

SUBJECT INDEX

Object-relations theory, 23

Parenting
    assigning responsibility, 112–113
    discipline, 388
        punitive, 114
        reinforcement, 114–115
    extrafamilial influences, 116–120
    ICPS research, 280, 282–284
    induction
        modeling, 111–112
        preaching, 110–111
Patriotism, factors supporting war, 89–90
Personal distress, 147
Personality traits, 167
    aggression, effects on, 168
        constructive behavior, 177–178
        destructive behavior, 173–177
        measuring, 172–173
        nonaggression, 169
        participant data, 171
        self-control, 169–170
Praise, reinforcement, 114–115
Preaching, inductive influences, 110–111
Predictability, functions of attachment, 40
Predicting
    achievement, 293–294
    high school completion, 295
    social adjustments, 194
Preschool, interventions, 277–280
Preventing
    aggressive behavior
        ICPS skills, 271–280, 282–287
        social-cognitive interventions,
           259–265
    juvenile delinquency, childhood
        interventions, 231–244
Preventive intervention, 264–265
Proactive aggression, 175
Problem-solving, 384–385
    aggression, preventing with, 271–276
        five-year longitudinal study, 285–287
        older children, 285
        parent research, 280, 282–284
        preschool and kindergarten
           interventions, 277–280
Propaganda, factors supporting war, 90
Prosocial behavior, 105
    aggression, associations with, 192,
        373–375
    assigning responsibility, 112–113

empathy, assessing in Italian
    children, 219
extrafamilial influences, 116–120
gender, 372–373
individual differences, 188–190
    different informants, predictive
        power of, 198–199
    gender differences, 190, 192
    psychometric characteristics, 190
    stability, 195–197
problem-solving, 384–385
punitive discipline, 114
reinforcement, 114–115
social adjustment, predicting, 194
stability, 368–372
Prosocial moral development, witnessing
    distress as a bystander, 62
    anger as motive, 68–69
    arousal modes, 62
    casual attribution, 67
    cognitively expanded bystander
        model, 66
    empathy, development of, 63, 65
    guilt and motivation, 68
    sympathetic distress, 66
Psychological autonomy, cathartic
    aggression, 322–323
Psychotherapy, expression, effects on,
    338–339
    catharsis, 339–344
    constructive expression, 355–358
    empathic workspace, 345–346
    stress and threat, 347–349
    therapeutic states of mind, 349–355
Punishment
    aggression, effects on, 51
    attachment theory, 33–35
    punitive discipline, 114
        inductive influences, 109
Puppy love, hazards of, 35–36

Quasi-egocentric empathic distress, 64

Reactive aggression, 175
Reinforcement, 114–115
Rejection and aggression, 32
Relationships
    adult
        educational and vocational
           settings, 330
        intimate, 329

ABOUT THE EDITORS

Arthur C. Bohart is Professor of Psychology at California State University Dominguez Hills, and an Adjunct Professor at Saybrook Graduate School. He is coauthor (along with Karen Tallman) of *How Clients Make Therapy Work: The Process of Active Self-Healing*, and coeditor (along with Leslie Greenberg) of *Empathy Reconsidered: New Directions in Psychotherapy*. His published works include articles on the role of the client as active self-healer in psychotherapy, experiencing in psychotherapy, and psychotherapy integration. He is also the coauthor of two textbooks: *Personality* (with Seymour Feshbach and Bernard Weiner) *and Foundations of Clinical and Counseling Psychology* (with Judith Todd).

Deborah J. Stipek received her PhD in developmental psychology from Yale University in 1977. She was a professor in UCLA's Department of Education for 23 years and director of UCLA's laboratory preschool and elementary school (Seeds UES) and the Urban Education Studies Center for 10 years. Currently she is the dean of the School of Education at Stanford University.

Professor Stipek's primary area of research is on the effects of different educational contexts on children's motivation and learning. She is currently directing a large study of the effects of home, community, and schools on very low-income children's development through middle childhood. She has strong interests in educational and other policies affecting children and families and experience working in policy contexts.